This is an illustrated volume of specially commissioned studies of the history of the cathedral foundation of Lincoln which traces its historical development, architectural evolution and musical history from its post-Norman foundation to the present day. The book synthesises the findings of modern scholarship and presents an important and comprehensible interdisciplinary survey for anyone interested in English cathedral history and architecture, and above all for anyone who visits or frequents this great landmark of England's heritage.

A history of
Lincoln Minster

A HISTORY OF
Lincoln Minster

EDITED BY

DOROTHY OWEN

Published by the Press Syndicate of the University of Cambridge
The Pitt Building, Trumpington Street, Cambridge CB2 1RP
40 West 20th Street, New York, NY 10011–4211, USA
10 Stamford Road, Oakleigh, Melbourne 3166, Australia

First published 1994

Printed in Great Britain at the University Press, Cambridge

A catalogue record for this book is available from the British Library

Library of Congress cataloguing in publication data

A History of Lincoln Minster / edited by Dorothy Owen.
       p.   cm.
Includes bibliographical references and index.
ISBN 0 521 25429 9
1. Lincoln Cathedral.   2. Architecture, Norman – England – Lincoln.
3. Lincoln (England) – Buildings, structures, etc. I. Owen,
Dorothy.
NA5471.L7H57   1994
726'.6'0942534 – dc20   93–1686   CIP

ISBN 0 521 25429 9 hardback

This volume is offered as a tribute to Kathleen Major,
who helped to initiate the plans for it and who has
continued to encourage and inspire all who have worked
on it.

Contents

❋

ix

Illustrations

✳

Foreword

❋

J. S. NURSER

In 1977 the Oxford University Press published an admirable one-volume *History of York Minster* edited by Gerald Aylmer, at that time Professor of History in the newly founded University of York, and Canon Cant, the Chancellor of the cathedral. It was readable, authoritative, and comprehensive. No remotely comparable book existed on Lincoln cathedral – all that was available (and that out of print) was Chancellor Srawley's brief history (*The story of Lincoln Minster*, London 1933). This situation was indefensible and absurd. Whether one is sympathetic or not to the popular media's need to arrange buildings in world rankings (and Lincoln appears fairly regularly in the 'top twenty'), it is clear that we have here an extremely important and beautiful building. And because it is found in one of the least 'developed' of English counties, and one of the proudest, there is a great deal of regional commitment to the 'cathedral as public symbol'. I suspect more firms have 'Minster' in their title in Lincoln than in any other cathedral city. So there is no lack of readership likely for a publication worthy of its theme.

If for a moment I may reminisce. When I came to Lincoln as Chancellor in 1976 it was one of my first concerns that chapter should review the publications available on the cathedral. There had been the two remarkable series of Minster Pamphlets produced by our Association of Friends under the inspiration of Kathleen Major and Joan Varley. And the Friends had also been responsible for another pioneering step in cathedral life in setting up a Minster shop after the 900th birthday festival year in 1972. But there was little in the way of productive chapter involvement in what was to be made available for sale to visitors and enquirers. So chapter resolved to ask the Vice-Principal of Bishop Grosseteste College, Dr Jim Johnston, to survey what material was currently obtainable to

xiii

meet the needs of visitors, including schoolchildren, and to indicate what gaps needed to be filled. He reported, and gave the highest priority to commissioning, a *History* along the lines of Aylmer and Cant's volume on York.

Chapter asked me to pursue the matter. I visited Canon Cant and I heard the story of the York project; how it had taken ten years to bring to fruition (ho, ho, I thought, will Lincoln beat York by doing the same task in half the time, or even in quarter the time?); and how Dr Owen Chadwick had heroically rescued the enterprise by writing a chapter virtually overnight. Reggie Cant was helpfulness itself, and encouraged us to go forward.

Lincoln is a city that has produced more than its fair share of notable people in the world of scholarship. Two were especially important in making it possible to get started. Dr Kathleen Major agreed in October 1979 to serve as Chairman of an Advisory Committee for the publication of a History of Lincoln; and Dr Stanley Aston used his good offices as a Syndic of the Cambridge University Press to persuade his colleagues to accept the *History* for publication. Other members of the Advisory Committee (for whose contribution chapter is grateful) were Dr Margaret Bowker, Professor Christopher Brooke, the Revd Professor Colin Morris, Dr Dorothy Owen and Professor Reg Ward. Minutes of the first informal meeting reveal that 'it was hoped that delivery of copy would take place within two years of the contract'. In the event, our pregnancy was not to be any shorter than York's.

The Advisory Committee, in consultation with chapter, appointed Dr Owen and Dr Bowker as joint editors, and they began work. It is remarkable that such a talented team of authors so readily allowed themselves to be persuaded to commit themselves to a project that held no prospect of financial reward. Sadly, after a year or so, Dr Bowker's health forced her to withdraw from her post as joint editor. In the intervening years, the progress of the *History* has been monitored by the cathedral's Library and Muniments Advisory Committee (now the Library Council). These laity-led committees and councils are now a *sine qua non* of our life, and among the principal evidence of the revolutionary changes that made the 1970s one of the major period-boundaries in the history of English cathedrals.

Chapter is therefore profoundly grateful to those who have offered their professional skills with such generosity and devotion, and produced this *History*. We address this appreciation with particular energy and warmth to the editor, Dorothy Owen. This must be the crown of a lifetime of distinguished contributions to the history of her adopted county.

In the event, this *History* concludes with the installation of Bishop Dunlop as Dean over forty years ago. There are few left in Lincoln now who were at that service. Historiographically it is a good cut-off point.

When chapter first discussed this project, however, we were anxious that there be a concluding essay that set out our present understanding of what the cathedral is about. Looking at minutes of those discussions, what comes through is concern that the extraordinary range of activities in which the cathedral is *active* in the life of our own time be spelled out, its role in the life of the church in the diocese and, more than anything perhaps, its openness, its hospitality to visitors, its accessibility. It is no longer strange to welcome a Roman Catholic diocesan Station Mass, or regular services of 'Pentecostal Praise'. Among those who sit in our prebendal stalls are a Belgian Roman Catholic priest and a Methodist District Chairman.

In 1949 it might have seemed unlikely that cathedrals of the Old Foundation should come to play such a relatively large part in the total witness of the churches to English folk-Christianity: the innumerable concerts, exhibitions, special services, as well as the provision of spaces for the lighting of candles, for prayer and private intercession, and the heartbeat of the daily offices. Choral Evensong could hardly be less 'contemporary' or populist, yet every year it seems to be received by more people as balm to their souls. Bishop Edward King's Old Palace next door has been converted to a cathedral-associated laity-centre cum retreat house that offers hospitality and a meeting-place for dialogue with the secular world. In addition, a major Sunday congregation worships in the 'parish and people' eucharistic tradition.

When the time comes for a revised edition of this *History*, there will be a story to add of our own generation's prayer and work in this ancient collegial foundation that will not be short of material for pious record and lively anecdotes. The Cathedral Church of the Blessed Virgin Mary is like that tree of which Job spoke (14.7), whose 'roots grow old' in the Lincolnshire earth, and whose life constantly illustrates the faith that 'if it scents water it may break into bud and make new growth like a young plant'.

Acknowledgements

❄

The volume editor would like to thank the members of the planning committee, Christopher Brooke, Colin Morris and Reginald Ward, with their chairman Kathleen Major. She is particularly grateful to Margaret Bowker, who was initially joint editor and who has continued to give help and advice.

The late Stanley Aston and Michael Black facilitated our approaches to the Cambridge University Press. In the course of the prolonged gestation of the book it was inevitable that changes and developments, especially in archaeology, should have emerged. Michael Jones and David Stocker ensured that none of these was missed. Members of a Battle Abbey conference heard an early version of the Introduction; the comments and suggestions they made greatly improved that section. A. E. B. Owen has been ready with advice and help at all points.

For help in providing support for the cover illustrations we also wish to thank Patrick Dean, Philip Gibbons, Bentley Nelstrop, Ian Walter, Kathleen Major, and two anonymous donors. Plates 1 to 13 are reproduced by kind permission of the Conway Library, Courtauld Institute of Art; Lawrence Elvin is thanked for plates 18 and 19, as is George Tokarski for plates 16 and 17.

Abbreviations

❋

AASR	*Associated Architectural and Archaeological Reports and Papers*
Anon.	No author or editor named
BAA	British Archaeological Association Bibliography
BAAL	British Archaeological Association, Lincoln
Berks. Arch. J.	*Berkshire Archaeological Journal*
BIHR	*Bulletin of the Institute of Historical Research*
CAS	Cambridge Antiquarian Society
CMS	Church Missionary Society
CYS	Canterbury and York Society
DB	Domesday Book
EC	Ecclesiastical Commissioners
EEA	English Episcopal Acta
EPNS	*English Place-Name Survey*
Ep. Reg.	Episcopal Register
HC	House of Commons Papers
JEH	*Journal of Ecclesiastical History*
LAASR	*Lincolnshire Architectural and Archaeological Society Reports and Papers*
LAO	Lincolnshire Archives Office
LAOR	Lincolnshire Archives Office Report
LAS	Lincolnshire Architectural Society
LCC	Lincoln Consistory Court
LCS	*Lincoln Cathedral Statutes*, ed. Bradshaw and Wordsworth

LIST OF ABBREVIATIONS

LDC	Lincoln Dean and Chapter
LDM	*Lincoln Diocesan Magazine*
Lincs. Hist. and Arch.	*Lincolnshire History and Archaeology*
LMP	Lincoln Minster Pamphlets
LNQ	*Lincolnshire Notes and Queries*
LRS	Lincoln Record Society
NGD	*New Grove Dictionary*
NMT	Nelson Medieval Texts
OMT	Oxford Medieval Texts
RA	*Registrum Antiquissimum*
RIBA	Royal Institute of British Architects
Rot. Litt. Pat.	*Rotuli Litterarum Patentium* (Record Commission)
RS	*Chronicles and Memorials of Great Britain and Ireland*, published under the direction of the Master of the Rolls
TCBS	*Transactions of the Cambridge Bibliographical Society*
TRHS	*Transactions of the Royal Historical Society*
VC	Vicars Choral

1

Introduction: the English church in eastern England, 1066–1100

✳

DOROTHY OWEN

The devastation which followed the Scandinavian invasions of the ninth and tenth centuries had seriously affected the Church in eastern England and produced a confused and confusing ecclesiastical picture which persisted until long after 1066. The two archbishoprics of Canterbury and York survived relatively unchanged, but the basic units of administration, the *parochie* or dioceses, ruled over by bishops, had been considerably confused. Small dioceses, corresponding to a shire, or folk territory, were common in the earlier church, but they were now merged, under pressure from the invaders, in large weak agglomerations. North Elmham, later to be known as Thetford, and eventually as Norwich, absorbed the Suffolk see of Dunwich, and its bishops administered Norfolk, Suffolk, and north-east Cambridgeshire from a small town in central Norfolk. Even more strange, the sees of Lindsey and Leicester were swallowed by the south Mercian bishopric of Dorchester; by this a small town in the very south of Oxfordshire was now the centre for the shires of Lincoln, Leicester, Rutland, Northampton, Huntingdon, Cambridge, Oxford, Buckingham and Bedford. The bishops of Dorchester and Elmham were neither well-endowed nor effective; their cathedral churches were unimpressive, their rule, in common with that of other contemporary bishops in England, was only moderately successful. As early as 1049 it was said that the Pope was urging their reform.

Meanwhile, other churches had been appearing throughout the country, and something of a detailed ecclesiastical pattern resembling what would be seen in later medieval England, could already be detected. The laws of the Anglo-Saxon kings already recognised several grades of church, loosely differentiated as

1

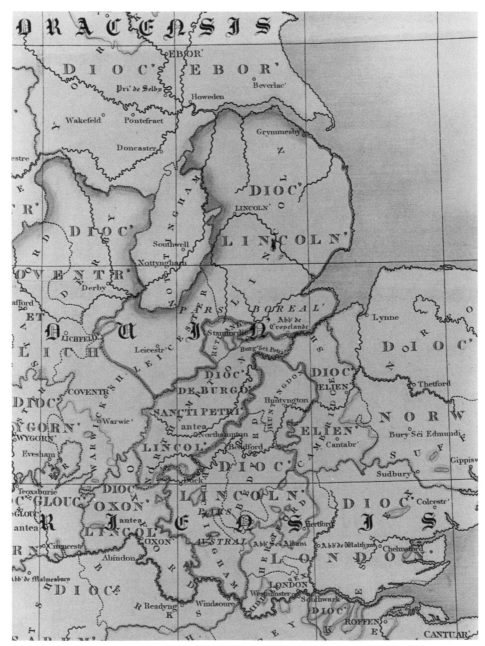

1 *The diocese of Lincoln from 1108 to 1536, after the* Valor Ecclesiasticus

minsters, manorial churches and field churches. The earliest of these were the
minsters, which in their largest and earliest form represented the first subdivision

2

of the bishop's *parochia*. The minster might draw on a whole shire for its support and be a species of episcopal church or 'head minster', it might, on the other hand, be confined to a parish covering a hundred or wapentake; it might be no more than the chief church of a large composite estate, usually, but not exclusively, royal in ownership. These minsters might have been founded by a king, a bishop or a lay magnate; they exercised rights, and collected church dues from the entire population of their parishes; they might be supported by considerable endowments in land and houses, and they were almost always served by a small community of priests or canons. There were never, it seems, enough of these minsters to serve the entire population and before the Conquest many had already disappeared, or had been given, with their endowments, to bishops and religious houses, by the descendants of their founders.

To meet the needs of an increasingly devout lay population as the numbers of minsters shrank, small local landowners had begun to build and endow churches on their estates. They appointed their own priests to serve these churches, they often continued to control the endowment (the glebe) as if it were their own, and they ensured that the area around the church, usually coterminous with their own estates, was designated as the parish of the church. These new manorial or proprietary churches were to resemble the minsters in owning the site on which they were built, and its curtilage or burial ground, in having priests with an endowment in land, in receiving from the inhabitants of their parish the customary payments which the royal laws enforced (tithe, church-scot, plough-alms, light-scot and soul-scot), besides 'voluntary' payments like mass pennies and corpse presents and many testamentary bequests. In return the new churches provided for all parishioners the sacraments of eucharist, baptism, marriage, confession, and the burial rites.

On a lower level lesser owners within such a manorial parish might build a 'field church' (a chapel) and cause it to be served by a priest for whom a small endowment might be provided. Here the only sacrament available would be the eucharist and that only on week days. All the rest were provided by the 'mother church' of the parish, with its font and burial ground and its inescapable right to the legal church dues.

Where older towns had survived the invasions the ecclesiastical pattern was confused. There might be one or more larger churches, occasionally called 'urban minsters', and sometimes served by a community of canons. Like many rural minsters these large churches were owned by kings or leading nobles, who gave them to religious houses. The parishes which these minsters must have had were by the eleventh century encroached on by smaller establishments serving a street, a quarter, or a specialised trading community. These had already begun to receive the customary dues, and provide all the sacraments to the inhabitants of their restricted parish.[1]

There was clearly no lack of vitality or enthusiasm within the local levels of the church yet it seemed in some quarters that confusion and disunity were probable unless the diocesan organisation could regain sufficient strength to impose orderly discipline on the parochial growths. The first steps towards this were taken in some parts of the country before King Edward's death, but only when the disgraceful Stigand was replaced as archbishop of Canterbury in 1070 by Lanfranc of Pavia could the changes begin. The see of Dorchester, like others in England, had already received a Norman bishop, Remigius of Fécamp, and with the full support of the King and of Lanfranc, Remigius was soon to decide that he must move his episcopal church away from Dorchester. He decided on Lincoln.

The new cathedral at Lincoln seems not to have been known as Lincoln Minster before the sixteenth century, but since the mid-seventeenth century the title has been universal in the town. This has led us, despite the lack of medieval precedent, to make this book the *History of Lincoln Minster*.[2]

The establishment of the cathedral at Lincoln

On the eve of the Norman Conquest the western Church was in the throes of a movement of reformation and renewal which had begun at least half a century earlier with monastic revivals, and which came to a head in the measures taken by Pope Gregory VII (Hildebrand) and his followers against such abuses as lay investiture, hereditary benefices and clerical marriage. Through their actions, and even more through their sermons, laymen came to be aware of the role churchmen were now playing in a sort of evangelical revival and a rebirth of learning, art and spirituality. In the context of this movement the reshaping by the Conqueror and his Norman clergy after 1066 of the rather old-fashioned Anglo-Saxon church can be seen as an attempt to bring it into the new clerical world of western Europe. Some bishops now removed their episcopal churches from remote rural centres to large and important towns like Exeter, Chichester, and Norwich, new monastic houses were founded, the episcopate was quickly Normanised. The new bishops, aided by the kings, and following examples set by King Edward, revised and strengthened the machinery of church government

---

[1] F.M. Stenton, *Anglo-Saxon England*, 2nd edn, Oxford 1947, 146–157.

[2] K. Cameron, *The Place-names of Lincolnshire* part I, *EPNS* 58, 1985, 29 and 116, notes Minster from 1525 and Minster Yard in 1601. The will of Sir John Rochford in 1401 described the cathedral as '*monasterium*', *Repingdon II*, LRS 58, 211–12. The usual phrase was 'St Mary of Lincoln'.

on Norman or French patterns, and proceeded to put into practice the reforms advocated by Hildebrand.[3]

This reshaping produced at Lincoln what seemed to be, at first, an entirely new institution, which would bring the largest diocese of eastern and midland England into the main stream of reform. The new foundation must nevertheless be seen against the Anglo-Saxon ecclesiastical arrangements which have already been briefly described. Here the work of a number of scholars investigating the Domesday Church has added to the picture drawn by Sir Frank Stenton, and provides an essential background for the story of Lincoln.[4] The archaeologists have also done much, especially, but not entirely, in urban settings, to add to the picture and we are fortunate that in Lincoln itself some of the pre-history of the parochial pattern has been elucidated.

The large diocese of Dorchester/Leicester/Lindsey to which Remigius was called almost immediately after William I's coronation had existed only since 1004.[5] It was a heterogeneous collection of shires, as the text of the profession of obedience made by Remigius to the Archbishop of Canterbury demonstrates:

> I R. (bishop) of Dorchester, Leicester and Lincoln, and of all the other *Provincie* over which my predecessors ruled . . .

This was a revision of the original profession made by Remigius to Stigand, and the use of the form Lincoln, rather than Lindsey, suggests that it followed the decision to transfer the episcopal centre to Lincoln.[6] The diocese of Lindsey, which was probably in existence from 678 to 1004, covered the former kingdom of this name north of the River Witham, and east of the River Trent. It is not yet certain where its episcopal church was: certainly post-medieval suggestions that it was at Stow cannot be substantiated. There may indeed have been several different episcopal foundations which could have served as cathedral towns at different times. It has recently been plausibly argued that Louth

---

[3] C. N. L. Brooke, *Medieval Church and society*, 1971, pp. 57–99; D. C. Douglas, 'The Norman episcopate before the Conquest', *Cambridge Historical Journal* 13, 1957, 101–15; D. Bates, *Normandy before 1066*, London 1982; F. Barlow, *The English Church 1066–1154*, London 1979; J. Blair, 'Secular minster churches in Domesday Book', in *Domesday Book: a re-assessment*, ed. P. Sawyer, Oxford 1985; B. Kemp, 'The mother church of Thatcham', *Berks. Arch. J.* 63, 1967– 8, 15–22; M. J. Franklin, 'The identification of minsters in the Midlands', *Anglo-Norman Studies* 7, 1985, 69–89. See also Pauline Stafford, *The East Midlands in the early middle ages*, Leicester 1985, p. 183 and figs. 66 and 67.

[4] The latest (3rd) edition of the *Handbook of chronology* (Royal Historical Society 1986), pp. 215, 218–19, has rather contradictory information about the date at which Leicester/Lindsey merged with Dorchester, and I have therefore retained the date given in the second edition.

[5] Ibid.

[6] M. Richter, *Canterbury professions*, CYS, vol. 67, 1973, no. 32.

5

contained such a church for a time[7] and David Stocker has pointed out to me that the church of St Martin in Lincoln seems to have been sufficiently important in the early tenth century to have qualified as an episcopal church. The town of Leicester must have had a cathedral and episcopal residence when the diocese was independent and these are presumably represented by the property held there by Bishop Wulfwig in 1066.[8] Dorchester itself had a large church, which was apparently served by secular canons, and which, since the establishment of the composite diocese in 1004, had served as its cathedral.[9] In the remaining shires which made up Wulfwig's diocese there was a series of large churches, many of which are regarded by John Blair as qualifying as minsters in 1086. Some, but not all, of these were hundredal churches, others had undoubted rights, still surviving, over neighbouring churches which must have been founded within the original *parochia*, or on a royal estate. In Oxfordshire Eynsham and Bampton, in Leicestershire and Rutland, Melton Mowbray, Oakham and Hambleton were such large churches. In Buckinghamshire the great church of Aylesbury, to which the freemen of eight hundreds paid a load of corn for every hide of land they held was an outstanding example of a great shire church (a head minster perhaps).[10] Huntingdon All Saints, soon to become the endowment of a priory, Luton, and Leighton Buzzard, Great Paxton, Leighton Bromswold, Hitchin and Welwyn, were equally important churches in the southern reaches of the diocese. In Northamptonshire Michael Franklin has been able to show that the churches of Fawsley and King's Sutton were also minster churches, substantial traces of whose status could still be detected in the later middle ages.[11] In Cambridgeshire Horningsea stands out, but in the Isle of Ely the abbey, which was soon to be the site of a new diocese, appears to have absorbed almost all ecclesiastical control.[12] Some, but not all, of these minsters had been served by a group of canons living a common life loosely connected with the rule of St Augustine, and sharing the endowments of the church in a rudimentary prebendal system. The 'portions' of the churches of Waddesdon and Bampton, which endured into the later middle ages, and those of Bedford St Mary, which was soon to pass to the newly founded priory of Newnham, fall into this category.[13]

The churches on royal estates often have an equally distinctive, though

---

[7] A. E. B. Owen, 'Herefrith of Louth', *Lincs. Hist. and Arch.* 15, 1980, 15–20.

[8] DB, f. 230v.

[9] *VCH Oxfordshire* 7, 1962, 52–3.

[10] DB, f. 143a.

[11] M. J. Franklin, 'Minsters and parishes, Northamptonshire studies', Ph.D. dissertation, Cambridge 1982.

[12] C. L. Feltoe and E. H. Minns, *Vetus Liber Archidiaconi Eliensis*, CAS 1917, 22–3.

[13] J. Godber, *Cartulary of Newnham Priory* I, BHRS 43, 1963, no. 7.

different, status, by which they are centres of networks of dependent churches and could be mistaken for minsters. The bishops of Dorchester had already acquired, or succeeded to a number of these larger churches, all of which now passed to Remigius, and were to become the endowment of his new cathedral. They were used, in particular, for the support of the new canons whom he was to introduce, so that individual members of the new chapter became the successors of the provosts or rectors of the Anglo-Saxon churches. Aylesbury, Buckingham (a secondary chapel, founded in a shire town, and linked with the great Northamptonshire royal church of King's Sutton), Leighton Buzzard and Leighton Bromswold were the most notable of these acquisitions. They had already put considerable power into the diocesan's hands, and would make the new chapter a powerful element in the newly designed diocese.[14]

The balance of emphasis in the Lincolnshire parochial arrangements was; if anything, more complex than elsewhere in the diocese. Here, because of the apparent interruption caused by the Danish invasions, it is difficult to distinguish genuine 'old minsters' among the many great churches, especially in Lindsey. Dr Blair notes Domesday evidence for important churches at Caistor, Wengale and Withcall and perhaps two Lincoln churches, All Saints in the Bail and St Martin. The two last-named are in fact no more than well-endowed proprietary churches. In Holland only Long Sutton appeared to stand out, while in Kesteven he names Threekingham, Boothby Graffoe and Wellingore, the latter of which, a well-endowed royal church, was said to belong to St Peter of Lincoln. Besides these there were a number of churches which reached royal hands through the disappearance from the political scene of Earls Edwin, Leofric and Morcar. Most of this group of churches were attached to the distinctively Danelaw organisations known as sokes, and exercised considerable control over lesser churches within the soke. Caistor was in fact of this type, and Kirton Lindsey, which has been suggested as a sort of minster for the northern part of West Lindsey.[15] Stow, before its re-endowment by Earl Leofric in 1061, may have played a similar part in the Wapentake of Well. Louth, the site of a pre-Danish monastic establishment, was the centre of a small group of dependent churches in Louthesk, and Horncastle the church of a soke which embraced dependent chapels in West Ashby, High Toynton, Mareham on the Hill and Wood Enderby. In Kesteven Sleaford stood in a royal manor, and had strong links with local churches such as Rauceby, while Grantham, which by 1086 had been given to the newly established cathedral of Salisbury, had very

---

[14] Dr Diana Greenway's discussion of these endowments in *Fasti 1066–1300* III, is the best summary available, but should be supplemented by the detailed introductions provided by the editors of *Registrum Antiquissimum*.

[15] *Fasti 1066–1300* III, 171–2.

clearly defined rights over a series of churches in Winnibriggs and Threo, and was evidently a hundredal minster.[16]

It is difficult to believe that the great church of Hough on the Hill, which stands close to the wapentake meeting-place of Loveden, does not also qualify as a hundredal minster, though its status, like that of Wengale, may have been obscured by its subsequent history as an alien priory. Both may, in fact, have been collegiate churches with canons serving nearby dependent churches, in much the same way as Castle Bytham was still providing in the late thirteenth century for 'portioners' in Little Bytham and Holywell.[17]

Against this complex background of 'important' churches, and of lingering survivals from pre-Danish religious life, as at Bardney and Partney, where attempts at refoundation were being made, together with the continual process of 'parochialisation' which was resulting from new manorial or proprietary churches, the establishment of a new episcopal church in Lincoln must now be viewed.

At the very outset of his reign William I had evidently appreciated the dangers inherent in the inchoate diocese held by Wulfwig of Dorchester and the death of this prelate enabled him to take immediate and decisive action. He appointed an enthusiastic and forceful successor, in the person of Remigius of Fécamp, a monk, and strengthened his position by a series of gifts along with, or soon after, his investment: the rich manor of Wooburn in Buckinghamshire, the monastic house and properties of Eynsham, the church of Buckingham and a house on the castle site at Huntingdon. Earl Waltheof followed up these gifts by the manor and church of Leighton Bromswold, which greatly strengthened his control of Huntingdonshire.[18]

To give the bishop comparable control in the north of the diocese, William made further gifts, which included the large manor of Welton by Lincoln, held for twelve carucates in 1066 by Swen, who is perhaps Swein the thegn who held land in Aisthorpe and Ingham, and the important churches of Caistor, Sleaford, Lincoln St Martin and Lincoln St Laurence.[19] It seems likely that, presented by the possibility of new Viking raids like that repelled by Harold at Stamford Bridge, William took immediate measures, including a strengthening of the bishop's power, to safeguard the area. Before 1068 he had constructed castles in Huntingdon, Cambridge and Lincoln to defend the route from London into the north; almost immediately the Atheling's determined attempt at a landing in north Lincolnshire showed how vulnerable the area still was.[20]

[16] For a general discussion of this point see Owen, *Church and society*, Lincoln 1971, 1–19.
[17] *R A* III, 343–59.
[18] *R A* I, 2.
[19] L R S 19, 47–54.
[20] J. W. F. Hill, 'Lincoln Castle, constables, and castle guard', *A A S R* 60, 1932–3, 1–22.

8

It must be with these conditions in mind that William promoted Remigius, a powerful and resolute supporter of the Norman rule, on whose assistance, most contemporary authorities are agreed, he could certainly rely. This may explain the large share of castle guard at Lincoln (forty-five knights) which was assigned to the bishop, along with a gift to him of a dwelling near to the castle, and in its Bail. There is no doubt that the strategic importance of Lincoln, and its relatively good communications, were also useful factors in preparing for a Viking attack: the need to control an area on which the royal hold was not entirely secure, together with the bishop's wish to strengthen his grasp of a remote and uncertain part of his diocese, evidently acted together. Remigius and William seem to have arrived jointly at the decision to transfer the headquarters of the diocese from Dorchester to Lincoln.

The town lay at the junction of Fossway, which led to Leicester and beyond to Oxfordshire and the south west and Ermine Street, which ran north from London to the Humber, through what would now be called the East Midlands, and passed within reach of the towns of Northampton, Huntingdon, Bedford and Cambridge. It was thus relatively easy for Remigius to reach the whole of his diocese from a centre in Lincoln. Lincoln was, too, a wealthy and important trading city, populous and attractive to foreign visitors, and entirely worthy to be the capital of a large and important diocese. It had excellent water connections with the east coast, and so with western Europe, and all told, must have seemed an attractive site for a new cathedral.

Ecclesiastical politics probably suggested more, and more pressing, reasons for the choice of Lincoln. Since the early eleventh century, when Lindsey was added to the Leicester/Dorchester diocese, the archbishops of York had been attempting to assert that, like Nottinghamshire, the area really belonged to the diocese and province of York. They had evidently also claimed Newark, Louth and Stow as episcopal endowments, but as recently as 1061 Wulfwig had appealed to Pope Nicholas II, who had pronounced that the bishop of Dorchester rightly held the *parochia* of Lindsey, and its properties in Newark and Stow, which Ailric the archbishop of York had improperly invaded. The York claim was revived in 1070 by Archbishop Thomas and was not finally withdrawn until Remigius' successor, Robert Bloet, succeeded in persuading (or bribing) William II to resolve the dispute in his favour.[21] It seems likely that Remigius' decision to move to Lincoln may have been influenced by the need to counter the claim of York and to secure a firm hold on the northernmost part of the diocese. Giraldus Cambrensis was perhaps repeating a commonly known fact when he reported that Remigius deliberately built his cathedral on the north bank of the Witham, in territory which York had claimed.

[21] *R A* I, 4, 247; Hugh the Chanter, *History of the church of York 1066–1127*, trans. C. Johnson, NMT, 1961, 8.

9

The first indication of the establishment of a cathedral at Lincoln seems to be the royal charter of about 1072, in which the King commanded Remigius to remove his chair from Dorchester to Lincoln, after he had taken counsel, presumably at or after the legatine council of 1070, with the Pope and his legates.[22] To establish his seat in Lincoln Remigius was given an area of toll-free land in the city, and here by 1086 he was firmly established:

St Mary of Lincoln in which the bishopric now is.

The chronicler Henry of Huntingdon, who was a schoolboy in Lincoln at the very end of this century, when the building of the cathedral church, dedicated to the Blessed Virgin, had already begun, recorded that it had been established at the very top of the hill, next to the castle, in *mercatis ipsis praediis*. The phrase he uses seems to imply an area of trading, if not an actual market-place, and since there is little doubt that a market would have grown up or been established at the main gate of the castle, it seems likely that on, or near its site, the cathedral was now begun.[23]

Orderic Vitalis, writing perhaps about the same time as Henry, does not report the building of the cathedral, although he mentions the castle, and another near contemporary, William of Malmesbury, suggested plausibly enough that Remigius chose to come to Lincoln because of its large and prosperous trading community.[24] None of these writers seems to have known any details about the events of the foundation, although a record, the 'Book of the Foundation', was certainly compiled and kept in the chapter library. This book was evidently used by Giraldus more than a century after the events it recorded, when he compiled a life of 'Saint' Remigius, in which he remarked on Remigius' intentions to flout the claims of York. This work of Giraldus was used, in common with the traditions he must have known throughout his life, by Bishop Sutton's registrar, John of Schalby, who had spent his whole life in the service of the cathedral and diocese, when he wrote an account of the foundation. Here for the first time, two hundred years after the events, the site on which the cathedral was built is described. Schalby tells us that it was founded where the church of St Mary Magdalen in the Bail of Lincoln had previously stood, and that the parishioners of that

---

[22] *R A* I, 2; D. Whitelock, M. Brett and C. N. L. Brooke, *Councils and synods* I, Oxford, 1981, 566 and note.

[23] Henry of Huntingdon, *Historia Anglorum*, ed. T. Arnold, *RS* 1879, 212. For an ingenious theory of the defensive purpose of the first church, see R. Gem, 'Lincoln Minster, *ecclesia pulchra, ecclesia fortis*', B A A L, 1986, 19–28.

[24] Orderic Vitalis, *Historia Ecclesiastica*, ed. M. Chibnall, O M T 1969–84, II, 219; William of Malmesbury, *De Gestis Pontificum*, ed. N.E.A.S. Hamilton, *RS* 1870, 312.

church were afterwards accommodated at an altar in the cathedral until Bishop Sutton established them in a new church outside the west gate of the cathedral yard.[25]

The topography of the town of Lincoln has been extensively discussed by Sir Francis Hill and by the archaeologists who have been working there in recent years, and much is now known about the site, on a crossing of the Witham where the limestone ridge, along which Ermine Street runs, was broken by the river.[26] The wide flood-plain of the Witham had been traversed, at least since Roman times, by a causeway (the Street) along which an extensive and populous trading suburb known as Wigford had spread. The upper town on the hilltop to the north of the crossing was enclosed by its Roman walls; south of it, on the lower slope of the hill, the Romans had later enclosed a further area which terminated just before the river crossing, where the Stone Bow still crosses the Street.

The south-west corner of the upper town, flanked on the west and south by the Roman walls, overlooked the flood-plains not only of the Witham, but also of the Trent a few miles to the west. It thus commanded a view along Fossway, the principal route from the south west of the country. It was here that William I had established his castle, and the rest of the area of the upper town within the walls became its bailey (the Bail). It was within this bailey, on a flat site in its south-eastern corner, bounded by the east and south walls of the town, that the cathedral was now begun. William's intention seems to have been to establish a cathedral at the castle gates and the spatial relationship between the two foundations, much the same as the contemporary arrangements at Old Sarum, is very marked. They lay not more than 200 yards apart, divided by a small, open square; between them they occupied at least half the area of the upper town.[27]

It is not easy to draw a complete ecclesiastical map of the upper city on the eve of the foundation of castle and cathedral. Archaeological evidence has established the existence since the fifth century of an ecclesiastical building, later known as St Paul's, on a site close to the Roman forum, in the north-west quarter of the city. By the time its parish was defined, its eastern boundary was the central street of the town, now known as Bailgate. There is documentary proof of the existence of a church dedicated to St Clement, close to the north

[25] Giraldi Cambrensis, *Opera*, ed. J. E. Dimoke, *RS* VII, 193–216; a translation was published by J. H. Srawley in 1949, *LMP* 2.

[26] J. W. F. Hill, *Medieval Lincoln*, Cambridge 1948; Michael Jones, 'Archaeology in Lincoln', *BAAL* 1986, 1–8; for an earlier view see L. A. Richmond, 'Roman Lincoln', *Archaeological Journal* 103, 1946, 25–56.

[27] J. W. F. Hill, 'Old Sarum', *VCH Wiltshire*, 6, 1953, 51–67 and plate facing p. 62.

gate of the city, and of All Saints in the Bail, which lay north of Eastgate and east of Bailgate.[28]

Nothing is known of any church which might have served the inhabitants of the houses cleared to make way for the castle, although one probably stood in that quarter of the city. It is possible that such a church, dedicated to St Mary Magdalen, was destroyed along with the houses which formed its parish, and that the dedication was subsequently revived in an altar in the cathedral to serve the lay parishioners. It may have been from knowledge of this fact that Bishop Sutton, defining the parish of the new church, added the castle and its inhabitants to it.[29]

Sir Francis Hill thought that the cathedral site had been occupied by an old minster or head minster dedicated to St Mary, and it has been assumed that this represented the episcopal church of the bishops of Lindsey. The case for an earlier church of some importance on the site of the future cathedral was fortified by a find of 'pre-Conquest stones' there. The origin and dating of these stones seems uncertain, and the size and importance of the church, if it existed, is not clearly established by them.[30] Further support for the theory of a head minster was provided in a suggestion by Sir Frank Stenton that because the cathedral claimed in the mid-twelfth century as an ancient right 'thraves called Marycorn' from the parishioners of Lincolnshire, it must have inherited such a right from an old minster dedicated to St Mary. If the thraves had been claimed only from Lindsey, this would have made a good case for an episcopal church for Lindsey at Lincoln, but the inclusion of the whole of Lincolnshire, that is of Kesteven and Holland, which were not part of the diocese of Lindsey, in this demand for Marycorn seems to invalidate the case. This mid-twelfth century claim made to the Pope, and a mention of non-payment in Bishop Dalderby's time, are the only occurrences of this due which have been noted: it is difficult to accept them as serious evidence for the antiquity of the precursor of the cathedral and easier to see them as no more than a twelfth-century attempt to manufacture evidence.[31]

There may well have been a church dedicated to St Mary on the site before the end of the Anglo-Saxon era, and this is perhaps borne out by the Domesday entry about St Mary, where the bishopric now is, which had and has (*habuit et*

---

[28] Hill, *Medieval Lincoln*, 104–5 and fig. 5, 'Lincoln *c*. 1100'; it should be noted that the site of All Saints in the Bail is wrongly indicated: there is documentary proof that it lay west of James Street, behind nos. 6 and 7 Eastgate.

[29] *R A* III, 1099.

[30] D. S. Davies, 'Pre-Conquest carved stones in Lincolnshire', *Archaeological Journal* 83, 1926, 1–20. I am very grateful to David Stocker for discussing with me the provenance of these stones.

[31] *R A* I, 255; for thraves as a payment to a minster church see A. F. Leach, *Memorial of Beverley Minster* I, Surtees Society, 98, 1898, 98–105.

habet) half a carucate of land in the fields of Lincoln.[32] Nothing in the entry suggests that this was an episcopal possession in 1066, and Wulfwig, making his assertion of a claim to Lindsey against York, in 1061, had not mentioned it. It had not at the death of Edward any possessions outside Lincoln and its half-carucate compares very badly with the whole carucate, and twelve tofts of nearby All Saints in the Bail. All told, it is impossible to believe that, if it existed, it represented an old and important minster.

It does not seem certain at what point Remigius began to build his cathedral, nor possible to say why it was ready for consecration only just before his death in 1091, but there is no doubt that by 1086 he had established firmly in Lincoln a chapter of secular canons. There seems to be no evidence to support Christopher Brooke's suggestion that until the very eve of the consecration Remigius was intending to set up a monastic chapter.[33] On the contrary, the Welton estate, which had been acquired by Remigius, was already held by six canons in 1086, and it seems certain that a full chapter had been planned, evidently as much to provide for the administration of the diocese, after the Norman example, as to serve the cathedral itself. Dr Diana Greenway's study of the first two centuries of the chapter's members has demonstrated that before the death of Remigius seven archdeacons certainly, and probably eight, all of them members of the chapter, can be distinguished, together with a dean, precentor, treasurer, and possibly a master of the schools or a chancellor. Henry of Huntingdon, whose father was among the first archdeacons, stated explicitly that before the death of Remigius twenty-one canons had been named, and had received prebendal endowments, although who they were, and what their endowments, cannot now be discovered. It is clear from the Domesday inquest that the bishop held, and had probably already assigned to his chapter, the churches (that is the rectorial endowments) of Sleaford, Louth, Kirton Lindsey, Caistor and Wellingore, Lincoln St Martin and St Laurence, Bedford St Mary, Leighton Buzzard, Buckingham, and Aylesbury and the manors of Leighton Bromswold and Wooburn. How quickly these became separate prebends, and were augmented by other acquisitions, cannot now be determined, for the process went on until the mid-twelfth century. The cathedral church and its chapter, then, were palpably in existence by 1091, when Remigius was succeeded by Robert Bloet; it is time now to consider the detailed development of both over the next three and a half centuries.

[32] L R S 19, p. 48; D B, f. 344a.
[33] G. E. Aylmer and R. Cant, *History of York Minster*, Oxford 1977, 25 and n. 73.

2

Architectural history

✻

PETER KIDSON

Although the actual building of the cathedral dates from 1072, when the seat of the bishop was transferred to Lincoln from Dorchester on Thames, the earlier history of both the city and the diocese had considerable bearing upon the origin and appearance of the Romanesque cathedral. There is a strong case for supposing that there was a bishopric at Lincoln in Roman times. This disappeared during or soon after the Anglo-Saxon invasions, but recollections of its existence probably explain the excursion of Paulinus to Lincoln on the way back from his missionary journey to the north of England in 627. On the other hand, when Archbishop Theodore of Canterbury set up the diocese of Lindsey fifty years later it was not based on Lincoln; and the fine stone church which Paulinus is said to have built – it must almost certainly have been a Roman building put into a state of repair – was lacking a roof when Bede wrote about it in 730. The independent diocese of Lindsey did not survive the Danish invasions. After the reconquest it was incorporated into the enormous Midland diocese of Dorchester, which spread northwards from the Thames to the Humber. This left Lindsey a part of the metropolitan province of Canterbury; but originally it seems to have been carved out of the ecclesiastical empire of Wilfrid of York; and for a short period in its early days it was regarded as part of the province of York. Later archbishops of York had long memories, and their claim to Lindsey became a bone of contention in their recurrent disputes with Canterbury.

It is against this background that the move from Dorchester to Lincoln has to be seen. Dorchester was obviously an unsuitable place from which to administer such a vast diocese; but Lincoln at its further end was not noticeably better. In any case the first Norman bishop, Remigius (1067–92), began to rebuild his

14

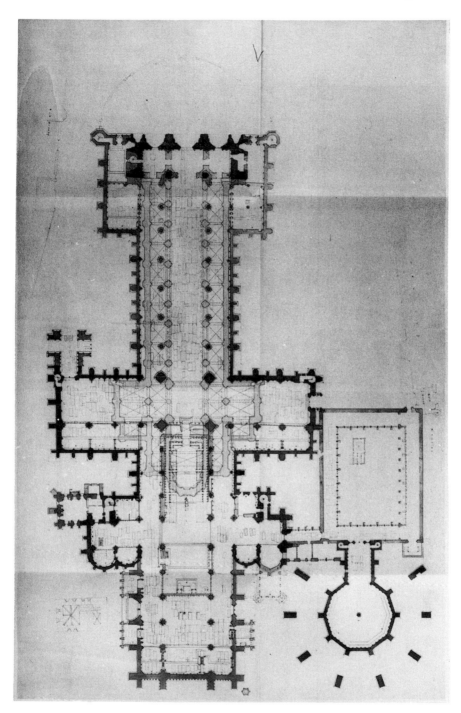

2   *Plan of Lincoln cathedral by E. J. Willson, Society of Antiquaries*

church at Dorchester soon after his appointment, a sure sign that at the outset he had no intention of moving. But there were rumours that Remigius obtained his bishopric as a reward for services to the Conqueror in 1066. Whether or not this was true, it laid Remigius open to the charge of simony; and when the matter of Lindsey was raised again in the course of argument between the two archbishops, Lanfranc of Canterbury and Thomas of York, this potential infringement of ecclesiastical law was gratefully remembered in certain quarters. Remigius went to Rome with Lanfranc and Thomas in 1071; and the whole case was thrashed out before the Pope. Exactly what decisions were reached at Rome is not clear; but at the end of it all Remigius returned home a loyal supporter of Lanfranc, with his title confirmed and his diocese intact. Shortly afterwards the move was made. In the light of the issues at stake the principal advantage of Lincoln, which lay within the confines of Lindsey, was that by making it the centre of the whole diocese, any attempt to separate Lindsey from the rest was effectively blocked. But another factor may well have been the belief that there were Roman precedents for the presence of bishops at Lincoln. From this point of view Lincoln was every bit as ancient as York; and arguments based on the seniority of York could therefore be countered.

So far as the building is concerned, reflections of the circumstances of its foundation can be detected in the character of its plan, and the peculiarities of its west front. Of the plan as a whole very little is actually known. The apse was found by E. J. Willson in 1852; and John Bilson, who carried out a series of small probing excavations in 1910, claimed to have found enough evidence to establish its outline and several dimensions.[1] His reconstruction presupposes an unusually high degree of regularity and symmetry for a large Romanesque church of the late eleventh century; but some of the masonry he found evokes extremely precise and suggestive analogies; and on the basis of these, opinions can be formed which are at least plausible. The crucial factor is the crossing. If this has been fixed correctly, then the extent of the transepts and choir are also known; and the presence of a support more or less in the middle of the north transept can be taken to imply that there were galleries across the extremities of the transepts. This sequence of inferences leads directly to the conclusion that the design of Remigius' cathedral was substantially similar to that of Lanfranc's Canterbury, which was itself closely related to another church with which Lanfranc had been connected at an earlier stage of his career, namely St Etienne at Caen. It may be surmised that Lanfranc brought his architect with him when he was translated from Caen to Canterbury; and that the man's services were made available to Remigius when he found himself in need of a new cathedral church at Lincoln.

---

[1] J. Bilson, 'Plan of the first cathedral church of Lincoln', *Archaeologia* 62, 1911, 553–64.

16

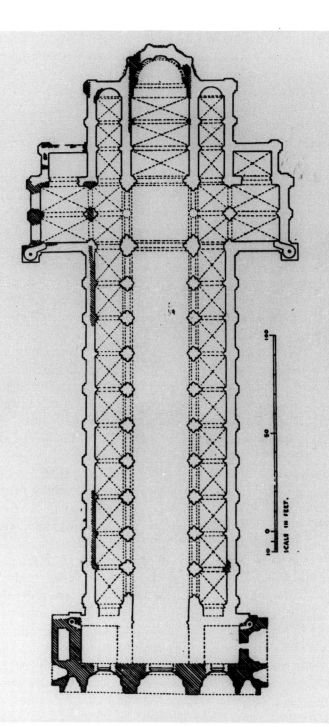

SCALE IN FEET.

3   *Plan of the Romanesque cathedrals by J. Bilson, Archaeologia 62, 1911.*

It is not necessary to press the affinities between Lincoln, Canterbury and Caen in every conceivable detail. What is important is that they allow us to form some general impressions about the elevation of Remigius' Lincoln. Of these by far the most valuable is the likelihood that there was a calculated contrast between the eastern limb and the rest of the building. The choir was certainly short. This could have been a necessary consequence of the position of the cathedral within the Bail, and owe little or nothing to architectural models. But the internal divisions between the choir and choir aisles must have been fairly substantial if not solid, and this suggests the presence of a vault over the choir. There are several eleventh-century analogies for such an arrangement. Solid walls in this position are normally associated with barrel vaults, but there is no reason why other types of vault should not have been used. The rest of the church must have remained unvaulted until the twelfth century, when Bishop Alexander is known to have provided it with a masonry roof. Traces that have survived on the Romanesque walls at the west end of the nave allow us to estimate that the original elevation was roughly equivalent to the arcade and triforium stages of the Gothic building, that is about 60 feet. This was divided into three not quite equal storeys.

The one part of the first cathedral for which there are no surviving analogies elsewhere is the west end. It is just as well that this imposing but curious design was never destroyed, because if it had been, attempts to reconstruct it, however ingenious, would almost certainly have got it wrong. Even so, the alterations it has undergone in subsequent centuries make it by no means easy to deduce its original form. As it stands today the west front at Lincoln may be described as a kind of two-towered facade. The towers themselves, however, can hardly have been a conspicuous feature of the eleventh-century facade. The upper parts were Gothic additions made in the fourteenth century by the treasurer of the cathedral, John de Welburne. The sections immediately below the Gothic work are covered with a rich display of late Romanesque ornament. These are the only parts of the towers that are in any real sense visible; but still further down they rest on square chambers concealed to north, south and west by twelfth- and thirteenth-century arcading and gables. These chambers and the passageway which connects them across the west front show every indication of having formed part of the original design. The chambers themselves may have been rudimentary towers, which were not unknown in the architecture of the time. It is also conceivable that they may have been intended to support timber towers. On the other hand they may have functioned purely as chambers, in ways that are no longer known to us. Below these chambers the basic structure must be fundamentally part of Remigius' work. On the outside this is not difficult to spot. But inside everything between the chamber and the ground was covered with a skin of Perpendicular panelling in Welburne's time; and then in

18

the eighteenth century John James, on the recommendation of Gibbs, strengthened the underpinning of the towers by filling what up to then had been open arches with solid walls. These convey the impression that the towers are continuous and recognisable entities from top to bottom. But it is a misleading impression; for if we think away James' walls, what we are left with is in effect a low western transept. It has often been supposed on the analogy with Caen and Canterbury that the galleries of the eleventh-century nave extended across the towers to reach the west front. But as these analogies manifestly fail to account for what we can see, it is gratuitous to invoke them, and in fact there is not the slightest shred of evidence for such an arrangement at Lincoln. On the contrary, on the north side, which is different from the south, there are extensive traces of a system of passageways and chambers in the thickness of the north wall which is quite independent of any gallery floor level under the towers, and unnecessary if there was such a floor. And on reflection it would seem bizarre madness to remove what would obviously have been a stabilising feature at any time after the mid-twelfth century, when serious masonry towers were added to the structure. In fact, it is clear that substantial modifications were made on the north side during the twelfth century to reinforce the walls that would have to bear the weight of the new stone towers, a concern that makes nonsense of the suggestion that the hypothetical tower galleries were removed on that occasion. The only other time when they might have been taken away was during Welburne's campaign in the fourteenth century but the same argument applies then. On the whole it seems better to accept the conclusion to which the evidence points, namely that the eleventh-century design included a low western transept, than to resort to a lot of special pleading in favour of an alternative.

Although the idea of a western transept at Lincoln is unfamiliar, there is nothing remarkable about it. Such a transept can still be seen at Peterborough, and there was something of the kind at Bury. In both places the facades bore a genetic resemblance to that of Lincoln. These two examples were considerably later than Lincoln. But at Winchester the foundations of the otherwise totally destroyed Romanesque west front indicate the possibility that the same idea was used in a more or less contemporary design. Old Sarum seems to have followed Winchester a generation later. Further afield similar western transepts were a feature of Romanesque churches at Novara and Pavia in northern Italy. One even turned up in the Gothic cathedral of Noyon.

Western transepts as such were common enough in pre-Romanesque church designs, especially in Germany. What is distinctive about Lincoln and the other examples just mentioned is that the transept occurs in direct conjunction with a properly designed facade. The facade at Lincoln which is now embedded in a thirteenth-century Gothic screen, was a striking affair of three tall and deep recesses framing doorways in the centre, flanked by smaller, blind niches at the sides. The whole composition combined a hieratic, triangular effect with a rectangular frame, the main horizontal element of which was the passage across the top of the facade on either side of the central recess. The sources of this design have aroused much speculation. Perhaps the most imaginative suggestion was Fritz Saxl's comparison with the facade of St Mark's at Venice.[2] But while it is not difficult to see what Saxl had in mind, it is exceedingly difficult to provide a plausible historical explanation for Venetian influence at Lincoln at the end of the eleventh century. More to the point is to recognise that the giant recesses of both Lincoln and St Mark's can be traced back to related if not exactly common sources in the monumental architecture of imperial Rome. In the case of Lincoln, what is required is a triumphal arch like the Porte-de-Mars at Reims to supply the formal inspiration, augmented by the more practical arrangement of fortified Roman gateways to explain the pas- sageways. It may be doubted whether Lincoln itself was able to supply these ingredients. The Roman gates in the walls of the Bail were still standing; but though they may have been noticed by the architects who built the castle at Lincoln, their scale was too modest for the cathedral. This does not rule out the possibility that there were monuments like the Porte-de-Mars elsewhere in England which have disappeared without trace. But while it would be nice to be able to track down the actual model, it is more important to realise that this is essentially a piece of theatrical architecture, in which contrived effects were being manipulated for what might almost be called propaganda purposes. The facade is at once both imposing and threatening. The threatening aspect has often been described in military terms. In the arches over the two side portals which still retain their eleventh-century form, an elementary sort of machicola- tion can be seen. No doubt there was originally something similar in the centre as well. The temptation to explain the presence of these features as defensive devices is hard to resist. However, the late eleventh century is rather early for machicolation in castles, let alone cathedrals; and it is not hard to think of alternative uses for narrow slits over doorways. One can imagine ornamental hangings being lowered through them on special ecclesiastical occasions. Certainly in any serious sense their military value can never have been great and can only have been effective at all against an enemy already established inside the Bail. Then there is the explicit statement of William of Malmesbury that King Stephen did actually fortify the cathedral when he besieged the castle in the winter of 1140–1. In itself this does not rule out earlier attempts at

[2] A. Clapham and F. Saxl, 'The cathedral building, the eleventh-century design for the west front', *Archaeological Journal* 103, 1947, 102–56.

fortification; but it could well explain the improbable presence on the north side of what have been identified as latrines, things which are not always easy to date. On the whole it seems prudent to view the defensive hypothesis with a certain amount of caution and reservation. The one context in which it could conceivably make sense is that precautions were considered necessary to anticipate sudden action by hostile ecclesiastical factions, among whom might be numbered supporters of the archbishop of York. Whether there was a genuine threat from that direction it is now impossible to say.

But the fact about which there can be no doubt at all is that the cathedral design which in its early stages was apparently content to follow a well-known Norman model, in the later stages of its execution gave up that model in favour of something altogether more grand and spectacular. At the very least, the theme of the three colossal arches turns one's attention in the direction of Rome. It would hardly stretch the limits of credibility to go further and suggest that they represent a calculated attempt to evoke impressions of Roman monumentality, not just to give the building greater dignity, but to remind those who knew about such things that the church of Lincoln had a Roman past. If so, Lincoln would not be an isolated case. At almost exactly the same time as Lincoln was going up, a new cathedral was under construction at York. Recent excavations have established the plan of this building, which turns out to have been very odd indeed.[3] But among the features that can be deduced with reasonable certainty is a giant order of blind arcades around its walls. This too could be construed as a way of laying claim to Roman origins. The reasoning would not be very different from that at Lincoln; and it could even be argued that the change of design at Lincoln was made in response to the example of York. Then at Speyer in Germany and Cluny in France, both of which were not far off being contemporary with Lincoln and York, extensive allusions to the vocabulary of Roman architecture were made with even more explicit intentions.

Not everybody who built Romanesque churches felt obliged to make such gestures, and among those who did, seriousness of purpose was not always of a very high order. Nor was it necessary for quotations to be more than nominal. What was understood to be a copy in the middle ages would seldom satisfy modern criteria. All this no doubt complicates the argument in detail, but whatever qualifications have to be introduced stop a long way short of disposing of it. Sensitivity about the past should have been particularly acute at Lincoln. There was no relic to lend its prestige to the new cathedral. Until one could be acquired, a claim to antiquity, even without continuity, would go a long way to provide suitable compensation.

[3] D. Phillips, *Excavations at York Minster II, the cathedral of Thomas of Bayeux*, Royal Commission on Historical Monuments, 1985.

The first cathedral was ready for consecration when Remigius died in 1092. The ecclesiastical establishment which he set up comprised a chapter of twenty-one secular canons under a dean. It may be supposed that in due course this body, which was gradually enlarged, came to regard itself as being especially responsible for its own part of the cathedral, namely the east end. Exactly when this happened is not clear. But so far as we can tell the first extensive modifications were confined to the western parts of the building and were specifically associated with the third bishop, Alexander (1123–48). Alexander had an insatiable appetite for building, and so there has been an understandable tendency to attribute to his patronage all the later Romanesque work at Lincoln. It is therefore worth remembering that there is only one item for which there is actual testimony. In his Life of Remigius, Giraldus Cambrensis says that the church had been damaged by fire, and that Alexander was the first to strengthen it with stone vaults.[4] This may seem to contradict the case for an early vault over the choir, but the apparent incompatibility with the archaeological evidence is not decisive. As there are clear traces of a Romanesque vault at the west end of the nave it can be inferred that, whatever else it did, Alexander's vault covered the nave. But the nave would not have been vaulted unless the choir had already been treated in this way. It therefore follows that in Alexander's time the cathedral became one of the first completely vaulted churches in England. It may even have been the first. This makes it unusually important to determine the date of Alexander's restorations. Elsewhere in the Life of Remigius, Giraldus tells us that in what was presumably the same fire the tomb of Remigius was cracked by a falling beam; the body was translated, and found to be uncorrupted. These events took place thirty-two years after the death of Remigius, i.e., in 1124. This is the sort of knowledge that could only have been acquired at first hand and in fact we know that Giraldus was living in Lincoln between 1192 and 1198, when he wrote his Life of Remigius. So he should be a reliable witness, and his date should command a certain amount of respect. Nevertheless, it was firmly set aside by E. A. Freeman in 1877, and most subsequent writers have been content to follow Freeman's argument in favour of 1141. The case against Giraldus' date is an intricate mixture of statements drawn from a variety of medieval chronicles, combined with stylistic theories about the sculpture on the west front. The author of the Anglo-Saxon Chronicle knew that the city of Lincoln was badly burnt in 1123. The Annals of Margam have it in 1122. This fire has often been taken to be the one Giraldus had in mind, although there is no reason why it should be. Anyone familiar with Lincoln will realise that a fire which affected the town at the bottom of the hill is unlikely to have also affected the cathedral at the top. Henry of

---

[4] Giraldi Cambrensis, *Vita Sancti Remigii*, *Opera* VII, ed. J. F. Dimock, *RS* 33 following.

Huntingdon, who should have known better than anyone else what happened at Lincoln in the second quarter of the twelfth-century, records no fire for either date; but as he did not start compiling his chronicle until *c.*1125, his silence is perhaps more serious for the second than for the first hypothesis. On the other hand, under 1146 he credits Alexander with a splendid restoration made necessary by an undated fire. Freeman, using the recently published Rolls Series, was able to dismiss the fire of 1122–4 on the authority of the Annals of Margam, where it is expressly stated that the 'monasterium' escaped the flames; as of course it did, whatever happened. For the fire of 1141 he relied upon chronicles from Peterborough and Louth Park. The latter alone connects the burning of the cathedral with the sack of Lincoln which followed the battle of 1141. What it comes down to is whether the Annals of Margam are really inconsistent with Giraldus and, if so, whether they are more reliable; and whether the chronicler of Louth Park knew more about the events of 1141 than Henry of Huntingdon. As a source of information about Lincoln the Louth Park chronicle is not impressive. It does not even mention the 'earthquake' of 1185. On the whole the verdict should go in favour of Giraldus. What has undoubtedly tilted opinion in favour of the later date are the portals and the frieze of the west front. Everyone has been agreed that these could not possibly belong to a campaign set in motion by a fire as early as 1124. while the 'splendid restoration' of Henry of Huntingdon positively invites one to suppose that they were part of what had been recently completed in 1146. But it is quite gratuitous to make this supposition. Henry does not specify what had been done, nor how long it had taken. He merely connects the new magnificence of the cathedral with a fire. This is precisely what Giraldus did later; and if the similarity means anything at all, what Henry had in mind was likely to have been the new vault over the nave.

The suggestion of 1141 was not a very happy one. Quite apart from the fact that Henry of Huntingdon would almost certainly have reported the burning of the cathedral if it had occurred, the Bail of Lincoln was the scene of intermittent violence between 1140 and 1145. William of Malmesbury, who was no friend to Stephen, claims that he used the cathedral for military purposes during this period in order to prosecute his siege of the castle. Henry of Huntingdon, whose sympathies lay with the King, does not mention this act of sacrilege, although he was equally horrified when the other side desecrated Hereford in the same way. But he refers to catapults and other warlike machines; and even if these were not actually installed on the cathedral, the west front was clearly no place for peaceful craftsmen. In any case five years were hardly long enough for the considerable operations involved. The vaults of the nave of Durham took five years to build, even though the walls were on a scale fit to support them. At Lincoln, to transform Remigius' nave for the purpose would have required something not far short of a total reconstruction. For this a starting date around 1125 would provide a much more spacious and satisfactory interval of time. It would also make the work at Lincoln coincide with the great period of Alexander's building activity elsewhere. This ended in 1139 when he was compelled by Stephen to relinquish his castles at Newark, Sleaford and Banbury. Not much is likely to have happened during the civil war.

The point of this lengthy excursion into chronology lies in the distinct possibility that Lincoln deserves the credit for being the first major English church to have been completely vaulted. This achievement is usually assigned to Durham, where the nave vaults are firmly dated to the five years between 1128 and 1133. But if the restoration of Lincoln began soon after the 1124 fire, in intention if not in execution, it may have anticipated Durham. Certainly a cosmopolitan prelate like Alexander, who must have known about the nave vaults being added to St Etienne at Caen and planned for the cathedral of Evreux at the time in question, is a better candidate than the remote monks of Durham when it comes to finding someone to promote such an ambitious project; and there is evidence that the nave of Durham had to be slightly modified in order to receive vaults. When this was done is not certain, but it could well have been inspired by the knowledge of what was happening at Lincoln. In the absence of hard evidence this intriguing idea must be left in the realm of speculation. But the mere fact that most of it no longer exists should not be allowed to obscure the extraordinary historical interest and architectural significance of the Romanesque cathedral of Lincoln.

The twelfth-century sculpture was no less important. Professor Zarnecki has demonstrated the influence of the portals at the famous French abbey of St Denis on those at Lincoln.[5] This provides a *terminus post quem* of 1140; and the most likely occasion for this influence to have made itself felt would seem to have been Alexander's second visit to Rome in 1145, when he could have seen St Denis. In 1775 James Essex, who at the time was engaged in restoring the cathedral, produced a drawing in which marks of damage are shown on two shafts, one on each side of the central door.[6] These would be compatible with the one-time presence of column figures. If the inference is correct, this would confirm the French connection in a most striking way. But for the most part, the Lincoln portals show little interest in the iconographical schemes that were the distinguishing feature of their French counterparts in the St Denis tradition. However, an extensive array of didactic imagery was deployed above the portals. Several stretches of a horizontal band of relief sculpture which once extended right across the facade have survived in position. This was concerned

[5] G. Zarnecki, *Romanesque sculpture at Lincoln*, LMP 2nd ser., 2, 2nd, edn revised 1970.
[6] Ibid., plate 28a.

with the first and last things, the two narratives reading outward from the centre. In this case Italy offers more promising analogies than France. Then there are some tantalising detached fragments in which Christ and the apostles were prominent, now lying in the north-east transept. The original location of these pieces can no longer be deduced from the fabric; but on iconographical grounds they ought to have occupied places in or near the centre of the facade. The whole programme seems to have been a comprehensive statement of the critical events in the Christian view of world history. But over and above this, there was evidently a great deal of interest in lavish displays of pure ornament. These are to be found not only on the portals, but also on the towers and gables which form the latest phase of the refurbishing of the Romanesque cathedral of the twelfth century.

The contrast between these intricate compositions and the stark, plain masonry into which they were set is a vivid reminder of the immense change which overtook the concept of the great church in the relatively short period which separated Alexander from Remigius. If the cathedral of Remigius offered an image of the Church Militant, that of Alexander, with all its finery and magnificence, seems somewhat closer to the Church Triumphant.

Alexander died in 1148. He may have been responsible for launching the campaign which transformed the west front; but it is unlikely that he saw much of it completed. The order in which the work was done is no longer easy to establish; and the complications of chronology have been compounded by restoration, which has destroyed some of the evidence and altered a lot of the rest. The side portals have creased mouldings, which seems to imply that they were somewhat later than the central portal. On the north side of the western block considerable volumes of twelfth-century masonry can be detected, and these indicate a concern to provide adequate supports for the new stone towers. They include few features which can be dated; but there is one base still visible in what is now the Morning Chapel which almost qualifies to be described as water-holding; and on the towers themselves waterleaf capitals, and bands of cusped ornament invite comparison with work done at Canterbury under Prior Wibert. A date not far removed from 1160 would be appropriate for all these details. The sculpture likewise does not seem to be entirely of one date. But however long it took to complete, the transformation of the west front gives the impression of having been a co-ordinated affair rather than a series of separate inspirations; and the role of prime mover should almost certainly be assigned to Alexander rather than his successor bishop Chesney.

The next chapter in the architectural history of the cathedral began in 1185. On 15 April of that year the Romanesque building suffered serious damage from what contemporary chroniclers called an earthquake. As the known effects seem to have been confined exclusively to the cathedral of Lincoln we may suppose that this was really a case of structural failure, and the most likely explanation is that some of the Romanesque vaults fell down. When reconstruction began, the first concern was to build a new east end; so we may perhaps go further and infer that the collapse took place in the old choir. This interpretation is confirmed by signs at the junction between the south-west transept and the south aisle of the nave which suggest that the transept was planned to join a narrower building than the present nave. This can only have been the Romanesque nave. So although work on the cathedral was more or less continuous for nearly a hundred years, and at the end of that time its appearance had been almost entirely transformed by a succession of modern Gothic idioms, it would be wrong to assume that a complete rebuilding was intended from the start. There is a major break in the design between the western transept and the nave; and what is left of the original eastern limb falls into two stylistically distinct parts: St Hugh's Choir and the main transept. Further changes separate the Gothic parts of the west front from the rest of the nave; and the west front seems to go with the lower parts of the central tower. The chapter house has features in common with both the nave and the Angel Choir; and the Angel Choir itself was virtually a separate operation. So was the cloister. Then, after a pause, a splendid addition was made to the tower over the crossing at the beginning of the fourteenth century, and later still the Romanesque towers at the west end were also heightened in a half-hearted attempt to bring the west front up to date. The result is at least nine separate operations not counting the screens, tombs and chantries, which contribute a great deal to the character and effect of the architecture. Put like this, the rebuilding of the cathedral might seem to have been a sequence of haphazard inspirations but it would be equally wrong to conclude that there were no comprehensive designs. So far as the main building is concerned, two basic phases can be recognised: the original eastern limb; and the nave. The rest was controlled to a greater or lesser degree by one or other of these.

The new building was not started until 1192. The interval of seven years implies that the situation was somewhat less than desperate; and no doubt the time was taken up with indispensable preparations. One would be the task of raising money; the other the acquisition of land needed for an enlarged choir. Remigius' cathedral occupied a site in the south-east corner of the Bail, and no expansion eastward could be made without breaching the Roman wall, which still formed the city limits in the immediate vicinity. A salient wall had to be constructed, and this would presumably have to be complete before the Roman wall could be demolished. A similar operation was required sixty years or so later when a further eastward extension of the cathedral was made in the form of the Angel Choir. It is important to note that the chapter house also lies beyond the line of the Roman wall; so unless there was yet another adjustment to the wall, provision for this ought to have been made between 1185 and 1192. As for money, we hear of a chantry for benefactors in 1205; and there are stories of offerings from pious peasants. But the burden of the cost must have fallen upon the clergy of Lincoln, the prebendaries and the bishop. As St Hugh's name has become inextricably attached to the first Gothic choir, there is perhaps a tendency to think of it as his work. No doubt he contributed generously to the building fund, and the fact that he was eventually buried there may allow us to suppose that he took an interest in its progress. But its sumptuous style can hardly reflect the austere taste of a distinguished Carthusian. The prime function of the new choir was to provide suitable accommodation in which the Dean and Chapter could conduct the prescribed liturgy of the Church. Although in many ways it was a remarkable and even unusual building, its basic dispositions represent attitudes and expectations that had become widespread among the higher English clergy of the time. The model was provided by the recently completed Gothic choir of Canterbury.

The scope of what was planned in 1192 can be deduced from a plinth which extends eastward from the corners where the western transepts and the nave meet. This is now interrupted by the Angel Choir; but it is beyond question that it once continued around the original east end. This means that the whole eastern limb (apart from the Galilee) was laid out in a single operation. It comprised eastern and western transepts, the choir in between, and the ambulatory and chapels which disappeared to make way for the Angel Choir. The form of the lost apse was partly recorded in 1886 (see fig. 3). Not everything was made clear in the brisk excavation which uncovered its remains, but enough was found to establish that, while it conformed in principle to the general pattern of apsidal east ends, in detail it was quite unlike any other apse known to us. The terminal feature on the axis seems to have been a large chapel, apparently hexagonal in shape. In the context of contemporary architecture, this chapel cannot easily be explained except as a kind of copy of the corona at Canterbury. This at once raises the question of what purpose it may have been meant to serve. At Canterbury the corona featured prominently in the new cult of St Thomas. At about the same time, at Trondheim in Norway, a large octagonal chapel was started at the east end of the cathedral in honour of St Olaf. Both can be regarded as belonging to a long tradition of eastern rotundas, in which special local cults were housed. But in 1192 Lincoln had no saint of comparable standing. In due course the omission was repaired by St Hugh himself. However, in 1192 any expectations in that direction would have been premature. At this point we may recall Giraldus Cambrensis and his life of Remigius written at Lincoln in the 1190s. That life was not a straightforward biography, but an undisguised essay in hagiography, complete

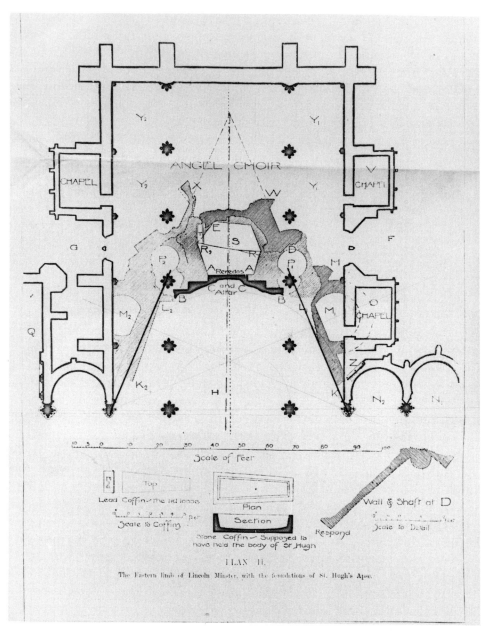

4 *The eastern limits of the cathedral, from a paper in* The Builder, *21 May 1887*

with miracles. It was the sort of thing that constituted the first move in procuring a canonisation. In the event the effort was discontinued in favour of a

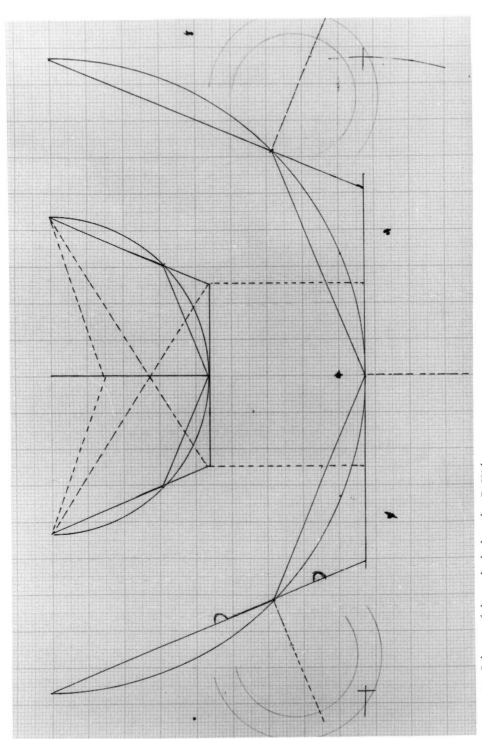

5   *Scheme of the cathedral vaults, P. Kidson*

more illustrious candidate. But if it had been successful, we would have encountered a founder cult at Lincoln in honour of St Remigius, located in the hexagonal chapel.

This may account for the presence of the chapel, but it does not explain the form of the apse. So far as we know, this was unique. Essentially it consisted of an irregular, wedge-shaped ambulatory with three chapels and two stair-turrets between them. It is possible to show that behind this curious arrangement there was a regular geometrical construction, namely half an octagon based on the eastern crossing, with the three chapels disposed symmetrically around the angles of the figure instead of along the sides. Experiments with polygons twisted out of their customary alignments were not unknown during the twelfth century, especially in the east of England; but nothing on the scale of the Lincoln apse had previously been attempted.

The somewhat perverse and mannered character of the apse design pervades the whole of the first phase of Gothic Lincoln. That the starting-point was William of Sens' new choir at Canterbury is as valid for the elevation as for the plan. This can be demonstrated by comparing sections of the two choirs, which are not only alike, but unlike every other choir section of the period in England. However, the architect was not content merely to follow Canterbury. Wherever possible he applied the principle that more was better than less. At Canterbury the choir piers were left plain and only those further east embellished; at Lincoln all the piers were surrounded by *en délit* shafts and some had crockets as well. At Canterbury the triforium openings were conceived in two planes; at Lincoln there are three. At Canterbury there was one clerestory window for each bay, and sexpartite vaults over each pair of bays; at Lincoln, in the eastern transepts, there are two windows, and a sexpartite vault over each bay. The result is a perceptible increase in both the number of shafts to be seen and the obtrusiveness of mouldings. On the other hand, there is a corresponding reduction in the extent of bare surfaces. Variety was also esteemed above uniformity. Piers which might have been expected to share the same form are different. The planes of the triforium are not regular in their arrangement, and a whole series of lobed perforations diversifies the tympana of the triforium. To do the same thing twice was evidently a confession of failure. The attitude is consistent, even if it is wayward.

The structure of St Hugh's Choir is as weird as its appearance is congested. Although the buttressing system can only have derived from Canterbury, the element of French logic which can still be detected at Canterbury has disappeared. Instead of being supported on sensible structural arches, the outer wall of the clerestory sits on a series of useless little arches corbelled out of the triforium. It is almost as though Baron Munchausen had taken charge. Then for good measure the whole upper part of the choir is honeycombed with apertures and recesses which have so far successfully defied elucidation.

30

The most celebrated of the eccentricities of St Hugh's Choir are its vaults. These do not conform to any symmetrical pattern of ribs. Instead each bay has two keystones; and each keystone receives two ribs from one side and one from the other, the asymmetries being in a sense cancelled out by being paired off together. The extra ribs qualify as the earliest known tiercerons. In addition there is a continuous ridge-rib which presumably helps to brace the keystones and keep them in position. So far as we can tell, no vaults of this kind had been conceived before Lincoln. Viollet-le-duc, who saw them in 1852, politely declined an invitation to claim them for the genius of France; and since then they have generally been attributed to an Englishman who was either 'mad' or 'dionysiac' according to taste. To German eyes they are decidedly reminiscent of vaults in eastern Europe which date only from the fourteenth century; and there have been sporadic efforts to argue that they formed no part of the original design, but were introduced during later alterations. These have usually been associated with the collapse of the central tower in 1237 or 1239. Ingenious theories have been proposed, connecting them with Bishop Grosseteste's views on optics and perspective.[7] Unfortunately, quite apart from the archaeological difficulties, these overlook the fact that for almost his entire episcopate (1235–53) Grosseteste was *persona non grata* in his own cathedral. It is extremely unlikely that the canons of Lincoln *c.*1240 had read Grosseteste on light and vision; if they had, whether they understood what they read; and if they did understand it, whether they would have done Grosseteste the recondite honour of placing over their heads an arrangement of ribs that would remind them for ever of someone they cordially hated. One may sympathise with those who are perplexed by having to date what is normally taken to be a late Gothic feature before High Gothic was properly launched; but the evidence seems to require this conclusion, and it should warn us against schemes of development which are too tidy and doctrinaire. The building itself makes it abundantly clear that although minds were changed on perhaps more than one occasion, when the upper parts of St Hugh's Choir were built no provision was made for buttressing a sexpartite system of the kind we find in the two transepts. All attempts to show that the building was altered to accommodate the present vaults create more difficulties than they solve. This was demonstrated with crushing effect by J. Bilson in 1911;[8] but wishful thinkers are not often persuaded by logic.

The evidence of the Fabric can be confirmed by two other considerations.

[7] F. Nordstrom, 'Peterborough, Lincoln, and the science of Robert Grosseteste', *Art Bulletin* 38, 1955, 241–72.

[8] J. Bilson, 'Lincoln cathedral: the new reading', *Journal of RIBA* 3rd ser., 18, 1911, 464–75, 551–4.

One is the problem of lighting the choir. Although there are two lancets in each bay of both transepts, they are not very effective as sources of light because they are largely enveloped by the adjacent sexparite vaults. The asymmetrical vault pattern is not only less constricting, but allows a third lancet to take its place in the clerestory of the choir bays. The second arises from the special circumstances involved in putting vaults over the wedge-shaped bay at the east end of the choir. Various possibilities were open to the designer; but given his evident predilection for dense networks of forms, a scheme with two keystones and a ridge-rib could recommend itself quite naturally. The asymmetry follows directly from the presence of an even, as opposed to an odd, number of keystones.

The most that can be conceded to the change of plan theory is that the design was modified in the course of construction. It may be postulated that when work began on the new eastern limb in 1192, a uniform elevation of sexpartite vaults over single bays was intended throughout. Evidence of this can be found in the buttresses along the aisle walls of St Hugh's Choir. The original design was retained for the two transepts, but altered in the upper parts of the choir proper, and presumably the apse as well, for reasons which were entirely pragmatic and which may have become apparent as work proceeded. That it was recognised as a kind of solecism at the time may be inferred from the fact that this particular feature of Lincoln was totally ignored in England.

Another feature of St Hugh's Choir is the double arcading of the choir aisles. This also has come in for attention from those who have wished to explain the complexity of the existing structures as the result of later alterations. In this case it has been supposed that the outer or order was added to the inner at some date after the aisle walls were first constructed. Again, one can appreciate the reasons for such a theory. But again, the explaination creates more difficulties than it removes. Not only are there zones where the two patterns are reversed, but anyone who wishes to adopt this solution has to account for the presence of a supporting shelf wide enough to hold the two orders. This has never been augmented. It supports the wall shafts as well as the arcading and these must have been there from the start. In fact there is something similar to these free-standing shafts in the retrochoir aisles of Winchester, which date from a period not much later than 1200. The same feature can also be found in the Trinity Chapel at Canterbury. These examples are more important for dating purposes than the contrapuntal triforia of Worchester and Beverly, which, though they owe something to St Hugh's Choir, are much later. Another dating control is provided by the north-west portal at St Alban's, which belongs to the period immediately after 1195 and where there are crocketed pilasters very close to the so-called 'Trondheim' piers at Linciln.

The visual opulence of St Hugh's Choir may have been an end in itself and require no further explanation. But there is one feature which may suggest certain iconographical overtones. A by-product of the conjunction of two different kinds of arcading along the aisle walls is the presence of a series of small blind niches above the arches and below the windows. Many of these are occupied by busts, the heads of which are free-standing. The heads are manifestly not medieval; but much of the drapery looks authentic. What seems to have happened is that the medieval heads fell victim to iconoclastic zeal after the Reformation, and were restored in the eighteenth century. In the middle ages such figures were unlikely to have been merely decorative. The closest parallels to them are to be found on a famous reliquary, the *Annoschrein* at Siegburg in the Rhineland, which was made in 1183. This analogy suggests that the Lincoln busts ought to have been part of the 1192 design; but it also conveys a sense of the choir sharing some of the characteristics of a reliquary. It would be foolish to press the idea too hard; but the basic imagery of the great church was continuously changing, and by the end of the twelfth century a feeling that churches, and especially cathedral choirs, were themselves large reliquary caskets, or had something in common with reliquaries, was beginning to receive acknowledgement in the way they were designed or at least decorated. Such a change of basic imagery almost certainly accounts for the disappearance of towers in early Gothic churches. For most of the eleventh century towers evocative of the Church Militant were still an essential part of a great church design. In the new east end at Lincoln there is evidence that a substantial tower was planned for the north end of the north-east transept. But it was never taken above clerestory level; and equivalent features inside the south-east transept were actually removed. That part of the building was finished off in a different style at a date well into the thirteenth century.

St Hugh's Choir was a seminal building and its influence on the subsequent development of ecclesiastical architecture both in England and abroad can hardly be overestimated. But it was also experimental, and it was some time before its example began to take effect. The man who built the main or western transepts at Lincoln does not seem to have been unduly impressed. The buttressing system implied by the plinth was designed for the same sort of sexpartite vault over single bays that is found in the eastern transept; and no further explanation may be needed to account for the change back from the asymmetrical to the symmetrical form. Then the western walls of the transepts have a different look about them when compared with the earlier work. The lancets are sharper, and closer together; the mouldings and ornament have changed. But while all this may be due to the arrival of a new man, it should be remembered that these walls have to take the full thrust of the vaults without the support of aisles or chapels; and their different character may to some extent reflect this structural function. However, there were changes of another kind. The double arcading was abandoned, and the facades altered so that rose windows could be introduced. That rose windows were not part of the original design can be deduced from two considerations. In the middle of the south transept facade there is a buttress which was anticipated when the plinth was laid down, but which stops short below the rose, and in fact buttresses nothing. That buttress must have been intended to support a descending ridge-rib. (There may have been something similar at the east end of the choir.) Such a rib would have been compatible with lancets, but not with a rose. Then the rose in the north-transept facade, the so-called Dean's Eye, is clearly too big for its position in the elevation, and cannot have been part of the original design. Yet it has never been altered and must have been constructed with the rest of the transept. As a result the vaults had to be deformed in order to accommodate the rose. Exactly what happened on the south side before its counterpart – the Bishop's Eye – was introduced in the fourteenth century, it is impossible to say.

There are two other modifications to the main transepts, represented by interruptions in the original plinth. These are the portals, attached to its north and south extremities. The latter, which opens westwards, is a grand affair. It is now called a Galilee, but both its splendour and its position suggest that it was really intended to be the bishop's entrance into the cathedral. The more modest doorway in the north face of the north transept was presumably intended for the dean. There was already a door for the chapter in the north-east transept.

Exactly what these changes signified is not easy to decide. They may have been made on an entirely pragmatic basis. On the other hand, they may have been connected, in ways that we can no longer recognise, with the decision to replace the Romanesque nave with an entirely new structure. This was the most important decision made between 1192 and 1280; but its date cannot be fixed with any accuracy. On grounds of general probability it ought perhaps to have been made after the Interdict, and the war which culminated in the capture of Lincoln by the supporters of Henry III in 1216; and indirectly it may have been connected with the efforts to get Hugh canonised. That was not finally accomplished until 1220, although the idea must have been in the air from the time he died, i.e., 1200.

The nave is distinguished by a higher and more elaborate plinth than the eastern limb. On the south side there is no proper corner between the south-west transept and the south aisle of the nave. The aisle wall simply abuts on to one of the minor buttresses of the transept. On the north side, there is a proper corner, which can be recognised both inside and outside. The reason for the difference lies ultimately in the fact that the Romanesque church did not lie on the same axis as its successor, but was somewhat to the north. Further consequences of this can be seen at the west end, where the Gothic nave has been grafted on to the western block of the earlier building. About half-way along, the south aisle wall starts to bend slightly to the north, in order to align itself with the south-east corner of the block, which it would otherwise have missed; as though it was only at that point that the decision was taken to retain the western block. The main arcades, on the other hand, go straight ahead, and meet the western block exactly as the difference between the two axes requires. The central arch of the western block, which is narrower than the nave, appears to be closer to the north arcade than to the south; and the ridge-rib of the vault makes a spectacular lurch as it passes from one axis to the other.

At first sight the nave gives the appearance of being a more symmetrical and coherent piece of architecture than St Hugh's Choir. Insofar as this is true it has to do with the enlarged scale. In the terminology of the middle ages, St Hugh's Choir was built 'to the triangle', that is, the cross-section can be defined by an equilateral triangle; whereas the nave was built 'to the square'. The difference in height is more than 10 feet. The increase has been apportioned more or less equally between the three storeys. Not only is there more room vertically. The bays were also lengthened. They are well over 26 feet. By the standards of the time this is very large indeed – considerably larger than the average bay lengths of the great French cathedrals. The piers, of varied design, are slightly more substantial than those of St Hugh's Choir before the latter were reinforced, but the predominant impression is one of greater spaciousness. In structural terms the ratio between load and supports was taken well beyond the recommendations of prudence and seldom if ever approached again during the middle ages. The sheer size of the arcade arches tends to eliminate any sense of division between nave and aisles. In effect, there is one vast space which extends from aisle wall to aisle wall. On the other hand, the upper walls and vaults of the nave are even more congested than the equivalent parts of St Hugh's Choir. Because of the greater bay length, there is room for more shafts and perforations in the triforium. There is also room for a third keystone in the vault, which allows the tiercerons of St Hugh's Choir to be reconciled with the symmetry of the transepts. For good measure further tiercerons were introduced, attached to short transverse ridge-ribs in each bay. This means that no less than seven ribs, not counting the wall-ribs, rise from each set of springers. Although the angles between the ribs constantly change, they endlessly reiterate the section of the nave. Visually, the result is something almost diametrically opposed to what we find in orthodox – one might almost say French – sexpartite or quadripartite patterns. Instead of broad expanses of surface, the spaces between the ribs are tiny, mostly elongated triangles; and instead of ribs converging on a point in the middle of each bay, they diverge from points on the walls between bays. The rhythm of the rib patterns is thus out of phase with that of the arcades. While it would be wrong to say that the traditional Gothic bay system has been superseded, it is clearly no longer a dominant consideration. The repetitions and contrasts which control the architectural experience were calculated by an unusually sensitive and pragmatic mind. The visual impact of the vaults depends to a very large extent on the interaction of the spreading ribs with the long receding horizontals of the ridge-rib and the string courses of the elevation. In a shorter or higher nave they would be far less striking. Then the tremendous concentration of small formal details in the zone between the two rows of windows has a cumulative effect which is certainly greater when seen as a horizontal band than as part of a diversified set of verticals. In these and countless other ways the nave of Lincoln qualifies as one of the most subtle achievements of medieval art; and the disposition to credit its conception to an architect of genius is understandably strong.

Nevertheless, there is abundant evidence that what we now admire was the result of second thoughts. There are as many solecisms or *non sequiturs* in the nave as in St Hugh's Choir if only we pause to look for them. In the easternmost bays of the nave aisles, there is a buttress on the south side with nothing to do; while on the north side there is a rib needing support, but no buttress to provide it. The wall arcading of the north aisle is out of phase with the bay system, with the result that the wall shafts coincide with the middle of one of the arches and are therefore partly free-standing. In the south aisle the arcading and the wall shafts are in phase, but the mouldings and ornament are not the same as on the north. Then the vaults of the north aisle have a continuous ridge-rib, whereas in the south aisle there is an interrupted ridge-rib. The most important difference, however, can only be seen in the galleries. On the south side the buttressing system was prepared for sexpartite vaults over single bays. On the north side, it conforms to the vaults that were actually erected. From this it can be deduced that the south side, at least up to gallery level, was built before the equivalent stage on the north; and that it was the work either of the man who did the main transepts, or at any rate someone who shared his views about the St Hugh's Choir vaults. The real man of genius at Lincoln was his successor. He was the one who realised that the way to improve upon St Hugh's Choir was not to go back to sexpartite vaults, but further in the same direction, by adding a third keystone and more tiercerons. The distinguishing characteristic of this man was his precocious ability to think of vault-ribs not as complete arches, i.e., something fundamentally two-dimensional, but as spreading clusters of arcs, grouped into three-dimensional cones. It took some time for the full implications of this shift of emphasis to be realised. The intention is clear enough in the high vaults of the nave; but the shape of the bays made some degree of compromise necessary. The vaults of the Morning Chapel at the west end of the nave (north side) took the idea a step nearer fulfilment. But it was the chapter house which produced the first really spectacular demonstration of what this new approach to vaulting could achieve.

The idea of the chapter house almost certainly goes back to the commencement of operations shortly after 1185 when the Roman wall was breached. The metrical life of St Hugh says as much, although the actual execution must belong to a later period. The metrical life also says that it was finished by the second bishop Hugh, that is before 1235. Its polygonal form must have matched that of the chapel at the east end of St Hugh's Choir. Lincoln was not the first polygonal chapter house, nor the first to have a central column. The central column as such was probably needed to support a vertical post in the middle of the timber construction above the vault. But so far as we can tell no previous centrally planned building had been associated with a free-standing cone of ribs. The chapter house has ten sides, and there are two ribs per side; so the complete cone has no less than twenty ribs. The cone is defined by a ridge-rib; and from each angle of the building what might be called partial counter-cones rise to meet the central cone. It is difficult to regard this extremely elaborate and costly pattern as anything other than an architectural conceit. Arguments have been put forward to show that the polygonal shape had certain practical advantages for the transaction of chapter business; but if so these were almost certainly discovered from experience. Cathedral chapters elsewhere, especially outside England, seemed to have managed well enough with simpler shapes. The shape, and the vault go together; and like the choir the chapter house gives a decided impression that the canons of Lincoln had a taste for conducting their affairs in sumptuous architectural settings. Some of the details which appear there for the first time were taken up in parts of the cathedral which were built after the chapter house; for instance the lozenges above the lancets on the exterior are a feature of the west front; and the foliated corbels in the angles of the interior were used to great effect in the Angel Choir.

The west front of Lincoln is usually called a screen, and classified with other thirteenth-century English screen facades such as Wells and Salisbury. This is no doubt correct, but there is much more to the Gothic west end than a wall of niches. The retention of the Romanesque facade can have been justified only on grounds of economy. In any case the screen extends well beyond the Romanesque facade on either side; and behind these extensions two considerable chapels were introduced into the design, the Morning Chapel on the north, and the Consistory Court on the south. For these there are no obvious contemporary analogies; and one may wonder whether at least part of the inspiration was provided by the old Romanesque western block which was enveloped within this new building. It is true that the chapels can hardly be called western transepts; but echoes from one generation of medieval cathedrals were often taken up in the next; and it is gradually becoming clear that past precedent was just as much a factor in the design process as current fashion. The two chapels are not identical. The Morning Chapel is treated as though it is composed of four cells which meet around a free-standing pier. This cannot be said to support a cone of ribs; but eight arches descend upon it at regular intervals. The Consistory Court on the other hand, dispenses with this central support altogether. Here the ribs form themselves into what in plan may be described as a net pattern of parallel lines; but structurally it has the character of a dome, or at least a shell. The ribs are entirely superficial. This vault is perhaps not as famous as some of the previous innovations at Lincoln; but it deserves recognition, and its influence on later medieval vaulting practice was no less profound.

The Consistory Court has another claim on our attention. The east gable and two of its lancet windows are filled with a rudimentary type of tracery – so-called Y tracery. In the windows this could be the work of restorers who may or may not have put back what they saw. But if the feature was original, it would not in itself be remarkable, nor is it likely that this was the first time Y tracery had been used in an English church. Its presence becomes interesting when we examine the central window of the west front. In its present form this window is filled with Perpendicular tracery which belongs to Treasurer Welburne's fourteenth-century alterations. But the frame of the window is not part of Welburne's work. It belongs to the thirteenth century, and there is no reason to suppose that it was not put there when the rest of the facade was built. Now this frame was intended for a very large window indeed, one which occupied most of the west wall of the nave. As we have no more than the frame, we cannot say how it was filled. But there are several surviving windows from the second half of the thirteenth century which have compositions of tracery made up of a series of overlapping Ys placed side by side. The result is an intricate reticulated pattern. It is at least possible that the model for such windows was the one in the west front at Lincoln. Not least among its characteristics would be an almost perfect concordance with the effect of the spreading ribs of the vault along the vista of the nave. But whatever the pattern, the thirteenth-century west window has a claim to be the first large window in an English church to have had a display of tracery. The date of the west front cannot be fixed with absolute certainty. However, it has many distinctive details not found in the rest of the nave but which turn up in the central tower. The diaper pattern is a case in point. For the central tower we have a date. A newly built tower is reported to have collapsed, in 1237 according to one authority, or in 1239 according to another. Whichever is correct, we cannot be far wrong in putting its replacement at the beginning of the 1240s. The diaper pattern, which is above the west window, makes it unlikely that the facade as a whole was later than 1240; and the west window ought to have been in position some time before that date. But if that is so, then the Lincoln window was considerably earlier than the traceried windows which appeared at Westminster Abbey after 1245, and which are usually taken to have been the first of their kind.

The collapse of the central tower entailed not only the reconstruction of the crossing piers and the lantern, but the adjacent bays of the western transepts and St Hugh's Choir as well. For good measure most of the piers of St Hugh's Choir were strengthened. Signs of this work are easy to spot. For the first time in the long period of construction taste and craftsmanship failed. The reinforcements are cheap and crude. But the lapse was short-lived. Soon after the repairs were completed, perhaps even while they were still in progress, work began on what has always been regarded as the most sumptuous of all the component parts of the cathedral, the Angel Choir.

The Angel Choir replaced the curious wedge-shaped apse of the 1192 design. The primary purpose of the new building was manifestly to house the shrine of St Hugh, and to facilitate the movement of pilgrims intent on offering their devotions to him. Exactly why the change should have been considered necessary it is now impossible to say. We do not know to what use the hexagonal chapel at the end of the wedge was put before it was pulled down; or why it was considered unsuitable for the purpose of housing the cult of the saint; or even where St Hugh was buried when he died in 1200. Adam of Eynsham, who wrote the *Magna Vita* of St Hugh, provides the meagre information on which all speculations have to be based. Hugh stipulated that he should be buried near the altar of St John the Baptist, and Adam adds that the tomb was placed on the north side of the building. As we have no idea where this altar was located, the further information does not help very much. The tomb could have been on the north side of the hexagonal chapel, or any other chapel for that matter; or the choir, or in the north-east transept, to which Hugh's predecessors had been translated. The hexagonal chapel recommends itself as the spot closest to Hugh's final destination. By and large the distances involved in the translation of saints were kept to a minimum. On the other hand the northernmost chapel on the north-east transept was enlarged not long after it was built, and given a separate entrance. (It was put back into something like its original form by James Essex in his restoration of 1772.) By the seventeenth century this chapel was known as the Lady Chapel, and the position is not unusual for Lady Chapels. But dedications were not always constant, and it may once have been the Baptist's Chapel. In any case, St Hugh may not have been left in peace between 1200 and 1280, when he was translated to the Angel Choir. If his original burial place had been anywhere east of the eastern transepts, this would have been necessary while the Angel Choir was being built. Wherever the tomb was, the Papal Bull, which proclaimed Hugh's canonisation, declared the position to be unfitting. But that was standard form and merely reflects that a decision in principle to move him had already been taken. From the point of view of the canons, unfitting may have been equivalent to inconvenient. What they seem to have been worried about was access. Although the architectural unity of the Angel Choir is impressive, liturgically it fell into two more or less equal parts: the western half which housed the high altar and went with the choir proper between the transepts; and the eastern half which was literally a retrochoir. This was given up to St Hugh and his cult. The two parts were separated by a double reredos which is now represented by an eighteenth-century screen into which Essex incorporated parts of the original. The retrochoir had its own entrance: the Judgment Portal on the south side; and its own exit: the smaller door opposite. These arrangements were designed to leave the canons in undisturbed possession of their own part of the cathedral. The desire of the clergy for privacy and seclusion behind their screens is spelt out so explicitly at Lincoln, by comparison with, say, the equivalent dispositions at Canterbury or Durham, that we may safely take it to have been the starting point of the whole conception of the Angel Choir.

The cult of Hugh was spontaneous, popular, and immediate. He was not canonised until 1220, but this was largely due to the ecclesiastical troubles of King John's reign. The creation of a new English saint was symptomatic of the reconciliation. The first we hear about the Angel Choir is in 1256 when an application was made to the King for permission to breach the city wall. It was presumably complete when Hugh was translated with great pomp and ceremony in 1280. A building period of twenty-four years is not in itself excessive; and in some respects a starting date c.1256 would be appropriate. Given the strained relations between Bishop Grosseteste and the chapter, it is unlikely that much was done before his death in 1253; that is, if the Bishop was expected to contribute generously to the building fund. It may be no accident that Grosseteste was buried at the south end of the south-east transept, that is as far away as possible from the clutch of episcopal tombs opposite. But there are other factors to be taken into account. As we do not know the precise line of the city wall between 1192 and 1256, it is not absolutely certain that the second breach was essentially connected with the construction of the Angel Choir. What it undoubtedly made possible was the enlarged precinct, which was duly fortified. But the 1192 perimeter may have left enough room for a start to be made on the new choir without further modifications. There is no very sharp break in style between some of the details of the lower parts of the Angel Choir, and the restoration of St Hugh's Choir after the collapse of the tower. It is difficult to know quite what to make of this, but the shorter the interval, the easier it is to explain. Then, however long it took to complete the building, nearly everything that is novel about it seems to be related to work at Westminster Abbey which was done in the decade after 1245. This is principally sculpture and window tracery. One has the impression of an unusually precise design being drawn up at the outset, whenever that was, and being followed through with unusual fidelity; and the date of the translation should not be taken too seriously as a clue to the architectural innovations.

40

Given its purpose, it was essential that the Angel Choir should present iself as a grand climax in the sequence of architectural experiences which the cathedral had to offer. In other words it was required to outshine the nave. This was no mean task, especially as the scale was reduced once more to that of St Hugh's Choir. But the architect was fortunate to have at his disposal the new decorative device of window tracery, which he used not only systematically, but with skill and imagination. The tracery patterns of the Angel Choir windows must be far more complicated than anything contained in the original west window of the nave. While they are straightforward developments from models at Westminster, concern for the effects of wall thickness and foreshortening can be deduced from the repetition of the stonework on the inner face of the clerestory passage. Both the problem and the solution were peculiar to Lincoln. The east window used to be reckoned the earliest of the great facade-filling compositions of tracery which are one of the conspicuous glories of English medieval churches. But even if it has to yield this distinction to its counterpart in the nave, it remains the earliest which has actually survived; and it marks the culmination of a particular method of designing windows out of paired lancets and oculi.

The architect also made more extensive use of architectural sculpture than his predecessor in St Hugh's Choir aisles. The angels from which the new work takes it name occupy the spandrels between the arches of the gallery openings. Visually, they intensify the ornament of the middle zone of the elevation to an even greater pitch than in the nave. They also contribute to the overall imagery of the choir by suggesting an aspect of the Church Triumphant not often stressed to such a degree: the orders of angels among whom saints like Hugh enjoy eternal bliss. The basic theme of this imagery is carried on to the bosses of the vault. It may also be regarded as an extension of that of the south portal, where the subject of the carved tympanum is the Last Judgment. While the sculptor clearly preferred elegance and harmony to the didactic thoroughness or vivid melodrama of similar portals in France and Germany, the message to those who pass through it remains serious and literal. The Kingdom of Heaven is to be entered only by way of the Judgment of Christ.

When St Hugh was translated into the new choir in 1280, the cathedral of Lincoln was virtually complete again after nearly a hundred years of continuous activity, infinitely larger and more complex than its predecessor, and wholly different in style. The one characteristic which it undoubtedly shared with Alexander's building was an evident determination to be the most magnificent church in England. In 1280 this is precisely what it was. Perhaps it was meant to be a reflection of the size and importance of the diocese of Lincoln. Certainly the investment of wealth and labour must have represented a disproportionate percentage of the resources of the diocese. But that amounts to no more than recognising the willingness of people in the middle ages to spend more than ourselves on beautiful buildings. Considering its splendour, its impact on contemporary taste was not overwhelming. The crowded, encrusted surfaces, which distinguish the great churches built in England during the thirteenth century, probably owe more to Lincoln than to any other source of inspiration. But such influence was of a fairly general nature, and there were always alternatives. Salisbury, which was exactly contemporary with the nave of Lincoln, could hardly be more different. The aspect of architecture to which fundamental contributions were made at Lincoln was vaulting. Here the achievement was technical as much as stylistic; and its effects were felt in far-away parts of Europe as well as England. Vaults similar to the spreading ribs of Lincoln nave can be found in East Prussia dating from the fourteenth century; and at Pelplin near Danzig in what is now Poland there is a remarkably accurate reproduction of the different patterns of the aisle vaults of Lincoln nave. Even the asymmetrical vaults of St Hugh's Choir have their counterparts in Bohemia. How these ideas were transmitted is entirely obscure; but short of finding a plausible common source, which no one has yet done, or falling back on sheer coincidence, which is intrinsically improbable, there seems to be no escape from the conclusion that late Gothic architects in eastern Europe drew some of their most characteristic ideas from Lincoln.

Apart from the screens, tombs and chantries which accumulated during the next 250 years, the interior of the cathedral is today much as it was in 1280. The one conspicuous modification is the rose window in the south-west transept. This can only be dated by its tracery, which has a distinctive undulating pattern, fashionable in the north and east of England during the second quarter of the fourteenth century. It may have had something to do with attempts to promote a cult of Bishop Dalderby, who died in 1320, and who was buried in the vicinity. On the other hand, the exterior has changed almost out of recognition. In 1280 the distant prospect of the cathedral was long and low, rather as Peterborough is today. There were stumpy towers to the west end and over the crossing. Otherwise the profile was broken only by gables and turrets. The transformation of this thirteenth century outline into the present configuration was a piecemeal business, spread over the greater part of the subsequent century. One gets a distinct impression that during the later middle ages there was far less money for building and that work was undertaken only when it became available.

The first important addition to the cathedral was the cloister. This occupies an unusual position on the north side between the two transepts. No doubt the determining factor was the chapter house, which had to open on to its eastern arm. The principal interest of the cloister is its sculpture in wood and stone, which shares the naturalistic style of the celebrated leaves of the chapter house at Southwell. This suggests a date not long after 1280. Then came the central tower. For this we have a contract. The mason in charge was named as Richard of Stow, and the date was 1306.

Although this is the first occasion on which it is possible to connect a particular mason with a particular part of the work, there is no shortage of references to masons in the surviving Lincoln documents.[9] The contexts in which they occur, usually legal transactions, suggest that they were men of substance; and it is tempting to suppose that they were in charge of whatever was going on at the cathedral at the time, and even that they were responsible for the designs in question. They may have been, but to reach such interesting conclusions often requires leaps rather than inferences. The best known of them is Geoffrey de Noyers, who was in some way responsible for St Hugh's Choir. He was called *constructor* of the cathedral in the *Magna Vita* of St Hugh, which leaves wide open the question whether he was the architect or the Clerk of Works, although the fact that he was in London with Hugh on his death-bed perhaps inclines somewhat towards the latter interpretation. To complicate matters, there was a Richard the Mason in Lincoln at the time. The trouble is that, until we can construct a career around a name, it tells us very little. In Geoffrey's case we do not know whether he came from Noyers in Normandy, or Noyers in Burgundy, or whether he took his name from a family long since resident in Lincolnshire. The style of the building sheds no light on these matters. Nor does it add much to one's understanding of the nave or chapter house to know that they may have been the work of the Master Alexander, who had property in Lincoln while they were being built; or that Simon Tresk may have been the author of the Angel Choir. We are on slightly firmer ground with Richard of Stow. He was related to another Alexander, who may perhaps be supposed to have been descended from the first, if only by reason of sharing the same name and the same profession. By such tenuous threads it is possible to detect the shadowy presence of a controlling dynasty in charge of building operations at the cathedral during the thirteenth century. That at least is compatible with what we find elsewhere. The easiest, and therefore the commonest, way of transmitting technical and craft skills from generation to generation in the middle ages was from father to son, or to son-in-law. Even so there was no stagnation. If Richard of Stow was a local man, as the name implies, and had married into the dominant masonic family of the cathedral, as the documents indicate, his style was anything but provincial. We may guess that the Eleanor Cross at Lincoln – on which he is known to have worked – was much the same as the other crosses, in which case it was cosmopolitan and up to date; while for the crossing-tower of the cathedral his inspiration seems to have been

[9] J. Harvey, *English medieval architects, a biographical dictionary to 1550*, 2nd edn, 1984, *passim*.

the one at Old St Paul's in London. This was another pace-setting monument. Both towers were surmounted by tall spires of wood, covered with lead; and both are supposed to have reached heights over 500 feet. They also shared the same eventual fate in so far as their spires succumbed to the weather. Even without its spire the central tower makes a tremendous difference to the external appearance of the cathedral. In this respect Lincoln was responding to a new criterion of imagery which left its mark on almost every cathedral in the land. One detail of the decoration of the tower is worth noting. It is covered with a type of ornament known as ball-flower, the overall distribution of which leaves Lincoln in spectacular isolation. It may have been known in London, but it is chiefly to be found in the west country. If Richard of Stow was personally responsible for its presence at Lincoln he must have had quite an interesting career, or else picked up a great deal from his colleagues in the Eleanor Cross enterprise.

The decision to add new storeys to the western towers may well have been taken at the same time as the central tower was heightened; but they were a separate operation, and carried out in an entirely different style. They were one of several works associated with the name of the treasurer of the cathedral, John de Welburne, who died in 1380. Welburne was a lavish benefactor. He paid for the magnificent wooden stalls in St Hugh's Choir, which vie with those of Chester for the distinction of having the most complicated canopy-work in the country. There is a similar opulence about the tracery panelling which was applied to the walls of the old western transept below the towers. This panelling goes with the Perpendicular windows which replaced whatever previously occupied the upper parts of the three Romanesque recesses in the facade. It seems clear that the ultimate purpose behind Welburne's interest in the west end of the cathedral was to obliterate the Romanesque fragment which had survived the Gothic reconstruction. No doubt by the middle of the fourteenth century it had come to be regarded as a discordant anachronism; but he did not have enough money to replace it entirely. The result is a curious hotch-potch in which bits from at least four different periods now sit uncomfortably side by side. Welburne's windows wreaked havoc on Alexander's frieze. The row of kings which was presumably meant to take its place finds itself squeezed into a narrow space between the central window and the Romanesque doorway, which had to be trimmed to make room for it. Confronted by such crude improvisions, it would be charitable to suppose that the perpetrator of this confusion did not actually intend to leave the facade in the state in which we now find it. It is a terrible anticlimax with which to end the building history of what is otherwise a remarkably distinguished monument. But however preposterous the present facade may be as an architectural composition, few of those interested in the history of architecture would have preferred to have it tidied up at the expense of the Romanesque fragment.

The cathedral is now rather more than 900 years old. The first half of that period was almost entirely given up to construction or reconstruction; and in any history of the building this is the part that is bound to loom large. The second half is less easy to characterise. For most of it nothing very much happened. Before the revival of interest in medieval architecture towards the end of the eighteenth century, the uneventful passage of time may have been a symptom of indifference and neglect. It is equally compatible with generations of unrecorded love. The cathedral certainly came in for its measure of desecration during the Reformation and the civil war; but it also acquired its Wren Library. Chapter records indicate fairly continuous, if modest, attention to the problems of maintenance, and the James Gibbs efforts to consolidate the western towers in the 1730s show that structural delapidation was both recognised and attended to, when occasion arose. The most considerable alteration to the appearance of the cathedral since the end of the middle ages was brought about by the disappearance of the wooden spires on all three towers. The central tower lost its spire in 1548; the others at the beginning of the nineteenth century after an abortive attempt to remove them in 1727 which provoked a riot. Clearly not everyone was apathetic all the time.

Lincoln was one of the first English cathedrals to undergo systematic restoration. This was started by the architect James Essex in a series of operations spread over the last three decades of the eighteenth century, and extended well into the nineteenth. Further restorations were carried out by J. C. Buckler in the middle years of the nineteenth century and by J. C. Pearson towards the end. Much controversy has raged around these activities, especially Buckler's, which provided plenty of scope for the favourite Victorian pastime of venting sense of outrage in print. No doubt mistakes were made, but the taste of any generation was seldom uniform, and it was impossible to please everybody. Whatever damage the restorers may have done, it is fairly certain that without their efforts the condition of the cathedral would by now be irretrievable.

In the twentieth century the difficulties of preserving the cathedral have been compounded in a number of ways. The rate at which vulnerable stonework is corroded by industrial pollution has increased alarmingly, and so also has the cost of trying to deal with it. Conservation work now has to be more or less continuous, and is developing its own highly specialised and expensive technology. It is becoming increasingly doubtful whether the Church can afford to maintain the effort, or even whether it wants to do so. Indifference to the architectural setting of Christian worship is widespread; and cathedrals are often conspicuous items among the residues of what passed for spirituality in former ages which the Church thinks it must shed if it is to adapt itself successfully to the expectations and standards of the modern world. Improbable monsters that have survived from a remote past, like the coelocanth, if they are to be preserved at all, cathedrals should be treated as museum pieces. This line of thought leads inexorably to ideas about state grants and cathedrals as part of the national heritage. It may turn out that in the long run this is the only practical solution; but it will be very sad indeed if the price of preservation is for Lincoln to become a dead husk like the Hagia Sophia in Constantinople. Cathedrals owe their existence to the connection between beauty and worship. They represent a distinctive mode of religious experience. But it is one which is out of fashion, even under threat. For it to be recognised at all now requires a considerable effort of historical imagination. Unless there is a widespread change of heart all that money and science will ensure for Lincoln is temporary reprieve or decent mummification.

3

Music and worship to 1640

❋

ROGER BOWERS

The medieval liturgy and its performance: the choir to c.1380

The great cathedral and collegiate churches of western medieval Christendom were erected by men to the active glory of God – not as mute and idle museums of ecclesiastical architecture, but as sounding, working buildings staffed by teams of men, youths and boys by whom the greater part of every day of every year was filled with the ritual worship of God.

There was very little that was arbitrary or discretionary about the pattern of worship conducted in a secular cathedral church such as Lincoln Minster. Of the ten major services a day, Matins, followed immediately by Lauds, was begun at midnight in winter and at around dawn in summer. The early morrow Mass was celebrated without music for the benefit of those travelling early from town, and soon afterwards a peal was rung to call the chantry chaplains and priest-vicars serving chantries to say their daily chantry Masses at up to a dozen of the side altars located around the building. Lady Mass at about 8 a.m. in the Lady Chapel was followed by Prime sung in choir, and then all proceeded to the chapter house for *Preciosa* and low Chapter Mass. Thereafter, Tierce, High Mass, Sext and None were sung in choir in succession, preceded on Sundays and major festivals by an elaborate procession; all was ended by about 11 a.m. In the afternoon Vespers was sung, followed by Compline. In addition, by at least 1220 the brief devotions known as the Hours of the Virgin had begun to be observed daily, each normally sung immediately after its corresponding Canonical Hour of the day.[1] These services were in no way congregational.

---

[1] *LCS* I, 364–96. *Registrum Antiquissimum* II, 56–7; III, 124–6. LAO DC A.3.3, f. 136v, Oxford, New College, muniment 5106.

The citizens of Lincoln and its suburbs worshipped not in the cathedral but in their own parish churches; the Minster was essentially the private chapel of its own chapter and clergy, to whose devotions the lay public had neither right nor need of access.

The liturgy enacted at these services was composed of three principal constituent elements – verbal text, music and ceremony, the latter involving dress as well as movement, sound, smell and much else besides. The authorised and traditional music of the liturgy was the unadorned monodic plainsong chant. Unfortunately very little can yet be written of the distinctive features of the particular liturgical Use observed at Lincoln, since little surviving material has yet been identified. Nevertheless, a thirteenth-century consuetudinary and a fragment of a fifteenth-century missal without music are enough to show that the ceremony and rite of Lincoln Use, while highly complex and elaborate, was no mere variant of the Uses of Salisbury or York, but was of independent character and origin.[2] Even though the Lincoln Use was being superseded in much of the diocese towards the end of the middle ages, it remained in observance in the cathedral until the Reformation, and was indeed revived during the Marian reaction until its final suppression was ordered in 1556.[3]

For the performance of a secular liturgy such as Lincoln Use, three distinct ranks of clergy were required. To the clergy of a rear and higher row of choirstalls (*superior gradus* or *prima forma*) was appointed the performance of those items in the rite and ceremony that were seen to be of greatest weight and significance; to those of the lower row (*secunda forma*) those of less importance and character; while to the clerks of the 'third form' (a bench standing in front of the lower row) were allocated those elements most appropriate for enactment by boys with unbroken voices, the choristers. In the late eleventh and early twelfth centuries the daily round of service may well have been conducted entirely by the resident canons, divided into two groups, and those boys of their households who were being trained and taught there for eventual ordination and service in the Church at large.

However, as the practice of non-residence grew among the canons in the twelfth and thirteenth centuries these pristine conditions changed. Growing administrative burdens caused the declining number of residentiaries to discharge themselves from all obligations to attend the services at all except for

[2] *LCS* I, 62–81, 125–9, 364–96. W. G. Henderson, ed., *The York missal*, 2 vols., Surtees Society 59–60, 1872–4, II, ix–xii, 341–8.

[3] C. Wordsworth, ed., *Tracts of Clement Maydestone*, Henry Bradshaw Society 7, 1894, 171–3. R. C. Dudding, ed. *The First Churchwardens' Book of Louth*, Oxford 1941, 152–3. Preface to The Book of Common Prayer, 1549. LAO DC A.3.6, f. 414r.

their hebdomadary duties and one participation a day at either one of the Canonical Hours or High Mass.[4] In choir the canons' places were taken by their substitutes, or vicars choral, and by the time of Bishop Hugh I (1186–1200) the residentiaries had become empowered to compel every non-resident to provide a suitable deputy to 'acquit him at divine service both by day and by night', and to provide sufficient maintenance for him. A system of examinations and probationary periods was established to ensure the diligence and competence of men presented to be vicars, and to equip them to sing the services largely from memory. As early as *c*.1190 the community of vicars was sufficiently numerous to begin to attract the gifts and bequests of the faithful to assist with their maintenance, and though the residentiaries and the canons of the six poorest prebends were exempt from providing vicars, yet by the late thirteenth century these provisions would still have been furnishing a substantial force of some 38 to 40 vicars to serve the choir. Vicars choral in priest's orders (and thus over the age of 24) constituted the *vicarii seniores*, and with the canons residentiary staffed the upper row of stalls; those in deacon's or subdeacon's orders (aged over 19 and 17 respectively) or in only minor orders were known as *vicarii iuniores*, and staffed the middle row as clerks of the second form. Eventually, between *c*.1295 and *c*.1330 residential courts were built to house each group on the south side of the cathedral Close.[5]

In choir the vicars were subject to the direction of the canon appointed to be Precentor, who exercised overall responsibility for the conduct of the services. On the greatest occasions he was to take personal charge of High Mass, and on others to appoint experienced vicars to be *rectores chori* ('rulers of the choir'), and to nominate those members of the choir entabled to take individual parts in the ceremony and singing. He also was responsible for the maintenance of the singers' reference books of chant. Characteristically, however, he was empowered to delegate the execution of these duties to a substitute of his appointment, an experienced and senior vicar designated as Succentor. Between them there could always be someone present at all the more important services who was empowered and authorised to control the conduct of the service and exact satisfactory standards of performance. As for the vicars, it was neither liturgically necessary nor vocally advisable for every one to attend every service each day. Provisions for minimum attendance compiled in 1309 would, if

---

[4] *LCS* I, 293–4, 384–5; II, 325. K. Edwards, *English secular cathedrals in the middle ages*, 2nd edn, Manchester 1967, 58–9.

[5] Edwards, *English secular cathedrals*, 71, 258–67. *LCS* I, 396–9; II, xlix–li, 144–6, 165, 316. E. Venables, 'The Vicars' Court, Lincoln, with the architectural history of the College and an account of the existing buildings', *AASR* 17, 1883/4, 235–50. LAO A.2.23, f. 9r. See also, for a full discussion of Vicars' Court, S. Jones, K. Major and J. Varley, *Survey of ancient houses in Lincoln* II, Lincoln 1987, 40–62.

faithfully observed, have ensured the arrival of some five-sixths of the full body of vicars at Matins, and of about half at all other services.[6]

The remaining participants in the execution of the liturgy were the boys of the choir, the choristers, whose full complement was deemed in 1264 to be twelve. The Consuetudinary of 1258x79 intermittently records the boys' contribution to the conduct of the services as candlebearers, crucifers at procession, thurifers and bearers of copes and books and the holy water. They might also read lessons, and as well as joining with all the choir in singing chants delegated for performance by all, might sing on their own brief items such as versicles and the occasional large set piece, such as the hymn *Gloria, laus et honor* from the top of the gate of the Bail during the procession on Palm Sunday. The Precentor had responsibility for their instruction, education and discipline, which he exercised by appointing as deputy an experienced senior vicar to be Master of the Song School. In 1264 Bishop Richard Gravesend acquired a house in the Close for the boys' habitation and care; here the Song School Master served also as their housemaster, and taught them their Latin grammar and vocabulary, reading and (presumably) writing, and all the technical intricacies of liturgical ceremony and of the chant and psalmody and the verbal texts accompanying it.[7]

Three other groups of cathedral clergy made some contribution to the conduct of divine service. All the chantry-priests were expected to participate in processions on feast days, and it was stipulated in the foundation deeds of a few chantries, for instance that of Richard Faldingworth, that the chaplains attend the choir service as vicars choral. To the extent that the canons resident observed the statute, sporadically complied with, that each maintain a chaplain to attend upon him at service, attendance in choir might further be increased. The Poor Clerks, however, made no substantial contribution to the choir service. Originally thirteen in number, they had contracted to eleven by 1290, and at that point their number remained fixed until the sixteenth century. Despite being recruited in part from choristers whose voices had broken, their function was merely to attend early each morning to serve the priests celebrating chantry masses at the altars to which they were attituled, spending the rest of the day thereafter at lessons in the city grammar school. Only on school holidays were they required to attend the choir service.[8]

---

[6] *LCS* I, 283–4, 370, 382–3; II, 141, 146–8, 157–8, 164, 348–9. *Registrum Antiquissimum* X, lv.

[7] *LCS* I, 281, 283, 292, 367–96 *passim*, esp. 369; II, 155, 157. Edwards, *English secular cathedrals*, 308–10. *Registrum Antiquissimum* I, 262–3; II, no. 478; X, x, nos. 2754–62.

[8] *LCS* II, 200–1, 208, 266, 327, 361–2, 366, 403–4. *Registrum Antiquissimum* II, 105, 109. A. H. Thompson, ed. *Visitations of religious houses in the diocese of Lincoln*, 2 vols. in 3 parts, LRS 7, 14, 21, 1915–27: I, pp. 133, 138. H. Salter, ed., *A clerical subsidy collected in the diocese of Lincoln in 1526*, Oxford 1909, 84–7. LAO DC A.2.23, ff. 5r, 5v, 17r; A.2.28, f. 4r; A.3.2, ff. 107v, 133r; A.3.19, f. 3r; A.4.9(6); Bj.5/13(18). Lincoln Ep. Reg. 9, ff. 30v–31r; 12, f. 478r.

The character and nature of the communities of vicars choral and choristers first come into focus in the early fourteenth century, the period from which date the earliest surviving accounts and Chapter Acts. At first, and indeed until the middle of the fifteenth century, the chapter evidently endeavoured to keep full the nominal total complement of vicars, normally standing at around 38 to 40. In April 1376 there appear to have been 36 present at the obit of a recently deceased residentiary; in 1405 37 were recorded, 23 being priest-vicars and 14 vicars of the second form. The surviving evidence likewise indicates that the choristers were maintained at their full complement of twelve. This was the number of admissions recorded in a short space of four years, 1351–5, and there were certainly twelve during 1366/7.[9]

Mere numbers, however, were not all that mattered, and it is clear that in terms of vocal quality and personal integrity the vicars choral were a mixed bunch. At any given time, it appears (the Macworth–Burton period, perhaps, excepted), a dependable majority of experienced and diligent men could be relied upon successfully to maintain a certain standard of conscientious competence; however, their efforts were always prone to derangement by the conduct of a minority (sometimes substantial) of their colleagues ill-motivated in choir and ill-behaved outside it. Notwithstanding the statutory system of probationary periods and qualifying tests, it was rarely possible to resist the casual presentation of an unsuitable vicar by an indifferent but powerful absentee canon;[10] meanwhile, instances of animal high spirits, and eventual disenchantment with the ecclesiastical life, were only to be expected among the youngest vicars only recently recruited from among the Poor Clerks and choristers. In choir there were instances of absenteeism, of work unprepared and incompetently performed, of wandering around the nave during service or talking and paying too little attention to its progress; outside church, of gambling, fornication and drunkenness.[11]

Nonetheless, far less prominent in the surviving record, yet far more representative of the vicars as a whole, was that substantial element among them whose devoted and loyal service, not only in the choirstalls but also in many of the lesser executive jobs in the cathedral's administration, was enough to maintain its capacity to discharge its obligations in a manner, if not wholly unblemished, then probably not unworthy either. Indeed, there

---

[9] LAO DC A.4.8 (9); A.2.30, f. 21v; A.2.26, ff. 19r, 19v, 21v, 26v, 46v; Bj.5.17/3, f. 27v; Bij.1.11 (5).

[10] *LCS* I, 351, 353, 396; II, 145, 347. LAO DC A.2.22, ff. 29v, 30v; A.2.23, f. 41v; A.2.26, f. 6r; A.2.28, f. 32r.

[11] LAO DC A.2.22, f. 9r; DC A.2.26, ff. 23v–24r, 37v, 42r; DC A.3.19, f. 10r. Lincoln Ep. Reg. 9, f. 30v; 12, ff. 477v–479v.

was a brief period between 1326 and 1340 when an administrative eventuality – a vacancy in the precentorship – caused the surviving archives to record many routine procedures in the promotion of the cathedral's music that at other times went unchronicled. This included much dutiful copying of service-books, and of text and chant for the sequences at Lady Mass and for feasts recently instituted, such as Corpus Christi and the Conception of the Blessed Virgin; one large *liber de cantu* of seventy-two folios – perhaps a book of motets – was copied in 1331/2 and another acquired by bequest in 1338/9.[12]

Throughout the middle ages the immense standard repertory of monodic plainsong chant formed the staple musical diet of the cathedral body at service in choir; but by as early as the thirteenth century there are indications that this was being supplemented on the greater festivals by instances of polyphonic elaboration of the chant, or even by free-standing composed polyphony, performed by *aliqui bene cantantes*, that is, a specialist ensemble of skilled executants. The Consuetudinary of 1258x79 records that the dismissal versicle *Benedicamus Domino* concluding second Vespers and Lauds on double and semidouble feasts was sung in unaccompanied polyphony (*organizetur*) – on greater doubles by vicars choral, on the other occasions by boys, trained by the Master of the Song School.[13] When performed by boys, the polyphony would have consisted of a single counterpoint of 'descant' improvised above the given chant; the vicars might well have sung some example of the type of motet, for two, three or voices, that was conceived as a *Benedicamus* substitute.

Certainly, therefore, polyphonic performance was cultivated at Lincoln as early as the second half of the thirteenth century, and probably these capacities were not limited to the occasions specifically prescribed, but were commonly deployed where appropriate as a means of distinguishing important feast days from other days of minor significance. By the 1320s polyphony was certainly sung on the anniversary of Bishop Grosseteste, and throughout the fourteenth century at High Mass on the two principal feasts of St Hugh.[14] The character of such items is not known, but motets with texts relating to the occasion would not have been inappropriate. Also during the fourteenth century polyphony was introduced into the conduct of the daily votive Mass in honour of the Virgin Mary. The Lady Mass, celebrated while the bells were being rung for Prime, was already being observed by 1220; Bishop Hugh de Welles' endowment of

---

[12] LAO DC Bj.2.5, ff. 34v, 116r, 129r, 174r; Bj.5.8 (9), f. 43r.

[13] *LCS* I, 369, 373, 381. F. Ll. Harrison, *Music in medieval Britain*, 2nd edn, London 1963, 74–6, 104–14, esp. 111.

[14] *LCS* I, 337. LAO Bj.5.16/1.

that year apparently proved abortive, but by *c.*1320 enough had been accumulated by way of benefactions to provide a daily attendance of a special team of a celebrant and four assisting vicars.[15] A high proportion of English fourteenth-century composed polyphony has texts and forms rendering it suitable for performance at this service, and at least by 1368/9 the vicars attending at Lincoln were being paid for 'ministering and singing polyphony' at the Lady Mass, a practice which continued uninterrupted until the Reformation.[16]

Characteristically, the late fourteenth century also witnessed the addition of two further Marian devotions to the daily round of services: the singing (to plainsong) following Compline of the votive antiphons *Mater ora filium* by the Poor Clerks at the tomb of Bishop Gynwell (from 1371) in memory of his benefactions to them, and of *Nesciens mater, Mater ora filium* or *Regina celi* by the choristers (from 1380) at the tomb of Bishop Buckyngham.[17]

Among the appurtenances of worship also to be mentioned for the first time in the early fourteenth century was its sole musical instrument, the organ. At this period the church organ was a small free-standing positive operated by one man and simultaneously blown by another; its role is obscure, but seems likely to have been not as an instrument of music but as a random generator of joyful noise, activated like peals and clashes of bells to distinguish the greater festival days. On 22 June 1310 the chapter delegated a vicar choral, Thomas de Ledenham, to maintain the instrument thenceforth, and very probably to work it also. Probably it was located in the choir, since a newly built successor of this instrument was described in 1332/3 as being *pro choro*; provisions made in 1322 for paying the organ-blower indicate that among the occasions on which it was used were the feasts of St Hugh and Robert Grosseteste. The organ appears to have been disused for some twenty years after 1343, but it was restored to use in 1363, evidently on the initiative of John Louth, vicar choral, who was also appointed its keeper and player, and whose successors as organist – at first, always chosen from among the vicars choral – can be traced with no substantial break to the present day.[18] By the late fourteenth century it is probable that the organ was being deployed as a more refined and considered contributor to the genuinely musical character of the liturgical service, but precise details of the manner and extent of its use are wholly lacking.

---

[15] *Registrum Antiquissimum* II, 56–8; IV 81–2, 131–2. LAO DC A.1.8, ff. 15r–16v, 133v–145v; DC Bj.2.7, f. 6v; DC Bj.5.2, f. 4v; DC Bj.5.13 (18), m. 1r.

[16] LAO DC Bj.2.6 (11), f. 8v.

[17] *Registrum Antiquissimum* II, 186–90. LAO DC A.4.9 (6); A.2.30, f. 48v.

[18] *LCS* I, 336–7. LAO DC A.2.22, f. 26v; A.2.27, f. 9v; Bj.2.5, f. 137v; Bj.2.6 (5), f. 8r; Bj.2.6 (6), f. 5v; Bj.2.10, f. 126v; Bj.5.16/1.

The evolution of a balanced chorus: the choir, c.1380–1547

The period between *c*.1380 and *c*.1420 was a time of regeneration and conservative reform at many of the secular cathedrals, marked at Lincoln by, for example, the creation of new prebends and the return of the major dignitaries to residence. It was also a time when significant strides forward in the music of the church (not least, in composed polyphony) were made at large in England, probably encountered and absorbed at Lincoln no less than in the other foremost choirs of the time. Supplements made to the payments to the four vicars attending Lady Mass suggest that from 1397/8 the performance of polyphony there was increased, being elevated perhaps to even a daily occurrence. Unfortunately, no music of this period survives at Lincoln, but there is a remote chance that the John Vaux who was resident in Lincoln Close in 1382 and 1394 may be identifiable with the John Vaux alias Pycard who was a principal singing-man in the chapel of John of Gaunt, Duke of Lancaster, in 1392/3 and 1397/8. Pycard is known as the composer of some eight or ten settings, for four or five voices, of the Gloria, Credo and Sanctus of the Ordinary of the Mass. These compositions are of great intricacy, and technically extremely demanding to perform; if any of this music was indeed sung at Lincoln, then the Lady Mass singers of this period must have been finely skilled and accomplished.[19]

Also at this time, a prevailing climate of at least modest spiritual regeneration manifested itself in the manner in which the liturgy was conducted. In 1390 it was ordered that the games, tricks, chatter and general rowdiness which disfigured the observance of the Feast of Fools each 1st January cease thenceforth. Perhaps in wholesome compensation for this suppression, these occurred between *c*.1380 and *c*.1420 a temporary multiplication of the occasions on which liturgical dramas, specially written though normally set to pre-existing chants, were inserted into the liturgy; these included plays of the Epiphany, Eastertide plays of the Resurrection and Christ's appearance to doubting Thomas, the Ascension, Pentecost, and a Christmastide play of the Salutation. Elaborate 'props' were procured and built for these ceremonies, including furs and crowns for the Three Kings, and a mobile star and descending angel and dove for Epiphany and Pentecost.[20]

---

[19] C. W. Foster, ed., *Lincoln wills*, LRS 5, 14, 17. LAO DC Bj.5.5, f. 20v; Bj.5.10.6 (5), f. 1r. Lincoln Ep. Reg. 12, f. 477v. PRO DL 28 3/2, f. 11v; DL 28 3/5, f. 8r. M. Bent, '(1) Pycard' *sub* art. 'Picard' in S. Sadie, ed., *New Grove dictionary of music and musicians* [henceforth *NGD*], 20 vols., London 1980, XIV, 720–1. A. Hughes and M. Bent, eds., *The Old Hall Manuscript*, Corpus Mensurabilis Musicae XLVI, Rome 1969–72, nos. 26–8, 35, 71, 75–6, 78, 123.

[20] LAO DC A.2.28, f. 32r. S. J. Kahrl, ed., *Records of plays and players in Lincolnshire*, Malone Society Collections 8, 1969, pub. 1974, 23–69, amplified by LAO DC Bj.2.5, f. 181v; Bj.2.10, f. 60r; Bj.5.16/1; Bj.5.9 (11), f. 3r.

Probably in much the same spirit, the education and training of the choristers was put on a more businesslike and professional footing at this period. Hitherto, the Master resident with the boys in the Choristers' House had been an unspecialised functionary, responsible for all aspects of their training, teaching and upbringing; however, a series of upheavals between 1390 and 1407 divided this work between no fewer than three specialists. A post of Steward was created, filled always by a chantry-priest who acted simply as general housemaster, manager and caterer, while a professional grammar school master was appointed to teach Latin. This allowed a specialist in liturgy and chant to be appointed Master of the Song School. The motive behind these departures appears to have been an intensified concern that the Master of the Choristers be able to concentrate specialised endeavours on the training of the choristers in their contribution to the ceremony and chant of the liturgy, and as the second appointee to this newly defined position the chapter attracted Walter Braytoft in 1395 from his post of Master of the Lady Chapel Choir at Westminster Abbey.[21] Hereby the role of the choristers as singers was for the first time elevated to that of top priority among their numerous contributions to the liturgy, so enabling them to participate in the major musical revolution of the later fifteenth century that finally established their role primarily as singing-boys. Meanwhile, the evidently high priority afforded to the expert singing of chant and, very probably, improvised descant by the boys at Lincoln could prove two-edged. When in 1420 Henry V licensed one of his singing-men, John Pyamour, to return to England from the French campaign to impress choristers for his Chapel Royal, it was with two boys commandeered from Lincoln cathedral that Pyamour returned barely three weeks later.[22]

The succession of disputes and conflicts that revolved around the reaction of the rest of the chapter to the character and behaviour of Dean Macworth (1415–51) are recounted elsewhere. The acrimony and even violence were not confined to the chapter house but spilled over into the choir service, and could hardly fail to cast a malign influence on all aspects of the cathedral's life and worship. The visitations of 1390, 1394 and 1410 had revealed no more than the usual impairments of the services arising from the chronic insubordination of a minority of unsuitable men. Those of 1432 and 1437/8, however, reveal a steady deterioration in the conduct of a rising proportion of the whole community of vicars, until plain absenteeism was sometimes reducing attendance to scarcely

---

[21] A. F. Leach, 'Schools' in *VCH Lincs.* II, 425–6. A. F. Leach, *Educational charters and documents*, Cambridge 1911, 386–93. LAO DC A.2.27, ff. 45v, 58v; A.2.28, f. 32v; A.2.29, ff. 24r, 27r–28v; DC Bj.2.8, f. 119v. Westminster Abbey, muniments 23188–92.

[22] PRO C66/402, m. 11v; E403/643, m. 16r.

three or four per side, rendering the services almost impossible to conduct.[23] The Minster ceased to be able to retain able men in its service, or attract others to take their places for very long. Among numerous instances, Gerard Hesyll, trained as a chorister since 1407 and promoted to a vicarage choral by 1416, left for service in the Chapel Royal in 1419; in 1429 John Retford, Master of the Choristers, resigned to join the service of the Earl of Northumberland and in 1433 William Jaye, one of the four expert singers constituting the Lady Mass choir, left for service with the bishop of Lincoln.[24] There was little chance of reform being imposed from above. Robert Burton, Precentor from 1427 until 1445, emerges from the records of the time as a tiresome man more concerned with the definition of the minutiae of his rights and privileges than with benevolent oversight of the conduct of the services; his nadir was a physical assault during the choir service on a luckless and inoffensive chorister whose perfectly proper censing of the Precentor in his stall had failed to meet with Burton's approval.[25]

Nevertheless, those aspects of worship in the Minster which relied for their execution not on the mass consent of all but on the enthusiasm of a few could continue to flourish and develop. By the 1430s the performance daily of polyphony at Lady Mass by the four expert vicars comprising the 'fellowship of the altar of the Blessed Mary' had become the chief identifying characteristic of the manner of its celebration; enhancing its musical content in some respect was a small organ, purchased new in 1428. By now these experts were performing polyphony in the main choir also, on the annual festival of St Hugh in Whitsun week, and evidently for the singing of certain of the Office canticles (Te Deum, Magnificat, Benedictus) on the greater festivals.[26] It is indeed tempting to identify the John Benet who was briefly a vicar choral from 1437 to 1441 with the mid-century composer of that name. The name is not uncommon, but at least nothing in Benet's surviving output – two or three cyclic Masses, seven or eight single Mass movements and three isorhythmic motets (one on St Thomas Cantelupe) – contradicts this tentative suggestion.[27] His music is representative of its period, more straightforward and far easier to sing than that of Pycard, while conceived on a larger scale.

---

[23] LAO DC A.2.28, f. 32r. Lincoln Ep. Reg. 12, ff. 477v–479r. M. Archer, ed., *The Register of Bishop Repyngdon*, 3 vols., LRS 57, 58, 74, 1963–82, I, 181–7. Thompson, *Visitations of religious houses* I, 128–43. *LCS* II, 364–425 *passim*.

[24] LAO DC A.2.30, ff. 6v, 49v; A.2.32, ff. 52v, 59v, 89r. PRO E403/63, m. 5r.

[25] *LCS* I, 160–3; II, 298–9, 463–7, 509–11, 519–20. LAO DC A.2.32, ff. 76r, 119v, 130v, 136v. Ep. records Vj.2, ff. 21v, 24r, 37r.

[26] *LCS* II, 366–7, 409. LAO DC A.2.29, f. 9r; A.2.32, ff. 46v, 59r, 59v, 97v, 98r, 99r, 104v, 114r; DC Bj.5.16/1.

[27] B. Trowell, 'Benet, John', *NGD* II, 481–2. LAO DC A.2.32, f. 126v; A.2.33, f. 45r.

The principal organ in the choir of the Minster, meanwhile, was not neglected; maintained by enthusiasts such as the vicars Robert Patryngton and William Quentyn, who jointly maintained and played it for thirty years between 1394 and 1424, it was repaired in 1428, and presently replaced by a new instrument altogether. The contract, specifying that the organ be built 'in the very best manner that can be achieved', was awarded to one Arnold (very possibly Arnold Mynhamber) of Norwich, and the new instrument was delivered by Christmas 1442.[28]

During the fifty years following Macworth's death in 1451, the regimes succeeding his unwittingly transformed the cathedral choir from its medieval to its Renaissance, and essentially to its modern format – from a somewhat protean, unwieldy and uncohering body of performers of plainsong to a balanced choir of singers, boys and men, able to realise composed polyphonic music conceived for chorus, rendering a coherent and developing repertory under the necessary guidance of a single, comprehensively skilled director.

In the first instance, the chapter acknowledged that in the face of the competition offered by the new collegiate churches and aristocratic household chapels, men having sufficient vocal ability and personal integrity could no longer be found in numbers adequate to keep full the statutory complement of vicars choral. In 1437 there had been 36 vicars, and as late as 1444 there had still been 39. By 1456, however, the number recognised as constituting the full complement had dropped to 32, and by 1501 to 25 – that is (when the lay *Magister Cantus* is counted in) to the standard 13 per side. Here the target complement remained until 1547, though usually with some three or four vacancies; there appears to have been an optimum ratio of some three to two between *seniores* (or 'old vicars') in priest's orders, and *iuniores* (or 'young vicars', of whatever age) in the lesser orders. The number of choristers, meanwhile, remained fixed at twelve. In October 1437, in addition to eight boys old enough to depose evidence to Bishop Alnwick's visitation, there were four others only recently admitted. Twelve was again given as the acknowledged complement in the draft code of statutes of 1440, and throughout the first half of the sixteenth century.[29]

This contraction in the number of those sharing the vicars' revenues, constituted as a self-governing college from 1440, produced a corresponding rise

[28] LAO DC Bj.2.8, f. 95v; Bj.2.11, f. 30r; A.2.32, f. 46v; DC A.2.33, ff. 51r, 60v. G. Paget, 'The organs in the parish church of St Peter Mancroft, Norwich', *The Organ* 57, 1978, 8.

[29] *LCS* II, 362, 392–415. LAO DC A.2.32, f. 119v, 122r, 123v; DC A.2.35, f. 140v; DC A.3.2, f. 115v; DC A.3.3, f. 63r; DC Bj.2.13, ff. 18v, 21r. Accounts of Macworth Chantry 1455/6–1467/8 in DC Bj.2.16; DC Bj.5.6 (2). Lincoln Ep. Reg. 24, f. 147r. DC Ciij.48.4. Salter, *A clerical subsidy*, 82–3. *Valor Ecclesiasticus* IV, 12, 22–5. *Seventh Report of the Deputy Keeper of the Public Records*, London 1846, 291.

in income for all those remaining. By 1535 each priest-vicar received some £11.0s.0d. per year and each junior vicar £7.10s.0d., which with lodging provided free was not at all unhandsome. Further, it appears to have proved possible at last to exclude almost completely that minority of ill-motivated individuals who hitherto had formed an apparently permanently disaffected and disruptive element. Black sheep there would always be, but by the early sixteenth century complaints of absenteeism and ill-conduct were surfacing but briefly and infrequently, and new, more rigorous standards of professional conduct and conformity had taken their place.

The progressive contraction in the number of adult voices also created a steadily improving balance between the men's and boys' voices, enabling the Lincoln choir to participate in, and possibly significantly contribute to, the series of decisive innovations which in the second half of the fifteenth century revolutionised the music of the church by creating, alongside but not replacing the traditional plainsong heartland, a repertory of choral polyphony involving all the members of a choir as a balanced chorus, and incorporating boys' voices for the first time in the performance of composed polyphony.[30] The vicars choral of the traditional school, competent only in the modest skill of singing plainsong, were perforce progressively replaced by professional singers, ideally possessing both the fine voices and the vocal training necessary to perform the virtuosic lines of sustained and finely spun counterpoint of which this polyphony is composed. Certainly by the late fifteenth century the chapter was beginning to ensure that even those newly appointed vicars not yet adept in the new skills of singing 'pricksong' (written-out polyphony) as well as 'Playnsong discant and Faburden' achieved competence within a year of appointment, and by the early sixteenth century it is probable that the great majority of the twenty-five vicars were so skilled.[31]

The writing and management of the performance of composed choral polyphony – for the Mass Ordinary and the Magnificat, and eventually also the hymn and certain responsories on festivals, and the daily Lady Mass and Marian votive antiphon following Compline – required the services of a specialist composer and choir-trainer; likewise, teaching the boys the unprecedented repertoire of skills and accomplishments involved in choral polyphony was no longer within the province of merely some one of the abler vicars choral. To meet both demands simultaneously, a new post was created, for which the title finally settled was *Magister Cantus sive Choristarum* – Master of the Music and of the Choristers. Apparently this innovation was

---

[30] M. F. Bukofzer, 'The beginnings of choral polyphony', in *Studies in medieval and Renaissance music*, New York 1950, 176–89. Harrison, *Music in medieval Britain*, 156–219. R. Bowers, 'The performing pitch of English fifteenth-century church polyphony', *Early Music* 8, 1980, 21–8.

[31] LAO DC A.2.37, ff. 15v, 19v, verso of folio unnumbered between 63 and 64; DC A.3.1, f. 89r.

decided upon and effected in 1461 with the appointment of the composer William Horwood; on this occasion, however, Horwood stayed at Lincoln only a few months before returning to London. The task of transforming the choir into a polyphonic chorus was therefore apparently undertaken by his successor, the otherwise unknown Nicholas Gray, and was presumably complete by the time Horwood returned to permanent employment at Lincoln from 1476 until his death in 1484.[32] His contract of 1477 accorded him a modest salary, soon augmented to £8.6s.8d. per year, in return for his serving as Master of the Choristers and master of the polyphony singers at Lady Mass, and in effect as general supervisor of all polyphonic music sung in the Minster; he also served as Lady Mass organist and eventually (from 1483) as choir organist also. As Master of the Choristers he was to teach the boys all the styles of singing then current – plainsong (and of course its attendant ceremony and ritual), 'pryksonge' and the three manners of improvising counterpoint to plainsong, 'Faburden, diskant et Cowntour'; to teach them to play the organ, and those most apt the clavichord also.[33] It seems likely that it was at this time that some of the choristers began to participate in the singing of Lady Mass each day, and that the singing of Bishop Buckyngham's evening votive antiphon began to be performed in polyphony and to be attended by the *Magister Cantus* and by adult as well as the boys' voices.

It is from this period that the earliest music of likely Lincoln origin survives. A fragment of an anonymous four-part Mass Ordinary, set for male voices (ATTB) without boys, survives at the parish church of Saxilby, 6 miles west of Lincoln, whence the cathedral seems to be its only plausible provenance. Dating from *c.* 1460 and written in a simplified notation capable of being realised by singers familiar only with plainsong, its sonorous texture and expansive idiom gives some idea of the manner in which High Mass (or more probably Lady Mass) would have been beautified on the major feast days. Of Horwood's five surviving compositions, one is a four-part Kyrie for Monday Lady Mass, one an *alternatim* Magnificat, and three Marian votive antiphons, all for five mixed voices. *Gaude flore virginali*, *Gaude virgo mater Christi* and the Magnificat all look, on stylistic grounds, as if they could date from the composer's last eight years at Lincoln, and each – at six to eight minutes of bravura counterpoint – makes formidable demands on the skill and technique of the singers.[34]

[32] LAO DC A.2.36, f. 60v; DC A.2.37, ff. 16v, 24v; DC Bj.2.16 (1460/1). London, Guildhall Library, MS 4889, ff. 5v, 9v, 19r. N. Sandon, 'Horwood, William', *NGD* VIII, 726.

[33] LAO DC A.2.36, f. 96r; DC A.2.37, ff. 15v, 16v; DC Bj.3.2 (1481/2, 1482/3).

[34] M. Bent and R. Bowers, 'The Saxilby Fragment', *Early Music History* 1, 1981, 1–27, with transcription of the 91 bars of music recoverable complete. H. Baillie and P. Oboussier, 'The York Masses', *Music and Letters* 35, 1954, 19. F. Ll. Harrison, ed., *The Eton Choirbook*, 3 vols. *Musica Britannica* 10–12, I, 101; II, 128; III, 69, 141.

Probably the years c.1460 to 1547 represent the apogee of the cultivation of fine music and elaborate liturgy in Lincoln Minster. The list of Masters of Music and of the Choristers between William Horwood and the Reformation includes a few men trained up at the cathedral itself (e.g. William Freeman, chorister c.1490–1495, Poor Clerk, vicar choral and eventually Master of the Choristers 1524–8) but most were professionals appointed from outside. For instance, Thomas Ashwell (1506–11) came from Tattershall College (Lincs.) and John Gilbert (1517–24) from Coventry, while Thomas Appleby (1537–8) moved to Magdalen College, Oxford, before returning to Lincoln in 1541. Contracts of employment surviving for two of Horwood's successors, Henry Ottringham (1511) and James Crawe (1539), show that the established nature of the duties of the *Magister Cantus* was maintained consistently from Horwood (1477) up to the Reformation, and except for an allegation in 1501 that John Sothey was teaching the boys for only one session a day, the voluminous Chapter Acts and other archives of the period contain no indication that the successive Masters exercised their duties with anything less than conscientiousness and competence. They were highly esteemed and appropriately rewarded, Robert Dove for instance receiving a total of £22.6s.3d during 1535/6.[35]

To the daily Lady Mass, sung in polyphony and with organ participation by a team consisting of the *Magister Cantus*, two expert polyphonists and some of the choristers, was added in 1542 a weekly Jesus Mass and daily Jesus antiphon sung by the same forces.[36] Such a performing resource was not large, but was adequate to realise the polyphonic votive masses of the period, normally composed à3 or à4 and often with organ alternation. In the main choir a new organ was erected in 1473; taking six months to build and install, it may have been the first instrument grand enough to be fixed into a particular location – either on top of the choir screen, or already in the gallery over the north side of the choir that was occupied by a successor and depicted by Hollar in 1674. A new instrument replaced it in 1536; it was built by the well-known builder John Clymmowe, but it was only after it had been inspected and rectified by the doyen of London organ-builders, John Howe, that expenditure on it could cease. It is at about this time that a native repertoire of solo music for organ first appears, and the choir organ at Lincoln began to be used with increasing frequency. In 1524 the *Magister Cantus*, John Gilbert, had been required to sound the instrument only on Sundays and principal and double feasts, which

[35] LAO DC A.3.1, ff. 103r, 163r; DC A.3.3, f. 135r; A.3.4, f. 30r; A.3.5, f. 50r, 85r, 171v; DC Bj.3.3 (1506/7, 1510/11, 1517/18); DC Bj.3.5 (1537/8, 1541/2–1549/50). Lincoln Ep. Reg. 24, f. 143v. J. Bergsagel, 'Ashwell, Thomas', *NGD* I, 654–5. R. Bowers, 'Appleby, Thomas', *NGD* I,509 (contains inaccuracies). *Valor Ecclesiasticus* IV, 8–25 *passim*.

[36] *Valor Ecclesiasticus* IV, 15, 22. LAO DC A.3.5, f. 76r; DC Bj.3.5 (1542/3); DC Bj.3.8, f. 95r; Dvj.13.3.

was probably the customary and historic requirement; in 1539, by contrast, James Crawe, on the new organ, undertook to play in addition on all feasts of nine lessons and on feasts of the Blessed Virgin Mary and St Hugh.[37]

The standard of music-making at Lincoln in the early sixteenth century was high enough to attract and retain the services – as a simple vicar choral – of at least one executant who had accumulated enough experience and expertise to have been admitted to the university degree of Mus.B.; this was John Watkins, vicar 1521–42, who had graduated at Cambridge in 1516. John Gilbert had graduated at Oxford in 1511. Unfortunately, no compositions by either survive, though Watkins was required to write a Mass and antiphon for his degree exercise.[38] John Sothey, *Magister Cantus* 1491–1506, compiled a large volume of polyphony for use at Lady Mass, which the chapter eventually bought for the cathedral's use from his widow Alice for the substantial sum of 40*s*., and indeed some idea of the manner and quality of the music-making at Lincoln at this time may be discerned in the technical demands made on their singers by the surviving compositions of the cathedral musicians. Thomas Appleby (*Magister Cantus* 1537–8, 1541–50, 1559–63) has left an extended and virtuosic Magnificat *à5* for solo ensembles and full chorus, and a four-part Lady Mass (with Kyrie and Alleluia) for men's voices. Somewhat superior in quality is the work of Thomas Ashwell (1506–11), of whom two complete six-part Masses, two fragmentary Masses and two fragmentary votive antiphons remain; conceivably the Mass 'God save King Harry' was written at Lincoln in 1511 on the birth of Henry VIII's first-born (and short–lived) son. Ashwell's work is characterised by its huge scale and great rhythmic intricacy and vitality; he was, perhaps, the most distinguished of the contemporaries of Fayrfax and Cornysh.[39] That the standards of singing were high is also suggested by the instances in which steps had to be taken to prevent – or at least minimise, the effects of – poaching by other choirs, including the Chapel Royal in 1463/4, that of the household of the Earl of Northumberland in 1483/4, and some unidentified institution which sought to appropriate the services of Thomas Ashwell in 1506. In 1514 Henry VIII, being 'credibly enformed that divine service is daily right well kepe [*sic*]

[37] C. Wordsworth, *Ceremonies and processions of the cathedral church of Salisbury*, Cambridge 1901, 196. L. Kirwan, *The music of Lincoln cathedral*, London 1977, plate 9. LAO DC A.2.36, f. 116v; A.3.5, ff. 50r, 172r; DC Bj.3.5 (1535/6–1537/8).

[38] C. A. Williams, *Degrees in music*, London 1894, 121, 134. LAO DC A.3.5, ff. 20r, 28r, 50r, 65v, 196v; Bj.3.3 (1517/18). A. B. Emden, *A biographical register of the University of Oxford 1501–1540*, Oxford 1974, 255.

[39] LAO DC A.3.2, f. 130v; DC Bj.3.3 (1510/11). J. Bergsagel, ed., *Early Tudor Masses I*, Early English Church Music 1, 1963. Cambridge University Library, Peterhouse MSS 471–4. London, British Library, Add. MSS 17802–5. Cambridge, University Library, MS Dd.xiii.27. Cambridge, St John's College, MS K31.

within our cathedral church of Lincoln' was pleased to issue Letters Patent granting immunity from such predation thenceforth; nevertheless, the chapter still deemed it prudent to buy off the Master of the Choristers of St George's Chapel, Windsor, on his arrival for recruiting purposes in 1536/7.[40]

The Reformation and the establishment of an Anglican repertoire, 1547–1584

The liturgical Reformation of 1547–9, rescinded during the Marian reaction 1553–8 but restored in 1559, transformed the cathedral choir from a body of participating tonsured clergy enacting the Catholic liturgy to a body of static performers merely witnessing and commenting upon its Protestant successor. The chapter lost little time in 1547 raising a huge sum exceeding £700 through the comprehensive sale of the cathedral's stock of plate, vessels, crosses, jewels, reliquaries and so on;[41] indeed, although liturgical change, massively reducing the number of daily services, and the mid-century inflation combined at this time to cause a severe curtailment of numbers, there is little indication that chapter and choir responded to the successive changes of liturgy with very much other than acquiescence.

Interim measures taken between April 1547 and the promulgation of the 1549 Book of Common Prayer included the dissolution of the chantries and the pensioning away and dispersal of the thirty-two chantry-priests, and the purge of the Latin rite of features considered to be tainted with error and superstition. Injunctions issued by Royal Commissioners in November 1547 and April 1548 enjoined the provision of vernacular Bibles and the increased use of sermons to expound the scriptures, with the use of the vernacular for the Epistle and Gospel at High Mass, and for the Litany which now superseded the procession preceding Mass. The daily Hours of the Virgin were to be omitted, and Matins celebrated no longer at midnight but at 6 a.m. The Marian votive antiphon following Compline was to be replaced with a vernacular anthem with a text in honour of God or Jesus, set not melismatically but 'therunto a playn and distincte note, for every sillable one' for ease of comprehensibility.[42]

Eventually, however, between January and May 1549 the Latin service was entirely discarded upon the promulgation of the vernacular Book of Common

---

[40] LAO DC A.3.3, f. 65v; DC Bj.2.16 (1463/4); DC Bj.3.2 (1483/4); DC Bj.3.3 (1506/7); DC Bj.3.5 (1536/7).

[41] LAO DC Bj.5.15 (9)-(10).

[42] LAO DC A.3.6, ff. 288r-290v (printed in R. E. G. Cole, *The Chapter Acts of the cathedral church of Lincoln 1520–1559*, 3 vols., LRS 12, 13, 15, 1915–17, III, 11–16). W. H. Frere and W. M. Kennedy, eds., *Visitation articles and injunctions of the period of the Reformation*, 3 vols., Alcuin Club Collections, 1910, II, 135–9.

Prayer, to be replaced in its turn by the revised version of 1552. For the former nine services a day, plus the Lady Mass and weekly Jesus Mass, a mere three were now substituted – Morning Prayer, Holy Communion and Evening Prayer. The total liturgy was contained in a single small book. For a cathedral choir the effect could not be other than traumatic. The Prayer Book contained not a note of music and, being conceived for parish church use, neither appointed anything for a choir to do nor gave any indication how one might be used, beyond a few stray, haphazard references to 'the clerks' and to items 'said or sung'. It was up to the chapter of a great church to decide how the choir could contribute, if at all.

At Lincoln the response was less radical than elsewhere; at least the choir was not – as at, for instance, King's College, Cambridge – disbanded and dispersed altogether. However, the progressive reduction in the number of vicars choral – a trend traceable from as far back as *c.* 1450 – was now sharply accelerated; vacancies left unfilled between 1547 and 1553 reduced their number from around twenty-two to twelve, at which point it remained pegged until the civil wars. There was no longer any necessity to maintain boys of the choir at all; probably it was only the educational value of the twelve choristerships that prompted their retention in 1549, though the private provision of Latin teaching in the Choristers' House was now terminated, and for this side of their education the boys had to go downhill to the Free School in the city. In the cathedral, the organ remained in service and continued to be played; but there was little that the choir could contribute to the services except sung renderings – to plainsong, no doubt – of the responses, Creed and Lord's Prayer, the psalms and canticles, and the Ordinary of Holy Communion. However, the Book of Common Prayer nominated twenty-seven feast-days, and on these there might still have been scope for the performance of simple four-part composed polyphony for the Ordinary of the Communion Service, and the canticles of Morning and Evening Prayer. Also, on a daily basis, there might still be scope for appending to Evening Prayer a vernacular anthem, in the spirit of the 1548 injunction. Nevertheless, the new liturgy certainly caused the extinction of the Lincoln choir's former repertory of expansive and virtuosic Latin polyphony, and very little may have taken its place. While the chapter duly purchased four new copies of the Prayer Book in 1549 and eighteen vernacular psalters for the use of the choir, none of the three surviving accounts for the reign of Edward VI (1547/8, 1550/1 and 1551/2 are missing) records payments for the copying of a new repertory of vernacular polyphony.[43]

---

[43] Frere and Kennedy, *Visitation Articles and Injunctions* II, 135–9, nos. 20, 22. LAO DC A.3.6, ff. 312r-437v, *passim*; DC Bj.3.4 (1549/50); DC Bj.3.6 (1552/3); DC Dv.2.2a (1548/9); DC Ciij.45.10, f. 3v-4r. P. G. le Huray, *Music and the Reformation in England 1549–1660*, 2nd edn, Cambridge 1978, 1–30.

During the reign of Mary I (1553–8) no attempt was made to restore the chantries or replenish the number of vicars choral, but most other aspects of the changes of the six years previous were thrown into reverse. Statute law enjoined that by Christmas 1553 all forms of Latin service in use in the last year of Henry VIII be restored. Consequently a substantial programme of rebinding old service books, including antiphoners, missals and processioners, was put in hand; others were bought new. In May 1553 only a minimum of communion and other plate had remained – four chalices and a pyx; new equipment now was purchased – processional crosses, an image of the Virgin Mary, cruets, censers, candlesticks and so on. The Subdean contrived to recover from the Queen's Wardrobe in London a quantity of vestments and copes lately confiscated; others were bought new. John Howe came up from London to repair the organ; the daily Lady Mass was promptly restored, and polyphony for use there or in choir was being copied by 1555/6. A grammar school in the Close was revived in 1556, and except for the chantry services and obits, a reasonable approximation to the revival of Catholic worship as it had been in the last year of Henry VIII may well have been largely accomplished.[44]

However, within a few months of the accession of Elizabeth I in 1558 the vernacular Prayer Book of 1552 had again been restored, with an Act of Uniformity requiring the abandonment of the Latin rite by 24 June 1559. On this occasion, however, a Royal Injunction supplemented the Prayer Book rubrics by expressly requiring that the great churches preserve their historic maintenance of places for singing men and choristers, authorising them to perform 'modest and distinct song' for any appropriate part of the Common Prayers, with, at the beginning and end of Morning and Evening Prayer, 'an hymn or suchlike song, to the praise of almighty God, in the best sort of melody and music that may be conveniently devised'. Thus was the historic cathedral choir preserved for the posterity of the Church of England. Other injunctions and orders allow the timetable of the new vernacular liturgy at Lincoln to be tabulated as follows:

5 a.m. or 6 a.m.	Early Prayers
9 a.m.	Public Theology Lecture (Tuesday, Thursday, Saturday)
10 a.m.	Morning Prayer
about 10.30 a.m.	Litany and Holy Communion (or Ante-Communion)
3 p.m.	Evening Prayer (and anthem).[45]

[44] LAO DC A.3.6, ff. 387v, 412r; Bj.3.6, ff. 11v, 23r, 24v, 56v; DC Dij.62.3.25. Leach, 'Schools', 431.

[45] Frere and Kennedy, *Visitation Articles and Injunctions* III, 22–3, no. 49. LAO DC A.3.2, f. 85r; DC A.3.7, f. 1v; DC A.3.8, f. 36v.

By the early 1560s the choir had already reached its standard post-Reformation disposition of personnel. The complement of twelve vicars choral was divided into four priests ('old' vicars) and eight laymen ('young' vicars). All were now able to marry and raise families, but under the new regime were conspicuously, even perniciously, underemployed; the priest-vicars could take on the incumbencies of neighbourhood parish churches, but the remuneration of all, in consequence of the mid-century inflation, was now reduced to meagreness, and probably Lincoln was soon again unable to keep, or even attract, the ablest men to the now devalued profession of liturgical singing-man. Unfortunately, no surviving document records the vocal distribution applied to the twelve singing-men, although the voice of individual vicars is occasionally mentioned, countertenor, tenor and bass being all encountered.[46] Meanwhile, in 1560 the Choristers' House had gone bankrupt; income no longer matched expenditure. The new liturgy offered nothing specifically for choristers to do; their role was exclusively musical, and given the meagreness of even their potential contribution, the chapter now saw fit to make ends meet henceforth by reducing their number from twelve to eight. Indeed, since there was now so little for the boys to learn in Song School, and so few services to attend, all the choristers were henceforth required to attend the Close Grammar School daily; by the retention as choristers of boys whose voices had in fact broken so that they could complete their grammar school education, the number of effective singing-boys may often have been but seven or even six.[47]

The ground rules for the new liturgy were presumably worked out by the time the veteran Thomas Appleby resigned as Master of the Choristers in March 1563; he was succeeded by the most illustrious of the musicians ever to have worked at Lincoln, William Byrd, then no more than 19 or 20 years old.[48] In so far as it was sung at all (much of what had formerly been monotoned now being merely read) the early vernacular cathedral service known to Byrd was, like its Catholic predecessor, sung predominantly to plainsong. Perhaps only the anthem concluding Evening Prayer (as the successor of the evening votive antiphon) was regularly sung in polyphony (quite possibly even daily), while a small repertory of relatively simple polyphonic settings of the canticles could be deployed to distinguish the greater feast-days. Need was slight, and only slowly, it seems, did a repertory of vernacular polyphony build up. Even so, Byrd at

---

[46] LAO DC Ciij.45.10, ff. 1r–5v. Cambridge, Corpus Christi College, MS 108, p. 221. C. W. Foster, ed., *Lincoln Episcopal Records in the time of Thomas Cooper (1571–1584)*, LRS 2, 1912, 150, 154–5.

[47] Foster, *Lincoln Episcopal Records*, 150, 154–5. LAO DC A.3.2, f. 84v; DC A.3.7, ff. 4r, 4v, 9r, 11v; A.3.8, f. 36v. Cambridge, Corpus Christi College, MS 108, pp. 223, 232–3.

[48] H. W. Shaw, 'William Byrd of Lincoln', *Music and Letters* 48, 1967, 52–9. E. H. Fellowes, *William Byrd*, 2nd edn, London 1948, 2–3. LAO DC A.3.7, f. 27r.

first distinguished himself with decisiveness and vigour. The sum of 53s.4d. was promptly spent on repairs to the cathedral organ, and he travelled to recruit boys for the choir in 1563 from Lancashire, and in 1564/5 and again in 1565/6 from the still surviving parish church choirs of Newark and Louth. If Byrd had to make do with only six to eight choristers, he evidently preferred to recruit them ready-trained. In 1563/4 and 1565/6 sporadic programmes of music-copying were undertaken – much of it, no doubt, of Byrd's own composing – and a new set of ten books (perhaps MATTB for each side of the choir) was prepared in 1571/2.[49]

Although the chronology of Byrd's earliest music is far from secure, it seems certain that while at Lincoln he launched into all the genres of composition at which he eventually excelled. To presumably the delectation of himself and his friends in his own front parlour can be attributed the early works for solo keyboard, and the Fantasias and In Nomines for viol consort; perhaps for the Christmas-tide vernacular plays acted by the choristers and other boys of the Close Grammar School (to 1567) were written his prototype consort songs. Given the character and premisses of the English Reformation at a provincial cathedral, it seems scarcely credible that any of the early motets could have been performed in the Minster; however, numerous works with Latin texts, including a number based on plainsong cantus firmi that depart in details from standard Salisbury Use and probably therefore adopt Lincoln Use versions, have been attributed to Byrd's Lincoln years. If he heard these pieces at all, it was probably in the context of domestic music-making in his own home, performed by the boys and by that majority of the singing-men whose careers stretched back not merely to the reign of Mary I but to that of Henry VIII. For use in the cathedral service, Byrd was limited to composing to vernacular sacred texts – responses and litanies, services and anthems. It seems probable that much of his Anglican service music dates from this period, and that the well-known Short, Second and Third Services, the Responses and the ecclesiastical verse and full anthems that circulated in manuscript were written for, and first performed by, the Lincoln choir.[50]

Byrd and the chapter, however, failed to remain in close accord. As the 1560s progressed such encouragement and enthusiasm for music as had survived since

---

[49] LAO DC Bj.3.6, ff. 138v, 152v, 166r, 179v, 224v, 235v; Dv.2.2(b), f.5v.

[50] J. Kerman, 'Byrd, William', NGD III, 538. J. Kerman, *The Masses and motets of William Byrd*, London 1981, *passim*. O. Neighbour, *The consort and keyboard music of William Byrd*, London 1978, *passim*. P. Brett, 'The English consort song', *Proceedings of the Royal Musical Association* 88, 1961/2, 73. Introductory material to relevant volumes of P. Brett and C. Monson, *The Byrd edition* (London, 1974–). LAO DC Bj.3.6, ff. 112v, 125v, 138v, 152v, 165v; DC Bj.5.12 (19), f. 1v.

1558 began apparently to evaporate, as the chapter came increasingly under the influence of the Puritan Archdeacon of Lincoln, John Aylmer. A purge of the Close in 1565 produced the departure of two canons resident and the master of the Close Grammar School, on grounds of their antipathy to the new religion. In 1567 the school was closed and amalgamated with the Free School in the city; the choristers now had to transfer twice a day downhill for their Latin education, reducing their availability for musical instruction. There was overt friction between Byrd and the chapter; the latter disapproved of his practice of leaving the singing of the (plainsong) psalms to the men, and instructed that the boys should participate also. For reasons unknown, his salary was withheld for eight months between November 1569 and July 1570. Then in September 1570 a chapter order effectively imposed a ban on the playing of the organ during service. Byrd was instructed that henceforth he sound the organ merely to give the pitch to the choir before the Office Canticles (instead of, perhaps, prefacing their performance – in plainsong on most days – with a brief voluntary); the application of this instruction to the anthem also, which Byrd was expressly enjoined, after giving the pitch, to sing with the choir, suggests that he might already have been experimenting with his earliest essays in the style of the accompanied verse anthem – to the chapter's evident disapproval.[51] There was thus good reason for Byrd to seek to move to greener pastures elsewhere; he was sworn a Gentleman of Queen Elizabeth's Chapel Royal on 22 February 1572 (not 1570, the date usually given), and left Lincoln to take up this appointment shortly after.[52] Contact was not entirely severed, however; in 1573, in response to an imperious request from the Queen, the chapter granted to Byrd an annuity of £3.6s.8d. per year, imposing a condition that he send regularly to the cathedral anthems and services (*cantica et servitia divina*) 'well set to music'. This was paid until 1582, but the identity of the music sent by Byrd – if any – is not known.[53]

Nevertheless,[54] probably no other provincial cathedral got off to so good a start as Lincoln in providing for the musical needs – such as they were – of the

[51] J. W. F. Hill, *Tudor and Stuart Lincoln*, Cambridge 1956, 97–8. H. Gee, *The Elizabethan clergy and the settlement of religion, 1558–1604*, Oxford 1898, 229. LAO DC A.3.7, f. 23v; DC A.3.8, ff. 36v, 44r, 45v.

[52] E. F. Rimbault, *The Old Cheque-Book or Book of Remembrance of the Chapel Royal*, Camden Society, NS 3, 1872, 2. LAO DC A.3.7, ff. 71r, 72v; DC Bj.3.6, f. 237r; DC Bj.5.12 (23), ff. 1r, 37v.

[53] LAO DC A.3.8, f. 52v; DC Bj.3.6, f. 257r; DC Bj.5.12 (33), f. 18r; DC Bj.5.12 (34), f. 15r; DC Bij.2.4, f. 61v; DC Bij.3.17, f. 46v.

[54] For almost all the raw materials used in compiling the remainder of this chapter, I am indebted to Dr Ian Payne, who most generously placed at my disposal his transcripts and notes from the cathedral archives for the period 1572–1642.

reformed liturgy, and under a new Dean, John Whitgift (1571), Byrd's successor appears at first to have been more than able to maintain this momentum. Thomas Butler came to the post with Byrd's personal recommendation, and briefly, from 1573 until its final abandonment in 1583, he enjoyed the benefits of the restoration of the grammar school in the Close for the choristers (and others). Moreover, exactly coterminous with the deanship of William Wickham (1577–84), the hitherto sporadic instances of music-copying expanded into apparently a sustained programme of repertoire-building. Every account surviving for that period records the payment of large sums to the choir scribe, Thomas Herbert, for making, writing and binding books of polyphony (*cantaciones*). Although the music concerned probably consisted of pieces characterised mainly by simplicity of counterpoint and absence of gratuitous extension, yet it seems to have been at this period that a body of music large enough to sustain the performance of vernacular polyphony on a frequent, and possibly virtually a daily, basis, rather than as hitherto only a festal and Sunday basis, was deliberately assembled and – presumably – performed. Thus, probably, was established (except for the psalms, still sung to plainsong) what has turned out to be the modern pattern of musical contribution to the choral Anglican cathedral service[55].

The choral service, 1584–1642

The plateau of endeavour and accomplishment achieved by 1584 provided a platform from which Lincoln apparently proved able to keep abreast of the developments in cathedral music which supervened between then and 1642, though probably without contributing very much to their original generation. For from the 1580s until *c*.1620 it was unfortunate that the progress of music and worship in the Minster was intermittently compromised and retarded by the insufficiency of the example set by a series of unsatisfactory occupants of the offices of Organist and Master of the Choristers, and by the insubordination and ill-motivation thus aroused among some of the singers.

After a productive start, Butler seems to have lapsed into indolence and inadequacy. Already in June 1580 he had been admonished for negligence in teaching the boys, and in 1584 his salary was briefly sequestrated and withheld.[56] At least by 1590 it is clear that the chapter was prepared to allow him to

---

[55] Hill, *Tudor and Stuart Lincoln*, 102. Leach, 'Schools', 440–2. LAO DC A.3.7, ff. 72v, 74v; DC Bj.2.1 (7), f. 3v; DC Bj.2.1 (9), unfol., DC Bj.3.6, ff. 245v, 269v; DC Bj.3.10 (4), unfol. DC Dv.2.2(d), f. 6v; DC Bj.5.12 (26), f. 27r; DC Bj.5.12 (29), ff. 6v, 7r; DC Bj.5.12 (33), f. 21r; DC Bj.5.12 (34), ff. 17v, 18r; DC Bj.5.12 (35), ff. 31r, 33v.

[56] Foster, *Lincoln Episcopal Records*, 152. LAO DC A.3.7, f. 104v; A.3.8, f. 64v; DC Bj.2.1 (7), f. 7v.

exercise his office by deputy, and fortunately the deputies were men of some ability. John Hilton (born *c.* 1566) had been a chorister in the choir before being appointed as a Poor Clerk in 1580 and, in 1584, to a vicarage choral in reversion, to have the next vacant place for a countertenor – an eventuality which never materialised. By 1590/1 Hilton was acting as both Master of the Choristers and as Organist, before departing in Autumn 1593 to the corresponding post at Trinity College, Cambridge. He briefly restored the annual choirboy play at Lincoln; also he composed madrigals, and wrote, among other church music, a seven-part setting of 'Call to remembrance, O Lord' and probably the well-known 'Lord, for thy tender mercies' sake' *à*4.[57]

Butler's neglect to replace Hilton on his departure led to complaints from the chapter in January 1595 that he was failing – among other things – to train up the musically abler choristers to play the organ so as to be able to substitute for him when absent; so within a few months, Butler found a new deputy, Thomas Boyce. As a composer, Boyce's work circulated widely; a whole Short Service survives even now in manuscripts of Durham, Ely, Gloucester and Oxford (New College) provenance, and Boyce was eventually admitted Mus.B. of Oxford in 1603. At last Butler resigned as Organist and Master of the Choristers as from Michaelmas 1597, and Boyce was appointed to succeed him.[58]

While Hilton and Boyce were effectively in charge, there was probably little danger that the cathedral's music could lapse into torpor. How much of their music was written at and for Lincoln cannot now be determined, but for the music scribe Thomas Herbert a recognised post with a modest salary was created from 1584/5, in evident anticipation of a steady renewing and updating of the repertory thenceforth. Another productive innovation of their period of office is disclosed by the account for 1594/5, which is the first surviving document to record expenditure on the maintenance of a chest of viols on which the choristers were taught to play by their Master. The chest was complete, of six viols (no doubt the standard two each of treble, tenor and bass), and was regularly maintained in new strings and bows until the civil wars. Principally, no doubt, they were used for the boys' general musical and aural training, though a single oblique reference from 1634 suggests that they may, exceptionally, have been used occasionally in service in the choir.[59]

For reasons unknown, Thomas Boyce never took up his formal appointment

[57] P. G. le Huray, 'Hilton, John', *NGD* VIII, 569–70. LAO DC A.3.7, ff. 104v, 117r, 125v; DC A.3.8, f. 63r; DC Bj.3.8, f. 277r.

[58] P. G. le Huray, 'Boyce, Thomas', *NGD* III, 138. DC A.3.7, f. 125v; DC A.3.8a, f. 46r (where Boyce's name is given as William Boys); DC Bj.3.8, f. 307r.

[59] LAO DC Dv.2.2(d), f. 5v; DC Bj.2.1 (7), f. 3v; DC Bj.3.8, f. 321v; DC Bj.3.9, f. 139r; DC Bj.3.10 (2), unfol.; DC Bj.3.10 (13), unfol.; DC Bj.5.12 (38), rear page. le Huray, *Music and the Reformation*, 128–9.

as Organist and Master of the Choristers; instead, Butler was succeeded at Michaelmas 1597 by John Allen, sometime chorister and lay clerk of Chester Cathedral, who was eventually to return there as Organist and Master of the Choristers from 1609 to 1613. Allen remained only two years at Lincoln, and was succeeded in September 1599 by Thomas Kingston, of whose previous career nothing is at present known.[60]

For Kingston's first ten years or so, the cathedral's music appears to have prospered once again. This was a period when, in the Church at large, an appreciation of the contribution which music could make to the beauty of institutional worship was coming increasingly to be restored to favour, in official circles at least. Composers responded with an increase not only in the sheer length and complexity of composition for the Church, but also in the technical demands made on the performers, especially on soloists in verse services and anthems. At Lincoln the chapter appears to have shown some concern that the choir keep up with musical trends at large. On two occasions ready-made collections of music were acquired. In 1599/1600 40s. was spent purchasing books of music from John Fido, already known as an entrepreneurial compiler and retailer of off-the-peg repertoires of church music; and in 1609/10 the large sum of £13.6s.8d. was given for various books of music acquired from one William Lawes, a Gentleman of the Chapel Royal.[61] The chapter also increased their provision for the performance of this music. In 1605/6 a part-time but permanent post of organ-blower was created, in response presumably to increasing use of the instrument for the performance of voluntaries and verse anthems and services;[62] and, far more importantly, it was resolved to augment the number of singing-boys.

Since 1560/1 there had been only eight choristers (reduced sometimes to seven or even six), a number perhaps adequate for Elizabethan church music, but scarcely able to support the boys' part in the more sustained and ambitious compositions of the Jacobean period and beyond. Since no new endowment was likely to be forthcoming for such a purpose, the chapter appropriated an ancient one. The original Burghersh and Buckyngham Chantries had been suppressed in 1549, but the Court of Augmentations had agreed to preserve the educational provisions associated with them. Prior to 1549 the seven boys resident in the chantries had been required to attend both lessons at the city

---

[60] LAO DC A.3.7, ff. 125v, 126v; DC A.3.9, f. 9r; DC Bj.5.12 (38), rear page. J. E. West, *Cathedral organists*, 2nd edn, London 1921, 17.

[61] LAO DC A.3.9, f. 78v; DC Bj.2.1 (11), unfol.; DC Bj.3.9, f. 153r. J. Morehen, 'Fido, John', *NGD* VI, 533. J. Morehen, 'The Southwell Minster Tenor Part Book', *Music and Letters* 1, 352. Rimbault, *Cheque-Book of the Chapel Royal*, 6, 7.

[62] LAO DC A.3.9, ff. 47v, 111v; DC Bj.3.9, ff. 51v, 111v.

grammar school and religious services, not in the cathedral but in the local parish church, St Mary Magdalen. After 1549, when the chantry houses were dissolved, their educational incomes continued to be disbursed, but simply as scholarships to the parents or guardians of boys nominated by the chapter, who lived at home and attended the city school, and were no more involved in the conduct of the services in the Minster following the Reformation than ever they had been before it.[63] The idea, however, of turning the Burghersh boys into additional choristers was perhaps in the air by 1607, and had received effect at least by 1609, when it was ordered that thenceforth no Burghersh boy should receive his grant unless the Master of the Choristers certified his diligent attendance at both the grammar school and the Song School. The Burghersh boys, living at home and in receipt of just their cash scholarships, and the choristers, living and fully maintained in the Choristers' House, could not be wholly assimilated; nevertheless, this group of potentially fifteen, though more probably (because of the 'dry' choristers) of about twelve voices, now constituted the singing-boys of the cathedral, and by 1626 the term 'Burghersh Chanters' was already in use to describe the boys on the Burghersh, rather than the choristers' ancient, Foundation – a distinction nominally retained to the present day.[64]

Whatever indication there may be that a degree of forward momentum in the conduct of the music of the cathedral was being maintained in the first decade of the seventeenth century has to be assessed in the light of at least the likelihood of its partial vitiation by a recurrent stratum of ill-motivation among some of the choirmen, especially among the four priest-vicars. By the 1590s this was manifest most clearly in persistent absenteeism. Especially on Sundays and holy days the priests were regularly failing to arrive to execute their duty of beginning the services by intoning the opening versicles and collects. On these days, they were perforce at service in their parish churches; they claimed (probably justifiably) to be unable to afford to pay deputies to substitute for them in the Minster. Essentially the problem was financial; it remained unresolved and a source of recurring trouble until the civil wars.[65]

In the second decade of the seventeenth century, however, such problems multiplied. Kingston lapsed into drunkenness and decline; in March 1611 the

[63] LAO DC A.1.8, ff. 312r, 315r; DC Bj.5.12 (14b), f. 64v; DC Bj.5.12 (32), f. 2v. Lincoln Ep. Reg. 12, ff. 482r–487r. London, British Library, MS Cotton Tiberius E iii, ff. 4v–5v. A. F. Leach, *English schools at the Reformation*, Winchester 1898, part 2, 138.

[64] *LCS* II, 642. LAO DC A.3.9, ff. 71r, 161r; DC Bij.1.11 (3); Cv.13.6.

[65] *LCS* II, 644. LAO DC A.3.7, ff. 119v, 120r, 132r; DC A.3.8a, f. 29v; A.3.9, ff. 3v, 49v, 55v, 82v, 113v, 114v; DC A.3.10, ff. 82v–90r.

chapter replaced him as Steward of the Choristers' House, and charged him with negligence in playing the organ and teaching the choristers, and with unreasonable severity in punishing them for their faults. He failed to keep his promises to reform, and in September 1612 was relieved of his office of Master of the Choristers. Briefly he remained as Organist only, until his conduct became too disruptive to tolerate longer. In September 1615 it was reported that 'he ys verye often drunke, and that by means thereof he hathe by unorderlye playinge on the organs putt the quier owte of tune and disordered them'. He was given a year in which to find a new job, and in September 1616 left to take up – incredibly – the post of Organist and Master of the Choristers at York Minster.[66] Thus from 1612 the posts of Master of the Choristers and Organist at Lincoln were divided between two separate men, an arrangement which obtained thereafter until 1850. The Organist appears to have been the senior musical officer of the church; the Mastership of the Choristers reverted to an appointment taken on by a man principally employed and remunerated as a vicar choral.

At first Kingston's departure led to little improvement; in particular, the new Master of the Choristers, Thomas Stanley, proved unable to teach his charges or even control them adequately, despite being allowed from 1616 to withdraw them from lessons at the city grammar school for an hour's rehearsal before 10 a.m. Matins and again before 4 p.m. Evensong each day.[67] The violent behaviour of the priest-vicar Nicholas Crosse, 1613–17, set a malign example to all, and by 1615 or so a genuine malaise was setting in and affecting even the junior vicars (the lay clerks) against many of whom little of ill had ever been hitherto alleged. In October 1619 an unprecedented catalogue of complaints was heard against members of all sections of the choir. The vicars were 'scandalous in drinkinge to muche', and the priest-vicars were prone to exceptional negligence and absenteeism, one preferring to play bowls to attending church. Thomas Stanley was negligent in teaching the choristers, and the boys were truant from Song School and grammar school; one was prone to addressing both Steward and Master of the Choristers as 'baldpate', and to Stanley had even offered violence, while two others had run away.[68]

The chapter which investigated these complaints was at least not complacent about the inadequacies of their staff, and although this may be an illusion arising from the increasing sparseness of the surviving documents, the 1620s appear to have been a calmer and more productive period than the previous

---

[66] LAO DC A.3.9, ff. 81r, 82r, 85r, 89r, 98r, 112v; DC Bij.2.6, f. 31v. P. Aston, 'Music since the Reformation', in G. Aylmer and R. Cant, eds., *A history of York Minster*, Oxford 1977, 405.

[67] *LCS* II, 623. LAO DC A.3.9, ff. 115v, 139v.

[68] LAO DC A.3.9, ff. 95v, 107v, 117v, 121v, 122v, 129v, 139v–140r.

decade, with men apparently more able than their predecessors being appointed to the principal musical offices. As Master of the Choristers Stanley was succeeded, apparently in 1620, by Ralph Standish, and by Henry Mace (1632–4) and John Heardson (1634–42); these are shadowy figures, though Heardson is known as a minor composer.[69] John Wanless, who succeeded Kingston as Organist in 1616, continued in office until the civil wars, and indeed, like Heardson, survived to be reappointed in 1660. He is known to have composed; an organ outline of a verse anthem 'Plead thou my cause' survives, and it is said that a setting of the Litany by him remained in use at Lincoln until about 1850.[70] From 1624/5 the choir music scribe, Richard Jameson, began to be paid bonuses for extra music-copying, and the set of ten *libri psallentes* bound during 1633/4 may well have been a double set of part-books for five-part polyphony.[71]

At least one visitor to the cathedral in the 1630s found that his expectations of its music were not disappointed. On 16 August 1634 a Lieutenant Hammond heard Morning Prayer, and recorded in his journal: 'Heere wee heard their solemne Service; the Organs, with other instruments, suited to most excellent voyces, were all answerable to such a famous Cathedrall.' The enigmatic 'other instruments' may perhaps have been the choristers' viols. Hammond's criteria, however, may have been those of an age earlier and more lax than those of the Laudian establishment of the 1630s. At the very moment of his visit, Archbishop Laud's metropolitan visitation of the cathedral was in progress. Already in July 1634 the Bishop's Chancellor had sent to Laud a preliminary but perhaps more trustworthy note of the state of the diocese, in which his report on the cathedral observed that the vicars were complaining of the irregular payment of their salaries; in return, the chapter 'complayne of their ill officiating the service, for there is not above 4 tollerable voyces in all the quire'. The articles of this visitation included the standard question enquiring 'whether the number of those that serve the Quire and all other ministres of this Church be kept full and the Quire sufficiently furnished with a skilfull organist and able singers and dayly service there sang according to the foundation of this Church'. Unfortunately, no formal record of the answers has survived, but a brief digest of the response includes: 'The communion table is not very decent, and the raile before it is worse. The Organs ould and naught. The fabrique

---

[69] C. W. Foster, ed., *The parish registers of St Margaret in the Close, Lincoln*, LRS, Parish Register Section 2, 1913, 42, 65. LAO DC A.3.9, ff. 145r, 176r, 177r, 183v; DC A.3.10, f. 228r; DC Bj.3.9, ff. 210v, 220v, 272v, 282v; DC Bj.3.10 (9), (10), (13), unfol. le Huray, *Music and the Reformation*, 228.

[70] LAO DC A.3.9, f. 129v. Oxford, Bodl. Libr., MS Tenbury 791, f. 453v. A. R. Maddison, 'Lincoln cathedral choir 1558–1642', *AASR* 18, 1885/6, 117.

[71] LAO DC Bj.3.9, ff. 219r, 224r, 281r; DC Bj.3.10 (9), unfol.

secretly ruinous ... The Copes and vestments are imbesilled, and none remaine.'[72]

Such questions and reactions eloquently bespeak some of the preoccupations of Laudian churchmanship and the ideals which the cathedral musical staff were now expected to live up to. The description of the organ was probably justified; the cathedral archives contain no indication that any new instrument had been acquired since that of 1536. The chapter did at least make a contract in May 1635 with Thomas Coats of Stamford to keep the organ in good repair and tune thenceforth, for 40s per year. The musical value of a subsequent chapter order is, however, rather more doubtful. In September 1637 it was decreed that the city waits be paid £4 per year in return for 'their service and paines in the Quier of the church upon everie Sunday and holyday at morning and evening prayer'.[73] It is unlikely that the waits could have substituted for, or complemented, the organ in the accompaniment of vocal polyphony; more likely perhaps is a contribution of fanfares and interludes at appropriate points in the services.

By the later 1630s evidence of demoralisation among the singers recurs, for which the reasons are not far to seek. Quite apart from the meagre salaries offered, irregularly and haphazardly paid, the elaborate choral service of the Caroline period was something with which not only much of the city and county beyond the Close wall was by now corrosively out of sympathy, but even the bishop, John Williams, and the canons of his collation. By 1637 a deep chasm of mistrust and suspicion had opened up between the priest-vicars and the type of residentiaries 'put in by my Lord Bishopp to worke his and their plotted ends', of whose demeanour towards them the vicars complained but in vain. Meanwhile, an enquiry by the chapter into absenteeism among the vicars choral revealed that by 1636 the old problem had reappeared – if indeed it had ever gone away. In the year previous each of the priest-vicars had recorded between 130 and 180 absent days, and all were clearly disaffected and incorrigible. On the other hand, of the young vicars, Robert Butler was never late, never left early, and was absent only twelve days; William Ellis was late eight times, but missed only seventeen days. Three other junior vicars missed between thirty and forty days each; the other three were as disreputable as the clergy. Meanwhile, although the choristers were almost all very irregular attenders at the grammar school, yet there is no record that they were absentee from the cathedral. Clearly, however, and not for the first time, whatever there was of quality and sincerity in the conduct of worship in the Minster was dependent

---

[72] L. G. W. Legg, ed., *Lt. Hammond: a relation of a short survey of twenty-six counties* [1634], London 1904, 6–7. LAO DC Dvj.23.4. PRO SP 16/271 no. 82, f. 1r; 16/274 no. 12, f. 1r.

[73] LAO DC A.3.9, ff. 190r, 196v.

almost entirely on the diligence and enthusiasm of a few, rather than on the uniform goodwill and dutiful conscientiousness of all. Overall, therefore, it seems unlikely that Lincoln Minster can have contributed much that was particularly distinguished or noteworthy to the glory of Jacobean and Caroline cathedral music.[74]

No surviving cathedral sources appear to record the date or manner of the final suspension of services sung according to the Book of Common Prayer in consequence of the outbreak of the civil war. The accounts for 1640/1 reveal the cathedral body functioning normally enough, but it seems unlikely that the choir could have continued singing services once an authoritative Parliamentary committee had been established in Lincoln at some time between August and December 1642.[75] The first, and only, interruption to an otherwise continuous history of music and worship in Lincoln Minster had begun.

[74] LAO DC A.3.9, ff. 188v, 190v, 192v, 195v; D C Bij.1.11 (3).
[75] LAO DC Bj.3.10 (13). C. Holmes, *Seventeenth-century Lincolnshire*, History of Lincolnshire VII, Lincoln 1980, 158–61, 169–71.

Table 1. *The Organists and Masters of the Choristers, to 1662*

	Organists	Masters of the Choristers	
		John Flur	1306–8
		William Seagrave	1308–
1310–	Thomas Ledenham	Roger Spaldyng	–1332
		John Claypol	1332–
		Nicholas Bautre	–1354–
1363–79	John Louth	John Welton	–1367
		Henry Langham	1367–
1379–81	Stephen Spaldying		
1381–91	John Louth		
1391–4	Robert Conyng		
1394–1424–	Robert Patryngton	John Tetford	–1395
	jointly with	Walter Braytoft	1395–1404–
	William Quentyn	John Tetford	–1413
		John Clare	1413–
		John Retford	1429
		William Fawkes	1431–
–1433–4–	William Fawkes	John Retford	–1434–
		Thomas Farford	1437–48–
–1440–5	John Ingleton		
1445–6	Richard Lescy		
1446–51–	John Tiryngton		

Table 1.—*continued*

	Organists		Masters of the Choristers	
−1452–8	William Mogham			
1458–61	John Tiryngton		Robert Burne	−1460−
1461	William Horwood			
1461–83	John Lytyll		Nicholas Gray	−1462−
			William Horwood	−1476–84
1483–4	William Horwood			
1484–90		John Davy		1484–91
1490–1	John Warcop			
1491–1506		John Sothey		
1506		Leonard Peper (acting)		
1506–11		Thomas Ashwell		
1511–16		Henry Ottringham		
1516–17		John Heghlay (acting)		
1517–28		John Gilbert		1517–24
			William Freeman	1524–8
1528–36		Robert Dove		
1536–7		John Brandon		
1537–8		Thomas Appleby		
1538–41		James Crawe		
1541–50–		Thomas Appleby		
−1552–9		William Monk		
1559–63		Thomas Appleby		
1563–72		William Byrd		
1572–97		Thomas Butler		
(−1590–3)		John Hilton (deputising)		
(1595–7)		Thomas Boyce (deputising)		
1597–		John Allen		
1599–1616		Thomas Kingston		1599–1612
			Thomas Stanley	1612–19–
1616–62	John Wanless			
			Ralph Standish	−1624–27−
			Henry Mace	1632–4
			John Heardson	1634–61

4

Music and worship, 1660–1980

❊

NICHOLAS THISTLETHWAITE

Dean Honywood was installed on 12 October 1660. The restoration of the choral foundation began at once. The problems were formidable.

Of the musical establishment before the wars, only three members remained to take up their duties. John Wanlesse, Organist since 1616, was now an old man, and John Heardson, appointed junior vicar and *Magister Choristarum* in 1634 (and later senior vicar) must have been well into middle age; both were dead by the end of 1662. Only John Blundevile (junior vicar, 1640) was to play a significant role in the years following the Restoration – he survived as Steward of the Choristers until 1692. To the vicars' houses, the 'Sones of Violence' had done their worst, and they were 'reduced into confused heapes of Rubbish'.[1] The Choristers' House seems to have suffered a similar fate, and the estates of both choristers and vicars had been seized. The fate of the music books is unknown, and as for the organs, despite claims to the contrary,[2] both Evelyn's comments[3] and the behaviour of the Parliamentary forces in other cathedrals[4] suggest that they were not spared. There was much to be done.

Two weeks after Honywood's installation the Chapter Acts record the admission of six junior vicars – Daniel Featley, John Jameson, Wm Jollands, Anthonie Boyce, John Ward and Richard Gardiner.[5] Wanlesse was paid as

---

[1] Vicars' petition to Dean and Chapter, 15 Apr. 1664; LAO DC Dvij.3.2.
[2] E. F. Rimbault and E. J. Hopkins, *The organ*, 2nd edn, London 1870, 93.
[3] E. S. de Beer, ed., *The diary of John Evelyn* III, Oxford 1955, 132.
[4] See, for example, Mercurius Rusticus, *The Country's Complaint recounting the sad Events of this Unparraleld Warr*, 1647.
[5] Chapter Acts, 25 Oct. 1660; LAO DC A.3.9, f. 213.

Organist from the beginning of the same month and must have had some sort of instrument to play upon, for a bellows-blower (Thomas Stevenett) was engaged, and was paid from about this time.[6] With these modest resources, the choral services were resumed, perhaps at the end of October 1660.

Admissions continued over the next few months. Thomas Cooke was appointed senior vicar on 5 December[7] and then a week later no fewer than seven choristers and seven Burghersh Chanters – all named (and we find among them familiar names such as Blundevile, Walter, and Heardson) – were admitted.[8] The same day, Hugh Walter was appointed senior vicar. He was later paid 'for prickinge out Anthems for the Church', but the sum involved is quite small (20 shillings) and cannot represent a wholesale replacement of the choir's books.[9] Choristers' 'gownes' were supplied by Thomas Beardshaw.[10] The choral foundation eventually regained its full strength in March, 1662, when Daniel Bull and Walter Powell were made senior vicars;[11] Heardson had died in August 1661,[12] and so this brought the number of 'old vicars' to four.

John Blundevile was appointed Steward of the Choristers – he may also have been their Master from 1660 but is not named as such until 1661–2. He was paid the usual sums for their board and feedings, for paper and ink, and for viol strings and bows.[13] The last two items suggest that the teaching of an instrument to the boys was revived as soon as possible, and, indeed, the accounts for 1660–1 record a payment of 12s.6d. to Blundevile 'for a Presse to keepe the Choristers viales in'.[14] The regular payments to Blundevile continue throughout the 1660s, with the occasional variation – a gratuity from the Dean and Chapter, or, for example, an extra payment 'for his paines in goeinge to Peterburgh to Fetch Choristars' (1665–6).[15]

It was not until October 1661 that the Dean and Chapter were in a position to turn their attention to the provision of 'a convenient house or place for the Choristers to Lodge in'.[16] It is not known what became of the 'little small Tenement ... built of Timber and Stone'[17] which had been used as the

[6] Draft Audit 1660–1; L A O D C Bj.3.11.

[7] Chapter Acts, 5 Dec. 1660; L A O D C A.3.9, f. 216.

[8] Ibid., 216 ?Dec. 1660.

[9] Draft Audit 1660–1; L A O D C Bj.3.11.

[10] Idem.

[11] A. R. Maddison, 'Lincoln cathedral choir A.D. 1640 to 1700' *A A S R* 20, 1889, 42.

[12] Ibid., 48.

[13] Draft Audit 1661–2; L A O D C Bj.3.1.

[14] Draft Audit 1660–1.

[15] Ibid. 1665–6.

[16] Chapter Act, 2 Oct. 1661; L A O D C A.3.9, f. 228.

[17] Revd Edmund Venables, ed., extracts from the Parliamentary Survey of the Minster Close, *A S S R* 19, 1887, 60–1.

Choristers' school before the wars, nor the old Choristers' House behind it. Both may have been derelict, or destroyed. Certainly, there was an empty 'peece of ground' to the north of the Chancery, and it was there that the Dean and Chapter resolved 'to build certaine roomes' for the lodging of the choristers (12 October 1661).[18] It is not clear when the building was ready for Blundevile and the boys but they were there by April 1665 when 'Stoopes & Rayles [were] placed before 2 windows of the Quiristers house'.[19]

The vicars' houses, too, presented problems, and these were not resolved so easily. According to the Parliamentary Survey of 1650, the 'College of the Old and Young Vicarrs' consisted of 'XIII dwelling Howses built of fair wrought free Stone, two Stories high, built about a Yard or square Court on foure sides'.[20] A gate-house is described and nine houses – three of them 'much out of Repayire'. Although some former vicars or their widows remained in the houses at the time of the Survey, one house had 'all the Rooms and Cellars full of poore people'.[21]

The 'poore people' were evidently still there in October 1663 when the chapter warned 'all the Inmates inhabitinge within the Old Vicars' to be gone before 25 March 1664.[22] Presumably, the vicars had meanwhile to make shift as best they could. The chapter was not in a hurry to do anything for them, and eventually, in April 1664, they petitioned the chapter, imploring their benevolence 'towards the speedie re-edif-ieing of our habitations' in the hope that an act of generosity on the part of the residentiaries would set an example to others.[23] The response was a gift of £100. Others followed (including a further £50 from the chapter) until a total of £335.9s.11d had been received. Work began in July 1664 and weekly payments to workmen continued until July 1665 – though the final payments were not made until the end of 1667;[24] a debt of £66.3s.2d remained, which was paid off in 1679–80, drawing in part upon a legacy from Bishop Laney.[25]

None of the records indicate the scope of this work. In 1665–6 the Dean and Chapter were still paying four vicars an annual allowance of £2 towards rent: the implication is that no houses were available for them.[26] Most probably,

---

[18] Chapter Acts, 2 Oct. 1661; LAO DC A.3.9, f. 228.
[19] Fabric Accounts 1664–5; LAO DC Bj.1.8; *Survey of ancient houses* I, 1984, 47–50.
[20] 'The old Viccars houses in Lincolne Close', in *ASSR* 17, 1883, 247–50; *Survey of ancient houses* II, 1987, 40–64.
[21] Idem.
[22] Chapter Acts, 27 Oct. 1664; LAO DC A.3.9, f. 238.
[23] Dated 15 Apr. 1664; LAO DC Dvij.3.2.
[24] LAO DC Bij.1.10.
[25] Fabric Accounts 1679–80; LAO DC Bj.1.9.
[26] Draft Audit 1665–6; LAO DC Bj.3.11.

the rebuilding had concentrated upon the senior vicars' houses.[27] Some confirmation that the junior vicars remained unhoused is found in a chapter resolution of 9 August 1673 when it was agreed to rent the 'Upper part of the Buildings called the Graneryes' (i.e. the so-called Tithe Barn) from the senior vicars, 'to build for habitacions for the younge Viccars of the said Church'.[28] The Granary lay on the south side of the young vicars' yard. This still did not solve the problem (perhaps the work was never executed) and in 1695 the chapter acquired a property in Turnagain Lane – now Greestone Place – and converted it into two tenements for junior vicars.[29] Three vicars continued to be paid an annual £2 towards rent 'for want of houses to live in',[30] and the difficulty was not finally disposed of until the early years of the eighteenth century, when these payments disappear (but without explanation).

The years following 1660 saw the restoration of familiar routines in and around the cathedral; it is therefore not, perhaps, surprising that familiar problems should have reappeared too. Occasional citations for negligence and disorderliness enliven the pages of the Chapter Acts in the second half of the century.

John Jameson, junior vicar, appears with some frequency. In 1662, it was alleged that he had behaved 'very sauciely and unmannerly' towards the Precentor in the vestry, and when rebuked, had replied that 'hee would speake, for if hee should forbeare the very Stones would speake'.[31] The Dean and Chapter were not impressed and he was ordered to make his submission in the presence of the choir. Eight years later, in 1670, he caused grave offence by absconding with the key of the Revestry, 'soe that Mr Subdeane and the Vicars of that Quire could not gett their habitts to putt on'.[32] Jameson made matters no better by protesting that the purpose of his journey had been to take out a writ at Westminster 'to sue Mr Heyht [the Organist] for strickinge him in the Church'. Told that he should have applied to the Lincoln chapter for recompense, he retorted 'that hee thought hee should have noe justice to him by them'.[33] Again, he submitted. Nineteen years later he appeared in the uncharacteristic role of plaintiff. The dispute concerned John Cutts, junior vicar and Master of the Choristers. Jameson complained that, on All Saints' Day, as he was going into the choir to do his duty as Clerk of the Vestry, Cutts

---

[27] Chapter Acts, 7 June 1669; L A O D C A.3.9, f. 265.

[28] Ibid., 24 9 Aug. 1673.

[29] Ibid., 16 Nov. 1695; L A O D C A.3.11.

[30] Draft Audit 1698–9; L A O D C Bj.4.2.

[31] Chapter Acts, 18 Mar. 1662; A.3.9, f. 230.

[32] Ibid., 269, 22 March 1670.

[33] Ibid., 12 Nov. 1689; L A O D C A.3.11, f. 129.

came behind him the Complainant and struck him so violently on his head with a stick
or Cane (being without his hat) that with the violence of the said blow he not onely
broke the Complainants head but also shiver'd and broke his stick or Cane.

Jameson traced the source of Cutts' hostility to the previous day, when,

Mr Thomas Wanlesse being playing on the Organ, he [Jameson] went into the Quire to
hear him play where he found Mr Cutts and his Dog, and the Complainant telling him
the Quire was not a fit place for his Dog, he thereupon lift up his Arm with his Cane
and swore and said God dam me I will beat out your braines, And the Complainant
verily believeth that Mr Cutts had then struck him had he not been prevented by Mr
Henry Wanlesse who was then also present in the said Quire.

For once, Jameson was vindicated: Cutts was expelled from all his offices.

Apart from the misdemeanours of its individual members the vicars choral as
a body presented the chapter with disciplinary problems. Some of these may be
inferred from the set of 'Rules Concerning the Vicars Chorall' which the
chapter laid down in November 1672.[34] First, it was agreed that no vicar should
be punished when absent upon leave, or on account of sickness. On the other
hand,

Those who goe out of Towne and absent themselves from the Church Service without
leave to be upon their perill of arbitrary punishment by Suspension or otherwise as the
Deane and Chapter shall think fitt.

Some concessions were made to old vicars who had to do duty in their parishes,
and they were not to be punished for absences on Sundays, or holy day
mornings – 'provided that there be alwaies one of them at home to assist then
at the Service at the Altar, otherwise all fower to be punished vid a piece'. A
history of troublesome irregularities perhaps underlies a further regulation:

They who come not into their Seates before the end of the Confession to be punished as
tardy, a penny. And those that come not in before the end of the Venite at Morning
prayer or the beginning of the Psalmes at Evening prayer to be punished as absent, two
pence.[35]

In the following year (1673) the senior vicars were rebuked for neglecting
their duty of officiating at early Matins 'to the Scandall of the Church',[36] and it
was decreed that they be fined 5 shillings for every lapse. Three years later
(1676) the whole body of vicars choral was again in trouble with the chapter,

[34] Ibid., 20, 15 Nov. 1672.
[35] Idem.
[36] Chapter Acts, 16 Aug. 1673; LAO DC A.3.11, f. 24.

81

when it was ordered that if any leave the choir 'before the Blessing bee pronounced' a fine of one penny was to be exacted.[37]

At the same time, the chapter turned its attention to the discipline of the singing-boys. The result was a series of resolutions which offer glimpses of the boys' life in the late seventeenth century. The chapter took notice

of the irreverence and undecency frequently committed by the Choristers in carrying of the bookes from one side of the Quire unto the other in time of divine Service, [and] they did therefore order and decree, that for the future the choristers shall deliver the bookes unto such Vicars as they sit under, and they to handle them unto one another in their Seates.

But there was a difficulty: 'the intermixture of severall services in the same book' – which perhaps had made necessary the traffic across the choir, until all the singers had sight of a copy of the service. So the chapter decreed that Walter Powell and Hugh Walter, respectively Succentor and Sacrist, should examine the books and devise means of reducing them into some 'order and method'.

The chapter then turned to the education of the choristers (presumably the four senior boys), throwing some light on their schooling and daily timetable at this period:

And whereas the Choristers are very remiss and negligent in resorting to the Free School at the usuall times, they did therefore admonish them (being all present) to frequent the Chappell Prayers, and immediately after they were ended, to get their breakfasts, and then to goe forthwith down to the Free School and there to stay and continue untill nine a clock, and then to come upp to the Singing School, and there to abide untill the bells ring in to Prayers: And that in the afternoone they in like manner goe down to the Free School at one a clock, and continue there so long; as that they may bee at Evening Prayers, sub poenâ censurae in delinquentem infligendae. And because the Choristers may have noe reason of pleading an excuse for want of their breakfasts, the said Chapter did admonish Mr Blundevile the Steward of the Choristers, being present, to take care that their breakfasts bee prepared against they [sic] return from Chappell Prayers.[38]

It would appear from this that the choristers were educated at the Free School in Grey Friars. No doubt the long haul up the hill from there to the cathedral offered irresistible temptations to youthful loiterers.

How (and indeed whether) the Burghersh Chanters received their education from the chapter at this period is unclear. From 1670 until 1690 the Master of the Choristers, as well as training the boys to sing, taught them 'to write, cast

[37] Ibid., 46, 17 June 1676.
[38] Idem.

up Accompts, and to Prick Song',[39] for which he received an additional £5 a year. Then, in 1690, this duty devolved upon a writing master, who was henceforth to be appointed annually, 'if it may out of the Quire'.[40] It is possible that this instruction was intended for both choristers and Chanters.

Before 1690, the Master of the Choristers was appointed under seal and patent; thereafter, it became an annual appointment, made at the Holy Cross Audit in mid-September, and the holder came to be referred to as the 'Instructor of the Boys'. One of the residentiaries was technically 'Master of the Choristers' (usually for a term of two years) and had charge of the Choristers' Accounts, and of their welfare. Blundevile, probably the first Master after 1660, was also the Choristers' Steward, living with them in the Choristers' House, and being responsible for their board. He continued as Steward after retiring as Master (in 1667) and died in office (1692). After this, the Stewardship was always combined with the office of 'Instructor', until 1850.

Blundevile's successor as Master of the Choristers was William Turner – one of the most distinguished of Lincoln's musicians – who came to Lincoln at the age of 15 or 16 from the Chapel Royal. As a composer his output was considerable. He composed anthems for the coronation of James II, and his mature style was strongly influenced by the contemporary French school; the ten or so anthems attributed to his 'Lincoln' period are altogether more modest. Lincoln only managed to hold on to him for two years, and in 1669 Turner returned to the Chapel Royal, where he remained until his death in 1740.[41] His connections with Lincoln did not cease entirely: in 1670–1 the Audit records that he was paid £1 'for a new Anthem'. Turner was succeeded at Lincoln by John Reading (possibly of a Lincoln family) who had been admitted two years earlier as junior vicar and Poor Clerk.[42] He was a minor composer of church music, songs and theatre music. Reading left Lincoln early in 1675 to be Master of the Choristers at Chichester Cathedral, and died as Organist of Winchester College (1681).[43] Little is known of his successor, William Holder (1675–83). When Holder died, John Cutts (who had been a junior vicar since 1665) was appointed. The dispute with Jameson seems to have been only the culmination of a generally unsatisfactory record, and it was Cutts' unreliability which inspired the decision to make the mastership an annual office (1690).[44] William Norris was thereupon appointed to succeed Cutts, but Cutts was appointed to

---

[39] Chapter Acts, 7 June 1670; LAO DC A.3.11, f. 2.

[40] Ibid., 29 1 Apr. 1690.

[41] *NGD* XIX, 281.

[42] Chapter Acts, 10 Oct. and 25 Nov. 1667; LAO DC A.3.9, f. 260.

[43] *NGD* XV, 633.

[44] e.g. Chapter Acts, 31 Mar. 1687; LAO DC A.3.11, f. 117.

the newly created office of Master of Instrumental Musick,[45] only to be removed and then reinstated at least once before his death in 1692. Norris was another minor composer – presumably less troublesome than his predecessor for he has left virtually no mark upon the cathedral records – and when he died (in July 1702) he left behind him a harpsichord, standing in the 'School Room'.[46] On 21 November 1702 another John Reading (probably the son of his namesake) was admitted, first, as junior vicar, then as Poor Clerk, and finally as Instructor of the Choristers.[47] This Reading had been a chorister at the Chapel Royal under John Blow, leaving to become Organist of Dulwich College in 1699 when his voice broke. He was thus only about 17 when he ventured north to Lincoln. He seems to have returned to London towards the end of 1707, and was chosen Organist of St John's, Hackney, in January 1708; he continued to hold posts in London until his death in 1764. Reading was an able composer, but is particularly remembered as a collector and transcriber of music – many of his manuscripts survive as an important source for music of this period and earlier.[48]

The Lincoln organists in the second half of the seventeenth century seemed less inclined to move on than the Masters of the Choristers – perhaps because they were better paid (£40, as opposed to £10 a year). The exception was Thomas Mudd, who succeeded John Wanlesse as Organist upon the latter's death in September 1662. Mudd was incapable of holding any post for much more than a year, and his appointment at York, as Master of the Choristers in 1666, is said to have lasted no more than two weeks.[49] The reason is plain enough from the correspondence of John Featley, Precentor of Lincoln. Mudd arrived towards the end of 1662, the chapter paying 30 shillings towards his removal expenses from Peterborough (another disastrous appointment). By March 1663, Featley was writing from Lincoln to Dean Honywood in London, that

Mr Mudd hath beene so debauched these Assizes; and hath so abused Mr Darby [the organ builder] that hee will hardly be perswaded to stay to finish his worke, unlesse Mudd be removed. And I have stuck in the same mudd too; for hee hath abused mee above hope of pardon. I wish you would be pleased to send us downe an able, and more civill Organist.[50]

Two days later, the crisis had worsened. Featley writes:

[45] Ibid., 117 1 Apr. 1690.
[46] Frank Dawes, 'Philip Hart and William Norris', *Musical Times*, October 1969, pp. 1074–6.
[47] Chapter Acts, 21 Nov. 1702; LAO DC A.3.12, f. 8.
[48] *NGD* XV, 633–4.
[49] Ibid. XII, 758.
[50] Featley to Honywood, 14 Mar. 1663; LAO DC Dvij.1.(7).

Although I wrote to you on Saturday last; yet I must trouble you with another letter. Yesterday Mr Mudd shewed the effect of his last week's tipling: for when Mr Joynes was in the midst of his sermon, Mudd fell to singing aloud: insomuch as Mr Joynes was compelled to stopp; all the auditorie gazed, and wondered what was the matter: and at length some neere him stopping his mouth, silenced him; and then Mr Joynes proceeded: but this continued for the space of neerer halfe a quarter of an houre. So that nowe we dare trust him no more with oure Organ; but request you (if you can) to helpe us to another; and with what speede may be.[51]

Featley went on to suggest an approach to a Mr Hinton, who was Organist of Newark, and who was said to be 'a very sober, civill, and quiet person'.[52] Honywood, however, had other ideas, and a few days later, Featley wrote again, consenting 'to have the Dutch Organist sent to us'.[53] Mudd was sent on his way, with his salary paid up to 1 May 1663, and next appears (briefly) as Organist of Exeter Cathedral, in March 1664.

The 'Dutch Organist' was Andreas Hecht; Honywood may have encountered him during his exile abroad. Apart from his brush with Jameson, Hecht seems to have led an uneventful life in Lincoln, contributing some compositions to the music books, and dying in office in 1693. His son, Thomas, was appointed in his place, but declined the office, and the place was filled by Thomas Allanson.[54] The chapter paid Allanson's removal expenses from Durham, and instructed him to see that one of the choristers was taught to play the organ.[55] When Allanson died in 1705, the chapter paid his funeral expenses.[56] His successor was George Holmes, a minor composer and Organist to the bishop of Durham. His works included an anthem to celebrate the Union with Scotland (1707), and a setting of the Burial Sentences which was used at Lincoln into the present century.[57] He, too, died in office, in 1721.

Most of these musicians made some contribution to the Lincoln music books. A few part books survive from this period, and the earliest (a bass part book, which was begun not later than 1685)[58] includes anthems by John Cutts, 'Andrew Hect', William Turner, Thomas Allanson and George Holmes – as well as contemporary composers from outside Lincoln. There is an incomplete set begun in 1685/6[59] with a number of anthems by William Norris (18), others

---

[51] Featley to Honywood 16 Mar. 1663; LAO DC Dvji.1.(5) [actually (8)].
[52] Idem.
[53] Featley to Honywood, 21 Mar. 1663; LAO DC Dvij. 1. (5).
[54] Chapter Acts, 3 Apr. and 5 May 1693; LAO DC A. 3. 11, ff. 156–7.
[55] Draft Audit 1692–3; LAO DC Bj. 4. 1. Chapter Acts, 5 May 1693; LAO DC A. 3. 1, f. 157.
[56] Draft Audit 1704–5; LAO DC Bj/4/2.
[57] *NGD* VIII, 657.
[58] Cathedral Library, MS 313.
[59] MS 311; Music MSS 48 and 49.

by Blow (14) and Purcell (13) out of a total of around 180. These books have services at the rear, and at least one of them (Music MS 48) was entered up with new music as late as 1762. The dates of the entries can be established with some accuracy; from 1685, the Succentor was charged with the duty of making regular inspections of the books, and having done so, he was to sign and date the last entry (this arrangement was in part to monitor the activities of the junior vicar employed to write up the music books at 1*s*. 6*d*. a sheet).[60] Most of the music copied into these early books was by contemporary composers, but it is interesting to see a block of twenty-three anthems by earlier composers (Farrant, 'Bird', Giles, Tallis, Mundy, Weelkes, Gibbons, Bull) being copied into the books in 1710–11 – clearly, this repertoire was still in use at the time.

It remains to say something about the cathedral organ during the half-century succeeding the Restoration. Nothing is known for certain of the instrument which Stevenett was paid for blowing in 1660–1: it may have been borrowed, or perhaps it was an old organ, patched up to do temporary duty. Steps were taken to provide a new (or largely new) organ in 1662. On 16 December the chapter resolved

that M[r]. Deane should pay fouer score pound to M[r].
Edward Darby the Organmaker towards the finishinge
of the Organs . . . And M[r]. Darby is
to have noe more moneys of them untill hee
hath fully finished the Organs.[61]

Darby, an organ-maker from Newark, received a further payment of £20 in the later summer of 1663[62] and, in view of the resolution of the previous December, this may indicate that his work was complete. Supporting evidence arises from the fact that Thomas Troope of Nottingham shortly afterwards entered into an agreement with the Dean and Chapter 'to painte and guilde the fronts of both the Organs, and the lofte on which they stand within and without, for the summe of fiftie pounds'[63] – work which would most likely have been left until Darby's work was substantially complete. The chapter paid extra for 'flower deluses for ye Organs'[64] and Troope received his final payment on 21 October 1665.[65]

Even so, Darby was not finally paid off until March 1666 when he received

[60] Chapter Acts, 14 Apr. 1685; L A O D C A. 3. 11, f. 108.
[61] Chapter Acts, L A O D C A. 3. 9, f. 232. 16 Dec. 1662.
[62] Draft Audit 1662–3; L A O D C Bj. 3. 11.
[63] Chapter Acts, 26 Oct. 1663; L A O D C A. 3. 9, f. 238.
[64] Draft Audit 1663–4; L A O D C Bj. 3. 1.
[65] Fabric Accounts 1664–5; L A O D C Bj. 1. 8.

£10 'in full for all Claimes . . . the said Edward Darby compleating & finishing all things needfull & necessary to be done about the said organs'.[66] This might imply a lingering dissatisfaction with Darby's work, or simply underline the rather casual way in which seventeenth-century organ-makers seem to have approached the completion of a contract. At the same time an agreement was made that Darby would 'preserve and keep the said Organs in good order and tune . . . during the . . . terme of his life' for the sum of £6 a year.[67] He seems to have come to live in Lincoln at some stage, for his will describes him as 'now of the Baile of Lincoln Organist'[68] and he died there in September 1670. Probably he had been a recusant, for he bequeathed £5 'to poore Catholickes in Lincolnshere'.[69]

Little is known of the organ which Darby built. It is shown in Hollar's engraving of the choir of 1672, sited in a loft, on the north side of the choir, but the perspective is deceptive and makes the instrument appear much larger than the available space would have permitted. There was a shallow case for the Great Organ, placed in front of the arch, and then behind the player's back, a Chair Organ projecting over the choir pavement. In all, the accounts record payments to Darby totalling £116.10s.6d. There must have been at least one other payment (upon signing the contract) which is not recorded. This would have paid for a new organ – perhaps reusing an existing case or cases.

The Fabric Accounts record various payments for mending the organs in the early 1670s, mostly made to John Cutts. Then, in June 1677, there is a payment of £20 'for Mr Smyth the Organ Maker'. Between then and January 1678 there are two further payments to Mr Smyth, making a total of £110, and the organ-maker is identified as 'Mr Bernard Smyth'.[70] Smith, an organ-builder possibly of German origin, had come to England c.1667; he was later to be known as 'Father' Smith, and it is interesting to find this man, who had worked in Holland for ten years, being employed at an English cathedral with a Dutch organist. The extent of his work is unrecorded. Darby's organ may well have been old-fashioned in conception and crude in execution, and perhaps provincial Lincoln looked to the King's organ-maker and his London workshop to provide something better.

The accounts record various payments for repairing the organs in the course of the next twenty-five years.[71] 'Mr Smith' was paid £35 for mending the organs

[66] Chapter Acts, 15 Mar. 1666; L A O D C A. 3. 9, f. 251.
[67] Idem.
[68] L A O: L C C Wills, 1670, II, 583.
[69] Idem.
[70] Fabric Accounts 1676–7, 1677–8; L A O, D C Bj. 1. 9.
[71] Idem.

in January 1690, and a Mr Smith appears again in 1698–9. Neither entry may refer to Bernard Smith, for in August of 1702, the Dean and Chapter made an agreement with Gerard Smith (nephew of Bernard) to repair and move the organs.[72] The Fabric Accounts record total payments to him in 1703–4 of £200. Nothing is known of Gerard Smith's work except that it presumably involved moving the organ from its loft on the north side of the choir, and rebuilding it on the screen (it cannot have been moved there in the 1670s because in 1680 it was agreed that a seat be set up on the screen, over the entrance to the choir).[73] Smith was paid a further £50 in 1706 (was this for repair or completion of the original contract?),[74] and £30 for 'the Reparation of the Organs in the Cathedral' in March 1722.[75] With this, the Smith family disappears from the records of Lincoln cathedral.

When one turns to contemplate the history of Lincoln's music in the period between 1721 (the death of Holmes) and 1850 (the appointment of J. M. W. Young) it is soon apparent that there are no figures of the calibre of a William Turner or a John Reading. Virtually no compositions by Lincoln musicians are to be found in the eighty or so manuscript part books surviving from this period, and the men who held the posts of Instructor of the Boys, and Organist, were (at best) unremarkable figures of modest ability. Culminating in the 51-year partnership of Whall and Skelton, this is not a distinguished era in Lincoln's musical history.

Many of these musicians were local men: George Skelton (Organist, 1794–1850) was the son of a Lincoln blacksmith, and first became part of the cathedral foundation when he was admitted as a Burghersh Chanter in 1782.[76] Among his immediate predecessors, William Middlebrook (Organist, 1741–56) and Lloyd Raynor (1756–84) had both been choristers at Lincoln, though each had briefly held a post elsewhere before returning to Lincoln – Middlebrook at Launceston, and Raynor at Newark. Raynor proved less than satisfactory. He amused himself by attempting to throw the soloists off their stride in the anthems. Brought before the chapter following one such incident in 1771 when a Mr Binns, one of the vicars choral, found himself singing one anthem, whilst Raynor 'play'd the Organ in the Tune of a different Anthem whereby the Singer was interrupted and the Choir put into Confusion',[77] he was rebuked; some years later (1784) he abused and threatened the Dean 'in the grossest manner',

---

[72] Chapter Acts, 27 Aug. 1702; L A O D C A. 3. 12, f. 5.

[73] Ibid., 12 June 1680; L A O D C A. 3. 11, f. 68.

[74] Fabric Accounts 1705–6; L A O D C Bj. 1. 10.

[75] Choristers' Accounts, 7 Mar. 1722; L A O D C Bij. 1. 6.

[76] Chapter Acts, 29 Apr. 1782; L A O D C A. 3. 15, f. 252.

[77] Ibid., 103–4, 10 Sept. 1771;

and his services were dispensed with.[78] Of the other two Organists of this period, one, Charles Murgetroyd (1721–41), had been previously Organist of York Minster; at Lincoln he survived suspension, rebukes for negligence, and debt, to die in office in 1741.[79] Nothing at all is known of John Hasted except the date of his appointment (1784)[80] and the date of his formal dismissal, some time after he was discovered to have 'withdrawn himself from the place' (1794).[81] None of this argues for particularly lofty musical standards.

The Instructors of the Boys were less prickly customers. Benjamin Whall, who served for fifty-one years (1799–1850), was probably a native of Norwich, and had been a pupil of Beckwith, the Organist of the Cathedral there. His three immediate predecessors were former Lincoln choristers: Thomas Weely (1707–30), Stephen Harrison (1731–56) and John Cowper (1757–99). All were junior vicars, all had sons who sang in the choir, and all (with the exception of Whall) died in office.

There were normally nine vicars choral. Of the five junior vicars, one would be the Instructor of the Boys, and another might be the Organist. The addition of a sixth junior vicar in 1803[82] and the engagement of four supernumeraries in 1838[83] reflects one of the problems arising from the vicars' freehold: in the days before pensions were provided, the vicars could not afford to retire when their voices failed. A high proportion of the vicars choral died in office – a number of them at an advanced age after holding office for more than fifty years – and if the tenures of a number of long-serving vicars coincided, the chapter was faced with the unenviable choice of allowing musical standards to slip (yet further, in Lincoln's case) or of appointing deputies at extra cost to themselves.

A further problem arose from the nature of the vicars' appointment. Patronage was a valuable commodity in the eighteenth-century Church, and it must not be assumed that the senior vicars, at least, were appointed for their musical abilities. The opportunity to 'reward' clients was fiercely contested, and it is no doubt significant that, in 1807, the residentiaries resolved that they would take it in turns to nominate senior vicars.[84] However, the income of a senior vicar was unpredictable, dependent, in any one year, upon fines and renewals of leases belonging to the Vicars' Estate; income from the Estate, together with the cathedral salary and various fees, might amount to £88 a year, or as little as £33. So a senior vicar must needs be a pluralist, and the Dean and Chapter

---

[78] Ibid., 274, 17 Sept. 1784.

[79] Ibid., 24 Mar. 1733, 16 Sept. 1734, 26 Oct. 1741; LAO DC A. 3. 13, f. 257, 272 and 343.

[80] Ibid., 29 Oct. 1784; LAO DC A. 3. 15, f. 277.

[81] Ibid., 15 Sept. 1794; LAO DC A. 3. 16, f. 20.

[82] Ibid., 19 Sept. 1803; LAO DC A. 3. 16, f. 183.

[83] Ibid., 17 Sept. 1838; LAO DC A. 3. 17, f. 344.

[84] Ibid., 21 Sept. 1807; LAO DC A. 3. 16, f. 225.

earmarked certain benefices in their gift as a means of augmenting the vicars' stipends. The account book of Thomas Sympson (senior vicar, 1749–86) has survived, and it reveals that in the late 1750s he had an income of around £300 a year from various sources – including no fewer than seven livings, and three sinecures.[85] Sympson employed curates, and paid deputies to preach for him, but it was in his financial interest to undertake as many of the duties as he could himself, and it seems unlikely that his musical responsibilities at the cathedral came very high in his list of priorities. Absences must have been frequent, especially on Sundays.

As for the junior vicars, they seem to have been largely local men at this period. The old distinction between junior vicar and Poor Clerk had become largely meaningless by *c.*1700, though at that date it was not unusual for the admission as Poor Clerk to take place a week or two later (oddly enough) than admission as a vicar; by the second quarter of the century, the man was invariably admitted to both offices at the same time, being presented by a residentiary, approved by the choir (a formality), and then reciting the Articles, making his declaration, and taking the oaths. Soon after this any distinction between the office of vicar and that of Poor Clerk ceases to be drawn; the only particular duty of the Clerks (the singing of the Litany)[86] comes to be spoken of as the responsibility of the junior vicars – Byng, in 1791, recorded hearing the Litany chanted at Lincoln 'by two lay-vicars with voices like bulls'.[87] With dogged consistency, the Audit continued to record separate annual payments to vicars and to Poor Clerks well into the 1850s.

The vicars and Poor Clerks were expected to sing at divine service twice daily; in the 1730s the hours were 10 a.m. and 4 p.m.[88] Individuals were, from time to time, reproved or even suspended by the chapter for misdemeanours (Isaac Spray, in 1787, for associating with 'Soldiers and idle disorderly persons', and James Wood, in 1799, for intoxication)[89] and we may guess that it is owing to the laxity of the times rather than the diligence of the vicars that the rebukes are not more frequent. An instruction that the Vestry Clerk should record absences (1799)[90] seems to have made little impact, and a correspondent in the *Gentleman's Magazine* (1836) reported finding only three singing-men in the choir on a Sunday (two of whom were present for only part of the service) and none on a weekday.[91]

[85] LAO DC CIV/95/10.

[86] Chapter Acts, 30 Aug. 1678; LAO DC A. 3. 11, f. 59.

[87] C. B. Andrews, ed., *The Torrington diaries* II London 1934–8, 345–6.

[88] Chapter Acts, 26 June 1731; LAO DC A. 3. 13, f. 223.

[89] Ibid., 1 Jan. 1787, and 16 Sept. 1799; LAO DC A. 3. 15, f. 303, and A. 3. 16, f. 134.

[90] Ibid., 16 Sept. 1799; LAO DC A. 3. 16, f. 134.

[91] *Gentleman's Magazine* NS 6, 1836, 562.

Like that of their senior colleagues, the junior vicars' income was irregular and, as the years went by, increasingly inadequate. Their assured income varied hardly at all between 1660 and 1830. A substantial part of it was the annual payment of £2 from each of the thirty-eight prebendaries – though, at least in the earlier part of the period, this was not always easy to extract, and the Provost of the Vicars had to endure letters calling him 'an impertinent Huffe, a knave, a foole, and an ill bred Clowne' when he solicited one prebendary for his arrears (1681).[92] Wages totalling £30.15s.0d., feedings worth £4.4.s.0d., and various pensions amounting to around £30 came from the Dean and Chapter, and the Vicars' Estate brought in outrents varying between £10 (in 1679) and £20 (by 1818). This yielded a sum rather in excess of £150 to be divided between nine vicars. Uncertain income arose chiefly from fines on renewals or sealing of leases, and small fees (a matter of shillings) for installations of prebendaries and residentiaries. Each vicar could hardly expect to receive more than £30 a year from these sources, and it might well be substantially less. A junior vicar would receive his share of the Poor Clerks' annual £24.14s.8d., and might secure a minor office or menial job around the cathedral (washing surplices, collecting rents, writing in the music books) but his total income might still be no more than £30 in a poor year.

Yet the life of a vicar choral must have had its congenial aspects, and there was ample scope for musical activities, within and without Vicars' Court. The possible extent of this is indicated by an inventory of the goods of Thomas Heardson, junior vicar, who died in 1685. These included one new and one old 'harpsicall', two spincts, thirty bows, eight violins, four 'base violls', and forty 'musick books unpricked'.[93] A few years later (1690) the chapter sought to stimulate the boys' interest in 'Instrumental Musick' (having just provided them with an Instructor in it) by instituting 'two publick consorts . . . one in every Easter week the other in the Audit week'[94] – but it may be that nothing came of this. Quarter of a century later, the music-making in Vicars' Court was dignified as the vicars' 'Musick Club', and the accounts record various payments towards it;[95] then, in 1726, Mr Drake was paid 'the sum of fifteen pounds fifteen Shillings for a Harpsicord for the Use of the Choire & Twelve Shillings for a Case'.[96] The chapter encouraged a different sort of musical celebration each year on St Cecilia's Day, when the choir was given 2 (later, 4) guineas for

---

[92] LAO DC Ciij. 45. 7.

[93] LAO DC Di. 40. 3. 47; I am most grateful to Mrs Joan Varley for drawing my attention to this document and for sending me a transcription of it, and also for other advice, particularly concerning Vicars' Court and the Choristers' House.

[94] Chapter Acts, 1 Apr. 1690; LAO DC A. 3. 11, f. 130.

[95] Choristers' Accounts, 2 May 1717; LAO DC Bij. 1. 6.

[96] Ibid., 2 Dec. 1726.

a feast – a custom not abolished until 1853[97] – and the choristers were allowed 5 shillings 'for bonefires'[98] to celebrate November 5th, the King's Birthday, Restoration Day, and other public festivals.

There continued to be (usually) four choristers and six Burghersh Chanters, some of the latter being no more than 6 years old upon admission. The distinctive gown made of black cloth, with 'white base' (i.e. baize) facings, 'Silk and Loops'[99] was worn by the choristers, whilst the Chanters wore surplices but no cassocks. In the mid-eighteenth century, the six Burghersh Chanters each received a half-yearly salary of 16s.8d.; the choristers only received 16s.3d., but a total of £40.8s.0d. was paid to the Steward of the Choristers for their board, and upon leaving the choir they were given £5 towards an apprenticeship.

In 1761, with not altogether typical reforming zeal, the chapter laid down new regulations for the education and government of the boys. They were, first, to be instructed in music 'as a liberal art or science by Rule & not by Ear only', and, to this end, the Instructor was to teach them himself and not entrust the junior boys to the senior. Then, only those Burghersh Chanters who 'have profited most by their former instruction' were to be promoted to the ranks of the choristers, and the Instructor was to ensure that there were boys trained to take over the solos when the older boys' voices 'go off'. Time was to be set aside each day for the boys to practise writing and accounts, and for those attending 'the Hospital School' or the grammar school to do so. The chapter was also concerned that the boys should grow up with a proper self-respect:

Whereas there is an Allowance of 10£ pr. Annum for the board of each Chorister (which is the same that is given by Gentlemen with their Sons at the Grammar School) besides a Sufficient Stipend for the Instruction in Musick, it is ordered, that they shall not be look'd upon & treated as Menial Servants but may wait upon their Master at Dinner by Rotation (as Sizars in the University do at the Fellows Table) provided such Attendance do not interfere with their busines in other places.[100]

It is not known whose reforming hand was behind these exemplary regulations: it is the only evidence from the eighteenth century that the chapter ever seriously considered the education of the boys. If the Acts are to be believed, a state of indifference prevailed for most of that century, and, indeed, well into the succeeding one. The true state of affairs is perhaps better represented in an anecdote from 1816. A musical gentleman and his family attended Evensong one weekday afternoon:

[97] Chapter Acts, 19 Sept. 1853; L A O D C A. 3. 17, f. 544.
[98] Draft Audit; various examples, e.g. L A O D C in Bj. 4. 6 (1727–33).
[99] Various examples in L A O D C Bij. 1. 6 (1710–29).
[100] Chapter Acts, 10 Oct. 1761; L A O D C A. 3. 14, ff. 146–7.

... the musical part was so extremely bad that they were shocked or disgusted. On walking down the nave to leave the church they were followed by the choristers, who came up to the gentleman, begging; saying, 'Please, sir, remember the boys': to which he replied, 'that I will; I never can forget you.'[101]

The modest ideals set out fifty-five years before had evidently been lost.

The impression of decline is created also by a consideration of the repertoire between 1721 and 1851. Services or anthems by Croft, Greene, Nares, or Stanley are copied into the part books in the earlier years, together with works by less distinguished figures of the period – King, and Kent, for example. As time passes, the repertoire comes to be influenced by compositions available in published collections. The chapter would subscribe towards a publication, taking one or two volumes, and the musicians would then choose anthems and services to be copied into the part books. Many of these published volumes survive in the Music Library, and the accounts record their purchase: Boyce's *Church Musick* (1760, 1781), Alcock's *Book of Anthems* (1768), Dr Nares' *Anthems* (1779), Dr Hayes' *Musick Books* (1796), Dr Clarke's *Cathedral Music* (1820), Latrobe's *Sacred Music* (1825), Wesley's *Cathedral Service* (1826), and Handel's *Oratorios* (1841). The music of these collections is heavily represented in two surveys of the Lincoln repertoire of the 1820s.[102] There are no longer any anthems by Byrd, and of the 136 pieces listed, nearly 100 postdate 1760. Best represented was Kent (15), followed by Handel (11), and then Jackson (9), Greene, (9) and Nares (8). Few of the sixteenth- and seventeenth-century composers are represented at all.

After 1721, little appears to have happened to the organ for the remainder of the eighteenth century. Anthony Parsons of Sheffield made an agreement to repair it in January 1729.[103] Mr Swarbrick (known elsewhere as 'Schwarbrook', and probably a German by birth) was paid the substantial sum of £40 for repairs in December 1735, and there were further payments to him in 1737 (£10) and 1743 (£20).[104] Regular maintenance and minor repairs were then undertaken, first by a Mr Brownless, and then, for a few years, by Middlebrook, the Organist. In 1757–8 James Broxscll was paid a total of £61 for repairing, cleaning, and 'new Works', after which the organ passed into the care of first William, and then James Casterton – local organ-builders, who received a regular payment of 6 or 8 guineas a year until 1811 for looking after the organ.

---

[101] *The Guardian*, 20 Sept. 1848 (no. 140), 602.

[102] *A collection of anthems used in the cathedral church of Lincoln*, Lincoln 1827; *The Quarterly Musical Magazine and Review* 6, 1824, 312–13.

[103] Chapter Acts, 22 Jan. 1729; L A O D C A. 3. 13, f. 201.

[104] Fabric Accounts, L A O D C Bj. 1. 13.

In 1767 the replacement of the organ (or an extensive reconstruction) was mooted, and it is from these discussions that we have the earliest surviving specification of the organ.[105] How far it had been altered since Smith's major work in 1702–4 is not clear, but possibly very little.

The Great Organ

2 Open Diapasons
A Stoped Diapason ♯ Bass
A Principal
A Twelfth
A Fifteenth
A Tierce ♯ Bass
A Sesquialtra ♯ Bass
A Cornet
A Trumpet ⎫
A Clarrion Bass ⎭ very bad

Choir Organ

A Stoped Diapason
A Principal
A Principal ♯ Bass
A Fifteenth
A Bassoon Bass, useless

Eccho

An Open Diapason
A Stoped Diapason
A Flute
A Trumpet, very bad
A Clarrion

The pipes must be new Voice'd, & them that have lost their tone
be Restor'd to it again, the keys and Movements must be all new,

It will be better to make new Sound Boards & add C♯ & D which is
very much Wanted, then the Organ need not be taken down till all
the new work is made

This was a singularly archaic scheme by the 1760s, and it is plain that the Organist (if it was he who copied out the specification) felt its shortcomings. Thomas Parker, a London organ-builder, offered to rebuild the organ for £400, or build a new one for £700, but nothing came of it.

[105] LAO DC A. 4. 14 (f).

Action was postponed for a further fifty years, until in 1823 the Dean and Chapter, acting upon the advice of Charles Wesley (elder brother of Samuel Wesley, the composer) commissioned William Allen of Sutton Street, Soho Square, London, to build a new organ at a cost of £1160. The Lincoln architect, E. J. Willson (1787–1854), a Catholic, an antiquary, and a friend of the Pugins, designed a new case in the Gothic style; it was, and remains, one of the most satisfying compositions of its style and period, and cost the enormous sum of £1392.14s.3d. – of which £662 was spent on employing carvers from London.[106] Work began in the cathedral in 1825, and the organ was complete the following year. Allen's final estimate (1822?)[107] gives the specification; only very minor modifications seem to have been made in the completed organ.

Estimate for a New Organ to be Built for
Lincoln Cathedral By Wm Allen Organ Builder
Sutton St Soho Square London

Exclusive of the Case, With the Two fronts to
be Gilt & Seperate Peddal pipes to a Octave
Below Double CC to Contain a full Organ Choir
Organ & Swelling D° With the following Stops
to Double G Long Octaves & up to F in Alt

Full Organ

Two Open Diapasons
Stop Diapason
Principal
Twelfth
Flute
Fifteenth
Sesquialtra 3 Ranks
Trumpet

Choir Organ

Stop Diapason
Dulciana
Principal
Flute
Fifteenth
Cremona Treble

---

[106] Ibid. (t).
[107] Ibid., (p).

Swelling Organ from F below Middle C & up to F in alt viz

Stop Diapason
Open Diapason
Principal
Flute
Twelfth
Fifteenth
Trumpet
Hautboy

The Whole of the above to be of the very Best Materials &
Workmanship fix'd up in the Cathedral in Tune With Every Expence
Packing Carridge &c for the Sum of Eleven Hundred & Sixty Pound

       Wm *Allen*

Twenty-five years later, Allen's organ was described as 'an inferior instrument'[108] but, in a modified form, it survived until the end of the century. William Allen's son, Charles, made an agreement with the Dean and Chapter in 1845 to tune the organ twice a year at a cost of £22;[109] five years later, he substituted a Viol de Gamba for the Choir Cremona.[110] In 1851 Allen undertook major work at a cost of £700.[111] No contract has survived, but the chief alterations seem to have been a downward extension of the Swell compass (to G), the addition of five composition pedals, the introduction of a 32-note pedal board, and the provision of Pedal stops.[112] The result of the last two alterations was a strange compromise between an independent Pedal of the German type, and the simple bass (designed to connect with the Great Organ) which the English had yet to reject. The Pedal specification was as follows:

Sub-Bourdon	32	32 notes
Open Diapason	16	32 notes
Principal	8	7 notes
Twelfth	$5\frac{1}{3}$	7 notes
Fifteenth	4	7 notes
Sesquialtera		7 notes
Trombone	16	7 notes

The addition of these extra pipes provided the occasion for 'the enlargement

---

[108] Sperling Note Books, Royal College of Organists' Library II, f. 177.
[109] Chapter Acts, 15 Sept. 1845; LAO DC A. 3. 17, f. 432.
[110] Vouchers, 8 Nov. 1850; LAO DC CIV. 60.
[111] Vouchers, n.d.; LAO DC CIV. 60.
[112] Rimbault and Hopkins, *Organ*, 531.

and embellishment of the Organ case', and this was done under Willson's own superintendence. Despite claims that the architect would not hear of any alteration to his case,[113] a document survives in which Willson confessed that he thought the case 'much improved by the additions lately made'.[114] Allen's last significant work on the organ seems to have been in 1859, when he altered both the cathedral and the school room organs to the newly fashionable Equal Temperament.[115]

No evidence survives (and perhaps there never was any) to contradict the view that the nadir of Lincoln's musical fortunes was reached in the first half of the nineteenth century. There are continual complaints about the irreverence of the choir, the absences of the vicars choral, and the abysmal standard of the musical performances. As early as 1816, discerning visitors to the cathedral found themselves 'shocked or disgusted' by the music, and twenty years later a correspondent in the *Gentleman's Magazine* asked why the music at Lincoln was 'so decidedly inferior to that of any other choir in the kingdom'.[116] John Jebb, writing in 1843, told how he long imagined 'that the acme of irreverent and careless chanting was to be found at Lincoln' (he eventually discovered that Gloucester was even worse) and spoke of the 'coarseness and want of feeling' with which the Litany was often performed by the junior vicars.[117] An illuminating description of a choral service at Lincoln, towards the end of Skelton and Whall's 51-year partnership, is to be found in the *Guardian* (1848):[118]

To say that the boys could not sing, and the organ could not play, and the boys and the organ could not go together, would only half describe it. It was sluggishness and torpor personified. It crawled like a wretched lame insect from beginning to end. Its excessive feebleness was such that it seemed every moment on the point of stopping from want of breath . . . At no point in the service did the organ rise to the substance or dignity of a street barrel. The organist – if he was one – was afraid of touching a bass note, and one man playing on a bad flute would have produced an equal or very similar effect to that of his playing. The voices of the choir were in keeping. I dare say there were good voices among them, but it did not seem to be expected that they should exert themselves in the slightest degree. I must confess that throughout the service I could not help feeling sincere and unfeigned astonishment at the exhibition which was going on, and asking myself repeatedly – What are these people doing? Is this Cathedral service, or is it something else?

At the time this correspondent put pen to paper, Skelton and Whall were both

---

[113] Andrew Freeman, 'The organs of Lincoln cathedral', *The Organ* 2, 1928, 195.
[114] Vouchers, 13 Sept. 1851; LAO DC CIV. 60.
[115] Vouchers, 15 July 1859; LAO DC CIV. 69 [sic].
[116] *The Guardian*, 20 Sept. 1848 (no. 140), 602.
[117] John Jebb, *The choral service*, 1843, 436.
[118] *The Guardian*, 23 Aug. 1848 (no. 136), 547.

in their seventies. Everything suggests that the music had been consistently bad during their long tenure, yet one might feel a sneaking sympathy for them as survivors from an age in which church musicians were held in low regard, and when many of the clergy cared little about maintaining decency and order in public worship. As the *Guardian*'s correspondent put it, 'no service half so bad . . . could possibly take place under the eye of any Chapter that did its duty'.[119]

Reform, clearly, was urgent. Finally, in September 1850, the chapter made it possible for Skelton and Whall to retire. Skelton was to receive a pension of £80 a year, and promptly went off to Hull to live with his son, another organist. Whall stepped down as Instructor of the Boys, but was allowed to remain Steward of the Choristers (and hence to live in the Choristers' House) during the Dean and Chapter's pleasure, and to retain his income as a lay vicar. He died in 1855. In their place, as both Organist and Instructor of the Boys, the chapter appointed John Matthew Wilson Young; he was to receive an initial salary of £100 a year, plus the stipend of a lay vicar, and upon Whall's death or final retirement he was to succeed him as Steward of the Choristers, and live at 10 Minster Yard.[120]

Young's comparative youth (he was twenty-eight) may have commended him to the chapter. Equally significant, though, was the fact that he had been articled pupil to William Henshaw, Organist of Durham Cathedral (Young was a native of that city), widely known as a strict disciplinarian and an excellent choir trainer. In 1844, Young went to York as Professor of Music at the Training College for Schoolmasters, and in the following years, took advantage of the proximity of Leeds to assist Dr S. S. Wesley at the parish church there. His credentials were thus impeccable, and the Lincoln chapter must have hoped for great things from him. They were not to be disappointed. He remained at Lincoln for forty-five years, establishing for himself a reputation as an organ accompanist and a gifted trainer of boys' voices, and for his choir, a reputation as one of the best in an English cathedral. Especially noteworthy was his accompaniment of psalms, the principles of which he described in his *Fifty-five Single and Double Chants as Sung in Lincoln Cathedral* (1887) dedicated to Dean Butler. The chants were his own, each written with a specific psalm in mind, and, in many, the voice parts were rearranged and the accompaniments varied to suit the meaning of different verses (the imitation of a harp in verse two of Psalm 137 is a characteristic device). Young claimed that his own care was a reaction against hearing (*c*. 1840) the seventy-three verses of Psalm seventy-eight sung to a single chant, accompanied throughout on the same two

---

[119] Ibid.
[120] Chapter Acts, 17 Sept. 1851; L A O D C A. 3. 17, f. 502.
[121] J. M. W. Young, *Fifty-five single and double chants*, Preface.

stops of the Choir Organ.[121] In general, Young was an able and willing collaborator in all that the clergy sought to do to raise the standard of the cathedral services.

But the appointment of a reliable and capable Organist was not the only matter with which the Dean and Chapter needed to concern themselves if the music was to be rescued from the doldrums. Two other matters particularly demanded attention, and in neither did the chapter act decisively or effectively for many years. There was, first, the reform of the vicars choral, and, secondly, the education of the boys.

In financial terms, the problems of the junior vicars (increasingly known as 'lay vicars') and the senior vicars ('minor canons') diverged as the century progressed. For many years, the junior vicars petitioned the chapter for an increase in their salaries, which they described as 'very small and inadequate to their maintenance and support'.[122] In 1832, the chapter took a modest step towards securing a regular income for each junior vicar by agreeing to stipends of £42 a year, and £60 for the vicar acting as Vestry Clerk.[123] These salaries would still be augmented by income from out-rents and fines, but presumably some sources of income (fees at the installation of prebendaries, income from prebends) disappeared during the reforms of the 1830s. A further increase in 1838 resulted in all junior vicars enjoying a salary of £60,[124] and, thereafter, salaries rose slowly until they reached £115–135 a year in 1923.[125] At some date between 1854 and 1881 the junior vicars commuted their interest in the Vicars' Estate,[126] and it seems that a pension scheme was established late in the century.

The senior vicars were especially badly hit by the ecclesiastical reforms of the 1830s. A survey of their incomes in 1826 reveals that four senior vicars held ten benefices and one curacy between them, yielding (once curates had been paid) an annual income each of between £207 and £372.[127] Of the gross income, less than one-tenth in one case arose from cathedral duties. Thus, the Pluralities Act of 1838, with its provision that no clergyman should hold more than two benefices at the same time, was of considerable concern to the senior vicars, for it meant that they could hold only one benefice apiece in addition to being a senior vicar. Replying to the Cathedral Commissioners (*c.* 1852), Richard Garvey, the senior minor canon, reported that the average income of each minor canon over the previous seven years (including payments from the chapter, and fines and out-rents from the Vicars' Estate) was no more than

---

[122] LAO DC Cii. 78. 2.
[123] Chapter Acts, 10 Nov. 1832; LAO DC A. 3. 17, f. 266.
[124] Chapter Acts, p. 344, 17 Sept. 1838.
[125] Ibid., 21 Mar. 1923; LAO DC CC. 2. 1. 6, f. 153.
[126] Chapter Acts, 31 Dec. 1881; LAO DC CC. 2. 1. 2, ff. 111–12.
[127] LAO VC 3. 1. 2. 4.

£42.1s.3½d., and that each minor canon was personally responsible for the upkeep of his house in Vicars' Court. Garvey made a further point. He would respectfully add, he wrote,

that he has faithfully served the cathedral thirty-two years, that he is nearly sixty-nine years of age, much enfeebled by a chronic cough, and no longer able to do the cathedral duty as he has done it. He would therefore beg the consideration of the Commissioners for such men who are to be found in most cathedrals, and would hope something may be done for the decent superannuation of worn-out servants of such establishments.[128]

The problem of minor canons' stipends did not become pressing until the 1860s, when three long-serving, pre-reform canons retired. The chapter then (somewhat grudgingly, one feels) agreed to make up the salary of any minor canon not holding a benefice to £100 (1865),[129] and, five years later, to £200.[130] Superannuation had to wait longer. In 1881 the Dean and Chapter applied to the Ecclesiastical Commissioners for funds to establish a superannuation scheme for both lay clerks and minor canons,[131] and the Supplementary Statutes proposed by the Cathedral Commissioners of 1885 provided for the retirement of minor canons at the age of fifty-five, with provision for a pension.[132] Finally, in 1903, responding to pressure from the chapter, the minor canons surrendered their Estate (apart from the houses in Vicars' Court) to the Ecclesiastical Commissioners in return for an annual payment of £1140. The chapter's annual payments were, at the same time, commuted to £60, and hence each minor canon secured an income of £300 a year.[133] In the following year, a pension fund was set up.

At the end of the Victorian era the vicars choral, as a body, were better disciplined, better provided for, and more musically efficient than had been the case at the beginning of the reign. From 1854, candidates for minor canonries had to submit to a competition, and their appointment reverted to the chapter as a whole.[134] Advertisements were placed in the newspapers when a lay vicar or supernumerary was required (unsuccessful candidates were reimbursed with 'the Second class Railway-fare')[135] and singers were increasingly recruited from

---

[128] *First Report of HM Commissioners appointed to inquire into the state and condition of the cathedral and collegiate churches in England and Wales*, 1854, 672–3.

[129] Chapter Acts, 6 May 1865; LAO DC CC. 2. 1. 1, f. 186.

[130] Chapter Acts, 15 July 1870; LAO DC CC. 2. 1. 1, f. 304.

[131] Chapter Acts, 31 Dec. 1881; LAO DC CC. 2. 1. 2, ff. 111–12.

[132] *Report of HM Commissioners for inquiring into the condition of cathedral churches in England and Wales upon the cathedral church of Lincoln*, 1885, 10.

[133] Chapter Acts, 13 June 1903; LAO DC CC. 2. 1. 4.

[134] Chapter Acts, 18 Sept. 1854; LAO DC CC. 2. 1. 1, f. 13.

[135] Chapter Acts, 15 Dec. 1870; LAO DC CC. 2. 1. 1, f. 316.

outside Lincoln. From 1891, lay vicars were required to give an undertaking not to apply for a post elsewhere until two years had elapsed.[136] There could still be problems; in the early 1870s two lay vicars were effectively pensioned off, one, on account of 'partial deafness' and another, because of 'a tendency to epileptic fits,'[137] and in 1873, the chapter had to instruct a Mr Plant 'to sing only in the Choruses and louder parts till the June Audit, when his case shall be reconsidered',[138] but the disappearance of the lay vicars' freehold, and the provision of adequate superannuation eventually made it easier to dispose of unsuitable singers. Other matters improved, too. In 1874, the lay vicars and supernumeraries were reminded of their duty to frame their lives 'by the rules of the Christian Religion' and were warned that 'any grave moral offence' would result in instant dismissal[139] – the tone is somewhat at odds with the laxity of the previous two centuries.

Education being the shibboleth which it was to the Victorians, it would have been strange had Victorian deans and canons not turned their attention to the educational provision for the choirboys. Once again, financial difficulties prevented them from doing as much as they might have wished until virtually the end of the century.

Miss Maria Hackett, a philanthropic lady who devoted a long life to obliging deans and chapters to fulfil their statutory obligations to choristers, describes the Lincoln boys' education as she found it in the 1820s:

All the boys, as well Choristers as Burgherst [sic] Chanters, attend daily choral service at ten and three on week-days, and at ten and four on Sundays. The Dean and Chapter provide for their instruction in Writing, arithmetic, and grammar; and those boys whose parents wish it, are allowed to attend the Free Grammar School . . . They attend these Schools from 11 o'clock to twelve, from two to three, and from four to five. They attend the Music Master from seven o'clock in the morning in summer, and eight in the winter, until prayer time.[140]

Surprisingly, Miss Hackett found Lincoln something of a model among cathedrals in her day, though thirty years later, these arrangements were deemed totally inadequate.

The Dean and Chapter made some half-hearted attempts to establish their own school for the boys during the 1840s; 'the room anciently called the Common Chamber now used as a Plumber's shop'[141] was to become their

---

[136] Chapter Acts, 28 Feb. 1891; LAO DC CC. 2. 1. 2, f. 385.
[137] *Report of HM Commissioners*, 1885, 22.
[138] Chapter Acts, 21 Nov. 1874; LAO DC CC. 2. 1. 1, f. 412.
[139] Idem.
[140] [Maria Hackett], *A brief account of cathedral and collegiate schools*, London 1827, 40.
[141] Chapter Acts, 21 Sept. 1846; LAO DC A. 3. 17, f. 451.

schoolroom (1846) and John Allen, a junior vicar, was appointed schoolmaster at a salary of £40 a year. It was presumably this makeshift arrangement which the chapter described to the Cathedral Commissioners as a school entirely under their control and superintendence.[142] Perhaps they sensed that this might not bear investigation and new arrangements were made in 1855–6. The choristers were to remain with Young in the Choristers' House, but now, for the first time, the Burghersh Chanters, too, were to be boarded and lodged – with a Mr Mantle, who established a private school in Lincoln about this time. Mantle was to be responsible for the education of all ten boys, for which he was to be paid (1856) £45 a quarter by the chapter. An additional £30 a year was to be paid for the board and lodging of each of the Chanters.[143]

It seems that the Dean and Chapter were not entirely satisfied with their arrangement with Mantle; when, in 1871, major repairs were undertaken at 10 Minster Yard, and the four choristers joined the Chanters as boarders at Mantle's school, this was spoken of as a temporary expedient until a house, large enough to lodge all the boys together, could be provided.[144] In fact, the choristers never returned to 10 Minster Yard (leaving the Organist in sole possession) and all the boys remained under the charge of the Mantles, father and son, as long as Mantle's school continued.

Young, the Organist, was one of those who had reservations about the suitability of Mantle's school:

Sometimes I am asked if I would send my own sons to the choristers' School; and to this, I feel bound to answer, that I would not. Thus we lose the very boys we are so anxious to get, and who would be sure to make the best singers. In addition to the education afforded being much below what I conceive cathedral choristers ought to receive, I consider it a serious drawback . . . that the choristers should be educated in a mixed school. To give an instance: the boys with whom the choristers mix at school do not speak well, and as the proper pronunciation of words is essential to good singing, the time spent in the Song School to attain this, is, in many cases, all but thrown away.[145]

Even so when W. H. Mantle died in 1884, the chapter recorded their 'high sense of the conscientiousness and ability with which for so many years he watched over and taught the Choir boys of the Cathedral', and agreed to the boys continuing at the school, which would henceforth be run by Henry Mantle.[146]

---

[142] *First Report of HM Commissioners*, 1854, 256.

[143] Chapter Acts, 17 Sept. 1855, 15 Sept. 1856, 17 Sept. 1861; LAO DC CC. 2. 1. 1, ff. 27, 37 and 115.

[144] Chapter Acts, 325, 18 Sept. 1871.

[145] *Report of HM Commissioners*, 1885, 20.

[146] Chapter Acts, 11 Nov. 1884; LAO DC CC.2. 1. 2, ff. 172–3.

At about this time, the school moved from The Grove to a large house in Northgate, at the junction with Nettleham Road (actually leased from the vicars choral) and it was the lease of this property which the Dean and Chapter purchased from Mantle in 1902, together with the furnishings and fittings of the school.[147] The circumstances are obscure, but it seems that Mantle was in difficulties (probably financial) and, in order to secure the future of the school, the chapter decided to take it over, and run it themselves. In June 1903 a Mr Cowburn was appointed Master at a salary of £260. He was to receive a further £520 a year for boarding sixteen choirboys, but had, from this sum, to pay the salary of a matron, whose appointment was to be approved by the chapter. An assistant master was to be employed and paid by the chapter.[148] At last, the cathedral had its own choir school.

Everything suggests that the more enlightened members of the chapter in the second half of the nineteenth century saw the musical foundation as having a vital role to play in the improvement of the cathedral's discipline, and the decency of its worship. A short office, to be used in the course of divine service, was adopted for the admission of choristers (1873);[149] the senior chorister on each side of the choir was to report any misdemeanours of the other boys to the Organist, and a lay vicar was to supervise them as they set out books before the service.[150] From 1871, clergy and choir assembled for prayer before processing to their respective stalls.[151] Cassocks were provided for the choir in 1886, in addition to the customary surplices.[152] In 1872, it was decided that the Friday morning Matins would be sung unaccompanied;[153] in 1887, that a processional hymn would be sung at the beginning of Matins and Evensong on the five great festivals;[154] in 1896, that the celebration of the Holy Communion on those festivals should be choral.[155]

All this came to pass during J. M. W. Young's long tenure of the organistship (1850–95). The chapter seems genuinely to have appreciated Young's contribution to the improvement in the services, but he was poorly paid, and was obliged to spend much of his time in private teaching. He had a succession of articled pupils who did duty for him at the cathedral, but by the late 1880s, a serious problem had arisen on account of Young's frequent and prolonged

---

[147] Chapter Acts, 15 Sept. 1902; LAO DC CC. 2. 1. 4, f. 85.
[148] Chapter Acts, 13 June 1903; LAO DC CC. 2. 1. 4, f. 131.
[149] Chapter Acts, 29 Nov. 1873; LAO DC CC. 2. 1. 1, f. 383.
[150] Chapter Acts, 16 Sept. 1879; LAO DC CC. 2. 1. 2, ff. 56–7.
[151] Chapter Acts, 23 Nov. 1871; LAO DC CC. 2. 1. 1, f. 333.
[152] Chapter Acts, 5 June 1886; LAO DC CC. 2. 1. 2, f. 246.
[153] Chapter Acts, 29 Nov. 1872; LAO DC CC. 2. 1. 1, f. 355.
[154] Chapter Acts, 17 Jan. 1887; LAO DC CC. 2. 1. 2, f. 272.
[155] Chapter Acts, 13 July 1896; LAO DC CC. 2. 1. 3, f. 210.

bouts of ill health. In 1887 he was warned that the chapter might not feel able to reappoint him as Instructor of the Boys – still, then, an annual office.[156] They held their hand, however, and various deputies were sanctioned until, in 1893, an Assistant Organist was formally appointed.[157] Matters came to a head in 1895. The chapter resolved that they must make arrangements 'for securing the *continuous* adequate performance of the Cathedral Services and due superintend-ance [*sic*] of the whole choir', and sent Young a copy of the resolution, together with an assurance (hardly necessary, one feels) that they would look favourably on an application for his retirement.[158] It must have been with relief that the chapter accepted Young's resignation on 22 June 1895, and set on record 'their high appreciation of his valuable services to the Cathedral through so many years and especially of his careful musical training of the boys'.[159] Young retired to West Norwood (he died in 1897). The chapter advertised the vacant post – £250 per annum plus house – and from a short-list which included the names of Walter G. Alcock and T. Tertius Noble, appointed Dr George J. Bennett.[160]

Young had remained essentially a mid-Victorian cathedral musician – a patriarchal figure, devoted to his choir, he found his relaxation in the study of astronomy. With the appointment of Bennett, Lincoln's music came under the direction of an altogether different figure.

Bennett had been a chorister at Winchester College. He had studied at the Royal Academy of Music in London, and then in Berlin and Munich – Rheinberger and Busmeyer were among his teachers. On his return from Germany, he was appointed Organist of St John's Church, Wilton Road, London, a fashionable suburban church, with a 'high' tradition in music and ritual. His experience when he arrived in Lincoln in 1895 was thus very different from that of his predecessors.

This was reflected in the distinction which Bennett brought, both to the cathedral music, and to other music-making in Lincoln during his tenure (1895–1930). His name is particularly associated with the series of 'triennial' festivals in the years preceding the Great War. These began, modestly enough, in Young's day as 'oratorio services'; they were held in the nave of the cathedral and drew upon the joint musical resources of Lincoln and Peterborough. The first reference to them is in 1887, and there seem to have been festivals at Lincoln in 1889 and 1891.[161] Bennett was instrumental in founding the Lincoln

---

[156] Chapter Acts, 16 Apr. 1887, 29 Oct. 1887; L A O D C CC. 2. 1. 2, ff. 278, 290.
[157] Chapter Acts, 16 Jan. 1893; L A O D C CC. 2. 1. 3, f. 36.
[158] Chapter Acts, 6 Apr. 1895; L A O D C CC. 2. 1. 3, f. 138.
[159] Chapter Acts, 22 June 1895; L A O D C CC. 2. 1. 3, ff. 163–4.
[160] Chapter Acts, 9 Aug. 1895; L A O D C CC. 2. 1. 3, f. 175.
[161] Chapter Acts, 18 June 1887, 27 Oct. 1888, 13 July 1891; L A O D C CC. 2. 1. 2, 282, 324 and 400.

Music Society (1896) and became its Honorary Conductor; this, with the recruitment of Ely and its musicians, opened up the possibility of large-scale choral and orchestral performances, and these followed in a series which included Lincoln festivals in 1896, 1899, 1902, 1906 and 1910. Among the visiting conductors at Lincoln during these years were Parry, Stanford and Elgar. The series ended at Lincoln with the 1910 Festival and the advent of Dean Fry, who was immovable in his opposition to any charges being made for seats in the cathedral.[162] Denied the necessary finance, the Lincoln series came to an end.

Bennett's relations with Fry highlight a certain intransigence in his character. For some reason (possibly, the discontinuance of the festivals) these two strong personalities clashed, with the result that they were not on speaking terms for some years and communicated only by letter; according to Fry's biographer, it was Bennett who finally opened the way to improved relations by admitting that the initial fault had been his.[163] Francis Woolley, Bennett's assistant at Lincoln in the last years of his life, tells of other stormy passages with the clergy, describing Bennett as 'a man of determination and hasty temper, particularly in regard to matters musical'.[164] Yet this was far from the whole story, and Bennett's election as City Sheriff (1925), and his appointment as Master of the Worshipful Company of Musicians (1927) indicate the regard in which he was held by many.[165]

One of Bennett's first tasks upon his appointment in 1895 was to persuade the chapter to do something about the cathedral organ – by then perhaps the most antiquated cathedral organ in the country. Little had been done to it since Allen's work in the 1850s, and in a period when organ-building was taking considerable technological strides, its inadequacies were all too apparent. Some of its shortcomings are apparent from the decision, in 1885, to install a temporary organ to accompany nave services; meanwhile, the organ-builder Henry Willis was asked to submit a plan 'for a large Organ' to stand on the screen.[166] When it became clear that there was no money to pay for Willis' proposals, a patching-up operation was attempted by Wordsworth and Maskell of Leeds at a cost of £220,[167] and then, in 1896, a Mr Shuttleworth and others promised £1000 towards a major reconstruction. The chapter, encouraged, agreed to plans being prepared but laid down certain conditions: the existing

---

[162] Francis Wolley, *Reminiscences*, LAO, 65.

[163] Derek Winterbottom, *Doctor Fry*, Berkhamsted 1977, 45.

[164] Woolley, *Reminiscences*, 56.

[165] Bennett's obituary, in *Lincolnshire Chronicle*, 23 Aug. 1930, 5.

[166] Chapter Acts, 7 Nov. 1885; LAO DC CC. 2. 1. 2, f. 215.

[167] Chapter Acts, 18 June 1887, 19 Sept. 1887, 17 Mar. 1888; LAO DC CC. 2. 1. 2, ff. 282, 286 and 308.

organ was to be reconstructed, rather than replaced; the Willson case was to be retained; and anything which would not fit into the case was to be placed in the triforium.[168] In the event, the Willis organ was effectively a new instrument, and the chapter had to agree to the case being raised by 2′6″. The contract was signed on 20 March 1897; the price was £3,605, with preparation made for additional work to cost a further £670.[169]

Work was completed by the end of 1898 and the new organ was dedicated at a service on St Hugh's Day (17 November). The choir on that occasion was augmented by singers from Peterborough, Ely, Southwell and London, and the service was followed by two recitals given by Sir Walter Parratt, Master of the Queen's Music, and Organist of St George's Chapel, Windsor.[170] The specification is shown on p. 107.

The 32′ reed was not added until 1901. The organ achieved some distinction by being the first in an English cathedral to have electrical blowing apparatus: three motors were installed in the triforium on the north side of the choir. All would have been well except that the city's generating plant was not in operation at the time of the opening service. The Lincolnshire Regiment was equal to the emergency, and supplied relays of men to blow the organ – their red jackets were clearly visible in the triforium, and the men were encouraged in their labours with an ample supply of ale, provided by the Dean.[171]

Like his immediate predecessor, Dr Bennett was a composer. A number of his works are to be found in the cathedral music lists of his day, and his small-scale orchestral works would appear from time to time in the Festival programmes. Inevitably, though, his chief preoccupation was the training of the cathedral choir, and it must therefore have been much to his sorrow when the Cathedral School was obliged, in 1920, to close. Bennett had had his reservations about the School. He particularly deplored the imposition (from 1902) of a fee of £15 a year upon the parents of the boys; it had been hoped that this would 'raise the class of boy, and . . . attract the sons of Clergymen in the Diocese' – but, as Bennett pointed out, this ploy had failed, and he urged the chapter to revert to the practice of giving the boys free education, board and lodging.[172] This was in 1915, and at about that time the School was moved from Northgate to the Burghersh Chantry in James Street. This does not seem to have been satisfactory. The standard of the singing deteriorated, and in 1920 the School closed.[173] With

---

[168] Chapter Acts, 28 Nov. 1896; LAO DC CC. 2. 1. 3, f. 224.

[169] Willis' contract; LAO DC deposit, 1959 (bundle 32).

[170] *Musical Times*, Dec. 1898, 801–2.

[171] A. Lindsey Kirwan, *The music of Lincoln cathedral*, London 1973, 13.

[172] LAO DC CC. 2. 5. 2 (report from Dr Bennett to DC 1915).

[173] Winterbottom, *Doctor Fry*, 46; Chapter Acts, 24 Sept. 1919; LAO DC CC. 2. 1. 6, f. 52.

GREAT ORGAN (C–a³)

Double open diapason	16
Open diapason No. 1	8
Open diapason No. 2	8
Open diapason No. 3	8
Stopped diapason	8
Claribel flute	8
Principal	4
Flûte harmonique	4
Twelfth	2⅔
Fifteenth	2
Mixture	III
Trombone	16
Tromba	8
Clarion	4

CHOIR ORGAN (C–a³)

Lieblich bourdon	16
Lieblich gedackt	8
Dulciana	8
Viola da gamba	8
Hohl flöte	8
Gemshorn	4
Concert flute	4
Piccolo harmonique	2
Cor anglais	16
Corno di bassetto	8

PEDAL ORGAN (C–f¹)

Double open diapason	32
Open diapason	16
Open diapason	16
Violone	16
Bourdon	16
Octave	8
Violoncello	8
Superoctave	4
Contra posaune	32
Ophicleide	16
Clarion	8

SWELL ORGAN (C–a³)

Double open diapason	16
Open diapason No. 1	8
Open diapason No. 2	8
Lieblich gedackt	8
Salicional	8
Vox angelica	8
Principal	4
Lieblich flöte	4
Fifteenth	2
Mixture	III

SWELL ORGAN —*Cont.*

Double trumpet	16
Trumpet	8
Oboe	8
Clarion	4
Vox humana	8

SOLO ORGAN (C–a³)

*Gamba	8
*Voix célestes	8
Claribel flute	8
*Harmonic flute	4
*Orchestral oboe	8
*Orchestral clarinet	8
Tuba	8
Tuba clarion	4

* enclosed in swell box

COUPLERS

Swell to Great
Solo to Great
Choir to Great
Swell octave
Swell suboctave
Swell to Choir
Solo suboctave
Solo to Pedals
Swell to Pedals
Great to Pedals
Choir to Pedals
Pedal to Great pistons
Pedal to Swell pistons
Swell pistons to composition pedals
Great pistons to composition pedals
Pedal *and accompaniment* to Choir pistons
Pedal *and accompaniment* to Solo pistons

ACCESSORIES

Swell tremulant
Solo tremulant (by pedal)
Swell pedals to Swell and Solo
5 pistons to Solo
7 pistons to Swell
7 pistons to Great
5 pistons to Choir
6 pistons (double acting) to couplers and
   accessory stops
7 composition pedals to Pedal
1 composition pedal, reducing Pedal to
   Bourdon 16′
3 double acting pedals to couplers

it, went the main boarding facility, and whilst it appears that some arrangements were, for a time, maintained to board non-local boys, it was not long before the choirboys were once again recruited largely from Lincoln itself. The chapter drew up new regulations in 1921: boys admitted as probationers would continue at their existing day schools and receive £2 a year; if admitted to the choir, they would attend either Christ's Hospital Terrace School or the Technical School, and, in addition to any fees, would receive £5 a year. Parents who wished their sons to attend Lincoln School would be paid the equivalent of the Technical School fees, and in all cases, the Dean and Chapter would pay school fees up to the age of 16.[174] This effective reliance upon local resources must have been a blow to Bennett, for in the years following his arrival in Lincoln considerable numbers of boys were admitted to the choir from all parts of the country, with comparatively few from Lincoln itself.

The pattern of choir duties, too, began to change in Bennett's day. In 1905, it was decided to discontinue choral services on Mondays,[175] and, about the same time, the whole choir was given an annual holiday, in August, when the choral services were suspended. (For some years the boys had been allowed short holidays in the periods after Christmas and Easter.)

Bennett was the last Lincoln Organist to live in the former Choristers' House at 10 Minster Yard. He declined the house at first, but then moved there in 1900. He seems to have found the house inadequate, added an extra bedroom at his own expense (1905), but finally moved out in 1909.[176] He died, in office, at the age of 67, in August 1930; the cathedral was packed for his funeral, at which Dr Edward Bairstow, Organist of York Minster, played. The *Lincolnshire Chronicle & Leader* recorded an impressive list of apologies from musicians unable to be present, including the names of Elgar, and Ethel Smyth.

In Bennett's place the Dean and Chapter appointed Dr Gordon Slater, Organist of Leicester Cathedral, and before that, of Boston Parish Church.[177] Dr Slater remained at Lincoln until his retirement in 1966. A further significant date should be recorded. In 1932, a Scheme was drawn up for the dissolution of the College of Vicars Choral (the minor canons). The income from the lands which had previously belonged to their Estate was henceforth to be paid to the Dean and Chapter, who were also to take possession of Vicars' Court.

All the manuscripts records books and documents and all furniture and fittings together

[174] Chapter Acts, 19 Apr. 1921; LAO DC CC. 2. 1. 6, f. 104.
[175] Chapter Acts, 20 June 1905; LAO DC CC. 2. 1. 4, f. 234.
[176] Chapter Acts, 1 Feb. 1909; LAO DC CC. 2. 1. 5, f. 31.
[177] Chapter Acts, 9 Oct. 1930; LAO DC CC. 2. 1. 7, f. 405.

with all other chattels belonging to the said Corporation shall be transferred and shall belong to the said Dean and Chapter.[178]

On 24 June 1934 the Scheme was approved by the King in Council, and the Corporation of the Vicars of the Cathedral Church of St Mary, of Lincoln, established in 1441, was no more.

Finally, a survey of the music books and service lists of the previous hundred years reveals a gradual process of change in the repertoire. In the early part of the period, it seems that little care was taken to match the text of the music to the liturgical season; a manuscript book of services and anthems compiled between 1843 and 1857 by H. Lumley (who sang with the choir in some capacity) gives three thirteen-week cycles of music, and the implication is that they were repeated *ad nauseam*. Most of the music in Lumley's book is to be found in the music lists of the 1820s, mentioned above, and only a handful of compositions were in any sense contemporary – there is, for example, a service by Mendelssohn (in A) and one by Wesley (in F).[179]

During Young's time, more contemporary composers began to appear in the lists, but his taste (dictated by a conservative temperament) ensured that the cathedral composers of the eighteenth and early nineteenth centuries continued to be well represented. Bumpus reports accompanying Young to the organ loft, and watching him play 'the grand old services and anthems from the first editions of the cathedral music of Boyce and Arnold, and of the collections of Croft, Greene, Boyce, Hayes, Page, and others'.[180] As late as 1893, the cathedral's first edition of Arnold's *Cathedral Music* (1790) was re-bound, as part of a working Organ Book. Bumpus also commented on Young's accompaniments; they 'were almost always independent of the voices, and some of the feeblest passages in the services and anthems of Kent, Clarke Whitfield, and others of the later Georgian school were rendered palatable by his musician-like organ parts'.[181] Despite an early performance of Stanford in B flat in the same year (1895) that he retired, Young's additions to the repertoire have a predominantly mid-Victorian flavour about them: Walmisley, S. S. Wesley, Goss, Elvey and Spohr, for example.

The old part books continued in use: as late as 1901, the Succentor inspected, and duly signed, one of them.[182] Much of the old repertoire continued in use, even under Bennett; King's mediocre Service in F received no fewer than nine performances in 1905. However, printed music was now widely available, and

---

[178] LAO DC 1. 3. 26 and 4. 6. 1.

[179] I am most grateful to Laurence Elvin for showing me the Lumley Book (which is now in his possession) and for further assistance with the preparation of this chapter.

[180] Thomas F. Bumpus, *The cathedrals of England and Wales* I, London 1905, 131–2.

[181] Ibid.

[182] Music MSS 95 and 97.

cheap. It had become much easier to expand the repertoire. Under Bennett, in the early 1900s, the later Victorian composers predominated, but contemporary works were introduced – by Parry, Stanford, Noble, Elgar, Bairstow and Bennett himself – and the number of performances of anthems by sixteenth- and seventeenth-century composers reveals a modest increase.

This last trend became more marked under Bennett's successor, Dr Slater. Taking advantage of the newly available scholarly editions of anthems and services by the Elizabethan and Jacobean composers, Slater drew widely upon this repertoire for his choir. Once again, the works of Byrd received the attention which they deserved from Lincoln, and indeed, Dr Slater was responsible for a week of music in 1943 to mark the Byrd Quatercentenary.[183] Among other composers, the appearance of Vaughan Williams and Howells, on the one hand, and of Palestrina and Vittoria, on the other, give an indication of how the tradition was being developed in the middle years of the present century.

When, in 1966, Dr Philip Marshall, Organist of Ripon Cathedral, succeeded Dr Slater at Lincoln, he was only the fourth Organist to be appointed since Skelton in 1794. The English cathedral tradition tends to prefer continuity to change, evolution to revolution. This is apparent when the recent history of the music at Lincoln, since the Second World War, is considered; there has inevitably been gradual change, but no clean break with the past. Trends which go back several generations have continued quietly on their way.

Weekday choral Matins was finally discontinued in the years following 1945. It had become increasingly difficult both for boys and men to attend this service, and in the early 1930s, Matins was no longer sung on three mornings a week. Some of the difficulties in maintaining this service arose from the growing demands which educational reform made upon the boys' time, and this was exacerbated by the fact that they attended a number of schools in different parts of the city. These difficulties were not entirely overcome by the abandon-ment of weekday choral Matins. They were only solved when the Cathedral School was reopened in 1961, housed in the Old Deanery, and with the boarders accommodated (appropriately enough) in the Burghersh Chantry in James Street.

Another significant date during Dr Slater's term of office was Whit Sunday 1960, when the cathedral organ was brought back into use following a major reconstruction. For some time it had been apparent that the mechanism of Willis' instrument, having functioned reliably for over half a century, was showing signs of age. An organ fund was established to raise £14,000. The

[183] Kirwan, *Music of Lincoln cathedral*, 14.

organ was dismantled by Harrison & Harrison of Durham in 1959, and when the reconstruction was complete, a new electro-pneumatic action and a new console had been installed. Some tonal additions were made, chiefly in the Choir Organ, but in other respects the builders sought to preserve the tonal character of Willis' original work.

Today, there is much to emphasise continuity with the past. There are still lay vicars living in Vicars' Court, and the Organist lives only a stone's throw from the cathedral (though no longer in 10 Minster Yard). The four choristers still wear their distinctive gowns or copes, and the choir continues to play a full part in both the daily offices and the many special services and events which take place in the Minster. In other ways, the pace of change has quickened. The advent of radio and television have brought new opportunities: the choir made over sixty broadcasts for the BBC during Dr Slater's time,[184] and television cameras are not unknown in the cathedral. Recordings made by the choir are now on sale in the cathedral shop, and in recent years, the choir has gone further afield, giving recitals in Germany and elsewhere. This blending of old and new in a living tradition is equally apparent when one turns to the current repertoire. At one end of the spectrum, there are the names of Palestrina, Shepherd, Taverner, and, of course, William Byrd. Victorian composers who disappeared from the music lists in the middle years of the present century have found their way back: works by S. S. Wesley, Goss, Steggall, Elvey, Stainer, Smart and Walmisley have a regular place again. Britten, Walton and especially Howells represent the earlier part of the twentieth century, and then a more recent generation figures with compositions by Adrian Cruft, Bryan Kelly, Francis Jackson, William Matthias and Peter Aston. Lincoln's own composers are not forgotten. The cathedral's chant book (compiled and produced by Philip Marshall in 1979) contains chants by Byrd, Flintoft, Young, Bennett, Slater and Marshall himself, and services and anthems by Lincoln's musicians appear from time to time.

The tradition goes on.

---

[184] Ibid.

5

Historical survey, 1091–1450

❇

DOROTHY OWEN

THE TWELFTH AND THIRTEENTH CENTURIES: ESTABLISHMENT AND CONSOLIDATION

General

The great establishment foreshadowed by the building of Remigius' cathedral took shape only slowly: it was to be another century at least before the numbers of prebendaries were complete, their endowments gathered in and allotted and the service of God within the cathedral fully provided for. The recollections of Archdeacon Henry of Huntingdon about the dignitaries and leading members of the chapter in his own day, and that of his father, who was his predecessor in the archdeaconry, although written between *c.*1134 and *c.*1146, went back to the early days when Remigius was laying the foundations. There were then, he says, a Dean, Precentor and Treasurer, who were the dignitaries, or *persone* of the chapter, and eight archdeacons, for Lincoln, Stow, Leicester, Buckingham, Northampton, Oxford, Huntingdon and Bedford.[1] No archdeacon was regarded as a dignitary, since his archidiaconal duties precluded the continuous residence nominally expected of the *persone*:

The first Chancellor to emerge into light seems to be Mr Hamo, who is known from about 1148; the first subdean, Humphrey, appears not much before 1163 and both were already also described as dignitaries. Humphrey's

---

[1] Henry of Huntingdon, printed in *Fasti 1066–1300*, III, 153–4.

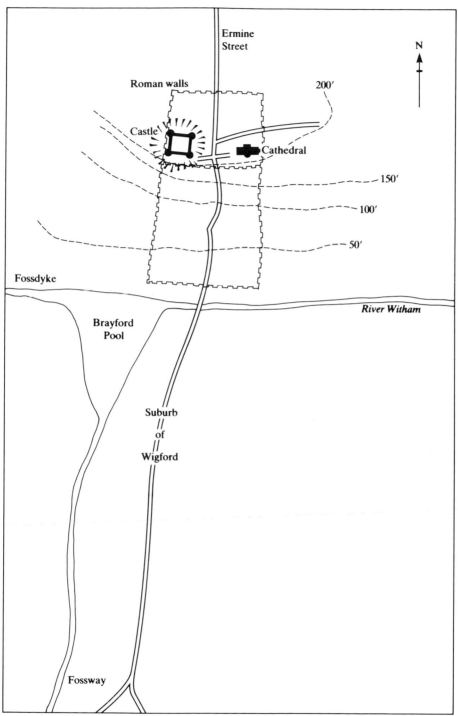

6 *Lincoln in 1091, after J. W. F. Hill,* Medieval Lincoln

113

office, and its prominence in the chapter, was evidently required because of the frequent absences of the Dean on the general business of the church and the necessity that he should have an efficient substitute. By contrast, the deputies of the Chancellor, Precentor and Treasurer, who were not expected to be absent, were no more than vicars choral.[2] Remigius and his successor Robert Bloet assigned to the three first dignitaries some of the manors and churches which formed part of the cathedral's first endowment, and later rulers of the see augumented these, besides giving other parts of the early lands to the Subdean and Chancellor, and to some at least of the archdeacons. The Dean received from the King a considerable estate in Derbyshire.

There were other members of the foundation, the canons, whose numbers grew steadily in the first century of its history. If we are to accept the conclusions of the most recent work on the subject, their numbers had, in fact, come close to the medieval total before 1135. In a list of the foundation written in the Great Bible, which enshrines some of the earliest records of the church and which seems to have been compiled about that year, the daily recitation of the psalter, which here, as in other cathedral churches, was a feature of chapter life, was shared by forty-three canons. By the time St Hugh revised the list in 1186–8, almost the complete tale of fifty-four was reached.[3] For each of the canons an endowment, or prebend, was needed before he could take his full part in the business of the chapter: in the age of papal provision to benefices a clerk might procure from the Pope the expectancy or promise of a canonry at Lincoln, but unless this was amplified by the naming of a distinct prebend nothing further would result. There was much shuffling, re-arrangement and division of prebendal endowment by the bishops until the mid-thirteenth century, when the names which derive from the lands and churches by which they were supported seem finally to have been fixed. These endowments vary considerably in origin, and, indeed, in annual value. Some were probably allotted by Remigius himself, from the churches and manors which he inherited from the bishops of Dorchester or had recently acquired by royal gift. The prebendaries of Banbury, Buckden and Leicester St Margaret all held properties which had been in the hands of the bishop of Dorchester before the Conquest; Caistor, Sleaford and Welton prebends were endowed from royal manors bestowed on Remigius by William. Other later prebends, like *Decem Librarum* and *Centum Solidorum*, seem to have originated in annual pensions chargeable on episcopal revenues and given to the chapter in compensation of some right appropriated by the bishop. Conversely, they may be no more than the

---

[2] Ibid., III, *passim.*
[3] Ibid., XV–XVI, 71, 87; *LCS* I, 300–2.

prebendal pensions known to have been paid from the temporalities of the see during vacancies.[4] Still other prebends were endowed with the lands and tithes (the rectories, that is) of churches in Lincoln and elsewhere which had been received from the King or local magnates, who in the case of Asgarby and Carlton Kyme had retained the advowsons of the prebends until the late thirteenth century.

These prebendal endowments were scattered throughout all the archdeaconries of the diocese even so early as the papal confirmation of 1149, besides the similar lands and churches held in the diocese and province of York. The Lincolnshire churches of Stow, Louth, Sleaford, Lincoln St Botolph, St Martin, St Mary Crackpole and Holy Cross all became prebendal endowments, as did Leicester St Margaret, Spaldwick in Huntingdon, which was given by the King as compensation for the loss of Cambridgeshire, as well as Leighton and Buckden in the same archdeaconry; in Oxfordshire Banbury, Cropredy, Milton and Thame, in Bedfordshire two churches in Bedford and Biggleswade, in Buckinghamshire Aylesbury and Buckingham, to which King's Sutton was added. Some of these endowments undoubtedly included the greater hundredal churches, notably Buckingham and Nassington; other prebendal churches may well prove to have similar origins when the evidence can be sifted.[5]

The first half of the twelfth century had seen the elaboration and diversification of duties assigned to the *persone* who were the principal agents in the maintenance of the cathedral's life, and to whom specific endowments were rapidly attached. The deanery itself seems to have enjoyed from the late eleventh century the Derbyshire churches of Ashbourne and Chesterfield with their chapels; before 1200 another church in the same county, that of Wirksworth, was also given to it, as well as the churches of South Leverton, Mansfield and Clayworth in Nottinghamshire.[6]

A precentor, with a song school over which he ruled, was mentioned as a dignitary before 1147; he was already endowed with all the Lincoln churches which had not been allotted elsewhere. The 'fee of the chancellor', with the church of All Saints in the Bail and neighbouring property in Bailgate, was well established before 1163. The Treasurer was, as we have already seen, in office before 1092, although his endowments seem to have been allotted much later. The subdeanery certainly existed as an office before 1133, but its possessions were not apparently bestowed until much later. Bishop Alexander had first assigned to it the prebendal church of Leighton Ecclesia, but this was later exchanged for another prebendal endowment, the manor of Welton Westhall,

[4] J. W. F. Hill, *Medieval Lincoln*, Cambridge 108.
[5] Ibid., p. 2 and n. 2.
[6] *Fasti 1066–1300*, III, 5–6.

the important hundredal church of Kirton in Lindsey, a portion of the church of Hibaldstow, and the demesne tithes in Elsham, Kingerby, Owersby and Kirkby cum Osgodby, which the chapter evidently acquired as part of the personal endowment of Adam de Amundeville, to whom they had later been assigned as his prebend.[7]

Each of these dignitaries had from the beginning his particular functions within the church and the chapter and although prescription rather than written statutes provided the only sanction for these customs for more than a century, it is clear that when, in 1214, the Lincoln customs were set down for the instruction of a newly begun chapter in Moray in Scotland, they were well established and clearly understood.[8] The Dean, who was to be elected by the chapter, was its ceremonial head, who admitted new canons, celebrated at the major double feasts and pronounced the benediction unless the Bishop was present. It was he who exercised ecclesiastical jurisdiction over the chapter and its servants, and took custody of the endowments of vacant prebends. The Precentor ruled and instructed the choir and Song School, with all that this implied, while the Chancellor ruled the Theological School, of which we shall hear more later, arranged for the preaching of sermons, provided and took care of the chapter's library of theological books, wrote its letters and had custody of its seal and muniments. The Treasurer's responsibility was the care of the ornaments and treasures of the church, its lights, bells and clock and the provision, through his servant the Sacrist, of all the necessaries for the services of the church. If the prebendaries were already well provided for by the mid-twelfth century, there was clearly some need for other funds to be assigned to the general service of the chapter and to the building of the cathedral and its maintenance. The second of these two needs would eventually be met by the Fabric Fund, which evolved in the late twelfth century and which will be discussed below, but a general fund, which may well at first have included provision for building maintenance, seems to have existed at a much earlier period, when it was known as the Common of the canons. In 1146 its sources of income were set out in a papal confirmation of the possessions of the cathedral; they then comprised tithe in Canwick and Kilsby, Stow and Greetwell, half of the offerings made at the Lady altar in the cathedral, two vineyards in Lincoln and the church of St Nicholas in Newport there.[9] The detailed elaboration and augmentation of this Common Fund was not to come until the thirteenth century but it was clearly an essential element in chapter organisation from the start. Its existence presupposed clerks to oversee and record its administration,

[7] Ibid., appendix contributed by Judith Cripps, 169–72.
[8] *LCS* I, 37.
[9] *R A* I, 252.

and these were evidently recruited from the priest-vicars who were already gathering around the cathedral. Traces of these shadowy figures can be seen in the witness lists of the charters of the Common Fund recorded in *Registrum Antiquissimum*, which is the cartulary of that fund, and even more in the early charters of the vicars' own cartulary. One such charter, to be dated between 1189 and 1195, concerns the grant of a rent of 15 shillings by Gerard the priest of Newport, out of land he held in Eastgate, to support his son William the clerk as a priest. It was witnessed by Hamo the Dean, Wynemer the Subdean and Mr Simon of Southwell, a prebendary, Ingeram and Odo, chaplains, William the writer and five other clerks, some of whom were perhaps the staff of the Common Fund Office.[10]

As the twelfth century passed, and as the cathedral came to be firmly enshrined in the affections of the bishop's subjects, the gifts it received increased in number, if not in size, donations were made not only by the tenants-in-chief of the counties within the diocese, or even by their mesne tenants. Many smaller landholders now gave small plots of land, houses or even minute rent charges, to the church of Lincoln. It is perhaps symptomatic of the cathedral's growing importance that, although pensions and rent charges on rectories continued to come from endowments of churches throughout the diocese, most of the lesser secular gifts came from the county of Lincoln itself and formed a second and different stage of the endowment of the chapter.

The territorial arrangement of the later parts of the *Registrum Antiquissimum*, which was devised in the early thirteenth century, was set out under Lindsey, itself divided into the west, north and south ridings, Kesteven and Holland (each with few properties), and the city of Lincoln and this reflects the strongly local basis of this second wave of endowment. It was accompanied, too, by a general movement to accept the donors into the confraternity of the chapter, as were Richilda and Maud, daughters of Walter Vilein, who gave property in St Peter at Arches to the chapter.[11]

The early phases of this confraternity movement can be detected in the mid-twelfth-century obit roll in the Great Bible, which shows how widely donors and their benefactions were already spread: they range from Robert, archdeacon of Lincoln, and William of Romara, earl of Lincoln, to Quenil, wife of William son of Ag, Moyses the clerk, Outi son of Unni, Richard the priest of Eastgate, Lewin, Turstin and Leverun, and Gilbert the clerk, son of Ernald the mason.[12]

There is very little to show how the community of clerks, created and endowed in this way, arranged its life and worship in the first century of its

---

[10] L A O V C 2.1.
[11] *R A* IX, 2390–91.
[12] Giraldus Cambrensis, Opera VII, Appendix B, 153–64.

existence. It is certain that by the mid-twelfth century the *Regula canonicorum cum martilogio* was read daily, and the daily repetition of the psalter by members of the chapter was, as we have noted, already in force in 1135; before the end of the century each prebendal stall was inscribed, as it still is today, with the *Incipits* (opening words) of the psalms allotted to its holder. Other ritual usages of the church can be discerned imperfectly from the 'customs and offices of the church of Lincoln', first written as we have seen, for the instruction of the church of Moray, and existing there, in their earliest form, but surviving at Lincoln only in a much amplified copy made by John of Schalby, a later member of the chapter.[13] The practices recorded in these sources are certainly reminiscent of those common in Normandy, although they can be paralleled in other cathedrals in England. Many were, in fact, based on decisions made by the chapter in solving the administrative problems presented when endowments grew in size and elaboration. Thus, for example, the chapter found itself called on to decide how to deal with the income and stock of prebendal estates after the death or resignation of a prebendary. Similar decisions were made about liturgical difficulties such as evidently arose in the course of one of the major feasts; it was not clear who was entitled to celebrate at such times at the high altar of the cathedral and the chapter pronounced that only the bishop and the dignitaries were eligible to do so. These great feasts, for which the Sacrist (the deputy to the Treasurer) was ordered to provide a special allowance of candles, were the centre of the liturgical year. They were Christmas, the five days before Epiphany, Candlemas, Easter Eve and the following fourteen days, Ascension eve, Pentecost eve, Trinity Sunday, the Nativity of St John Baptist, the Feast of Saints Peter and Paul, the Feast of Relics, the Nativity and Assumption of the Blessed Virgin.

There were to be weekly sermons preached 'to the people' each Sunday and, in addition, sermons at Christmas, Easter, All Saints, the Nativity and the Assumption of the Blessed Virgin, and Ash Wednesday. All these sermons were to be arranged, if not preached, by the Chancellor. On Palm Sunday and the three Rogation Days there were processions and stations, when sermons were preached out of doors, for which the chapter carpenters provided seats for the canons participating in the procession. On Palm Sunday, in addition, the choir sang the hymn *Gloria, laus et honor* from above the west door as the procession passed below, on its return to the church, and palls or cloths were hung on the gate of the Bail where one of the stations was made. (It is not clear whether this is the east gate or the south gate at the top of Steep Hill.) On Maunday

---

[13] *LCS* I. For some remarks on this see D. E. Greenway, 'False *Institutio* of St Osmund', *Tradition and change*, Cambridge 1986, 77–101.

Thursday the altars were bared of ornament and washed; for this the carpenters provided warm water, which was also needed for the ritual washing of the canons' feet. On Ascension Day the relics of the church were washed, and a pall was hung on the front of the church (that is, the west front), where the choir halted to sing *Non vos relinquam orphanos*. There were three festivals immediately after Christmas for which the carpenter had to make provision: St Stephen for the deacons, St John Evangelist for the priests and Holy Innocents for the boys.

This fragmentary and dimly seen liturgy has a marked resemblence to the Rouen customs which were thought to derive from the usages described in the treatise *De officiis ecclesiasticis* of Archbishop John of Avranches. Certainly at Rouen the Host was carried out to the church of St Gildard on Palm Sunday and on its return six boys climbed the tower of the city gate which had been adorned with hangings and sang from the height, in festive manner, *Gloria laus et honor*. The Holy Thursday and Ascension Day practices, and the three post-Christmas festivals are also found at Rouen. There are similar usages at Hereford, as Edmund Bishop has pointed out; in Canterbury on the other hand, the three Christmas festivals are attributed to an importation by Lanfranc from Le Bec. It seems very likely that the Lincoln usages described here were fully established by the time when St Gilbert was a schoolboy in the town in the early twelfth century: certainly, when he came to devise a rite for his new order, in the middle of the century, he adopted the Holy Week Practices and other observances which are known from this source.[14]

The church in which this liturgy was first celebrated is even harder to discern and only a few things can be established about it. From the earliest times it had several altars, for Remigius gave the offerings from them to the canons. They included the high altar itself, dedicated presumably to the Blessed Virgin, before which Bishop Bloet was buried, and a rood altar at the entrance to the sanctuary, where the grave of Remigius was made.[15] There was a gallery over the west door, where the boys stood to sing their Palm Sunday sequence. On the west front there were facilities for the attachment of a pall for certain feasts. In the choir were the seats for the chapter, including the bishop, who also had a separate throne or seat placed perhaps behind the high altar, as seems to be the case at Norwich. There were benches for the priest-vicars who appeared very early in the cathedral's history as substitutes

[14] E. Bishop, *Liturgica Historica*, Oxford 1918, 276–300; R. Delamare, *Le De Officiis Ecclesiasticis de Jean d'Avranches*, Paris 1923; E. Martène, *De Antiquis Ecclesie Ritibus*, Rouen 1700–2, III, 76. I have discussed this more fully in *Anglo-Norman Studies* 6, 1984, 188–99. For St Gilbert's rite see R. M. Woolley, *The Gilbertine rite*, Henry Bradshaw Society 51–2, 1921–2, 26–8.
[15] *The book of John of Schalby*, trans. J. H. Srawley, LMP 2, 1949, 5–6.

for absent canons, and for the deacons and junior vicars who assisted in the church. A *pulpitum* served for the reading of Scripture: it was presumably a stone screen at the western entrance of the choir, behind the rood altar. Before the high altar was a beam on which candles were placed, and a bronze candelabrum; this was perhaps what fell down in ill omen at the Candlemas celebration before Stephen's disastrous attack on the supporters of Matilda, early in 1141.[16]

This building had many vicissitudes. The successive stages of its development are treated elsewhere, but the hazards and difficulties attending its early days are inevitably reflected in the institutions of the chapter. In these early days, according to contemporary record, the lead in building was always taken by the bishop. John of Schalby, recording in the early fourteenth century the traditions of the foundation and of the first century of the church, and Giraldus Cambrensis, almost a contemporary of the later stages of the twelfth-century building, each declared that it was invariably thus.[17] Remigius, they implied, decided on the form, and arranged the building of the first church, and when accidental fire destroyed parts of it, Bishop Alexander restored it and strengthened it with stone vaults. The church already had four servants, a glazier and three carpenters. The glazier's duty was to repair defects in the windows but the carpenters had a variety of responsibilities in addition to the maintenance of the Fabric. They installed the Lenten veil before the sanctuary, supplied and lit candles on the candelabrum and beam, hung palls, curtains and tapestries of linen, silk and woollen cloth and guarded the church while they were in place. It was the carpenters, too, who fitted new clappers to the bells, swept the church at Passiontide, provided water for the altar-washing and kept chairs for the canons' seats at procession stations.

When, in 1186 the Carthusian monk Hugh of Avalon became bishop of Lincoln he almost immediately found himself obliged to devote himself to the rebuilding of the cathedral.[18] In April 1185, a year before his consecration to the see, the church had been 'split from top to bottom' by what contemporaries spoke of as an earthquake. The work of rebuilding seems to have begun about 1193/4, and before Hugh's death in 1200 the eastern transepts, and perhaps the easternmost bays of the nave, were complete. In March 1193 Hugh had dedicated the building in honour of the Holy Trinity and the Blessed Virgin, and Bishop Sanderson recorded that an inscription commemorating this dedica-

---

[16] Orderic Vitalis, *Historia Ecclesiastica*, ed. M. Chibnall, OMT 1969–84, II, 541.

[17] *Schalby, passim.*

[18] *Magna Vita Sancti Hugonis Lincolniensis*, ed. D. L. Douie and D. H. Farmer, OMT, 2 vols., 1961–2, II, *passim*; H. Farmer, 'Canonization of St Hugh', *LAASR* 6, 1955–6, 86–117; EEA IV, no. 20 gives the precise year.

tion could still be seen in 1640 on a pillar 'over the font';[19] it is tempting to speculate that if the font were then in its present position at the south-west end of the nave, and if the inscription had been placed at the point which the work had reached, at the time of the dedication, all was further advanced than has been supposed. Hugh had taken the closest personal interest in the progress of the work, and continually visited the site whenever he was in or near Lincoln. The record of miracles prepared for Hugh's canonisation process included an account of the cure of a cripple effected by handling a hod which had been used by Hugh for carrying stones and cement in the building of the cathedral, and Hugh's biographer recorded another such visit to the building site:

I was present on another occasion at Lincoln on the morrow of Christmas when he had reverently said the mass of the glorious proto-martyr of Christ Stephen, he was asked by a mason who was working on the fabric of the cathedral to absolve by his episcopal authority the soul of his brother who had died the previous night . . .

Again when his last day on earth seemed to be approaching he said to Geoffrey de Noiers the Chief Mason of the magnificent cathedral at Lincoln which Hugh's immense zeal for the beauty of the house of God had caused him to begin to rebuild from the foundations 'make haste to finish so that it may be consecrated'.

His own burial place was also selected 'before the altar of my patron St John Baptist in any fitting place under a wall so that it does not obstruct the passage'.[20]

Such stories clearly illustrate the astonishing attraction Hugh had for the people of the city and diocese, and this seems to have produced a constant flow of gifts to 'the chest where alms are collected for the repair of the church'. He had greatly increased this fund by the issue of an indulgence for eighty days' remission for all making contribution, and followed it up by instituting a gild of St Mary for the raising of further contributions to the work. This gild was evidently the precursor of the Works Chantry established by his successor William of Blois to pray for the welfare of all helping the 'work of rebuilding.[21] There had been since at least 1160 a specific fund set aside by the chapter for the maintenance of the cathedral Fabric, and to this the contributions now made in increasing number were assigned. They constituted a very great resource, with considerable funds in houses and rents within the city of Lincoln. The Fabric Fund was administered at first by a layman and a canon but they were replaced by two of the resident prebendaries, who were elected each year to serve as Masters of the Fabric, and who accounted annually to the chapter at the audit in September, as those responsible for other cathedral funds were

[19] F. Peck, *Desiderata Curiosa*, 1735, 321: Hec ecclesia dicata est in honore sancte Trinitatis et Sancte Marie Virginis, 3 non Mar. a domino Hugone Lincolnie episcopo anno ab incarnatione domini M C X C II.

[20] *Magna Vita* II, 80, 89, 192.

[21] *Rot. Litt. Pat.* 57; Giraldus, *Opera* VII, 217, n. 219.

required to do.[22] They kept accounts, hut none has survived for the medieval period and it is not therefore easy to see how the Fund was then run. During the height of the rebuilding considerable sums were accumulated and held in the cathedral treasury and when in May 1217 the close was pillaged by the royal troops who were attacking the French Prince, and his allies the barons, from whom they had just seized the castle, the Precentor Geoffrey of Deeping, evidently the Master of the Fabric, was said to have been robbed of 11,000 marks which were in his charge.[23] It seems likely from this account that despite the interdict on England pronounced by Pope Innocent III in 1209, and not lifted until 1213, the accumulation of funds, and the building of the cathedral went on unhampered.

The chapter and its community

The intrusion into a major commercial town of an episcopal household and a large clerical community, which followed hard on the heels of an incoming and even larger secular establishment in and around the castle, generated in Lincoln social and economic problems of some magnitude. From the first, given the indiscriminate charity practised, in accordance with canonical precept, in the households of many churchman, beggars of all types must have flocked to the vicinity of the cathedral. They can be seen fleetingly in the stories collected for St Hugh's process of canonisation. Simon, a blind pauper, who after begging for many years among the canons of Lincoln was cured of his affliction at St Hugh's tomb and retired to an honourable maintenance under the protection of Roger the Dean, is a good example from among many.[24] A floating mixed population of innocent countrymen, rogues, vagabonds and thieves undoubtedly moved into the town for every festival and every royal visit, and this sort of attraction exercised by the cathedral reached its peak after Hugh's death, when 'Great crowds flocked there . . . Night and day men and women holding lighted candles in their hands walked continuously in a circle round the son of light lying in their midst, forming a garland to honour and glorify the saint crowned by God.'[25]

The civil disturbances of Stephen's reign, when in 1140–1 three successive changes in the control of the castle, a full-scale siege by Stephen, and his defeat and imprisonment by Earl Ranulf of Chester, and a second, unsuccessful siege by Stephen in 1144, made the vicinity of the cathedral for a long period no better than a battleground. It is hard to detect any physical effect this may

[22] *R A* IV, 1213, 1218 to 1223, grants to the Fabric; *L CS* III, 168; *R A* IV, 1457.
[23] A Gibbons, *Liber Antiquus Hugonis de Welles*, Lincoln 1888, Vii.
[24] Farmer, 'Canonization', 99.
[25] *Magna Vita* II, 230.

have had on the cathedral building itself, but the disorder, and the destruction of property which followed the sieges undoubtedly increased the difficulties of the cathedral community. Where, in all this turmoil, did the bishop house his *familia*, always numerous, and evidently growing? Where did the first dignitaries and canons, the clerks who served them and the *ministri* and labourers who built and maintained the great church, find houses in which to live? Those dependent on the castle for shelter and maintenance were already well established in the area of its Bail, which was defined by the north, south and east gates of the upper Roman city. Within this area, it is true, some houses were available for others, and some of the canons, and many of the lesser clergy of the cathedral, besides the cathedral servants, were building, owning and living in, houses within the Bail. This we know because by one route or another their property came to form part of the cathedral endowment. As early as the middle of the twelfth century, for example, Hamo, the first known Chancellor, had acquired land near the church of All Saints in the Bail (to the north of Eastgate), and had granted part of it to a Mr Nicholas, who was related to a canon named Ilbert. On this land, Nicholas, who had meanwhile become a canon, and was also a physician, had built houses which, before the end of the twelfth century, he had granted back to the chapter.[26]

The site of the first bishop's dwelling in Lincoln is something of a mystery. After the Domesday reference to his 'little manor' of Willingthorpe, which Canon Foster assigned to the north side of the castle dyke,[27] he must soon have needed other more extensive accommodation. We do not know where Robert Bloet's palace, in which Henry of Huntingdon had his first schooling, can have stood, and he may still have been in the 'little manor', but there is no doubt that his successor Alexander found it necessary, perhaps as a result of the civil wars, to acquire from the King, for his lodging, the east gate of the Bail and its tower.[28] This too would have provided meagre enough accommodation, and before his death in 1148 Alexander had procured a fresh site to the south of the upper city wall and had laid the foundations of the Old Palace on the hillside there. Here he was close to the south side of the cathedral and had royal permission to breach the Bail wall in order to make a gate through it, facing what would be the site of the great south transept.[29] The Old Palace now clearly delimited the cathedral enclosure on its southern side, and perhaps encouraged the development of that part of the Close, and also of the hillside below it, as a domestic quarter.

By the mid-twelfth century the dignitaries had begun to build or acquire

---

[26] *R A* IX, 2494–8.
[27] *R A* I, Appendix I, where successive episcopal dwellings are described and discussed.
[28] *R A* I, 130–3.
[29] *R A* I, 137.

houses for themselves, which eventually formed part of the endowment of their successors. Before 1190 Dean Richard Fitzneal had given to the chapter a house on the north side of the cathedral which would become the nucleus of a site on which successive deans were to have their official residence until 1960. The house just within the western gate of the Close (the Exchequer Gate) which is now called the Subdeanery, was evidently acquired for the Precentor's residence about 1260, and its neighbour, the 'old' Subdeanery had served for this purpose since the mid-twelfth century. The Chancellor seems to have had no fixed abode until 1321, when he was given the site of the present Chancery.[30]

Meanwhile, individual canons were also building or acquiring houses near to the cathedral, in what would later be known as Minster Yard. At first they bought and owned the houses but later, by a series of transactions which can be traced in *Registrum Antiquissimum*, the properties came into the hands of the chapter. It is difficult to be certain that conscious decisions were made to buy up or acquire all available properties within the area. Certainly some reached the chapter as bequests, or as endowments for chantries, yet the final result was the creation of a species of ring-fence estate, from which at first at least lay owners or occupiers were excluded. The evolution of the whole area has been described by Miss Major, and she and her collaborators are now engaged in tracing the detailed history of individual properties. One such property still standing was 12 Minster Yard (Graveley Place) which Roger of Raveningham, archdeacon of Huntingdon, was occupying in 1250/1, and which, after a short spell in the occupancy of the priory of Stainfield, was in the hands of one prebendary after another until after the sixteenth century.[31] The development of Minster Yard reflects and parallels the way in which the chapter itself, and its administrative machinery, focused upon the hilltop site. It seems likely, from two passing references in charters of the mid-twelfth century, that despite the acquisition by and for dignitaries of specific houses which could be passed on to their successors, some at least of the prebendaries lived a common life together, such as could be paralleled at, for example, Beverley, in buildings known variously as the Bedern and the Common. Interestingly enough, the first mention of a cloister, just before St Hugh's pontificate began, and predating by half a century the start of the present cloister, was related to a plot close to the so-called Bedern, and evidently to be associated with it, on the south side of the Minster.[32] Here, in the Bedern, if the customs recorded by Schalby are to be trusted, common meals were taken and most of the non-liturgical business of the chapter transacted. All reference to it ceased by the thirteenth century and it

[30] K. Major, *Minster Yard*, LMP 2nd ser. 7, 1974, 5–14; *R A* III, 990.
[31] S. Jones, K. Major and J. Varley, *Survey of ancient houses in Lincoln* I, 1984, S14.
[32] *R A* IX, 2603.

may have been overtaken by buildings in individual ownership such as the Sacrist's house on the north side of the Old Palace.

Minster Yard had not always had a separate parish church to serve its lay inhabitants. Its southern and eastern boundaries, the walls of the Roman city, excluded St Margaret in Pottergate until the first breach of the walls. This was, it now seems from recent excavations, clearly made by the eastward extension of St Hugh's rebuilding about 1200, and was followed by the creation of a burial-ground close to the breach outside the cathedral, which was still in use in the later medieval period. The other 'cathedral' parish, the western end of the enclosure, St Mary Magdalen, was served, as we have seen, by a nave altar in the cathedral until the end of the thirteenth century; such burial places as it provided were at the western end of the cathedral yard. There were considerable numbers of inhabitants and parishioners to be provided for, members of the foundation and their dependants, servants of the cathedral and of the numerous great households, the keepers of shops at the west end, close to the gates, and the unspecified laymen who inhabited the many dwellings which appeared within the church yard, like so many mushrooms, during the twelfth century.[33] This lay intrusion into the enclosure was clearly no threat in the twelfth century but pressure on accommodation steadily increased and during the next century serious, and for a time successful, attempts were made to restrict the houses in Minster Yard to the occupation of those associated with, or employed in, the service of the cathedral. In about 1263–72 John de Nassington, one of the masons, granted land in the parish of All Saints in the Bail to the chapter, and when the houses built on this land were leased to one of the vicars, a clause was inserted in the lease restricting their occupation to members of the cathedral body, or those approved by the Dean and Chapter.[34]

It is not easy to decide whether there was within the cathedral precinct a building set aside for learning, a school with a local habitation. By 1400 a building later known as College House seems to have served as the Chancellor's School. Certainly some form of instruction was from the chapter's earliest days provided for young clerks associated with the cathedral. Henry of Huntingdon, who was reared in the household of Bishop Robert Bloet, named Albinus of Angers, the second Precentor, as his master, and remarks in passing on the literary distinction of Gilbert, then archdeacon of Buckingham, 'famous for both prose and verse', and of Nicholas, archdeacon of Lincoln, '*inter eruditos praeclarus*'.[35] Miss Rathbone has shrewdly remarked that from Albinus, if not from the two archdeacons, Henry had acquired considerable classical learning.

---

[33] *R A* X, 2934, 2937.
[34] *R A* IX, 2514, 2516.
[35] *Faste 1066–1300* III, 301–2.

There is no doubt that Bloet and his successors tried to recruit for the cathedral chapter the most able and learned churchmen of the day, who were expected to advise the bishops on theological and even more on legal questions.[36] Peter de Melida was a well-known legal expert of the period 1159–79 and this was certainly a continuing practice. The *familia* of Bishop Grosseteste included several canons whose function was chiefly to offer legal advice, notably John of Crakehall, later archdeacon of Bedford, and Nicholas the Greek who assisted in the Bishop's translations from the Greek.[37] The tradition persisted to the end of the medieval period in the recruitment from among the chapter of men learned in the law (*iuris periti*) to preside over the episcopal courts and especially that of the audience.

At times these legal scholars may well have lectured on the common and civil laws but the canon law was even more their subject of study, and for a time there certainly was a legal academy (one of four only in England, according to Peter of Blois (*c*.1160–1204)), at which students heard the lectures of distinguished canonists who were members of the chapter. In this connection it is known that Robert Blund, of Bologna and Oxford, was lecturing in Lincoln, where he was a prebendary in 1176. Nothing has survived, however, to suggest that this was the first step towards a well-established school.[38] On the contrary, the reputation of Lincoln as a place of higher learning was rather transitory. Some elementary instruction to fit clerks for the priesthood was provided in the cathedral or its vicinity throughout the twelfth century and the decrees of the Third Lateran Council of 1179 undoubtedly strengthened the practice. So late as the episcopate of Hugh of Wells, clerks were being told that institution to benefices would be conditional on attendance at the Cathedral School. There was also, presumably at this school, a continuing tradition of classical and literary training, and some Lincoln clerks were learned enough to write satirical verses reminiscent of Walter Maps. More advanced studies were undoubtedly intermittent, and dependent on the presence in the chapter of sufficiently able scholars willing to lecture to students. If Giraldus' account of his youth in Lincoln is to be accepted, the school was made remarkable in his time by the presence and teaching of William de Montibus.[39] William was a theologian who

---

[36] E. Rathbone, 'Intellectual influence of bishops and cathedral chapters', Ph.D. thesis, London, 1935, 150; *Fasti 1066–1300* III, 133.

[37] K. Major, '*Familia* of Robert Grosseteste', in D. A. Callus, *Robert Grosseteste, scholar and bishop*, Oxford 1955, 229.

[38] S. Kuttner and E. Rathbone, 'Anglo-Norman canonists', *Traditio* 7, 1949–51, 279–359; Rathbone, 'Intellectual influence', 309. For Robert Blund see also Giraldus, *Speculum Duorum*, ed. M. Richter *et al.*, Cardiff 1974, 57.

[39] R. W. Hunt, 'English learning in the late twelfth century', *TRHS*, 4th ser., 19, 1936, 19–42; H. Mackinnon, 'William de Montibus', in T. A. Sandquist and M. R. Powicke, *Essays in medieval*

popularised the 'new' sacramental theology in a whole series of works intended to assist the young priest and the new preacher. The works are now thought of as elementary compositions which use such popular devices as mnemonics to make their points but were, in their day, very generally attractive. William, who is said to have been born in Wigford and who had studied in Paris, where Giraldus had heard and known him, was brought to the cathedral as Chancellor by St Hugh, and it was perhaps in this time that responsibility for the cathedral schools was first assumed by the Chancellor, and had become part of his office. Most of the regular pupils of the school were lesser clergy of the cathedral and young clerks from elsewhere in Lincolnshire; those looking for more advanced teaching were beginning to go elsewhere, as William himself and Robert Burnham had done. It was only by the fortuitous presence in Lincoln of one or two able teachers that the school achieved more than local fame and, as Richard Hunt and others have said, 'One master will make a school famous and when he dies the school dies.' Thus the Law School vanished after *c*. 1175, and perhaps with the death of De Montibus in 1213, or with the end of Richard Le Graunt's period as Chancellor in 1229, the School of Theology at Lincoln undoubtedly came to an end.

The episcopal households of twelfth-century Lincoln certainly provided some literary patronage and encouragement, which intermittently attracted attention to those living and studying in Lincoln. Robert Bloet and Alexander fostered theological and legal studies, and received dedications of many treatises and poems. Even as late as Giraldus' time the tradition lingered, and something of the flavour of the household academy provided in the episcopal palace can be detected in his account of his studies at Lincoln. When his nephew was studying in Lincoln, there were plenty of scribblers at hand to take advantage of the younger man's criticism of his uncle, and there were many lively young wits in the cathedral precincts.[40]

Besides encouraging study in the schools the bishops were solicitous to provide the latest scholarly texts for the members of the chapter. In one case Bishop Chesney seems to have been so eager to add Peter Lombard's Sentences, which was a new work, to the chapter library, that he bestowed it before it had been condemned by the Council of Tours in 1163. The library so fostered was already of some size when Hamo was Chancellor, and caused a list of the books it contained to be entered in the Great Bible. This list has attracted much scholarly attention. Zachary Brooke, for example, remarked on the presence in it of the most important canon law texts of the day, including two copies of

---

history presented to Bertie Wilkinson, Toronto 1969, 32–45; F. J. E. Raby, *A history of secular Latin poetry in the middle ages* II, 90–1, 109–10.
[40] Giraldus, *Opera* VII, 1–80.

Lenfranc's False Decretals, Ivo of Chartres' work and Gratian's *Decretum*.[41] M. R. James, in contrast, thought the holdings of law and theology almost negligible, in contrast with the plentiful supply of the classics of Christian and secular learning.

Most recently Frank Barlow has written of it as 'not very impressive. What was wanted evidently was classical authors and theological collections, including Augustine, Jerome, Ambrose and Gregory the Great'. Certainly gifts of books seem not to have qualified the donors for the prayers of the foundation, and only one such gift of a book, sermons for the whole year, given by Peter, abbot of Missenden, who was Hamo's brother, is noted in the twelfth-century roll of benefactors which is entered in the Great Bible.[42] Nevertheless, almost all the books which reached the library in the twelfth century are known to have been gifts, either from bishops or from members of the foundation. The two volumes of the Great Bible itself, for example, had been given to the cathedral by Nicholas, archdeacon of Huntingdon.[43] Bishop Alexander bequeathed seven biblical texts and Bishop Robert Chesney gave nine books, which included a text of Eusebius. Other books, of various types, had been given by Archdeacon Hugh of Leicester, Jordan the Treasurer, Richard the Precentor and by Hamo himself, and by a number of prebendaries. There is evidence that the manuscripts were borrowed and read by prebendaries: one named Gerard is recorded in the library list as having borrowed and lost Boethius' *De Consolatione* and having replaced it by copies of Eutropius and Vegentius.

The responsibility for the library rested from the first on the Chancellor. At no time is there very much evidence that the chapter spent much on the library, and at this early period it was small enough to be housed in a single cupboard (*in armario*) though where the cupboard was placed has not yet been ascertained: the cloister or chapter house, when they were constructed, are the most obvious locations until a room for a separate library was at some point set aside. Such a room already existed well before 1420, when a *new* library, which survived until a fire in 1609, was constructed above the north range of the cloister, where the Wren Library now stands.

In the twelfth century the library had other functions besides the service of scholarship and it is important not to overlook them. The library list mentions

---

[41] Z. N. Brooke, *The English Church and the Papacy*, Cambridge 1931, 78, 95, 97, 106–7.

[42] The catalogue of the forty-five books found by Hamo '*in armario*' on assuming office as Chancellor, and of the volumes he himself added, was printed by R. M. Woolley, *Catalogue of the manuscripts of Lincoln cathedral library*, London 1927, v–ix; for comments Z. N. Brooke, *The English Church*; F. Barlow, *English Church 1066–1154*, London 1979, 236; the catalogue also appears in Giraldus, *Opera* VII, 153–64, and *LCS* II, ccxxxv–ccxlii. For recent comments, *Fasti 1066–1300* III, xvi.

[43] Nicholas *de Sigillo*, the successor of Henry; *Fasti 1066–1300* III, 27.

a 'little book about the foundation of the church' and a 'volume containing all the charters of the church' (thought by Canon Foster to be the so-called *Registrum pre-Antiquissimum*, fragments of which still survive) and these clearly represent part of the writings and muniments of the church for which the Chancellor was responsible, and which at this time were kept in the library. On the other hand the Martilogium, containing a copy of the customs and the Rule of St Augustine, which was read daily in chapter, remained, like the service books, homilies, missals and collects, in the Treasurer's care, while the song books (*libri de cantu*) were the responsibility of the Precentor. Overall care of most of the chapter's books, replacements of losses and regulations for borrowing, nevertheless remained the business of the Chancellor, and it is clear that from the first he regarded his responsibilities with seriousness.

The bishops within the chapter

References to the identity of the early canons and the manner and reason for their appointment, in narratives like those of Henry of Huntingdon, make it clear that for the first half-century or more of the cathedral's existence the bishops not only controlled appointments to vacancies by retaining in their own hands collations to almost all canonries (it is a pleasing touch that they signified their choice by a letter naming the new canon to be posted on the vacant stall), but, by a careful selection of canons who could act as their own clerks and advisers, maintained in the most influential part of the chapter a strong party of episcopal interest. There were, of course, times, as Dr Brett has reminded us, when the bishop's rights were denied, as in the case of a dispute about the prebend of Asgarby.[44] On another occasion when the King endowed a new prebend, such as Sutton cum Buckingham, the beneficiary for whom it was intended was actually named. Dr Brett also suggests that family and local influence must have played some part in the nomination of some canons, however earnestly the bishop maintained his claims. This perhaps explains the election of Corringham into a prebend from Brand the priest there and his son.[45] Nevertheless, episcopal relatives were numerous in the first years of the chapter, as Henry of Huntingdon recorded. William, archdeacon of Northampton, was the nephew of Bishop Alexander and David, archdeacon of Buckingham, was his brother, while Dean Simon was the son of Bishop Bloet.[46]

There were, of course, other factors which influenced the bishops' decisions in the nomination of prebendaries, and as the thirteenth and fourteenth centuries

[44] M. Brett, *English Church under Henry I*, Oxford 1975, 189, citing *R A* I, 56–9, 118, 130.
[45] *Fasti 1066–1300* III, 62, 171–2.
[46] Ibid., 30, 39–40.

passed, increased royal pressure to provide for clerks in government service pre-empted a number of prebends. In the same way papal reservation and provision absorbed many others. At the height of the system, in the early fourteenth century, there were seventy-nine successful provisions in the nine years 1305–14.[47] Almost all the men so promoted to the chapter became total non-residents, and the accounts of 1327 contain a surprising memorandum showing that the non-resident foreigners holding prebends in that year included four cardinals and eleven other Italians, besides two cardinals who were archdeacons of Oxford and Leicester and an Italian archdeacon of Buckingham.[48]

The predominance within the chapter of episcopal clerks, advisers and officials constituted a marked party at times, and this, taken in conjunction with the leading part played by the bishops in the rebuilding or refurbishing of successive phases in the cathedral building, is reflected in the cathedral customs, which, though not set down until the latethirteenth century, had crystallised a century earlier.[49] William of Malmesbury's history of the bishops (*De Gestis Pontificum*) indicates clearly the role in his cathedral church of, for example, Robert Bloet 'who adorned with most precious ornaments the church where his throne was'.[50] The customs, however, suggest a more active role for the bishop, who was to take a lead in all the divine offices, always preceding the Dean. He was to come in state for his own enthronement, and at the beginning of his first visitation of the chapter. When he returned to his diocese from a journey abroad he was to be met by all the canons in procession at the west door, and escorted by them to move to the high altar, the Dean on his right, and the next senior dignitary on his left. He had, as we have seen, a stall and also a chair or throne in the sanctuary, and at the Ash Wednesday ceremonies, and when the chrism and holy oils were consecrated he had his own special part in the proceedings. As early as 1132 he took part in the recitation of the psalter, his name being inserted in the list immediately before that of the Dean.[51]

Despite this ceremonial predominance in the chapter and the apparent respect paid to the bishop, it is clear that even so early as Robert of Chesney's time the chapter was successfully asserting its right to independence of the episcopal jurisdiction. It was at this point that the prebendal churches, and those of the Subdean and the Chancellor, were adjudged to be as free of the bishop's and archdeacons' jurisdiction as were those belonging to the canons of

---

[47] J. R. Wright, *The Church and the English Crown 1305–1344*, Toronto 1980, 24.

[48] LAO DC Bj.2.5, f. 81v.

[49] *LCS* I, 273.

[50] *Malmesbury*, 313.

[51] *LCS* II (2), 789–92; *RA* IX, 257, n. 7; *Fasti 1066–1300*, Appendix 2, 151–2.

Salisbury.[52] St Hugh supported even more effectively the rights of the chapter, declaring publicly before King Henry II that it was the right and duty of members of the chapter to elect a new bishop when a vacancy occurred, in their own chapter house, and emphasising strongly that they must and should proceed against, and even excommunicate, those who infringed their rights. At the same time he continued to regard himself as their leader, he expected them to reside personally, and was not in his own words 'mild and gentle . . . when I am presiding at chapter the least thing often rouses me to anger'.[53]

Hugh's conception of the rights of the chapter was nevertheless very strong, and is matched by a development of its role as complementary in diocesan affairs to the bishop. Already during the twelfth century many important transactions were conducted in the cathedral, in the presence of the chapter, or were confirmed by its members, and the cartularies of the religious houses of Lincolnshire include many examples of this process. Bishop William of Blois, for example, resolved in the cathedral, in the presence of the chapter, a dispute between Ralph de la Mare and the abbot and convent of Bardney about the church of Spridlington St Mary. At times gifts made to religious houses by laymen were announced before the chapter, and witnessed by its leading members, as happened with a grant of land made by William, son of Roger of Huntingfield, to Kirkstead Abbey. The synod, presided over by the Archdeacon in Lincoln cathedral, was often the occasion for the solemn announcement of such a gift. The presence of many laymen at the synod and the inclusion of a symbolic act such as the laying of his knife on the high altar by Roger Basuin, gave increased importance to his gift to Stixwold Abbey of his land in Bassingthorpe.[54]

This use by the bishop of the cathedral for his synod, and later for his visitations, and for some of the more important sessions of his courts, underlines the part it was to play as the 'mother church of the diocese'. 'Our cathedral church of Lincoln which is the mother and mistress of all other churches in the diocese of Lincoln' was how it had come to be regarded by 1321, but the process had begun very early in its history, as the story of Pentecostal offerings and processions demonstrates. This Pentecostal custom,[55] apparently Norman in origin, by which a levy was made of (say) a farthing on each hearth alight in the parish (hence the later name of smoke farthings) towards the support of the cathedral, deeply involved the inhabitants of outlying parishes once a year at least, in the affairs of the cathedral. Representatives of each parish brought

[52] *R A* I, 249–50, 253.
[53] *Magna Vita* I, 92–5, 124.
[54] *Bardney*, f. 197; *Kirkstead*, f. 179; *Stixwold*, ff. 69v, 14.
[55] Brett, *English Church*, 162–4; E E A I, 26, 116–19, 156; *R A* II, 322.

their contributions to Lincoln in a procession headed by a banner, although in a diocese the size of Lincoln the difficulties this presented must have been apparent from the start, and some decentralisation practised. As early as the mid-twelfth century the north Hertfordshire Pentecostals were being claimed by the abbot of St Albans, and the claim was acknowledged by Bishop Robert Chesney.[56] The Northamptonshire offerings may have been collected originally by Peterborough Abbey, though the archdeacon of Northampton was later responsible, and even earlier Bishop Alexander had granted the collection of Oxfordshire farthings to the abbot and convent of Eynsham. Two centuries later all archdeaconries except Lincoln and Stow were making bulk payments of Pentecostals to the chapter through the archdeacons' officials; if processions were made in those archdeaconries they went to local centres, as we know happened in Leicester, where there were fights when the men of Wigston Magna came with their procession in Whitsun week. For Lincolnshire itself, however, there is abundant evidence that local processions continued to advance upon the cathedral, bringing parishioners into the mother church and giving them boundless opportunities for jostling, rioting and disorder, which are best known from the warning injunctions of most bishops from Grosseteste onwards and are not, indeed, peculiar to this diocese.[57]

There is much less evidence about an offering known as Maricorn which it is said the chapter claimed from all parishes within Lincolnshire, and which has been identified by a few scholars as the plough alms or thraves payable to an ancient minster church. Since it is known only from two complaints about non-payment, widely spaced in time, and since, unlike Pentecostals, it makes no figure in the accounts of the common fund when these survive to be consulted,[58] its significance is doubtful. All told, the regular contributions from the diocese to the cathedral are of a token nature, and the early endowment sufficed for its maintenance until the great rebuilding, to finance which St Hugh and his successors set themselves to raise funds on a vast scale from the whole diocese. Yet even before St Hugh's time the importance of the cathedral in the life not only of the city and its two neighbouring archdeaconries, but also throughout the diocese cannot be doubted. It was, after all, the bishop's own church; here his chair was placed, and it was used by him for the benediction of abbots from every part of the diocese, occasionally for ordinations, and for every other sort of ecclesiastical ceremony. Even more, it retained a special significance for the

[56] Idem.

[57] D. M. Owen, *Church and society*, Lincoln 1971, 107; the Leicester incident is recorded in M. Bateson, *Records of the Borough of Leicester*, 3 vols., Cambridge 1899–1905, I, 375.

[58] Hill, *Medieval Lincoln*, 68, sets out the evidence; Maricorn is mentioned once later, in the register of Bishop Dalderby, LAO Ep. Reg. 3, f. 291v, when the parishioners of the north-eastern deaneries of Grimsby, Yarborough and Walshcroft had refused to pay it.

people of the city and county, and nowhere can this be seen so well as during and just after St Hugh's own lifetime. The wife of the Mayor of Lincoln prayed at his tomb, valuables were stored in the cathedral by wealthy families, hostile crowds flocked into it to ventilate their grievances against rivals and attract the Bishop's attention. The author of the *Magna Vita* recounted that on one occasion when this occurred the Bishop was in no way disconcerted but rushed between angry men clenching their fists and waving swords, and pacified them.[59]

The cathedral was particularly useful as a theatre or exhibition place for the punishment of malefactors. Penances were regularly performed there from the twelfth century onwards, and one particularly detailed mandate entered in Sutton's register describes a procedure which was plainly very well established. Sir Ranulf de Rye was sentenced, in expiation of an attack on the church of Gosberton, to join the cathedral procession at the west, or castle end of the church, and to continue with it, carrying the arms with which he had made the attack, until he reached the high altar, where he was to lay them upon the steps.[60] The significance of such a public display, at such a time, seems to have been the presence in the cathedral at procession time of large numbers of the population of the city, for whose edification it was partly intended. Similar arrangements were made when a solemn excommunication was pronounced, as in 1293, against all concerned in a sacrilegious attack on the church of Thame, where church and churchyard were desecrated. The announcement was made first in Latin, then in English, so that the congregation would understand it.[61] The lay congregation must have been particularly edified by the punishment in the cathedral in 1378 of a local clerk who was convicted of necromancy, magic arts, sorcery, spells and invocations, and who, among other things, was condemned to go barefoot and bareheaded as a penitent, before the procession there on three successive Sundays.[62]

The close link of the cathedral with diocesan life at all levels was in these ways securely forged, and would be maintained throughout the middle ages and beyond. The difficulties created by Bishop Grosseteste's claim to Visitation of the Chapter made no serious interruption in the strong bonds which united the bishop and his chapter. Formal acts of the bishop were constantly attested by the dean and some of the canons. In 1222, for example, Bishop Hugh of Wells had summoned the Dean and four canons to the outskirts of Horncastle to witness his installation of a new Master (administrator) in the Cistercian

---

[59] *Magna Vita* II, 17; Farmer, 'Canonization', 101.
[60] *Sutton* V, LRS 60, pp. 169–70.
[61] *Sutton* IV, LRS 52, pp. 104–5.
[62] LAO Ep. Reg. 12, f. 161v.

nunnery of Stainfield; it is not perhaps purely coincidence that immediately afterwards the Dean's chaplain was promoted to the living of Ewerby.[63] In 1236 the Dean and Chancellor may have served with Bishop Grosseteste as papal judges delegate in a dispute about the hospital at Brigg but there is nothing to suggest that even so early as this the bishop and the chapter had common interests and common aims.[64] When first Richard Gravesend and then Oliver Sutton, after successful terms as deans of the cathedral, became bishops of the see, the fusion of interests of the bishop and chapter might well seem to have been achieved.

Gravesend was particularly effective in his efforts to aid the chapter after he became bishop. It was he who granted a series of indulgences, between 1257 and 1266, to all who went to hear the sermons preached by members of the cathedral foundation, who contributed to the cathedral Fabric Fund, or performed other 'manual alms'.[65] This appeal especially to the people of the cathedral city was followed by a successful attempt to organise and regulate the life of the choirboys.[66] These boys had until Gravesend's time depended for their maintenance on the erratic almsgiving of members of the chapter and had no lodging: the Bishop now encouraged the chapter to assign to them the revenues of the rectory of Ashby Puerorum, and a portion of those of Hibaldstow, to provide an independent living, and a common house. In general Gravesend's relations with his chapter, like those of Sutton, were outstandingly good, and he was able to draw more members into the main stream of contemporary ecclesiastical reform by establishing vicarages in the prebendal churches and so avoiding the scandal of non-resident incumbencies.[67]

Sutton, like Gravesend, made much use of prebendaries as members of his household; his registrar, John of Schalby, of whom both Canon Foster and Professor Hill have written warmly, was also the recorder and guardian of chapter rights and chapter customs, for whose work the writer of this chapter has as good reason as Canon Foster had before her to be grateful. The chapter functionary known as Keeper of St Peter's altar (the auditor of chapter causes) was also Sutton's regular commissary in legal and administrative matters, not only in Lincoln but throughout the diocese and indeed, Sutton's register, the first surviving record of diocesan memoranda, which thanks to Schalby is unusually full and interesting, bears witness to the Bishop's constant effort to fortify and preserve the rights of the chapter.[68]

[63] Wells III, LRS 9, pp. 127, 138.
[64] Grosseteste, LRS 11, p. 9.
[65] R A II, 408–20.
[66] R A II, 429–30.
[67] Gravesend, LRS 20, pp. 209, 210–11, 225, 232, 254.
[68] Sutton III, LRS 48, pp. xiiii–lxxxvi, 180, 183–4; LMP 4.

The very strong concern of the bishops of the twelfth and thirteenth centuries with the repair, maintenance and replacement of the cathedral building is, of course, best represented by, or best known from, the Life of St Hugh, but in fact Hugh's work was only completed by Hugh of Wells, who ruled the diocese from 1209 to 1235. It was left to Bishop Henry of Lexington to initiate the repairs needed after the fall of the central tower in Grosseteste's time, and to begin to build the Angel Choir so as to provide a fitting new shrine for St Hugh. Much the most important element in St Hugh's contribution to the cathedral fabric was his posthumous sanctity, which attracted pilgrims and gifts, at first in dazzling profusion, even before his formal canonisation in 1219. The chapel of St John Baptist in the north-east transept of the choir where he was first buried had been enlarged, but could not accommodate the droves of pilgrims who came to venerate, and offer at the tomb. The Angel Choir was therefore begun to provide a more suitable setting for his shrine, and the body was translated to a new tomb which lay in the full centre of the Lady Chapel, behind the reredos of the new high altar. There were now two shrines, for the saint's head had been detached from the body in the process of translation, and was now replaced in St John's Chapel in the north-east transept, in a new and very impressive setting.[69] Both shrines were richly jewelled and were despoiled at the Reformation, but the fabric of the principal tomb survived until the mid-seventeenth century, when Bishop Sanderson recorded that he saw in 1640 'a beautiful shrine of Bishop Saint Hugh of great height in pyramidal fashion'.[70]

It was, no doubt, the success of St Hugh's cult which prompted the various unsuccessful efforts made by the chapter to procure the canonisation first of Grosseteste and then of Dalderby, the records of which have been discussed and published by Canon R. E. G. Cole and Dr Eric Kemp. The tombs of both bishops continued, without benefit of canonisation, to attract pilgrims and offerings, and to maintain their separate chantries.[71] The Dalderby shrine stood in the great south transept, on its western side, and was soon marked by a silver chest which was paid for by the offerings of those coming to the shrine to enjoy the

[69] E. Venables, 'Shrine and head of St Hugh', *Archaeological Journal* 50, 1893, 37–61; an original view was presented in the 1985 Grosseteste lectures by John Bailey, 'The struggle and the light, the built legacy of St Hugh'.

[70] Bishop Sanderson in Browne Willis, *Survey of the cathedrals of Lincoln, Ely, Oxford and Peterborough*, London 1730, 8.

[71] R. E. G. Cole, 'Proceedings, relative to the canonization of Robert Grosseteste bishop of Lincoln', *AASR* 33, 1915–16, 1–28, and 'Proceedings relative to the canonization of John Dalderby', *AASR* 33, 1915–16, 243–76; E. W. Kemp, *Canonization and authority*, Oxford 1947, 120–1; David Stocker has recently discussed Grosseteste's tomb, in W. M. Ormerod, ed., *England in the thirteenth century*, Woodbridge 1986, 143–8.

benefits of an indulgence proclaimed by Dalderby's successor, Henry Burghersh. Very soon chaplains were assigned by the chapter to 'keep the tomb' and a special office was devised, fragments of which have been preserved by J. F. Wickenden.[72]

Johannes Lincolnie
Presul Christo care
Vas divine gratie
Nomen habens a re
Gemine sciencie
Doctor nos dignare
Precibus milicie
Celi sociare
O doctor tuos famulos dignare tueri . . .

It might also be permissible to see a similar motive in the rescue and burial by the chapter, in 1255, of the body of the child Hugh, who was allegedly the victim of a Jewish ritual murder. His tomb in the south choir aisle was much visited by pilgrims during the rest of the thirteenth century and though its popularity declined as memories of the Jews faded after their expulsion, 'St Hugh junior' continued to exercise some drawing power until the end of the fourteenth century at least. The story has been thoroughly discussed by Sir Francis Hill in *Medieval Lincoln* and the tomb and its history have recently been described by D. A. Stocker.[73]

FOURTEENTH AND FIFTEENTH CENTURIES

The administration of the chapter

Offerings at all the shrines came twice each year, on the morrow of St Denis (9 October) and at Pentecost, into the hands of the Provost of the Common Fund, and the money provided by the *aperture* (openings) of the boxes fixed next to the shrines for the gift of pilgrims forms a continuous feature of his accounts. He in his turn paid for fresh embellishments of the shrines, such as a new coffin lid for St Hugh, with images in gold and silver, which was ordered from the London goldsmiths in 1310.[74] The Provost was also required to distribute part of the offerings to the 'staff' of the cathedral and the list of recipients of these monies in 1334 provides a convenient *aperçu* of the complicated community which by the beginning of the fourteenth century had grown up in and around

---

[72] *Archaeological Journal* 40, 1863, 215–24.
[73] Hill, *Medieval Lincoln*, 224–32; D. A. Stocker, 'The shrine of Little St Hugh' BAA, 1982, 321.
[74] Venables, 'Shrine', 43.

the cathedral.[75] The offerings were to be divided among the twelve canons then keeping the Great Residence, the Keeper of the altar of St Peter (that is the Provost of the Common Fund), two other canons, the priest celebrating at the shrine of St Hugh, with his chaplain, deacon, sub-deacon, and eight singers, the two principal shrine-keepers with their chaplain and clerks, the day keeper of the shrine and head, with his clerk, the two night keepers, the vicars choral, four clerks, the choirboys, the Succentor, the Sacrist and his clerk, the Clerk of the Common, the Chapter Clerk, the Clerk of the Fabric, the Masters of the Grammar and Song Schools, the master masons and carpenters, two thurifers, the organ-blower, the door-keeper of the Close, the candle-lighter, the sweeper, the bell-ringers, the candle-maker, two clerks 'who rouse the people' and the clerk 'who brings the dove'.

Nothing displays so well as this list the elaboration of chapter administration and liturgical practice which had been reached by the early fourteenth century, which it now becomes necessary to examine in more detail. The Lincoln chapter, with its five *persone*, the greater residentiaries, and its body of prebendaries was apparently completely established before the end of the twelfth century but at no point is it clear when its members laid down the rules by which their own lives, and that of the cathedral, were governed until the nineteenth century. Dr Diana Greenway has recently discussed in full the uncertainties and variations to be found within the chapters of English secular cathedrals, in relation to the so-called foundation document of St Osmund for his new cathedral at Salisbury.[76] She concludes that there, at least, the elaboration of custom came belatedly and gradually, and the same must have been true at Lincoln. Here, as we have seen, the first version of the customs was set down in 1214 for the instruction of the new chapter at Moray, but the copy preserved at Lincoln is embedded in further elaborations of the thirteenth century, which were unravelled by Henry Bradshaw in the first volume of *Lincoln Cathedral Statutes*. There is no sign that at this stage of the cathedral's development any received body of statutes was formulated by a bishop, or any other external authority. Instead a series of customs, some of which, as we have seen, were liturgical practices, perhaps imitated from Rouen, were gradually adopted. Their principal objects were the maintenance of liturgical life and the business administration of the chapter, in the circumstances in which dignitaries and prebendaries alike had the cure of their prebendal churches and other ecclesiastical and secular duties to take them away from Lincoln, and hinder their constant residence there.

Thus, it seems plain, the central feature of the custom of the cathedral must

---

[75] Ibid.
[76] Greenway, 'False *Institutio*'.

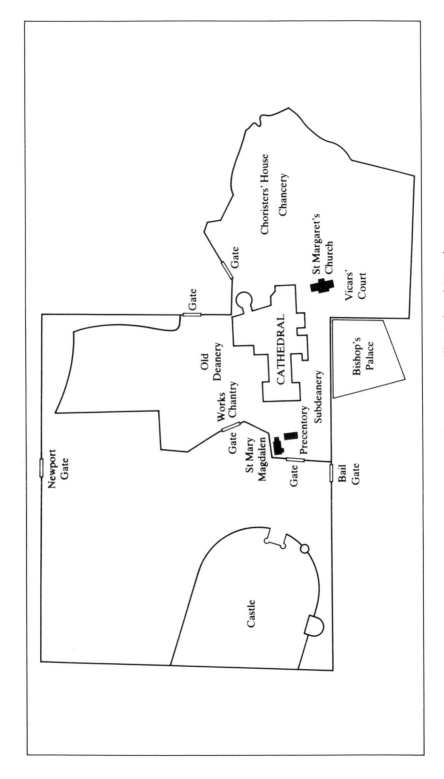

7   *The Minster Yard and the upper city c.1300, after J. W. F. Hill, Medieval Lincoln*

from an early time have been the arrangements arrived at for residence at Lincoln. The *persone* or dignitaries (the Dean, Precentor, Chancellor, Treasurer and Subdean), each of whom had his own specific area of responsibility within the chapter, were bound to continual residence, although their interpretation of what constituted residence was often varying and ambiguous. The prebendaries, after installation, had an initial period of residence during which, in form at least, they served their weeks as hebdomadary canon in choir. Then they would make a choice between living away from Lincoln and, presumably, serving their prebendal churches or engaging in secular affairs, and 'protesting' in chapter their intention to 'make the greater residence', which would oblige them to be in Lincoln for two-thirds of the year for the following few years. After their period of greater residence came to an end they might make the lesser residence of one-third of the year. Only by the formal protestation of residence in chapter could the prebendaries obtain a voice and a vote in chapter, and it is scarcely surprising therefore that prebendaries who had been completely non-resident for many years, and absent on royal or episcopal service, should towards the end of their lives return to retirement and the greater residence, as John of Schalby did.

The non-resident's place in the liturgical duties of the cathedral came very soon to be supplied by a vicar, whom at first he appointed and paid himself. After the time of Pope Alexander III (1159–81) and St Hugh, the vicars were apparently supported by the Common Fund, for the chapter had been empowered by episcopal and papal authority to make a levy of one-seventh of the income of all non-residents, known as septisms, to meet the charge.[77] These vicars, who were themselves continually present in Lincoln, often served as witnesses of charters and holders of offices. They could be recruited as shrine-keepers, chaplains, sacrists, succentors and even clerks of the Common and Fabric Funds. Before the end of the twelfth century they already represented an important property-owning group within the cathedral community and had received many gifts of land, houses and rent charges. They were to be organised by Bishop Sutton into a community, with a common life in a collegiate building close to the gates of the Palace, which survives today as Vicars' Court.[78]

Meanwhile, a newly constituted residentiary found for himself, or from the end of the thirteenth century had assigned to him, a residence within easy reach of the cathedral, and invited his fellow residentiaries, his *confratres*, to eat bread with him there, as a ceremonial introduction to his life. Then he settled to residentiary life, which was taken up by attendance at the daily hours and chapter meetings, by the reading of a chapter or singing of a verse in choir, if

---

[77] R A I, 257.
[78] L A O V C 2.1, *passim*; A. R. Maddison, *Vicars choral of Lincoln cathedral*, London 1878.

the Precentor or Chancellor assigned this to him, and by the regular duty of acting as hebdomader (canon of the week), either in his own turn or to fill the place of a non-resident. His prebendal church, meanwhile, was served by a competently endowed vicar, at least after Gravesend's time. Changes of residence were carefully noted by a clerk of Re[deundi] and Ve[niendi] who kept a roll on which were based the payments of the daily commons and the calculations of the dividend or share of the residue of the common fund which each might receive at the year's end. Dr Kathleen Edwards has calculated from the accounts of the common fund for the year 1304–5 that eleven prebendaries, including the Chancellor, Treasurer, Subdean and the Archdeacon of Stow, made the greater residence, and there were forty non-residents who were assessed for septisms. Six of the non-residents were with the Bishop, one was Royal Treasurer and seven others, who had been papally provided, were still at the Roman curia.[79]

An average of twelve or thirteen canons continued to make the greater residence throughout the fourteenth century, but by 1420 the number had dropped to seven. Those who resided, if they were administrators, lawyers, scholars, or preachers, or even if they were no more than adequate social entertainers, found plenty of scope for their talents in the service of the cathedral or the diocese. Many were book-owning scholars and a few came later to be Fellows of Oxford or Cambridge colleges. As residentiaries they had the laborious discipline of the Office, Matins at midnight or 5 a.m. according to the season, followed by Lauds, the Lady Mass at 9 a.m., followed by Tierce, High Mass at 10 a.m., Sext and nones, before breakfast at midday, Evensong at 3.00 p.m., Vespers and Compline, supper at 6.00 p.m. and curfew. Festivals of varied complexity prolonged the day and when the residentiary was hebdomadary canon he himself celebrated Mass at the high altar on those days. In his week of duty the hebdomadary had also the heavy duty of hospitality. Each day he provided meals for a hebdomadary deacon and subdeacon and a vicar choral. On Sunday he entertained the choir to midday dinner, except on the greater festivals when the Dean himself entertained the whole choir.[80]

The regular habit for all who took part in the choir service was a black cope of plain Deuxsevers cloth, worn over a surplice, with an almuce lined with fur. Festivals, processions, and certain of the canonical hours called for silken copes, and arrangements for the changes, which were already customary when Schalby was writing, are set out clearly in the Black Book.[81]

[79] K. Edwards, *English secular cathedrals in the middle ages*, Manchester 1949, Appendix 1, 'Canonical residence at Lincoln during the fourteenth century', 334–6.
[80] C. Wordworth, *Notes on medieval services*, 1898, 262.
[81] Ibid., 128–9.

The complexity of the ritual life in which the residentiaries played their part was firmly established by Gravesend's time, when, for fear of unsuitable innovations and 'for the memory of old men and the information of young ones' the customs of the church were first set down in writing.[82] It is not of great moment whether they derive from Bayeux or Rouen, but it is important to note that they have certain features which have been very long-lasting. The bells, for example, were continually marking the hours, as in a manner they still do, and the three bell-ringers, otherwise known as the lay sacrist, the lighter of candles on the high altar, and the lighter of the choir candelabra, were sworn, on taking office, to ring the bells at all the prescribed times. Due reverence was very carefully observed. All on entering or leaving the choir bowed to the Dean in his stall. When a canon entered, all who sat on his side except the Dean rose. On entering choir everyone bowed to the altar before the steps. Those crossing the choir bowed to the altar, and always bared their heads. The processions on Sundays and semi-double feasts set out from the choir, proceeded along the southern aisle as far as the westernmost column of the nave, and then returned along the northern side. The choir and vicars came first, followed by the rest of the foundation with three cross-bearers, a holy-water carrier, three light-bearers, two thurifers, three clerks carrying relics, a subdeacon bearing before his breast the Gospels, bound in silver and gold with images of the crucifix, John and Mary, a deacon bearing before his breast a silver and gold crucifix, the celebrant at Mass, and two servers. The continued importance of these processions is underlined by the fact that stones were fixed in the floor of the nave to mark the places of the participants before the return to the choir was made. Bishop Alnwick asked in his will to be buried on the north side of the nave close to the stone where he regularly stood in the processions and these stones are said to have remained visible until the repaving of 1782.[83] The ritual importance attached to the regular processions is emphasised by one of the charges against Dean Macworth that he would not walk in line after the canon in the last rank during the procession.

Other more elaborate processions inside and outside the church marked special occasions, and none was more imposing than that which escorted Bishop Sutton's corpse from Nettleham, where he died, to burial in the cathedral.

On the same Saturday all the canons rode to the place [Nettleham] and after a spoken commendation of the spirit his relatives and noble neighbours carried the bier on their shoulders for half the journey, their resting place being now marked by a cross. Meanwhile the canons then hastened to the cathedral so as to robe themselves to meet

---

[82] LCS I, 69–71.
[83] Wordsworth, *Notes*, 261–2.

the corpse in the traditional way and after a little time the relatives again took up the bier and carried it as far as the city gate. Here the leading citizens claiming this as their right, took it up on their shoulders and carried it to the cathedral door.[84]

The ceremonial meals of the hebdomadary week and, even more, those prescribed for the great feasts are also provided for in great detail. Each canon was to take with him his chaplain or clerk and his squire, who were to carry each his own cup and knife. All were to stand until grace had been said if the bishop or dean were present. It is no doubt from an occasion of such overwhelming protocol that St Hugh escaped by his offer to bury the cathedral mason's brother and three other corpses.[85]

Some of the provisions for the ritual life were in part the concern of the Chancellor, who was to arrange for, or to preach in person, courses of sermons which were associated with the Palm Sunday, Ascension Day and Rogation Day processions, when the preacher stood at the various stations visited by the Host, and when presumably there was a great concourse of citizens. By 1432 it was the Vice-Chancellor who wrote on his board the names of those to read the lessons. There were other recurring ceremonies provided for by the customs: the procession of the deacons at Christmas and St John, the festivals of Holy Innocents led by a boy bishop, and the descent of a dove from the church roof at Pentecost. The Treasurer's duties were central to much of this activity: he was charged with the provision and care of the clock, the lights, the bell ropes, and the necessaries for Mass (cruets, thuribles, water and wine), as well as the strewing of rushes for the floor.

The maintenance of this great establishment and of the cathedral building itself had, it seems, been arranged and systematised before the end of the twelfth century. The Common Fund had by this time emerged as the machinery by which the regular needs of the cathedral and chapter were met.

The acquisition of this endowment is recorded in detail in *Registrum Antiquissimum*; its surviving accounts begin in the late thirteenth century and its expenditure can be clearly traced, as Miss Major has demonstrated.[86] Its income came from the endowments of a series of churches, in land and tithes, that is to say, rectories, from four manors in lay fee, from house rents, tithe portions, the endowments of chantries and obits, from pensions ordained by the bishop as compensation for lost revenues when he authorised a religious house to appropriate a rectory to its own uses, from the Pentecostal pennies of the laity, the septisms collected from non-resident canons, and the offerings at all shrines within the church. The total income in 1318 was £999.11s.5½d. Out of this,

---

[84] LCS II, cxxii.
[85] Magna Vita II, 80.
[86] K. Major, 'The finances of the Dean and Chapter of Lincoln', *JEH* 5, 1954, 149–67.

1   *General view of Lincoln Minster from the south west*

2   *View through the vestibule into the chapter house, looking east*

4 *Romanesque frieze above the south niche: 'Daniel in the "lions" den'*

3 *Romanesque frieze above the south niche: 'Noah's ark'*

5 *Decorated screen between the main crossing and St Hugh's Choir, looking east*

6   *Angle of the north aisle and the north-east transept, looking north west*

7   *South gallery of St Hugh's Choir: the inner wall of the central bay*

8 *North-west transept, north facade*

9   *South aisle of St Hugh's Choir, looking east*

10 *North side of the Angel Choir, second bay from the east: an angel with crowns*

11 *South side of the Angel Choir, the Judgment Portal tympanum: Christ blessing, and displaying the wounds of the crucifixion*

12 *South-east corner of the cloister, looking north west*

13 *Romanesque west block: second-floor chamber on the north side, showing the deformed entrance to the former stairway*

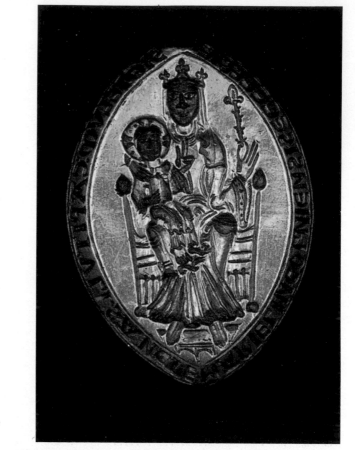

14 *Silver matrix of the second chapter seal, attributed by T. A. Heslop to about 1150–60. Dean and Chapter of Lincoln*

15 *Drawing of the Works Chantry, Eastgate*

16 The first donors' list of the cathedral library, entered on the flyleaf of the Great Bible, Lincoln cathedral library no. 1 f. 2

17   *The Wren Library*

18   *The 'Father Willis' console, 1894*

19   *The organ from the choir*

20   *Organ-blower Tommy Dodd, c.1895*

21   *J. M. W. Young*

22   *G. J. Bennett*

as we have seen, the offerings at shrines were distributed among the members of the foundation. Beyond this were the annual fees which were paid to the staff of the Fund: the Provost, a canon from the fourteenth century onwards, was elected annually by the chapter, but might well serve the office for many years, and the clerk, who between them administered all the business of the Fund. There were also payments to the keeper of the high altar, the janitor of the Close, the watcher of the church and to a number of chantry chaplains. Less predictable payments went in purchases of wax, cloth for liveries and for distribution as alms (*les duddes*), timber for the repair of houses and farm buildings (which was seasoned in the Galilee garth), repairs and new furniture for the churches of the common. In 1318 at the audit which was kept on the Monday after the feast of the Exaltation of the Holy Cross (14 September) there remained a surplus of £220 to be divided among the eleven residentiaries.

There are no such detailed accounts for the Fabric Fund, although it is known that before the end of the twelfth century there was a chest (*arca*) into which alms for the repair of the church were put, and that a canon and a layman accounted for it, but by the fourteenth century two canons were elected annually at the audit to be Keepers (later Masters) of the Works, and accounted for the contents.[87] They also accounted for the income from some endowments, although since this fund had started later than that of the common, these were neither numerous nor large, and consisted chiefly of houses and rent charges in Lincoln. A characteristic Fabric property, which can be identified and traced in the late medieval rentals, was the building known as St Andrew's Row in Wigford. It had begun in the fourteenth century with a rent-charge payable from St Andrew's Hall, a Norman house once owned by Philip Marmiun of Scrivelsby, to the obit of John de Sutton.[88] Another was a former Jewish property in Dernstall, which after the banishment of the Jewish community passed to the Fabric as part of the endowment of Henry Welbourne's Chantry, and was ultimately known as the Cardinal's Hat.[89] The Fabric Fund also benefited handsomely from bequests from testators in every part of the diocese. In 1293 the archdeacons of Oxford and Buckingham were permitted by Bishop Sutton to assist in the collection of alms for Dorchester Abbey, provided that they did not thereby prejudice the cathedral Fabric Fund. In the same year the collectors of alms for a hospital at Anagni were warned not to interfere with either crusading alms or the cathedral Fabric Fund and in 1297 Sutton urged on the rural deans of the whole diocese the obligation to exercise greater diligence

[87] R A X, 295.
[88] C. L. Exley and D. M. Williamson, 'Some notes on St Andrew's Hall, Wigford', *LAASR* 6, 1955–6, 118–20.
[89] J. W. F. Hill, W. A. Pantin *et al. The cardinal's hat*, Lincoln 1953.

in the collection of legacies.[90] The moral obligation to arrange a bequest to the cathedral fund continued to work on all makers of wills in the diocese until the sixteenth century, fortified by repeated indulgences which waived forty days of penance to all so contributing. Testators in sixteenth-century Bedfordshire were still leaving small legacies to 'the red chest of the fabric' in the last few years before the Reformation.[91] How much these bequests and contributions produced, or how the money was spent is not now known. The two Masters of the Fabric, who were elected annually from among the residentiaries, supervised its administration and it is clear that the Treasurer of the chapter often had a considerable hand in it, either by personal gifts or by influencing decisions. It is known that Thomas of Louth (Treasurer 1321–9) provided the first clock in 1324 and Treasurer Henry of Welbourne (1349–81) is credited with the provision of a new clock for the cathedral, with the installation of the statues of the kings on the west front, with the making of the canopies of the choir-stalls (which still remain) and with the insertion of new vaulting under the central and west towers.[92] Since the benefactors of the Fabric enjoyed the benefits of the prayers of the foundation, by the agency of the Fabric or Works Chantry, and since the Fabric Masters published each year the indulgences proclaiming these and other benefits for donors, there was undoubtedly a steady flow of legacies and gifts.[93]

The beginning of the fourteenth century had marked an important stage in our knowledge of the internal history of the cathedral for the systematic records of Chapter Acts and, as we have seen, of the finances of the Common Fund survive. As Miss Major has pointed out, it is possible to reconstruct some of the earlier financial and economic history of the chapter, at least for the thirteenth century, from conveyances, leases and grants in fee, which survive either in originals or in the *Registrum Antiquissimum*, but with the start of the annual accounts of the Clerk of the Common, in the last decade of the century, a more systematic view can be taken.[94]

As we have already seen, the Common revenues were distributed and accounted for, at the audit on Holy Cross Day, by the Clerk of the Common, who was not usually a canon, and nominally at least acted under the supervision of the Provost. This last office, which had certainly existed since the late twelfth century, was said by John of Schalby to include responsibility for the chapter's daily seal, and for one key of the Great Seal; the Provost examined and acted on the daily correspondence of the chapter, kept the charters and muniments,

---

[90] Sutton IV, LRS 52, pp. 43, 56, 70.
[91] A. F. Cirket, *English wills 1498–1526*, BHRS 37, 1957, *passim*.
[92] Venables, 'Shrine'.
[93] Edwards, *English secular cathedrals*, 235 and n.
[94] Finances, *passim*.

oversaw the Clerk's distribution of the revenue and twice in the year visited the churches of the common.[95] The Clerk himself, working from the Common Chamber, which can still be seen between the chapter house and the northeast transept, received rents, held the audit, supervised the work of subordinate clerks like him of *Re* and *Ve*. It was he who arranged for the repair of chapter houses, inside the Close and beyond; he reported on dilapidations in the Close and in the various chapter properties, to the leases or farms of which the prebendaries in residence succeeded in turn. He also procured new fittings, furniture, and books for the cathedral life. When the Provost made his tourn or visitation the Clerk went too, to receive rents, view dilapidations and record the proceedings of the secular and ecclesiastical courts held during the tourn. Side by side with the Clerk of the Common worked the Keeper of St Peter's altar, who was the auditor of the chapter court and incidentally often an episcopal commissary. It was he who gave legal advice and prepared the chapter's brief in the various legal causes in which it was embroiled.

The Chapter Clerk seems from the mid-thirteenth century to have taken on the secretarial duties, letter-writing and act-keeping that had originally been performed by the Chancellor, and became an important member of the group which now maintained the administration. Many of the holders of these offices, and notably Richard of Stretton II, progressed by a series of professional steps culminating in the provostship and often a canonry, serving the chapter almost continuously for more than twenty years. The provision of this sort of ladder of promotion is indeed one of the more important, though not much noticed, contributions of the secular cathedrals to the clerical profession in the later middle ages; Lincoln, with its wealth, and the complexity of its system, had a very large share in this.[96]

The Act Books of the chapter survive as an almost continuous series from the early fourteenth century; some earlier chapter decisions are recorded in the copies entered by John of Schalby in his Martilogium, while he was a residentiary, and it is possible to reconstruct from them something of the main preoccupations of chapter life.[97] The buzzing gossiping world of the community of the Close, the continual visits of laymen from the town and the country, the presence in all ranks in the church of mischief-makers wishing to profit from daily business, made secrecy essential. The scribe was required to take an oath of secrecy and at times, as in 1408, the watcher and other cathedral servants

[95] LCS II, 168.
[96] K. Major, 'Office of Chapter Clerk,' in M. V. Ruffer and A. J. Taylor, *Medieval studies presented to Rose Graham*, Oxford 1950, 163–88.
[97] D. M. Williamson, *Lincoln muniments*, LMP 8, 1956.

were warned to expel lay persons from the chapter house after the Dean and Chapter had entered and the door had been closed.[98]

The chapter proceedings have some constants: corrections of vicars and other clerks, and of the inhabitants of chapter parishes, haphazard entries of leases and grants of land, records of gifts such as the new clock given by Thomas of Louth in 1324,[99] collations to the masterships of grammar schools in the county, and to the chantries and churches of the common, admissions and protestations of residence of the canons, and petitions by the newly admitted to succeed to the hospice of their predecessors, examinations and admissions of choristers.

At intervals particular emergencies called for a specific order: in 1385 chantry-priests were warned to take their places in all processions, and then and later the affairs of the Song School, the Cathedral Grammar School and its relation with the town school, were dealt with.[100] The lay sacrist's duties were defined in 1409; casting light on social grades within Minster society. It was emphatically declared to be the office not of a gentleman, but of a valet, and he was not to bear a mace except before the Treasurer, who was his master. It was his business to pull the bells, and cut up and restore old vestments.[101] In 1403 there was an informative elucidation of the consuetudinary in relation to the feeding of ministers by the residentiary canon on Sundays: the Vice-Chancellor, the Chapter Clerk, the Clerk and Writer of the Common Chamber, the Clerk of the Fabric, the lay sacrist, the Keeper of St Hugh's tomb, and the cathedral janitor were alone entitled to this meal.[102] In 1425 the holy-water carrier complained that his right to carry holy water to the canons in their houses was being usurped by John Luminour, Roger Couper and William Hundon, officers of the parishes of St Margaret and St Mary Magdalen.[103] Infrequently it is possible to catch the tone of actual discussions: in 1439, for instance, the Chancellor and the Archdeacons of Oxford and Huntingdon, with three other canons, opposed the Precentor's attempt to control the appointment of choristers, and again in 1443, an order was made for the removal of the iron gates hanging between the altar and the aisle on the north side because they seemed unsuitable (*inhoneste*) in the opinion of many. Details of disciplinary action are also given on occasion: in 1443 proceedings against Robert Buy, chaplain of the Ravenser Chantry, who had been accused of adultery with the wife of a layman living in the Close and had purged himself, ended with the

---

[98] LAO DC A.2.30, f. 7.
[99] Ibid., A.2.23, f. 4.
[100] Ibid., A.2.27, ff. 7, 31; A.2.29, ff. 27v. -28; A.2.30, f. 4.
[101] Ibid., A.2.30, f. 14.
[102] Ibid., A.2.29, f. 5v.
[103] Ibid., A.2.31, f. 23v.

advice to abjure suspect places, especially the hospice in which the Countess of Westmoreland used to live (4–5 Pottergate).[104]

The obligations and demands involved in the ownership by the chapter of landed and house property and churches, and in responsibility for the community of clerks in and around the cathedral enclosure, forced upon it the provision of a legal forum, a court, to hear cases and complaints arising from their tenants and the clerks. As early as 1219 the Crown had given a form of recognition to this necessity: in that year the chapter was permitted to hear pleas of the Crown and other assizes and to receive and return royal writs concerning thc prebends of Welton, and the manors of Asgarby and Friesthorpe 'at the door of the church', and was still exercising this right in 1256, doubtless in the Galilee Porch at the south end of the south-west transept.[105] Here, in the room above the Galilee Porch, a species of court leet had also developed, and after 1263 its suitors were declared to include the four statutory servants of the church (the carpenters and glazier) and their wives. This year saw the drawing up of an elaborate composition with the town authorities which defined the elements of the jurisdictional liberty. Those able to claim it, as tenants or servants of the cathedral, were to be free of all town jurisdiction, and of all duties of watch, except during wars and sieges; they need not make oath or presentments at assizes, they were to be free of all tallages and contributions levied by the city; they were not liable to 'aletol' and 'backestrigeld' (fines for permission to brew and bake) in the city, and they could not be called on to answer any pleas or causes except of possession, land or bloodshed, outside their own court.[106]

The chapter also claimed and exercised ecclesiastical jurisdiction in the cathedral and its enclosure, and in all the churches belonging to the common fund. Twice each year the Provost of the Common made a tourn of the outlying churches to visit the parishioners, inspect the fabrics and prove wills. Cases arising from the misdemeanours detected on the tourns were usually resolved on the spot, although they appear occasionally among the deliberations of the chapter, along with similar causes concerning the inhabitants of Minster Yard. Defaulting cantarists, lecherous vicars, and the occasional practitioner of magic are the staple of the court's hearings, along with neglectful churchwardens failing to repair roofs or provide service books. The chapter itself plainly took very seriously its own responsibilities and obligations to its churches. The careful provisions made for the ordination of a vicarage in Bottesford demonstrate this, as do the frequent details of expenditure on the churches

---

[104] Ibid., A.2.33, ff. 8v, 54, 56v.
[105] R A II, 597–8.
[106] R A III, 963.

themselves.[107] Chancels at Hainton, Wellingore and Castle Bytham were all reconstructed at the chapter's expense in the second half of the fourteenth century, and there were continual purchases of ornaments, vestments and books for all the chapter's churches.[108]

Vicars choral, cantarists and minor clergy

We have seen that every non-resident prebendary was obliged to provide and maintain a vicar to serve in his place; the numbers of such vicars were already great before 1200; they undoubtedly bore the heat and burden of the day in the progressive elaboration of the daily services, and became an important and useful element in the cathedral foundation. It is clear that a few non-resident prebendaries were already providing vicars to supply their place in choir before the beginning of St Hugh's pontificate. Chaplains, who may well be the ancestors of vicars, occur in the witness lists of cathedral charters in the first half of the century but it was two grants by St Hugh which for the first time enjoined upon all non-resident prebendaries the duty of providing a vicar to serve their place and at the same time laid on the chapter the obligation to select and approve the men chosen.[109] Small properties had been granted to the support of the vicars from about 1200 (there is a surviving cartulary of their properties) and in 1280 Dean Oliver Sutton assigned to the vicars the control of the decayed hospital of St Giles outside Lincoln, to provide for the retirement of their aged fellows.[110] Then in 1293 Sutton, now bishop, allotted to the vicars a site on the south side of the cathedral (the Boungarth) to allow them to build a common hall and dwellings. He still further helped the project by a bequest in his will, and the work was finally completed almost a century later by Bishop John Buckingham. At first only the senior vicars (priests) of the first form were accommodated in the new building, but in 1328 a dwelling was provided by the chapter on the same site for the junior vicars (acolytes, subdeacons and deacons) of the second form.[111] The vicars were not yet a corporation but they elected annually two provosts, one from each form, to administer their common property and the income received from the chapter.

Similar provision had already been made by Bishop Gravesend for the choristers who had depended on the alms of the canons, and been subject to the rule of the precentor. Now Gravesend arranged for them to live (there were to

---

[107] R A II, 534; Hill, *Medieval Lincoln*, 214; R A II, 5–34.
[108] Finances, *passim*.
[109] R A I, 300, 301.
[110] R A III, 1049; X, 2867–8.
[111] L A O D C A.2.23, f. 9.

be twelve of them) in a common hall on the east side of Minster Yard.[112] A series of small grants of pensions and tithe portions followed, and the endowment was completed by Bishop Sutton's appropriation in 1289 to the Dean and Chapter of the rectory of Ashby Puerorum for the maintenance of the choir boys.[113] A mysterious grant by the prior and convent of Caldwell in 1264 to the twelve wax-bearers and incense-bearers, of a pension of 2 marks, is perhaps also intended for the choir boys, whose various functions it seems to reflect.[114]

A further foundation provided for the Poor Clerks, whose numbers provided the servers at masses and from among whom the vicars were often recruited. For them, too, Sutton provided a house, which seems now to be represented by 3 Minster Yard, and arranged for their regular attendance at the grammar school.[115] These foundations for choir boys and Poor Clerks symbolise the eastward movement of the cathedral yard, once the Angel Choir and the new east end were completed, and the cathedral enclosure finally walled. They also concentrate, in a small area, a considerable number of young people, clerks and others, with inevitable problems for the future.

Meanwhile, a whole series of chantries had been founded within the cathedral and so many were they, and so elaborate and varied their statutes, that it became necessary to compile a special cartulary of chantries, the *Liber Cantariarum*, to record them. Some of these chantries, because they required cantarists who were explicitly not vicars, augmented the clerical population round the cathedral, while some others provided further occupation and emoluments for the more fortunate of the vicars. The earliest of them, the Works Chantry, seems to have been founded, as we have seen, in the time of Bishop William of Blois, perhaps with an informal origin in St Hugh's time, to pray for the souls of benefactors to the Fabric. Its altar was in the most northerly chapel on the east side of the great south transept, where the cantarists are still depicted in the spandrels of the door. Its priests, perhaps four in number, were housed in a large and commodious house, which remained until the early nineteenth century, on a site to the west of the Old Deanery. The Masters of the Fabric administered this chantry, although at times a layman was associated with them in the early days. There were a number of other chantry foundations soon after this. Hugh of Wells endowed in 1232 a chantry for St Hugh at the altar close to his tomb, endowing it with pensions from the episcopal churches of Paxton and Great Carlton and a bovate of land at Owersby.[116] It was to be

---

[112] Jones *et al.*, *Survey of ancient houses* I, S12.
[113] R A II, 429, 445, 449–51, 454.
[114] R A II, 405.
[115] Jones *et al.*, *Survey of ancient houses* I, S4.
[116] R A II, 360, 363.

served by a priest, deacon and subdeacon from among the vicars, the priest to receive 4*d*. and each of the others 3*d*. every Saturday, and the masses they were to celebrate were prescribed in detail. Within twenty years the 'wardens and ministers of St Hugh's altar' were appealing to the Pope against the rectors of Paxton and Great Carlton who were withholding their pensions.[117] Members of the foundation themselves joined in the chantry movement quite quickly:[118] the earliest was perhaps Peter of Hungary's endowment for a single priest at the altar of St Nicholas, established in 1223–4; in 1243 Dean William de Thornaco founded a chantry to be served by a vicar choral at the altar of the Blessed Virgin. Two larger chantries belong to this period of the thirteenth century, Faldingworth, founded in the chapel of St Giles by Richard son of Herbert of Newport, rector of Faldingworth, for two chaplains who were not to be vicars, and who were to dwell together in a separate house, and Lexington, founded about 1260 for the soul of Bishop Henry Lexington at the altar of St John Baptist, for two chaplains. This also provided for a regular distribution to Poor Clerks, boys, and the servants of the church when the anniversary Mass was celebrated. Bishop Sutton, methodical as ever, ordained his own chantry before his death and laid down explicit instructions by which the cantarist, whether he were a vicar or not, was to 'follow the choir', that is, to be present at all choir services. The amounts payable at the obit are also specified: 32 shillings to the canons, 18 shillings to the vicars, 3 shillings to the Poor Clerks, fourpence to the Clerk of the Hospital (of St Giles), eightpence each to the Sacrist and Clerk of the Common, sixpence to the Faldingworth chaplains, fourpence each to the wardens of the shrines of St Hugh and Blessed Robert Grosseteste, providing they are present at the obit. All of these chantries except the Works were to be administered by the Clerk of the Common Fund, and the complexity of accounting they called for is very marked. So, too, are the 'fringe benefits' which could be gathered from these various sources, by the clerical proletariat of the cathedral.

Some chantry foundations proved to be inadequate. Early in the thirteenth century, William son of Ulf, priest of St Swithin, had established a chantry for a single priest, and this was augmented by Mr Richard of Stretton, a canon, in 1334–5, with the aid of the prior and convent of St Katherine at Lincoln. Another canon, Mr William of Thorneton, in 1312 augmented the Barton Chantry founded about 1275 at the altar of St John the Baptist by an archdeacon of Stow. Other small chantries founded during the fourteenth century, usually

---

[117] R A II 385, 387.

[118] For what follows see C. W. Foster and A. Hamilton Thompson,. 'Chantry certificates for Lincoln and Lincolnshire I,' *A A S R* 34, 1922, 1–28.

for one chaplain, by various donors, seem to have been more successful: among these were the foundations of Canon John Edenstow in 1350, Gilbert Umfraville lord of Kyme in 1308, King Edward II in 1315/16 at the altar of the Blessed Virgin, and Bishop John Buckingham for two chaplains and two clerks.

By far the most impressive and important of the fourteenth-century foundations are those of the Burghersh family, founded by Bishop Henry Burghersh and his brother, and of Nicholas Cantilupe. The original intention of Bishop Burghersh seems to have been no more than to provide for a chaplain who would live with the eleven Poor Clerks, but this was revised by Bishop Bek and the Dean and Chapter in 1345 to provide maintenance for five chaplains dwelling together in a specified house, one of whom was to be named warden, and for six boys, who were to be instructed in grammar, and to share the same house. The life of the boys after their admission at seven until the end of their eight years' maintenance, is firmly laid down: they were to come in able to sing and acquainted with Donatus; each year they were to receive a winter tunic, a cloth cap, and as many shirts as could be provided for them out of 30 shillings. Each was to read for a week while the chaplains were eating, but they were not to eat with the chaplains, nor lie in the same chamber. They were to go to and from the grammar school in a body on school days, to say Vespers in the chapel of the house when they returned, and on feast days to attend the parish church (St Margaret) together. Bishop Buckingham, ordaining a chantry on his own account for two priests and two poor boys, added to the 'chantry quarter' by arranging accommodation for them at the entrance to the Burghersh House, with the chaplains each in upper rooms above the gate, and the boys together in a tower room.

Nicholas Cantilupe's chantry had been founded in 1558 for five chaplains, in a chapel dedicated to St Peter which was on the site of a former house of the Sack Friars, but before it can have been really established it was transferred to the control of the Dean and Chapter; by 1366 it had become a college of a warden and seven chaplains, not vicars choral, who were to celebrate at the altar of St Nicholas, and to live together in one of two houses built by Nicholas before his death, near the east gate of the bishop's palace.

Thus there came to be, by these foundations created round the cathedral, a very large clerical population within its close or enclosure. Despite the ravages of the Black Death, from which only two of the residentiaries survived, by the time a clerical poll-tax or subsidy was levied in 1379,[119] the numbers had recovered. There were in the Close, when the subsidy was levied, nine canons (that is presumably residentiaries) and ten other beneficed clerks, thirty vicars choral, forty-two other chaplains wearing the habit of the cathedral, eleven

[119] LAO DC A.2.26, f. 4v.

151

other Poor Clerks, four adult choristers and nineteen chaplains and clerks who neither wore the habit nor were beneficed.[120]

Later development of the Close

The area within which this clerical population lived had during the thirteenth century become far more clearly defined than at first. It had been limited on the south and east at first by the Roman wall of the upper city, and then, after St Hugh's extension of the church it was supposed, by a rebuilt wall on a more easterly line which cannot now be determined. Recent excavations by the Trust for Lincolnshire Archaeology immediately to the south of the south-eastern transept have made it more possible to define some of the changes which were needed to make the 'old' city wall part of the foundations of the new building and to create level ground on which to build. Mr David Stocker, who reports on this excavation, has not yet been able to decide whether the east wall of St Hugh's church was now regarded as the city wall or whether a new wall was in fact built in an arc round it.[121] Whichever course was followed, it was soon rendered useless, for in 1256, when the chapter was proposing a further extension of the cathedral to house a new and more splendid shrine for St Hugh, that is, the Angel Choir, the King permitted them to break through the eastern wall of the city to do so and to build a new wall further to the east.[122] Finally, in 1285, when perhaps a new town wall had not yet been built, Edward I permitted the canons to build and crenellate a wall 12 feet high, including within it Pottergate, and two lanes to the north of Eastgate, and to erect and man gates leading to it. The enclosure thus created was substantially that which can be traced today, and its gates included the double gates on the west, of which Exchequer Gate is the surviving member, Pottergate Arch, and a northern gate now represented by the nineteenth-century 'Priory Arch'.[123]

Safety of the inhabitants and protection from robbers, thieves and murderers were the reasons for this new move: the walls and gates created an inner world independent of the city and Bail communities outside, and apparently sheltered from their hazards, but still possessing its own special features and problems. One of the most pressing of these was that of a burial place. A cemetery had indeed come into use in the area south east of St Hugh's church, which was made available by the removal of the city wall, but it was still too small to cater

---

[120] PRO E 179/7/35; I am very grateful to Dr Alison McHardy, who has communicated these figures from her forthcoming edition in the Lincoln Record Society series of the Lincoln portion of this subsidy.

[121] 'Excavations to the south of Lincoln Minster', *Lincs. Hist. and Arch.* 20, 1985, 15–20.

[122] R A I, 244–5.

[123] Cal. Pat. Rolls 1281–92, 161.

for the entire population of the enclosure and in 1295 the 'poor church' of St Bartholomew behind the castle wall was acquired by the chapter from the abbot and convent of Selby to provide a larger cemetery for the inhabitants of the Close.[124]

The buildings within the wall and around the cathedral were by the time of the crenellation almost entirely owned by the chapter, whether as residence houses for canons, common halls for the lesser corporations of vicars, Poor Clerks and boys, or as chantry houses. All were substantial dwellings housing in addition to the nominal inhabitants large and often unruly households of chaplains, clerks and servants. It was a markedly congested and overcrowded community and it is clear that tranquillity and good behaviour were not easy to achieve. Sutton's enclosure for the vicars choral and his provision for them of a common life was addressed to this aim; the ordination of the Burghersh Chantry enjoined on the chaplains that 'they should not wander overmuch in the town or elsewhere, nor go out of the close by night but should be bound to assemble every day in their house before the ringing of curfew, or at least while it is ringing, and no one should afterwards go out any where except to lauds and after the ringing of curfew the door shall be closed by the principal chaplain, with a good lock.'

Despite these precautions, fresh problems were continually appearing until the end of the period because of the disorderly conduct of the minor clergy, of whom John Tetford, who in 1350 kept a tavern and was always brawling with his fellows, was a good representative.[125] No doubt the social problems created by the Black Death accentuated the difficulties, and in the second half of the fourteenth century and beyond there were continual troubles, especially among the vicars. They were accused of absenteeism, noise, fornication and rape. More unexpectedly perhaps, they were said to purloin candles from the high altar for their own celebrations. They in turn had grievances which came increasingly before the chapter, and which raise some echoes today. In 1404 for example, the two cantarists of the Buckingham Chantry objected to having to use the altar at St Hugh's shrine for their celebration: 'in misty and windy weather the winds blow so hard through the two doors at each side of the shrine that the host is blown about on the altar, and the cold is intolerable'.[126]

The accusations of disorderly living increased in the fifteenth century. The vicars made fun of the Succentor's singing and reading in 1408, the Poor Clerks imported a lewd woman into their hall at twilight in 1409, a vicar called Markby who was constantly corrected for disorder, when excluded from the

---

[124] R A X, 2867–8; II, 465–72.
[125] LAO DC A.2.26, f. 42.
[126] Ibid., f. 10v; A.2.30, f. 11v; A.2.29, f. 9.

153

choir, came back to mock, wearing an extraordinary hood. A number of cantarists wasted time playing bowls and other games, or in blasphemous talk and archery, and fomented riotous behaviour of all sorts, while the warden of the Burghersh Chantry went out a-hunting in 1426.[127]

The regular liturgical life of the cathedral offered unexpected diversions at times: in 1441 for example, we know from the accounts of the common that the Clerk of the Common bought apples to be blessed and distributed to the choir on the Feast of Saints Felix and Agapittus (6 August).[128] There were other recurring variations: at Christmas, for example, the processions of deacons and priests were perhaps an excuse for the Feast of Fools at the Circumcision, which is said to have originated in France.[129] As early as 1236 Grosseteste pronounced vehemently against it: as 'full of folly and pleasures odious to God and acceptable to the demons'.[130] In the next century Archbishop Courteney, visiting the chapter in 1389, after forbidding the cathedral clergy (the chaplains and cantarists that is) to hold drinking parties at their altars on the feasts of the saints to which they were dedicated, uttered an outright condemnation of their activities at the Feast of the Circumcision when they put on lay dress and 'interrupt the divine office by noise, tricks, scoldings and plays which they call the feast of fools'.[131] The boy bishop ceremonies on Holy Innocents Day were evidently less obnoxious and other dramatic performances even had an official existence. At dawn on Christmas morning, Mary, Elizabeth (portrayed by boys, it seems) and the angel regularly received gloves for their performance (of a play one supposes). At Epiphany there was also a play, for which on one occasion at least a woollen head for a king, a star and three crowns were provided, and on Easter Monday the play of the Resurrection, or St Thomas Didymus, was presented in the nave. At Pentecost came the earliest of these performances, when a dove came down by a cord from the church roof, and an angel appeared.[132]

The laity and the cathedral life

The coming of the laity into the cathedral, which was a continually growing feature of church life, inevitably disturbed the even tenor of liturgical practice. As the centuries passed there was a marked tendency for the children or

---

[127] Ibid., A.2.30, ff. 7, 14v, 45; A.2.32, f. 40v.; *Repingdon* I, LRS 57, 181.
[128] LAO DC Bi.2.12, f. 10.
[129] LCS I, 290.
[130] Epistole, p. 119.
[131] LAO DC A.2.28, f. 23.
[132] Ibid., Bi.2.8. ff. 74v, 119v; Bi.2.7, f. 119v.

retainers of local gentry to become part of the cathedral foundation, which was no longer a body of clerks detached from the surrounding county, but a landowner with claims and responsibilities not unlike those of the lay gentry. At the same time many of the higher gentry came to take their place in the fourteenth and fifteenth centuries as familiars of the chapter, members of which were fellow magnates. This had important results for cathedral life. In the first place there were resident lay households in the Close, magnates who had many followers. Perhaps Catherine Swinford, mistress and later wife of John of Gaunt, and mother of the Beauforts, is the best-known example.[133] These lay folk symbolise perhaps a decline in the standards of cathedral life and a general tendency to succumb to external, and particularly aristocratic, pressure. At the same time 'the people' for whom they were devised continued to frequent the cathedral sermons despite the challenge offered by the friars, who once at least went so far as to advertise the attractions of their own sermons in a notice on the cathedral doors.[134] Nevertheless, the lay congregation continued to make substantial offerings at the shrines during the feasts and flocked into the nave at all times. There was occasionally much pushing and even some violence; it was reported in 1410 that a miller named Richard Spendluffe attacked Robert Tras, who had accused him and other millers of stealing grain, and when he moved over to the holy water stoup by the door on the south side of the choir, 'stouk him in the side with a daggar'.[135]

At times unnamed persons abandoned orphan children in the nave during service and the chapter was at the expense of conveying them to St Katherine's across the town,[136] at other times there were spectacular penances to watch, performed by laymen or women or, sometimes, by members of the foundation. In 1343 William of Walcote, a vicar choral, was called to purge himself six-handed (that is to find six other clerks willing to swear that he was innocent) of an accusation of heresy in the course of which he was alleged to have said in the Creed 'Credo in Jesu Christo' instead of 'Credo in uno Deo', and to have indulged in spells, incantations and demon-raising.[137] A different sort of show would be provided by a criminal seeking sanctuary in the church, and even more if there were attempts by a lay authority to remove him, as happened in 1422. There were even occasions when, for some reason unspecified, the Galilee court for lay cases was brought into the nave, when the press of suitors and spectators must have filled the area. Even worse were the times in the early

---

[133] J. H. Harvey, *Catherine Swinford's Chantry*, LMP 2nd ser. 6, 1971.
[134] Repingdon III, LRS 74, 180.
[135] LAO DC A.2.30, f. 18v.
[136] Ibid., Bi.1.3., f. 1.
[137] Ibid., A.2.32, f. 13v.

fifteenth century when laymen selling jewels and vestments actually set up their stalls inside the nave, on whose authority it is not clear, to the great scandal of all right-thinking men.[138]

The official occasions when the townspeople came into the cathedral must always have enlivened the scene; in the fifteenth century at least there were regular processions, which began from Bargate at the southern limits of the town.[139] Many, though not all, of these processions were the concern of the town gilds, and especially those dedicated to Corpus Christi.[140] Members of the Corpus Christi gild in the parish of St Michael on the Mount, all wearing garlands, carried a great torch to the Minster on their feast and the tilers' gild on the same occasion processed from St Botolph below hill bearing a great candle to burn before the choir gate, while the sailors' gild brought another candle to St John Dalderby. There were other feasts similarly honoured: the Exaltation of the Holy Cross, for instance, was signalised by the weavers' gild bringing a candle to the High Cross in the mother church on that day, and the Assumption of the Blessed Virgin by the gild of St Mary in All Saints, bringing a candle to the statue of St Mary near St Hugh's tomb, while the mercers' gild of the Blessed Virgin carried one to a side altar. What is perhaps most significant in all these ceremonies is not the enlivenment of the Minster community itself, but the light in which the townspeople regarded the cathedral as the honourable centre of their religious life.

Further enlivenment and a species of dissipation must undoubtedly always have been provided for the clerks of the cathedral community, and more distantly for the townspeople, by the succession of royal visits to the town, beginning with Stephen's ill-fated campaigns, and by the parliaments and convocations which during the fourteenth century used the chapter house as an assembly place. The honours paid to St Hugh at his burial by King John of England and King William of Scotland, and by numerous bishops and archbishops, created immense excitement, which the narrative of the *Magna Vita* clearly reflects.[141] Everyone's ambition was to touch the coffin, and those who were unable to do so on account of the crowds surrounding it felt it no mean achievement to have seen and venerated it at a distance.

When we arrived at the foot of the hill almost a mile outside the city we were met by the kings of England and Scotland, the archbishops, bishops, magnates, abbots, and nobles and an immense crowd of clergy and people . . . Those whose greater physical force had secured for them the opportunity of carrying the bier advanced triumphantly . . . they were soon driven out by others.

[138] Ibid., A.2.30, f. 7.
[139] Repingdon III, LRS 74, 216, 278.
[140] For what follows see H. F. Westlake, *Parochial gilds of medieval England*, London 1919, 167–8.
[141] Magna Vita II, c. xix.

The reputation of St Hugh's shrine itself attracted important visitors and their attendant retinues. Earl Richard of Cornwall, for instance, came there in 1257 at the very moment when the hullabaloo attending the 'martyrdom' of 'Little Hugh' was beginning. Even the turmoil of the barons' wars, when the followers of Montfort sacked the castle, did not seriously affect the cathedral community, it seems, though the city itself suffered severely, and its trade perhaps never really recovered.[142] Edward I and his queen were present in 1280 at the consecration of the Angel Choir. In 1290 Edward returned alone after his wife's death at Harby, and buried her viscera in the cathedral.

The first meeting of parliament in Lincoln, in Hilary term 1301, was provoked by the dangers of the Scottish war; the meetings which followed in 1315, 1316 and 1327 arose from the same circumstances. They required the amassing of considerable stores to feed the royal household and brought large crowds into the city, and to the cathedral itself. The strain on the chapter was considerable: not only were they forced to make a loan of 900 marks to the King after the Bannockburn defeat but the Deanery was used as well as the chapter house for the later meetings, and the burden of keeping order among the camp followers of the royal household must have been very great. Enlivening though these royal visits must have been, the subsequent tranquillity of the later fourteenth century can only have been a relief to those living and working about the cathedral.[143]

Episcopal visitation thirteenth to fifteenth centuries: the Dean in conflict with the chapter

In the first century and a half of the cathedral's existence the bishops' relation with the creation of their predecessors was relatively untroubled. The canons were their nominees for the most part, they had contributed very largely to the building of the cathedral, the possession of the relics of the greatest of them made an important contribution to the prosperity of the foundation. No bishop had, it seems, interfered with the internal affairs of the chapter, and certainly none had tried to exercise visitatorial power over it. Changing views of the episcopal function, and especially of the bishop's duty to visit and correct his subjects, regardless of the claims to immunity they might make, were already being felt before the end of the twelfth century and came to a head so far as Lincoln was concerned, in the pontificate of the very remarkable Robert Grosseteste. Early in his dispute with the Dean and Chapter, in 1239, he prepared for them a long statement of the ideal relations which should exist

---

[142] Hill, *Medieval Lincoln*, c. x.
[143] Ibid., c. xii and *Memoirs illustrative of the history and antiquities of the county and city of Lincoln*, 1850, 19–38.

between a bishop and his cathedral chapter. The gist of his argument was that the bishop, from outside, must visit and correct the cathedral chapter as the dean, who is himself a member, cannot do.[144] This met with resistance from a chapter already discontented at Grosseteste's supposed lowly birth, and even more at his protection of the mendicant orders. Despite a cogently argued case composed by the Chancellor, Mr Nicholas of Wadingham,[145] Grosseteste was able to win the support of Pope Innocent IV for his stand, and in the end to carry his point, but only after six years of acrimonious wrangling. When he first announced his intention of visiting the chapter and the prebendal churches, for which last he had papal authority, the Dean and Chapter instructed the clergy in the prebendal churches to ignore him, and he in revenge suspended the Dean, Subdean and Precentor. Then in October 1239 he gave notice that he intended to visit the chapter itself and the Dean and Chapter promptly summoned all canons to the chapter and received from 'the people' a mandate to appeal to Rome against him. On the day appointed by the Bishop for the Visitation the dignitaries had left for Rome and all other members of the foundation failed to appear. Attempts at arbitration failed and the Dean, William de Thornaco, was deposed for contumacy. This was perhaps the occasion when the stonework of the new central tower collapsed just at the moment when, according to the chronicler Matthew Paris a canon preaching against the Bishop's oppressions, had proclaimed, 'If we should hold our peace the very stones would cry out on our behalf.' It seems that the chapter declined to accept William's deposition and refused to elect a successor, and Grosseteste thereupon nominated Roger of Weseham, and carried him off to Lyons, where Pope Innocent was preparing to hold a general council in 1245. Here, fortunately for the peace of Lincoln, Weseham was provided to the see of Lichfield and Grosseteste was wise enough to leave the choice of his successor to the chapter. Perhaps as a result of this, or because the Pope was genuinely convinced of the justice of the Bishop's cause, he six months later gave judgment in his favour, with only the slightest of reservations.[146]

Henry of Lexington, whom the chapter now elected as Dean, in due course succeeded Grosseteste in the bishopric. Richard Gravesend and Oliver Sutton similarly became bishops after holding the deanery. While this period lasted, until the end of the thirteenth century, relations were good and the bishops did much to promote the welfare of the chapter, the Close, and the subordinate corporations; disputes were few. With the beginning of the new century,

---

[144] Epistole, 127.
[145] Bodley MS 760, ff. 176v–178v. The late Dr R. W. Hunt discovered this text in 1953 and generously allowed me to make use of it.
[146] R A I, 273.

however, almost 150 years of litigation began, not now between the bishops and the chapter, but between the deans and their chapters. It is perhaps worth remarking at this point that almost all the deans involved were canonists, in some cases, such as William Bateman, later bishop of Norwich and founder of two Cambridge colleges, very notable men, and all very aware of the rights of their office, which they felt obliged to defend.

The first dispute was initiated by Roger Martival, who in 1314 had appealed to Bishop Dalderby to interpret various customs which restricted his powers to exercise jurisdiction over the chapter, and to visit the chapter, the prebendal churches and the choir.[147] Martival's successor, Anthony Bek, appealed unsuccessfully in 1333/4 to the papal curia for confirmation of his sole power to admit vicars, canons and altar-keepers. His complaints were revived in the curia in 1340/1, by William Bateman, who succeeded him. Bateman had been provided to the deanery in this year, but before the cause could be decided he was promoted to the see of Norwich. The next dean, John of Offord, exacted from Archbishop Stratford an award in his favour against the chapter, from whom he now gained control of the important post of Keeper of St Peter's altar. After this there was a respite for half a century, until 1404, when John Shepey acquired from Bishop Beaufort a confirmation of his rights of visitation, and of nomination to all chapter offices.

Finally, during the long tenure of the deanery by John Macworth (1412–52), with which this section of the history will end, there was a series of three separate disputes between the Dean and his chapter. The quarrels of 1418, 1421 and 1434 seem to have been precipitated by his neglect of duty and positive absenteeism.[148] When Bishop Alnwick visited the cathedral in 1437, the entire foundation seems to have spoken against Macworth, and to crushing effect. It was clear that a great many things had gone astray at all levels. It was alleged, for example, that in 1435, when many pilgrims were in the cathedral, the Dean, with an armed band, had made a personal attack on the Chancellor Peter Partrich, whom the soldiers dragged away by his almuce. This was of course Partrich's complaint to the Bishop, but there were other facts equally damning. The vicars and Poor Clerks complained that their stipends were not paid, their vestments not washed, and their service books wanting. In the event Macworth was constrained to accept the Bishop's arbitration, and this resulted, in 1439, in the formation of a 'new book of customs', the *Novum Registrum*, which finally ended the disputes.[149]

It is a contentious, disorderly society which is reflected in the events of

---

[147] LCS I, 319–22.
[148] LCS II, 257–8, 259–67.
[149] Ibid., 268–363.

Macworth's period of office, and the few years which preceded it. The Dean himself had the train of his cope borne by a servant and went about the Close, and even the town, 'as if he were a pontiff'. He was opposed by a 'league' of all the residentiaries, Partrich, Southam, Haket, Warde and Ingoldisby, only the Precentor Burton being on his side. The great households of the Close fomented the trouble. Partrich was accused of giving shelter in the Chancery to an excommunicated fortune-teller, and said to have secreted and sold some of the library books in his charge. The Dean's servant (or one of them) was convicted on two counts of adultery, in one case with his master's cook. The Dean himself was undignified in church, chattered during the processions and regularly broke rank in a regrettable way. Moreover he had allowed, or caused, the north wall of the cloister, next to the Deanery, to be demolished so that he could use the site for a stable to be built from its stones. The bell-ringer was allowed to keep a dog, which sorely defiled the church, in his chamber at the west end of the building, near to the Pele altar. Equally scandalously, the verger had been allowed to bring cattle into the churchyard.

The Feast of Fools continued to be celebrated, despite many previous condemnations from Grosseteste's time onwards; in its course the chapter met many heavy demands for food, and the young vicars and other junior clerks, after a token appearance at Matins, spent their days in taverns in the lower town, in entirely unsuitable company. A woman who had been suspected of adultery with one of the canons, and who had sworn to avoid his company, still lurked in the Close, near to his house; when she had been watched she pretended to go off into Pottergate, but soon came back into Eastgate and her old haunts. Worst of all, money was scarce, houses were decaying and often empty, so that they produced no rent, the stipends of the vicars were paid only irregularly and the church was badly neglected. There was only one candle, instead of ten, on the high altar, neither mason nor carpenters were employed about the building and in a rainy season the floor was awash.

A 'cash-flow' difficulty was nothing new. As long ago as 1383 two canons journeying to London on chapter business were driven to borrow funds for their expenses from the funds of St Hugh's shrine and from the Fabric chest.[150] The rest of the gloomy picture painted for Bishop Alnwick was no doubt produced by a combination of neglected properties and overweening personalities, which seriously affected the quality of life in Lincoln at the turn of the century and was still doing so thirty years later. The whole English Church was in fact in some confusion, between conciliar troubles coming in from the continent and threatenings of Lollard heresy, and the disturbed atmosphere clearly affected the Close. Heretics at intervals recanted and did penance in the

---

[150] LAO DC Bi.2.7, f. 71v.

cathedral, Bishop Repingdon was very critical of the state of chapter properties, archbishops proclaimed processions of intercession with what must have seemed to the ordinary churchman alarming frequency, and Franciscan friars preached revivalist sermons in the town.[151] In the chapter itself the numbers of non-residents again rose; those who did reside harboured in their households large numbers of gentlemen and valets who are named in their wills. A few of the resident canons were men of great wealth, who left vestments, plate and furniture in great quantities; their servants often wore the bishop's livery and they themselves were distinguished local magnates, who talked on equal terms with leading laymen of the county like Lyndewode of Linwood, Moulton of Moulton or Copledike of Harrington. They supervised the wills of these gentry, acted as guardians to their orphaned children and at intervals allowed their widows to find a house in the Close.[152] It was also a period of great civil unrest and disorder, a run-up, as it were, to the Wars of the Roses, during which a canon of Lincoln, who was also vicar of Horncastle, might be murdered while on his way, wearing full canonicals, from Horncastle to Lincoln.[153] It was no wonder that, when another canon set off for Laund on chapter business in 1399, he needed the escort of Richard Belrynger and Thomas Clere.[154]

The disturbed conditions and the demoralisation, for it is no less, of the cathedral community, beginning no doubt after the revolts of 1381, together with the continuing difficulties of the royal government, seem to have encouraged the rulers of the town to attack the chapter liberty, in 1386, and to press home their assaults on it for a number of years.[155] The resulting disputes were often attended with great violence, and in the end it was necessary to call in the help of an external arbitrator. This was John of Gaunt, a powerful landowner within the county as well as a leading political figure of his day. His award went entirely in the chapter's favour, and it is scarcely surprising after this that his mistress Katherine Swinford, after she had returned as a widow, was welcomed to the close, and eventually admitted to burial in the cathedral, and that their son became bishop of Lincoln in 1398.

The episcopal visitation of the chapter by Bishop William Gray in 1432, which preceded Alnwick's vigorous and decisive action against Dean Macworth, and which is fully reported, affords a final opportunity to look at the chapter without the distortion produced by dislike of the Dean.[156] There were in all

---

[151] Memoirs, 310–27; A. Gibbons, *Early Lincoln wills*, Lincoln 1888, *passim*.
[152] Repingdon, *passim*.
[153] Gibbons, *Early Lincoln wills*, 71, John de Rouceby.
[154] LAO DC Bi.2.10, f. 11.
[155] A. H. Thompson, ed., *Visitations of religious houses in the diocese of Lincoln* III, LRS 21, 1929, 128–45.
[156] *Medieval Lincoln*, 266–8.

sixty-three prebendaries, of whom ten were resident: the Dean, Precentor, Treasurer and Chancellor, Southam, Tealby, Baldyng, Marchalle, Leek and Castell. The archdeacon of Lincoln and two other prebendaries were also in the town, and appeared before the Bishop, but had not protested residence.

There was by now only one foreigner in the chapter and a number of the prebendaries actually bore such local names as Tealby, Depyng and Ewerby. At least sixteen members of the chapter were canonists and ecclesiastical administrators, and although some of this number, such as Thomas Bekyngton, archdeacon of Buckingham, and William Scrope, prebendary of Asgarby, were far removed from Lincoln affairs, a number of the rest, and especially John Southam, archdeacon of Oxford, the Treasurer John Haget and John Depyng, were deeply involved in diocesan and chapter business. Only one prebendary, Thomas Chichele, was absent for the purposes of study in a university. The will of John Tealby alias Cotes, who died soon after the visitation, allows us to see the sort of life led by an 'average' member of the chapter. His will, made on 4 April, and proved on 16 October 1433, shows him to be a client of the all-powerful Willoughby d'Eresby clan, from whom some of his Lincolnshire preferments came, and to whose college at Spilsby he left a bequest. His bequests to his brethren in the chapter and to the gentlemen and valets of his own household show him to have been moderately wealthy, and his piety is attested by the arrangements he made for a twenty-year chantry. His care for cathedral observances is demonstrated by the clause restricting his legacy to chantry chaplains, Poor Clerks and choristers who were present at the entire office and not roaming through the middle of the church like vagabonds at the time of service.[157] Nothing in the will suggests that Tealby was a man of learning or culture, and he may well have been fairly typical of the late medieval prebendaries. The contrast of his will with that of Richard Ravenser, who died in 1386, is very marked.[158] Here we have an archdeacon of Lincoln with interests in York and Beverley, a royal servant but also a man of the bishop's household (he bequeathed to his sister-in-law a robe of the bishop's livery), a canonist who owned not only legal texts but chronicles and other secular literature. He had a great deal of plate in his houses in Lincoln and Stretley and a fully equipped chapel, and an abundance of furniture. He was characteristic of the non-local canon who was something of a magnate. He almost became Dean in 1378, he held three different prebends from as early as 1359, besides the archdeaconry, two other members of his family were prebendaries after him and Henry of Brauncewell, also a prebendary, was his servant and follower, who in 1396 asked for burial in the cathedral 'near my late master

[157] Gibbons, *Early Lincoln wills*, 158.
[158] Memoirs, 310–27.

Richard de Ravenser'.[159] Ravenser belonged to a type of churchman often found at this period, engaged far less in the affairs of Lincoln that in those of the church at large yet concerned to found obits, to reward faithful servants and acknowledge the local claims of friends and relatives. Once the demoralisation produced by Macworth had ended, men like Ravenser regained their place in the cathedral affairs, and the next eighty years or so was a relatively peaceful period.

[159] Gibbons, *Early Lincoln wills*, 35.

6

Historical survey, 1450–1750

❋

MARGARET BOWKER

The cathedral before the storm: 1450–1530

The Reformation in England, which took place in the middle decades of the sixteenth century, was to require of the Dean and Chapter the implementation of statutes and injunctions which were to abolish much of what belonged to the very heart of the organisation and worship of the Minster. But, in the late middle ages, change of so radical a kind did not appear likely, nor would it have had the support either of the residentiary canons or of the lesser office-holders, from the most senior vicar to the youngest or newest chorister. The Minster boasted no 'early' Protestants who raised their voices against the ritual, expressive of Catholic doctrine, which dominated the worship of the cathedral church. If High Mass was interrupted in the late fifteenth and early sixteenth centuries, it was not because there were doubts that the Host after consecration was the actual body of Christ, but because a cart was taking a short cut across the Close and rumbling through the north door to the south. In the morning, the murmur of masses and of offices for the dead might cease, but this was not because the efficacy of prayer for the departed was in doubt, but because a chantry-priest had overslept, perhaps because of imbibing too heavily the night before. The presence or absence of such devotions tended to be drowned by the steady procession of laity who came to pay their respects to St Hugh, the great saint whose wealthy shrine the cathedral harboured, or who used the church as shelter as they made their way round the Close, thereby avoiding the bitter wind and driving rain which still ravage the Fabric of the Minster itself and remain to harass pilgrim and tourist alike. There is nothing at all to suggest, in the eighty years before change was even mooted, that it would be welcomed –

164

though there are signs that reforms were necessary and that some effort was being made to effect them.

Who, then, was responsible in this period for running the cathedral and its affairs? That responsibility, whether it was the ordering of the cathedral itself or the administration of its lands, or the moral, probate and marriage jurisdiction over those who lived in the Close or its parishes, belonged to the small body of canons who had chosen to be residentiaries. The residentiary canons varied in number in the later middle ages from as few as three to as many as seven.[1] They were responsible, not only for chapter meetings where accounts were audited and duties allocated, but also for the many small meetings which were held for everyday matters of business.[2] A canon could undertake major residence of two-thirds of the year or minor residence of seventeen weeks and three days; minor residence was regarded as a privilege only earned after a proper stint at major residence, but the whole subject of the precise duration and obligations of residentiaries was good for many arguments, not least because they carried with them the vexed subject of pay.

These matters were supposedly fixed and recorded in the statutes and customs of the cathedral but that did not prevent a cunning, disgruntled or impecunious canon from testing for possible loopholes or eventually from trying to maintain that the statutes were contrary to the law of the land.[3] The arguments about residence at Lincoln were derived from an arrangement which appears unique: residentiaries received a carefully divided share of the profits of the Common Fund when all other payments had been made.[4] It was, therefore, in the interests of the residentiaries to keep their numbers low – but not so low that the work was too onerous.[5] They also needed to ensure that no one claimed to be a residentiary who was not properly entitled. If a residentiary was away on the business of the chapter, the bishop had decreed in 1465 that this should count for residence.[6] Quarrels arose in the late middle ages over defining what 'business' was and whether there was enough leave. In 1467 the annual leave of seventeen weeks and four days had been increased by forty days. In 1503, the Dean maintained that his permission was necessary for a residentiary to leave the Close for more than one night, and the Treasurer, John Cutler, was asked to seek pardon for not observing this statute. The Treasurer protested his wish to preserve the statutes but denied he had violated them. The whole

---

[1] M. Bowker, *The secular clergy in the diocese of Lincoln 1495–1520*, Cambridge 1968, 161.
[2] Ibid., 162.
[3] See below p. 175.
[4] K. Edwards, *The English Secular cathedrals in the middle ages*, 2nd edn, Manchester 1967, 44.
[5] Bowker, *Secular clergy*, 161.
[6] LDC A.3.6, f. 17.

matter was referred to the Bishop.[7] In 1507, Cutler was again on the warpath; he raised the question whether absence from the Close during Lent might legitimately be counted as residence. The point was cleverly made. Residentiaries had churches which they either held by virtue of their residence to augment their income, or by a dispensation which allowed them to hold more than one living at a time. Some would simply appoint a deputy and leave all duties to him, but others might deem Lent a good time to hear confessions and preach in their churches, or use the arrival of spring to take a short break in the country under the pretext of 'business'. To include absence in Lent as residence would significantly curtail the number of days which a residentiary was bound to spend in the Close: but the work load would be greater, especially in Lent. Cutler lost this concession but death claimed him before he was inconvenienced by Lent more than once.[8] Others were more fortunate. The Chancellor, Nicholas Bradbridge, burned with a fervent desire to go on pilgrimage to Rome in July 1516; he was allowed to go and his devotion was counted as residence.[9]

In 1525 Bishop Longland clearly decided that the number of residentiaries, which stood at six, was too few, and he yearned for a greater number to lend dignity to his cathedral church. He particularly wanted the Treasurer in addition to the Dean, Precentor and Chancellor to reside: 'the treasurer has cure and charge and ought specially there to be, and hath of long season been absent from the said church whereby many things are more out of order in the same.'[10] He attributed, wrongly as he was to discover, the lack of a treasurer to the unprincipled but ingenious scheme, which the residentiaries were poised to make their own, of using retirement as though it were residence, and many had the wit to see that early retirement set them free to seek their fortunes elsewhere.

The plan to use the Common Fund as the basis of a pension scheme had innocent beginnings. In 1528, an archdeacon who had spent twenty years in residence was, it seemed, so ill that he could not perform the duties of major or minor residence. It was resolved to give him a fixed pension of £16 rather than his share of the residue of the Common Fund, which, in that year, would have been slightly more.[11] By 1529 the chapter had granted the same privileges of an annuity, irrespective of age, health or service, to 'every other residentiary then present in the chapter'. In a space of five months Richard Parker, the recently appointed Treasurer, who had held office for four years and had been in major

---

[7] L D C A.3.2, f. 682; *L C S* II, 574–5.
[8] J. Le Neve, *Fasti Ecclesie Anglicane*, 3 vols., Oxford 1954, 22; D C A.3.2, f. 145.
[9] Bowker, *Secular clergy*, 163.
[10] Bowker, *Henrician Reformation*, 31
[11] L D C Bj. 3.4. unpaginated; Bowker, *Secular clergy* 162

residence for rather less, claimed his £16. No doubt the others would have put in a similar claim had they not been stopped by the intervention of a new residentiary who clearly reported the whole matter to the Bishop.[12]

Most of the canons of the Minster were not resident, and their contribution to the life of the cathedral church as such lay only in their paying a fixed sum to the Common Fund; this became smaller and smaller, as the sixteenth-century inflation was not matched by increases in customary payments. The stagnation of the Common Fund also played its part in the unseemly quarrels over residence, since residentiaries received a share of that fund once all other claims on it had been met.[13] In the early fourteenth century he might receive as much as £100.[14] By the 1520s it was more likely to be about £20, but it could be less[15] – though free food, housing and payments for other duties, arrears and other parishes augmented that sum in the case of any one individual. In 1526, the residentiaries, who included the Dean, received £18.8s.8d.;[16] the Dean augmented the sum from his other benefices and from the income of his prebend to the sum of £396.6s.1¾d.[17] In contrast, the Treasurer received £71.3s.6¼d. He was liable for expenses within the cathedral including the purchase of bread and wine for mass and for candles which totalled £37.2s.0d.: his net income was £34.1s.6¾d. – almost half that of any of his colleagues.[18] To alleviate this situation which arose from his heavy obligations,[19] he may have been given half of the offerings made to the high altar but there is no mention of the payments in the accounts.[20] Not surprisingly, therefore, the Treasurer was touchy where his expenses were concerned. In 1510 he was ordered to pay for the wine used at the high altar and for all other priests for whom he was bound to provide; that appears to have been extended to include all chantry-priests, and not surprisingly the demand met with an outspoken protest: 'By god I wil fynde noe wyne to any of them for nothing, that I know, yet they get noone of me. Doe what ye wille.'[21] In 1507, he vigorously refused to extend the right to 'commons' (that is, to eat with the residentiaries) to the Custodian of the altar of St Peter. He was more than a superior chantry-priest who celebrated at that altar for all past bishops; he

---

[12] Bowker, *The Henrician Reformation*, Cambridge 1981, 33–4.
[13] R. B. Walker, 'Lincoln cathedral in the reign of Queen Elizabeth', *JEH* 11, 1960, 194.
[14] Edwards, *Secular cathedrals*, 44–5.
[15] LDC Bj.3.4, unpaginated.
[16] Ibid.
[17] R. E. G. Cole, *Chapter Acts*, LRS 12, 208.
[18] Ibid., 208–10.
[19] *LCS*, I, 302–5.
[20] LDC Bj.3.3 and Bj.3.4, unpaginated.
[21] Bowker, *Secular clergy*, 168.

was usually a canon lawyer and presided over the Galilee Court which heard most of the cases which fell to the jurisdiction of the Dean and Chapter.[22] He was to receive a bare £8, but, no doubt, legal fees augmented the sum considerably.

Before the Reformation to ensure that a suitable number of canons resided and to avoid the self-centred wrangles which occurred, the stipends of the residentiaries needed to be raised. In the case of the Treasurer his dividend from the Common Fund was less than his expenses arising from the cathedral. Much of the Common Fund income was from pensions, visitation monies, incomes from churches and chantries, which were fixed and show no variation at all;[23] but the chapter did possess various lands, the proceeds of which either went to the Common Fund or to the Fabric Fund, or, in the case of prebendal lands, to the canon who held the relevant prebend. In fact, very little property was annexed to the Common Fund,[24] and this yielded only just over £70 throughout our period.[25] The most wealthy manor annexed to the Common Fund was that of Navenby, which brought in £23.15s.1¼d.;[26] its rectory was let for twenty-five years in 1528,[27] but there is no sign that the manor and its lands were subjected to any increase in rent, or that the Fund received entry fines on its leasing, or that it was made more profitable by being farmed as demesne land. The income of the Common Fund, therefore, proved very hard to augment, and the obligation of residence was likely to prove increasingly unpopular as the sixteenth century progressed.

It was also increasingly difficult for the residentiaries to look after the Fabric of the great cathedral. Their greatest source of revenue for the purpose was bequests, and the average annual income of the Fabric Fund between 1504 and 1517 – a period for which accounts survive – was £35.[28] In 1525, this plunged to £16.18s.5d. and thereafter its highest peak was to be in 1528–9 when it was £26.4s.3½d.[29] Obviously, when radical changes were required in the cathedral, and sensibilities were ruffled, the level of bequests would fall,[30] but it looks as though the faithful on the eve of the Reformation were less generous and perhaps less concerned about the cathedral fabric than their ancestors had

[22] See above, p. 147.

[23] K. Major, 'The finances of the Dean and Chapter of Lincoln from the twelfth to the fourteenth century: a preliminary survey', *JEH* 5, 149–53

[24] Ibid., 151; D. M. Williamson, *Lincoln muniments*, LMP 8, 1956, 31.

[25] LDC Bj.3.3 and Bj.3.4, *passim*.

[26] LDC Bj.3.3, unpaginated.

[27] Cole, *Chapter Acts* 12, p. 109.

[28] LDC Bj.1.4 f. 217v, 344, 355, 372v, 398v, 417.

[29] LDC Bj.5.19.

[30] This seems to be the case in the diocese, see Bowker, *Henrician Reformation*, 175ff.

been. This left the Minster very vulnerable. A major accident would find them without funds; as it was, they had enough money to maintain the glass and repair the roofs and guttering, but the only sign of building in this period, in contrast to Canterbury or Westminster, was the private concern of Bishop Longland, who set about building himself a chantry some time after his elevation to the see in 1521.

Major accidents could happen, especially as a result of the pranks practised by those whose offices were less exalted and whose responsibilities could induce boredom and bonfires. Certainly this was the case in April 1516, when six Poor Clerks went up one of the towers with burning torches intent on catching pigeons either to sell or to eat. They started a fire, and it was fortunate that the tower was not set ablaze.[31] The incident was only one in a whole series which suggest that reprimands, suspensions and even episcopal injunctions had no influence whatsoever on the large number of people, clerical and lay, who were employed in some capacity within the Minster. They were ubiquitous, though they varied in number, since the chantry-priests who were additional to the senior vicars were dwindling in number and the senior vicars were taking over their duties. In addition there were junior vicars, Poor Clerks and choristers, as well as a host of laymen who might act as watchmen or vergers, bell-ringers or cleaners.[32]

It was the vicars, chantry-priests, Poor Clerks and choristers who caused the most trouble. Not only had their lawful activities to be timetabled to ensure compliance with the conditions of those who had chantries in the cathedral, but their unlawful activities had to be kept to the minimum. The first masses usually began at 6 a.m.[33] and they continued until High Mass at 10 a.m.; the offices of Prime, Lauds and Tierce were all said before High Mass, and Sext and None immediately followed. Breakfast was at midday, and Vespers, Vespers of the Blessed Virgin and Compline started at 3 p.m. and probably took an hour. The canons and vicars supped at 6 p.m. and curfew was rung at sundown, or, in the winter, at a suitable hour. The senior vicars had the chief responsibility to maintain these services, and to rise for Matins at 2 o'clock in the morning.[34] Chantry priests had much the same obligations but these were differently stipulated in the case of any one chantry.[35] In addition to their liturgical duties the Poor Clerks and choristers had obligations to learn both grammar, to assist them with the Latin of the liturgy, and music to improve

---

[31] Bowker, *Secular clergy*, 172.
[32] Edwards, *Secular cathedrals*, 309ff.
[33] LDC A.3.2. f. 132v.
[34] LDC A.3.2. f. 108v.
[35] LDC A.3.2. f. 132v–133.

their singing. This proved difficult. In 1501 the Bishop found the Poor Clerks 'scarcely sufficiently learned or instructed' in either, and the choir boys were allegedly appointed not because they knew any grammar or how to chant but because they were related to the choir master.[36] Mention of a song master for the choristers who might also teach the organ is explicitly made in 1477, and grants of this kind continue though it was not until 1524 that the 'Song Master' was always the same person as the Organist. The choristers were taught grammar by a master in their own house.[37] A grammar school in the city was in existence in 1521, and this provided tuition in grammar in addition to any teaching available in the Close.[38] The Poor Clerks clearly felt that schooling with the choristers was beneath them, and in spite of the Bishop's orders they were still learning no grammar in 1504.[39]

Schooling was one way of keeping clerks and choristers out of mischief. Communal living was, supposedly, another: choristers, Poor Clerks, vicars and chantry-priests were obliged to eat together, but, in this, the vicars, chantry-priests and choristers were incorrigible: in 1505 the choristers had to be reminded that they might not leave their house without the leave of the master;[40] in the same year the chantry-priests were told to eat together and not to take advantage of the hospitality of the resident canons.[41] The vicars were accused of the same offence. These orders did little to curb the violence within the communal houses or to prevent their members seeking their pleasure elsewhere. While the vicars got drunk, missed Matins and hurled abusive language at the residentiaries, the Poor Clerks fought, got tight and frequented brothels.[42]

Several bishops tried to bring the lower clergy to heel. In 1501, Bishop Smith visited his cathedral church and found that the choristers had all the office books in their house with few in use in the Minster, the chantry-priests played at dice and cards, and fines for the vicars who failed to attend Office mysteriously found their way back to the offenders themselves.[43] In 1524 Bishop Longland drew up new statutes for the Poor Clerks, and his personally annotated copy of them shows that other records do not quite capture the extent of the

---

[36] LAO, Ep. Reg. 24, 234.
[37] A. F. Leach, 'Schools', *VCH Lincs*. II, 434; Bowker, *Secular clergy*, 173.
[38] There is considerable doubt about the existence, on a continuous basis, of a grammar school in the Close distinct from the 'chorister school' which was centred on the Master of Grammar and presumably only met when the choristers were free. Leach, 'Schools', 428ff.
[39] Bowker, *Secular clergy*, 173.
[40] LDC A.3.2, f. 107v.
[41] LDC A.3.2, f. 110v.
[42] Bowker, *Secular clergy*, 172–3.
[43] LAO Ep. Reg. 24, ff. 230–4.

misdemeanours, actual or potential.[44] The gates of their house were left open, and behind them, in the yard leading to the hall, the walls of the yard were used as a urinal. In the house itself the common games were cards and dice, at which the clerks were adept cheats. Arguments abounded and could lead to fights where knives came out to threaten and to wound. Servants were actually bitten or hit, perhaps as a result of a visit to a tavern. Women 'of evell or suspect conversation' were dated in the taverns and brought to the common house where they might encounter the dogs, hawks or ferrets which were the preferred amusement of some Poor Clerks.[45] Yet the Bishop, much as he might order the Dean and Chapter to keep the Poor Clerks chaste and virtuous, could find no punishment for them but fines and he rarely suspended them from office. A reformation of a more radical nature was necessary: the Poor Clerks needed a sense of purpose and vocation, and the attendance at services which they poorly understood and poorly sang was unlikely to provide that.

In addition to the clergy, there were many laymen within the Close who had leased property there; there were also laymen who had secular duties such as that of running inns which, like the Angel Inn, could provide hospitality for guests of the Dean and Chapter.[46] Few laymen required the pastoral care of the residentiaries since their properties frequently lay within the boundaries of one of the many parishes which were situated just within or just without the boundaries of the Close itself.[47] The clerks who kept the minutes of chapter meetings were frequently married men during this period, and they and their families normally lived in the Close. John Carter, who was admitted as Chapter Clerk in 1507, for instance, lived in the parish of St Margaret in the Close, as did his successor; while Peter Efford, admitted as Chapter Clerk in 1522, lived in Northgate and is buried in the church of St Peter of Eastgate.[48] Less welcome in the Close were the women who made their houses into brothels and could not be removed, although in 1503 the Dean and Chapter had a good try.[49] Additionally there were pilgrims and visitors who disturbed services with chatter and clatter.[50] Although many of the laity in the Close had a nuisance value (and they were not alone in this) they were also an asset. Bequests to the cathedral came from all over the diocese, but offerings at the high altar (which

---

[44] LDC A.2.10 (8).

[45] *LCS* II, 559–63; LDC A.2.10 (8).

[46] For a lease to the landlord of the Angel see LDC A.3.2, f. 108v.

[47] J. W. F. Hill, *Tudor and Stuart Lincoln*, Cambridge 1956, map facing p. 16.

[48] K. Major, 'The office of Chapter Clerk at Lincoln in the middle ages', in M. V. Ruffer and A. J. Taylor, eds., *Medieval studies presented to Rose Graham*, Oxford 1950, 175, 186–8.

[49] LDC A.3.2, f. 72v.

[50] LDC A.3.2, f. 110v.

could total £36) were likely to be from local folk and visitors.[51] Their presence posed the need for evangelism, a need already very apparent in the behaviour of the lower clergy.

Special cathedral sermons in Advent and Lent were primarily intended for the cathedral clergy, and that is why, in Advent, they were preached in the chapter house.[52] A preacher's library was clearly in existence, and in 1501 William Skelton stated in his will, 'I lyvieth certane bookes to be chenyd in the quere or in the librarie as it shall please them, that be necessarye to them that use preching ther.'[53] For the illiterate, or for those who found the preaching of the time too allegorical and turgid, a visual means of instruction was more helpful. At high festivals, plays were performed in and from the Minster, for which payments were made from the Common Fund; gloves and shoes were required for the Virgin, clocks and a crown for a play at the Feast of St Anne, and for such educational festivities one of the vicars acted as stage manager and producer.[54] These plays answered the need of certain of the lower clergy and the majority of the laity to receive instruction. By the beginning of the sixteenth century printed books were becoming available to assist lay faith and devotion, but by 1530 these were not widely enough known or understood for a widespread destruction of religious imagery and pageantry to be desirable. The Minster existed, until the Reformation, not primarily to instruct in religious truth but to glorify the Godhead, the Virgin and the saints. This meant that Lincoln Minster, though a secular institution housing clergy and not monks, performed in effect a similar function to its monastic counterparts. When the emphasis changed to understanding the faith rather than accepting it, the role of the cathedral would then be called in question. But until that happened, the offering of Mass and liturgical prayer for the Church Militant, Expectant and Triumphant was the main function which the Dean and Chapter needed to see performed. And the signs were that that was proving increasingly difficult.

Reformation and deformation from Henry VIII to the civil war: 1530–c.1629

King Henry VIII (1509–47) is normally seen as laying the foundations of the change in England from a Catholic state under the Pope, at least in matters of faith, to an autonomous Protestant one with an emphasis on the use of the vernacular in worship, on the Bible and on sermons, combined with a disregard

---

[51] Bowker, *Henrician Reformation*, 93.
[52] LDC A.3.2, f. 108v.
[53] LDC A.3.2, f. 12v.
[54] LDC. Bj.3.3, unpaginated.

for the Blessed Virgin and saints, and for intercession for the departed. It is undoubtedly true that under Henry VIII, after 1533, and under his son Edward VI (1547–53) much legislation, which made such a transformation possible, was passed. In fact, however, progress was gradual, if only because in matters of faith immediate conversions are not very usual. To slow down the pace still more, Queen Mary (1553–8) tried to take England back to Catholicism, while Elizabeth had an eye for the possible, for the gradual conversion within a Protestant structure, rather than an immediate one which would force so many of her subjects into a state of tension between national loyalty and religious affiliation. During her reign and that of her successor, James I, an indigenous form of Protestantism was to appear, but it would fragment between 1626 and 1640 as the basically Calvinist theology on which it rested was increasingly called into question, eventually to the point of persecution.

The religious changes which occurred from reign to reign manifested themselves in various ways which can be seen in the history of the cathedral. There would be greater interference after 1533 in the work of the chapter by the monarch or by a vicegerent acting on his behalf. By 1548 shrines and eventually chantries were to be removed and we begin to see the introduction of new forms of worship in 1549 and in 1559, and some effects on the personnel of the cathedral, a few of whom, like chantry-priests, would lose their jobs. We should also expect that during the reign of Mary (1553–8) there would be an attempt to reverse these changes, while under Elizabeth and James I, their permanence would not be called in doubt.[55]

Henry VIII was anxious to secure the loyalty of his subjects to the offspring of his second wife, Anne Boleyn, as well as seeing that none of his clergy continued to acknowledge the supremacy of the Bishop of Rome after his own supremacy act of 1534. To this end oaths were required of the Dean and Chapter. Unlike their bishop, John Longland, the Dean and Chapter were prepared to receive a visitation which was linked with an oath to the succession[56] from the archbishop of Canterbury, through his representative. They were also prepared to take an oath that they would preach that the Bishop of Rome alias the Pope had no greater jurisdiction in England than any other bishop possessed outside his own see.[57] In place of the visitation of archbishops or papal legates, the chapter could expect and did experience royal visitations: these were not made by the monarch in person but by especially empowered commissioners acting on his behalf. There was a royal visitation by deputies in 1548[58] and

---

[55] Bowker, *Henrician Reformation*, 65ff. For the impact of the English Reformation on cathedral churches see Stanford E. Lehmberg, *The reformation of cathedrals*, Princeton 1988.

[56] L A O D C Wills II ff. 1–4 (first numeration), 1–13 (second numeration).

[57] Bowker, *Henrician Reformation*, 89.

[58] For their names see L C S III, 591.

another took place in 1559 which included among the visitors Francis Knollys and William Cecil.[59] When Mary was on the throne, visitation was by Cardinal Pole, acting as legate for the Pope, in August 1556.[60] Archbishops of Canterbury occasionally seized the opportunity to visit. Cranmer tried it, and, in 1633, so did William Laud, but in both cases, though they succeeded, the Bishop, Dean and Chapter objected to interference which they thought was against the statutes.[61] Visitations by the Bishop from time to time continued as they had before.[62] As a result of so many inspections, we have sidelights on the life within the Close which are not even glimpsed in the Chapter Acts. We can begin to see where and when change came to the cathedral. Those changes, however, took place within the medieval organisation of residentiary canons, who continued to fight for their rights with considerably more zeal than some seem to have shown for the worship of God.

Throughout the sixteenth century and in spite of new orders relevant to it, the problem of residentiary canons continued to disturb chapter meetings and create a high level of discontent – so much so that letters came from the Privy Council about it. By a statute of 1529, designed to limit non-residence in the parishes, the cathedral dignitaries throughout England were not obliged to reside.[63] This, of course, was at variance with the Lincoln statutes which required major or minor residence from a few office-holders or senior canons, and it was totally opposed to the ideas of the Bishop, who thought that six residentiaries at the least were necessary. In his visitation of the cathedral in 1539, Bishop Longland made sure that there were six in residence; he also changed the customs over residence by requiring fourteen years of major residence before minor residence was permissible.[64] But this was not to last: at the royal visitation of 1548, when the residentiaries seem to have been three in number, the commissioners acquiesced:

because that the canons residenciaries be ofte tymes but fewe in nomber, and many tymes trobelyd with syknes and deceasys, yt shall be lawful for them to appoynt some of the olde vicars and officers of the churche beyng prists to execute at evensonge, matens and highmasse.[65]

By 1548, the office of Treasurer had been abolished. The claim made by former

---

[59] LDC Dvi. 26(5).

[60] Cole, *Chapter Acts*, 15, 132ff.

[61] LAO DC Wills II, f. 5.

[62] For examples see, Bowker, *Henrician Reformation*, 90ff.; Cole, *Chapter Acts* 15, 18, 74; LDC Dvi. 17 (17); Dvj 24(5).

[63] *Statutes of the Realm* III, 21 Henry VIII, c. 13.

[64] Bowker, *Henrician Reformation*, 92–3.

[65] Cole, *Chapter Acts* 15, 16.

treasurers that the office was financially unremunerative seems to have been finally accepted and the treasury was depleted by Henry VIII.[66] By 1559 there were still only three residentiaries, but they were up to four by 1563, all of whom were office-holders.[67] At their head under Elizabeth I, as Dean, was Francis Mallett, and he seems to have petitioned the Queen to be allowed to be non-resident *and yet* have the emoluments of a resident canon. The Queen through her secretary wrote to the chapter on 13 July 1568 ordering that Mallett should have the same rights whether present at or absent from the cathedral, and she added 'that you should have more regard to her princely graunte, groundcd upon her prerogative, and not to abridge him of anie parte of his commodities and lyving that should be in any wise dew unto him'.[68] On 1 August at Hatfield, a group of councillors, with the Dean on one side, and the archdeacon of Lincoln and the Chancellor on the other, heard from the chapter representatives that a non-resident could not have the stipend of a resident. Notwithstanding their interpretation of the Statutes, it

was resolved and decreed by their lordships for the quiet of both sydes and final ende of the matter . . . Mr Mallett shall from henceforth have and enjoy the benefyt of the soul [sic] graunt aswell inrespect of his deanery as of his prebend and commonship of the said church. And further . . . touchinge his divident for his residenciaryshipp he shall receave so much thereof as shall fall owt to be dewe unto him at this next Audite.

It was further resolved that after the next Audit his initial deposit on becoming Dean should be repaid and he would cease to receive his dividend.[69] The result of this decision would be to remove the Dean from the Close, and to revive the old question whether few residentiaries with better dividends (or shares in the Common Fund) were to be preferred to more, each of whom would receive less. The matter was finally settled in 1591 by Bishop William Wickham and clarified in 1601 by William Chaderton: there were to be four residentiaries provided that the Dean was not excluded if he wished to reside.[70]

Throughout the same period of the sixteenth century, the income and convictions of the residentiaries did not remain constant. In 1564, each residentiary received £8.6s.8d.[71] while in 1591 each received £41.3s.7d.:[72] the

---

[66] Le Neve, *Fasti*, 23.

[67] LDC A.3.7, ff. 20, 33 (there are two conflicting sets of pagination in this volume; I have used one throughout: in the conflicting pagination f. 20 = f. 2).

[68] LDC A.3.7, f. 62.

[69] LDC A.3.7, ff. 62v–70.

[70] *LCS*, III, 599–602; cf. LDC A.3.9, f. 17v; R. B. Walker, 'Lincoln cathedral in the reign of Queen Elizabeth I', *JEH* 11, 1960, 189.

[71] LDC Bj.3.8 (*sub* 1564), ff. 106ff.

[72] LDC Bj.3.8, ff. 276ff.

difference was largely a matter of the number of residentiaries and the extent of royal subsidies. Within this time-honoured structure, there were striking changes which overtook the personnel of the Minster. Not all residentiaries were Vicars of Bray, changing their beliefs cynically with each change of royal religious requirement, and the lower clergy were as hard as ever to wean from their usual distractions of wine and women. For all, there was the question, posed first in the 1530s, but with increasing clarity thereafter, of the headship of the Church and the morality of royal marriages, especially that to Anne Boleyn. The combination of the curtailment of saints' days, the commissions to examine Church property in connection with first fruits and tenths (taxes on income payable to the Crown) as well as doubts about the past, erupted in Lincolnshire in October 1536 in the Lincolnshire Rebellion, the spark which spread to wider rebellion in the Pilgrimage of Grace.[73] The Lincoln rebels found their way to the cathedral, and it is clear that there was some sympathy for them in the Close: Henry Litherland, who had been a resident of the Close as Custodian of the altar of St Peter since 1522, was appointed Treasurer in 1535. He did not take an oath of residence, partly because he joined the Pilgrimage of Grace in Yorkshire and was executed in York in August 1538.[74] Others were less dramatic about their beliefs.

In 1539 John Taylor was made Dean of the cathedral, largely because the Bishop was tricked into his appointment. He had clearly shown some Protestant leanings, and he was aware of the conservatism of the Bishop and the chapter.[75] He did not take up major residence until August 1546.[76] He seems to have enjoyed the changes which came to the Minster during the reign of King Edward VI[77] and was promoted to the bishopric of Lincoln in August 1552;[78] his place as Dean was taken by Matthew Parker, later to be archbishop of Canterbury under Queen Elizabeth.[79] Taylor and Parker were the first to go through the ceremony of installation while the vicars sang the Te Deum and Psalms in English,[80] but they were not alone in taking advantage of the permission given under Edward for priests to get married. As a result, under Mary, they were deprived either specifically as a result of marriage or as a

---

[73] Bowker, 'Lincolnshire 1536: heresy, schism or religious discontent?', in *Church history*, vol. 9, *Schism, heresy and religious protest*, ed. D. Baker, Cambridge 1972, 195–212.

[74] Cole, *Chapter Acts* 12, 192.

[75] Bowker, *Henrician Reformation*, 101.

[76] Cole, *Chapter Acts*, 13, 125.

[77] See below, p. 182

[78] Cole, *Chapter Acts* 15, 72.

[79] Ibid., 74.

[80] Ibid., 72, 78.

result of their views or behaviour.[81] Some cathedral canons, as well as the senior office-holders who were residentiaries, are listed as having been deprived specifically because of their marriages: some dozen of the canons were so described in the scanty records which have survived for this period.[82]

The personnel of the cathedral church were not all evicted at the accession of Elizabeth. Indeed, it was not until about 1565 that two conspicuous Catholics, Roger Dalyson the Precentor and Roger Bromhall the Subdean, were removed in favour of ardent Protestants or less awkward Marian clergy; but the Dean, Francis Mallett, who had been a chaplain to Queen Mary, remained. Indeed, it may have been their hostility to clerical marriage quite as much as to the Protestant settlement which proved the undoing of the two residentiaries. Others, like Thomas Robertson, canon and prebendary of Cropredy under Bishop Longland, could not take the oath of supremacy under Elizabeth and were forced into resignation at that point.[83]

These tests of loyalty to monarch or consort largely ceased after the accession of Elizabeth. But the Queen was known to be unsympathetic to clergy wives and children. As early as 1561 she sent out an injunction urging cathedral churches to avoid the offence which arose from women and children in the Close, and in September of 1561 she enjoined that no cathedral clergy 'be permitted to have within the precincte of some such college [in this case the Minster yard] his wife or other women to abide . . . or . . . to frequent or haunt any loginge within the same'.[84] Her idea of matrimony was for a variety of apartheid, guaranteed to cause maximum strain even for the best adjusted couple. As her attitude relaxed, so the number of wives in the Close increased, and the problem of children playing and making a noise was to vex bishops and deans and chapters alike.[85] But the problems of the sixteenth century were largely those of disciplining either the residentiaries or the more junior clergy. In 1607 it was reported to the Bishop 'that the D[ean] and Chapter are verie dissolute and careless in the Government of the Church'.[86] We may infer that this was the situation long before, since they remained unable to control the lower clergy under them, whose pranks continued whoever was on the throne.

The vicars and Poor Clerks, as well as the choristers, lost a chance of promotion (and certainly, for those of them who held two offices, a large part of their work) with the dissolution of the chantries in 1545–8. The process of dissolution had to a degree taken place before 1548: there were some fifty-three

---

[81] Bowker, *Henrician Reformation*, 173.

[82] Cole, *Chapter Acts* 15, 179ff.

[83] Ibid., 79; Walker, 'Lincoln cathedral', 186–90.

[84] L D C A.3.7, ff. 23–23v.

[85] See below, p. 208.

[86] L D C Dvi. 27. i; *L C S* III, 642.

chantry-priests in 1536 and only eleven in 1548. Their disappearance was largely due to impoverishment, but it left the Close to the senior and junior vicars, Poor Clerks and the choristers.[87] Their record throughout the sixteenth and early seventeenth centuries shows a quite astonishingly uniform pattern. No matter what the theology or the discipline of the day might be with regard to moral failings, they continued to indulge in many of them. At the royal visitation of 1548, they, as well as their seniors, needed to be reminded not to 'haunte' taverns or alehouses, indulge in drinking, dicing, playing cards, hunting or hawking, nor were they to slip away to the women of the town. They were to cease to swear or use abusive language.[88] Fifty years later they had to be reminded of the statutes, and they were accused of 'intolerable' behaviour.[89] What precisely this was became clear in 1607. One Poor Clerk was accused of being 'a comon haunter of Alehouses and tipplinge houses and often tymes hath beene drunk within these two yeares'. He was frequently absent from services, and when present he would neither sing nor apparently wear a surplice – whether because he disapproved of the garment or because he had lost it we are not told. But as he also sometimes failed to light the candles and at other times lit far too many, we may assume that carelessness enhanced by alcohol, rather than conviction, was his chief trouble.[90] One vicar choral called the Dean foul names just like his predecessors a century before.[91] The Organist in 1612 was no better: he beat the choristers and neglected the organ, and was known to call people names – apparently out loud when a service was in progress.[92] Most of the vicars were accused of drinking in service times, one was accused of playing bowls, and the choristers annoyed one vicar by calling him, as Elisha had once been called, 'balde pate', and by waking him at night with similar taunts.[93]

Such behaviour was particularly regrettable because the aim of committed Protestant deans was to educate young clergy in the truths of the Bible and the Fathers (not in the taunts of the ungodly in the Book of Kings) and by learning from their own reading that bad behaviour was not a passport to the Kingdom of Heaven. It was envisaged in 1548 that in place of the time devoted to riotous living the vicars and choristers would 'gyve them selves to redyng and studyeing of Scripture' and in place of the 'sclaunderose and unfruitful talkyng' at dinner 'the Scripture should be read in English to them'.[94] It was a pious vision, but vision it remained.

---

[87] Bowker, *Henrician Reformation*, 101.
[88] *LCS* III, 585ff.
[89] LDC A.3.9, ff. 2, 5.
[90] LDC A.3.9, ff. 53–4.
[91] LDC A.3.9, f. 74; see above, p. 170.
[92] LDC A.3.9, f. 82.
[93] LDC A.3.9, ff. 139v–140.
[94] *LCS* III, 585–6.

There were many causes for the continued quarrelsome behaviour of the lower clergy. Their poverty was increased by the need to support wives in some cases (though the obligation on the vicars choral to reside together remained). The position was an unattractive one, and by the end of the sixteenth century, laymen were appointed as vicars in order that the services should be properly sung. Poor Clerks and choristers were unlikely either to appreciate the study of Scripture or to improve their lot unless they became educated. Provision for such education improved but it was not always taken up or appreciated.[95]

In 1548 the Royal Commissioners specifically stated that revenues of the church were to go to a grammar school with a master, paid at 20 marks and with free accommodation, and an usher paid £6.13s.4d., with a free room; and they envisaged that choir boys whose voices had broken were to go to this school or another. Normally, the choristers were to have their own teacher.[96] This arrangement may have continued and become formalised in the Marian idea of 1556, when a 'New College of Thirty Poor Clerks' within the close is mentioned with a list of pupils.[97] It seems to have lasted under this name for a short time only, but there are continual references to schoolmasters, either for the choristers or for a grammar school in the Close until 1585 when its place seems to have been taken by a grammar school in the town.[98] By 1580 negotiations were in hand between the Dean and Chapter on the one hand, and the city council on the other, to see whether the grammar schools of Close and city could be combined. In January 1584 an indenture between them for a free grammar school was agreed: overlapping was to be avoided, and costs and buildings were to be shared. The schoolmaster, capable of teaching Latin and Greek, was to be chosen by the Dean and Chapter and paid £20 by them and £6.13s.4d. by the city. The city was to appoint an usher, also able to teach Latin and Greek, and to be paid £13.6s.8d. a year by them alone. The school was to be visited by representatives of both parties.[99] The questions raised by one such visitation survive and indicate what was the expected behaviour of the school in 1615. The master and usher were asked the hours they kept and whether they went to taverns. They were examined on whether they heard sermons and whether they asked their pupils to take notes on them. Had any of their pupils been 'fitted for the universities or for other scholler like imployment'? How did they keep order: 'whether they have menuaged their schollers by gentle allure-

---

[95] Walker, 'Lincoln cathedral', 192–4.

[96] LCS III, 589, 595.

[97] Cole, *Chapter Acts* 15, 131–2; for the detailed proposals for seminaries within cathedral closes see N. Orme, *English schools in the middle ages*, London 1973, 286–7.

[98] Leach, 'Schools', *VCH Lincs* 435, 446–7.

[99] Ibid., 441–2.

mente or otherwayes daunted directed their schollers by churlish behaviour and severe correction – correction (that is by) uprisinge by the eares, beatinge them on the heade and handes rashlye and intemperately?' They were also asked if they took poor men's children for no fee, and whether scholars were asked for extra fees.[100] Though no answers to these searching questions have come down to us, the school seems to have survived and remained unscathed, even when the revenues of the chapter were confiscated.[101]

Educational provision there may have been, but it still remained unused. The Poor Clerks, who were meant chiefly to profit, were accused from time to time of not attending the school, and one confessed that he had been 'all together absent from the gramer schole these two years past'.[102] The choristers continued to have their own schooling arrangements,[103] and they were supposed to be at school between 9 a.m. and 3 p.m.[104] but by 1619 they appear to have attended to neither the choir master nor the grammar master.[105] Four of them had to attend Song School for eight weeks without a break, and another was said to be illiterate.[106]

Schooling does not appear to have done much to increase the dedication of the vicars, Poor Clerks and choristers to their duties in the Close. Yet changes had taken place, particularly in worship, to make their liturgical functions lighter and easier to follow; and one would have supposed more attractive. If we look at these changes, it becomes clear that at a certain level formal religious obligation had as little meaning to certain sorts of people in Protestant England as in Catholic England. It was not that they were agnostic – we have no evidence of that – they were apparently indifferent.

At first the changes which took place in the Minster would have savoured more of greedy iconoclasm than of religious reformation. They involved the stripping of the shrines which had made the ancient church a place of pilgrimage. Henry VIII would have gained some knowledge of the value of the treasure actually affixed to the shrine of St Hugh and to the other shrines in the Minster and in the Treasury in his enquiries in 1535 for the tax of first fruits and tenths. But that tax was primarily concerned with income; for the capital value of the shrines we need to turn to a list of jewels made in 1520, another made in 1536 and another of 1557. These do not quite agree with one another, either in what was there, or what was taken, but they indicate that the plundering hand and

[100] LDC A.3.9, ff. 118–19; cf. A.3.10, ff. 151ff.
[101] Hill, *Tudor and Stuart Lincoln*, 211.
[102] LDC A.3.9, f. 53.
[103] LDC A.3.9, f. 28v.
[104] Ibid., f. 81.
[105] LDC A.3.9, f. 139v.
[106] Ibid., f. 140.

destructive might which was to be associated with a church free of papal jurisdiction was not popular. Sapphires, gold images and crosses as well as pearls were said to have adorned the shrine of St Hugh. There were also chained books of his life either in the library or on book stands near the shrine itself. In addition to these there were chalices, copes and mitres belonging to the cathedral and numerous other jewels belonging to the cathedral itself and other shrines in 1520. The Commissioners who were to strip the shrines were at work in June 1540, and they carted away from Lincoln quantities of gold and silver and innumerable pearls and precious stones, mostly from St Hugh's shrine. Undeterred, if dismayed, by the loss of what they considered the proper adornment due to a saint's remains – and he, moreover, a former bishop of the great see of Lincoln – the good people of Lincoln continued to venerate the shrine, and some seemed still to come on pilgrimage, causing the King anger – and perhaps a passing realisation that belief is not always changed by pickaxe and shovel.

But clearly the dignitaries of the cathedral, aided and abetted by the Bishop, were also anxious to see that all treasure given to the Minster over many centuries should not be melted down for bullion to buy the cannonballs to kill the French. Some valuables were quietly 'taken away' by the chapter according to the Treasurer's notes on the 1536 list. A mitre, probably given by the then bishop, embroidered with stones and pearls, was kept from the King, as was an elaborate silver and gilt image in which on Easter Day the sacrament was placed: it weighed 36 ounces. These all found their way back into the church under Mary, together with vestments of cloth of gold and a mass book covered with jewels and gold leaf. There many of them were to stay, in spite of the reigns of Elizabeth and the first two Stuarts; but the civil war in England may well have seen the end of the richest of them.[107]

In place of the attractions of the visible it was the aim of Edward VI in 1548 and again of Elizabeth to make the Minster a place of readily understood worship, fine singing of a more limited range of anthems and, above all, regular preaching. Even before the Church in England had a Book of Common Prayer (first that of 1549 and then that of 1552), Edward VI's Commissioners had gone far towards changing the traditional worship of the Minster.

At the centre of worship and of all Christian life was the Bible, first ordered by the injunctions of 1538, if not earlier, and there were to be public readings of the Scripture for all chapter clergy in 1542.[108] By 1548 there were to be two Bibles of a large size to be used in choir and two smaller ones available in the church 'in suche mete and convenyent places as every other person comyng

[107] Bowker, *Henrician Reformation*, 93–5.
[108] Ibid., 101.

181

thether may have recourse to the same'.[109] Under Henry VIII, Archbishop Thomas Cranmer had composed a litany in English which was ordered for use in 1544. Full clarification of when this litany was to be used also comes from the injunctions of Edward VI: every Sunday, Wednesday, Friday and every festival day, the Litany and suffrages were to be sung in the middle of the choir before High Mass,[110] and under Elizabeth it was to be sung by the priest who was to preside at the Communion Service with assistance from the choir. The Litany of 1544 ended with six prayers, but to these there were added in 1552 variants or additions such as prayers for rain, fair weather and for divine aid in time of dearth and famine (these were removed by Elizabeth and restored in 1662). The ancient liturgy used before 1544 at Lincoln, which was called the Sarum rite, also had a litany but it was used sparingly and usually in processions. The novelty, therefore, of the Use as envisaged in 1548, was one of language. Those present were not likely to forget their sins when they prayed 'Remember not, Lord, our offences nor the offences of our forefathers: neither take thou vengeance of our sins.' Such a phrase in the old usage was disguised in Latin and actually kept to an anthem.[111] Indeed the whole Litany underlines the frailty of human life which in its deepest sense looks as though it was not fully appreciated among the lower cathedral clergy in spite of repetition.

The night office of Matins, which had in the past provided the excuse for the sleepiness of vicars and their non-attendance or dishevelled appearance at Mass, was also abolished in 1548, together with any 'syngyng of dyvine service in the nyght tyme'. In future, Matins was to be sung at six in the morning, and as the church moved towards only two offices, Matins and Evensong, so it was ordered that each should have two lessons read in English: one from the Old Testament and one from the New. The old offices of Prime, Tierce, Sext, None and Compline had very little biblical reading outside the repetition of the Psalms in them; and the move to an emphasis on Scripture and the Psalms was a feature of Morning and Evening Prayer in the Prayer Books of 1549 and 1552, and the revision of the 1552 Book accepted in 1559. In consequence, the worship of the cathedral became possible for everyone to follow. This trend was increased when the Mass was put into English in 1549 and remained so in 1559. But in the emphasis on plain vernacular liturgy with a large admixture of Scripture, there were losses and problems.

One loss was that of the awareness, particularly in a cathedral such as Lincoln, that, in worship, the choir was joined by unseen heavenly hosts. The

---

[109] *LCS* III, 586.
[110] Ibid., 593.
[111] *The Prayer Book interleaved with ... notes*, ed. W. M. Campion and W. J. Beamont, Cambridge 1870, 75–9.

presence, as it were, in the cathedral, of the 'Angel Choir', together with shrines to saints and the carved statues of the mother of Jesus and all the saints which adorned the interior and exterior, tended to remind the worshipper that his voice was not alone. But under Edward VI the desire to rid the Church throughout England of what was held to be superstition resulted both in the removal of much imagery and certainly a deliberate movement away from celebrating the Virgin and the saints and towards concentrating on God as revealed in Christ alone through the Spirit. So the Edwardian injunctions order that 'no anthemes off our lady or other saynts but onely of our Lorde' shall be sung in English and no other.[112]

The use of the vernacular both in Scripture and in the services of Morning and Evening Prayer and Holy Communion was tried in 1549 and, after the reversion to the Sarum rite under Mary,[113] was tried with considerably more success and permanence under Elizabeth and the first two Stuarts. This put a very high premium on explaining what Scripture actually meant. The move away from allegorical and figurative interpretation, which had characterised the middle ages, was a feature of the early sixteenth century. By the reigns of Edward and Elizabeth, the sermon was a fundamentally important part of worship. Yet not all the residentiaries nor the non-residentiary canons held a degree, nor had they much experience in preaching; there was obviously both difficulty and reluctance on their part – which eventually gave way to extreme dexterity in passing the duty to another or using the pulpit for personal ends.

In 1548 it was ordered that the Dean, if in residence, should preach on Christmas and Easter day; the Chancellor (who was the scholar of the Close) had to preach on four Sundays in Advent and on the Sundays of Septuagesima, Sexagesima and Quinquagesima, and on the first five Sundays in Lent. In the summer he was to rest. Of the others, the dignitaries should preach once by virtue of their office and once on account of their residence; and the non-resident canons were to fill the remaining Sundays provided that the yearly value of their prebend was over £20. The objective was to have one preacher every Sunday. Following the 'preaching rota' set out in 1548, others were made and a practice grew up of paying some for taking a 'turn'.

This practice was continued after the reign of Mary, and non-resident canons, whose income was below £10, were expected to participate in preaching: fines were imposed on defaulters but this did not coerce some reluctant canons who were accused of not preaching in 1575. Clearly the sermon assumed a place in Protestant worship which it did not have in the pre-Reformation Church, and provision was made at this time by the city for a special preacher who was

---

[112] *LCS* III, 592–3.
[113] Cole, *Chapter Acts* 15, 133.

to preach in the cathedral on Wednesdays and on Sunday afternoons.[114] The city provision lapsed within the decade, but the duties of residents and non-residents remained, though the 'rota' seems to have changed a little by 1629: the Dean was still to have Christmas and Easter; the Precentor and the Archdeacons of Lincoln, Leicester, Buckingham, Bedford and Stow were to preach on the Sundays in Epiphany, and the Subdean took over Sexuagesima from the Chancellor, who was left with Septuagesima and Quinquagesima in addition to five Sundays in Lent and four in Advent. All Sundays after Easter, including Whit Sunday and Trinity Sunday, were covered by the canons.[115]

Not all these sermons seem to have had the content or the attention which they deserved. In 1591 a letter was written to the Bishop by the chapter, complaining that the Dean had preached 'at them' or, in their words: 'iii several times to the greate disturbance of the peace of the church and the wonderfulle discredite of us the Chapter proclaiming us, and that not covetlye, proscutors [*sic*], seckers of his bloode, theaves, men of inveterate malice.'[116] In 1607 the Archdeacons of Leicester and Buckingham and the canon and prebendary of Aylesbury were accused of neglecting their preaching altogether, and this may have been one of the causes for extreme unrest among the congregation. It was said that preachers were 'usually much troubled in their sermons by the prophane walking, and talking of idle and irreligious persons' and that such behaviour 'disturbing and distracting the preacher' needed reform.[117]

Yet the contents of sermons by the end of the sixteenth century should have grown more weighty. The 1548 injunctions had ordered the improvement and extension of the cathedral library by editions of the Fathers,[118] and by the end of the century most senior clergy in cathedrals and parishes held a degree – and, what is more, would have probably studied under someone who had been in exile in Calvinist Geneva and was tutoring extreme Protestant theology at Oxford and Cambridge. This, however, did not mean that their preaching was any less boring – at least to some. But there is one letter which suggests an appreciation, not only of change, but of the ministry exercised in the cathedral. Henry Howard, Earl of Huntingdon, wrote in February 1605:

synce I was a littell one and brought up at Lincoln with Bishop White I have loved and reverenced that church . . . I doubt not but in this greedie world god will ever rayse upp some faithfull ministers under the most faithful and just Kinge that lyves upon earthe to

---

[114] *LCS* III, 587–8; Walker, 'Lincoln cathedral', 198–9.
[115] LDC D. vii. 3D. 1.
[116] LDC A.3.8, f. 73.
[117] LDC Dvi. 27.1.
[118] *LCS* III, 585.

dryve away those Jackedawes and Carren Crowes with the staff of Abraham that watch onely to devowere that holye sacrefice which is offered to god.[119]

Only one of the clergy seems to have objected to the use of the sign of the cross in baptism and another refused the surplice,[120] a garment of 'popish' origin and an anathema to the extreme Protestants. Laity who were more extreme in their views could usually take themselves to the parish churches. Yet there was concern for some who appear in 1607 not to have been to *any* church for nine years: 'due care is not taken to cause those that are negligent to frequent divine service so that diverse in this place have not for these naine years been known to frequent any church.'[121]

The sixteenth century saw the rise to prominence of the laity in the Minister. Not only did laymen gain the custody of prebends and the control of certain offices which had before gone to clerks (notably that of Bishop's Chancellor and that of Chapter Clerk): there was the inevitable laicisation involved in having within the Close the families of cathedral residentiaries and of the lower clergy. Where laymen took over from vicars and Poor Clerks the duties of singing in the services, the gain to the cathedral was considerable. But not all the laymen in the Close were so helpful, and the poor constituted a problem.

Dearth and price increases created a scale of poverty in England which caused fear and savage legislation from Henry VIII onwards. The poor were the concern of the parishes in which they were born, and if found elsewhere were to be encouraged by flogging to return to their place of birth. Hospitality for the poor had been a feature of some monastic houses, and was ordered by the Edwardian injunctions of 1548 to be practised by the corporate houses of vicars, Poor Clerks and even choristers. They were to keep hospitality, and in particular 'shall releve therwith the pore wayfaryng men, honeste and nedy persons and specially such as be poor Mynisters of the churche'. The latter would probably refer to the elderly vicars, some erstwhile chantry-priests and the disabled.[122] All seems to have been well until after the war with Spain (1604) when, in Lincoln as elsewhere, old soldiers appeared without pay or keep. From 1607 onwards there is evidence of begging inside and out of the cathedral. It was said that 'there is no course taken for beggars who, in very ungodly maner both abuse the Church . . . and trouble every stranger with there importunitie contrarie to the statutes of the realm.'[123]

---

[119] LDC A.3.9, f. 44.
[120] Walker, 'Lincoln cathedral', 187.
[121] LDC Dvi. 27. 1.
[122] *LCS* III, 586; Walker, 'Lincoln cathedral', 190–1.
[123] LDC Dvi, 27. 1.

In 1611 a pauper called Lambert was paid 6s.8d. on condition that 'they [*sic*] dooe not begge in the churche'.[124] He was presumably a leader of a begging gang. He was perhaps fortunate not to have been at the receiving end of falling masonry. Then as now the Fabric of the cathedral sometimes deteriorated to the point at which it was unsafe.

While the responsibility for the Fabric remained in chapter hands, it was teams of lay masons, glaziers and pewterers who bore the brunt of the work in keeping the Minster in good order. Similarly, it had been the devotion of the laity which kept the Fabric Fund reasonably healthy. Legacies and payments to the Fund steadily declined after 1530[125] and it is hard to see how financially the chapter could cope with an emergency such as the collapse of the steeple of the cathedral tower in 1547. But if laymen were no longer giving so much to the Fabric Fund and supporting the Minster in that particular way, they were giving to the bells. In 1593 five bells of 'our lady's steeple' were 'new caste'[126] and their ringing was the duty and the pride of a lay guild.

The ringers of Our Lady Bells and St Hugh Bells were gradually organised throughout the sixteenth century into a company. The bells were central to certain customs practised in the cathedral and announced Mass and other services as well as telling all within earshot that day had come – 'the Day-bell and the Peal' – and that it was over – 'the Curfew'.[127] They were used to mark honoured occasions and they continued to be used throughout the Reformation. Their ringers were mainly artisans who were to form a company, and gentry who were interested were known as Associates. The Ordinances of the Ringers, together with a schedule of their names, survive from the seventeenth century. The Ordinances provided for a dinner to which wives could be invited on the Sunday 'next after the Feast of St Luke the Evangelist' and ringers who were absent from their appointed duties were fined, as was anyone who did not come to the feast. The ringers clearly had their own Common Fund for which accounts were made, augmented by bequests and fines, and the Master was responsible for appointing two wardens and paying them 10s. each for arranging the ringing times and other meetings of the company; refusal to take the office cost 13s.4d. The company cleaned the chapel where they rang (it is at the foot of the south-west tower) in addition to the ringers' lofts elsewhere, they oiled the bells and laid the 'Chyme hammers upp' before ringing commenced. All the company undertook to behave themselves honestly, modestly, orderly and quietly whether in Lincoln or when invited to ring elsewhere. Penalties were

[124] LD C A.3.9, f. 84v.
[125] LD C Bj.5.19, ff. 142vff.
[126] LD C Bij.3.2, unpaginated.
[127] *LCS* I, 71.

imposed in the form of fines for stepping out of line. A member who died was of right entitled to 'a peale or twoe' of St Hugh Bells at burial; some financial arrangements were made for widows and children. The names of the bell-ringers from 1614 to about 1634 are recorded, and so are those of six associates. The names of the masters were painted in the ringers' chapel until 1725 and the company of ringers seems to have provided a closely knit and supportive group until at least that date.

The evidence seems to suggest that the Dean and Chapter weathered the storms of the English Reformation reasonably well. In spite of disagreements about residence and insubordination among the lower clergy which had preceded the Reformation as well as followed it, a change had been made in worship and the understanding of the faith of staggering proportions. With the exception of the reign of Mary, worship was in English and centred on Matins, Evening Prayer and Communion with a large teaching ingredient in the sermon and intercession provided by the Litany. That no regime claimed the allegiance of all is certainly true, but deprivation was of the few not of the many, and the gentle pace of change, which the century as a whole provided, does not detract from the sudden and traumatic choices which confronted individuals, like Matthew Parker over the question of marriage and papal supremacy.

The difficulties of change may for some have been offset by the financial advantages which the new regime, especially of Elizabeth, brought. Leases of prebendal property might, in 1560, be for as much as ninety years on apparently favourable terms,[128] or even in kind. In 1571 and 1575, Parliament limited the duration of leases to twenty-one years or three lives but, even thereafter, individual lessees seem to have done very well. The actual rent charged remained unchanged until the eighteenth century in most cases, and though entry fines may have increased, they are unlikely to have reflected the large difference in value between the real income of the property and the customary rent.[129]

Money might make the chapter friends of 'the mammon of unrighteousness', but it did not test the sincerity of the allegiance of the Minster and its staff to the new order. Archbishop William Laud was to try to do just that.

Abolition and restoration c.1620–1680

The change from a broadly uniform Protestant state to one in which there were many individual Protestant churches and groups, and in which neither Roman Catholicism nor Anglicanism were even tolerated, is associated with the English

[128] LDC A.3.7, ff. 19–21, 24v.
[129] LDC A.3.9, f. 197v; Walker, 'Lincoln cathedral', 195–6.

Civil War and the Interregnum (1642–60). The Restoration of Charles II (1660–85) saw the restoration of the Church of England and a very limited toleration for other groups. These dramatic changes in the status of the Church of England were expressed initially in the abolition and, thereafter, the reinstatement, of bishops, deans and chapters, accompanied first by the confiscation of their endowments, and the destruction and pillage of the Minster and its treasures, and second by an attempt to make good the loss. In a sense, after 1649 and until 1660, the Minster had no independent status and no recorded history. But it is instructive to know how such a situation came about, what damage we believe to have been done, and what problems confronted a new Dean and Chapter in the 1660s and how they tried to solve them.

English Protestantism, which had been partially imposed by Elizabeth I (with its peculiar insistence on the slightly amended Book of Common Prayer of 1552, its adherence to the monarchy, and its use of an element of ritual in its services, such as kneeling to receive Holy Communion, making the sign of the cross on the forehead at baptism and using a ring in the marriage service), had raised cries of dissent from some congregations. This was particularly the case where the parish priest preached with an eye to the Protestantism of the Continent and especially to Geneva. On the Continent Protestants used a different vernacular Bible and different forms of worship, and there were different expectations of behaviour from those who thought themselves the elect of God. English Protestantism and Continental Calvinism held to the doctrine of predestination: God had predestined some to salvation and others to perdition; to which destination, that any Englishman held a ticket was obvious from his devotion and behaviour. Articles of Religion, compiled in 1552 and revised in 1562 and 1571, closely followed the idea that salvation was decreed in advance and damnation, for some, inevitable: 'so, for curious and carnal persons, lacking the spirit of Christ, to have continually before their eyes the sentence of God's Predestination, is a most dangerous downfall, whereby the Devil doth thrust them either into wretchedness of most unclean living, no less perilous than desperation'. That this creed made a sinner desperate (and many others too) was hardly surprising and the faithful might ask, 'How do I know that I am saved?'

It was in response to this question that, within the Church of England voices were raised to suggest that no one was predestined to damnation, all received the grace of God, which was renewed by the sacraments. This change in the understanding of the 'economy of salvation' gained adherents in England, particularly after the accession of Charles I. The expression in practice of a change of this nature was mainly detectable in the increased reverence with which sacraments as such, and the furniture necessary to them, were regarded. Altars could no longer be treated as hat stands; they must be pushed to the east end and rails installed, so that the laity could be kept at a distance and supported on their knees for receiving Communion. It was no longer a matter of indifference what the clergy wore at services, the surplice or not, nor whether they used the sign of the cross in baptism: for those among them who believed in the universality of grace and of constant recourse to it by the sacraments, these things were important.[130] Misleadingly known as Arminians, or followers of the Dutch theologian Arminius who held these views,[131] the divines in England who espoused this understanding of salvation were welcomed at the court of Charles I, and one of them, William Laud, was to become archbishop of Canterbury in 1633. At that time, the bishop of Lincoln was John Williams, who was basically Calvinist in his attitude to predestination. Just as the enforcement of changes of the Henrician Reformation were heralded by an archbishop's visitation of the Dean and Chapter, thereby circumventing an obstreperous local bishop, so William Laud tried to make his views known in Lincoln by visitation.

The questions to be asked at visitations were, by the late sixteenth and seventeenth centuries, apt to be stereotyped, so departures from the common form tell us what Archbishop Laud wished to introduce into the Minster, or at the very least, what he wished to ascertain was actually the expected practice. After asking questions about the number of people serving the cathedral, whether as residentiaries, choristers, vergers or grammar school masters, and whether there was simony, Laud was very concerned with the singing of the daily service:

Is the number of those who serve the Choir, and all other Ministers of the Church, kept full, and the choir sufficiently furnished with a skilful organist and able singers? And is the daily service there sung according to the Foundation of this church and the Statutes of this realm?[132]

Laud also asked whether the sacraments were administered in due time and according to the Book of Common Prayer. He further required the wearing of not only a surplice but an academic hood if the clerk possessed a degree. Like other bishops, he was anxious to know about the extent of adultery, drunkenness, incest and fornication in the Close. He was also concerned with attendance at Communion for a minimum of three times a year. He, like former bishops of

---

[130] *The Book of Common Prayer*, ed. Campion and Beamont, 378; H. C. Porter, *Reformation and reaction in Tudor Cambridge*, Cambridge 1958, 323ff; N. Tyacke, 'Puritanism, Arminianism and counter revolution', in *Origins of the English civil war*, ed. C. Russell. London 1973, 130.

[131] The term is misleading because English Protestants had reached similar conclusions before Arminius: see N. Tyacke, *Anti-Calvinists: the rise of English Arminianism c 1590–1640*, Oxford 1990, vii–xv, 1–86.

[132] *LCS* III, 648; LD C Dvj. 23. 4.

Lincoln, asked about the standard of preaching and the state of repair of the Minster.[133]

We have no means of knowing the answers to these questions. Even if Laud rebuked a cathedral chapter, with a local bishop hostile to his ideas and residentiaries likely to attend to neither of them, it would be hard to establish whether his visitation made a difference. There are suggestions that the lower cathedral clergy, quite apart from an antipathy to authority, were as intransigent as ever, and that the Dean and Chapter had enough on their hands with the status quo. Innovation was beyond them. In 1636, for example, just after the visitation, the chapter acts record that Richard Jameson, a junior vicar choral, was negligent in his duty on Sundays and holy days, and poor in his behaviour

by talking, laughinge, writinge or readinge of such bookes as are unfitt to be writt or redd in that place and for frequentinge the Company of Widowe Blundmilo [*sic*] in suspicious manner and also for not livinge orderly and peaceably with his new wife and for frequenting Alehouses.[134]

If 'new wives' could not keep their husbands, the attractions of an ordered liturgy, the oft-quoted 'beauty of holiness' which Laud saw as so important, could hardly be expected to succeed. Yet as England moved towards a war between King and Parliament (or more accurately some of Parliament) it was inevitable that many members of the Church of England, however ambivalent they were about Arminianism, saw King Charles I as the guardian of the Church of England, even though he was to betray it and his friends; death concentrated his mind on his real priorities. But fickle as was the King, the Parliament of 1641 attacked bishops and the whole ecclesiastical establishment[135], and the King's enemies in the Westminster Assembly continued to do so. It was, therefore, likely that bishops and deans and chapters should side with the King, thereby making their fate as catastrophic as his own in the event of his defeat. Sir John Wray, one of the knights of the shire returned to Parliament, spoke against the 'popery' which became equated with Anglicanism. Deans and canons were the subject of opprobrium and one member said of them:

[We] will never bee safe nor well at quiet, until these heave drossy Cannons with all

---

[133] LDC Dvj. 23. 4; for the attitude of the Bishop of Lincoln to Laudian innovation see H. T. Blethen, 'Bishop Williams, the Altar Controversy and the Royal Supremacy', *The Welsh History Review* 9(2), 1978, 142–54.

[134] LDC A.3.9, f. 195v.

[135] Edward, Earl of Clarendon, *History of the rebellion and civil wars in England* I, ed. W. D. Macray, Oxford 1888, 308ff.

their base mettle, be melted and dissolved: let us then dismount them, and destroy them, which is my humble motion.[136]

Not surprisingly, the 'heavy drossy Canons' heard the message, and, as both sides contended for the allegiance of Lincoln, the men from Parliament, in forming the view of arms found

most of the Close of that Great Church neglected to appear ... the truth is ... that the Recorder of the City whom we may justly suspect not to be well affected to the service and some others of his leaven (Popishly inclined) near the Cathedral were so far from sending in their own arms ... that we rather apprehend they endeavoured to dishearten others therein as much as in them lay.[137]

The loyalties of the Close, led by the City Recorder, rather than the Dean, influenced many, as was shown in July 1642 when the King visited the city and was widely acclaimed. He spent the late summer in the East Midlands and returned to Lincoln on at least one occasion. Finally, it was near Nottingham he raised his standard and began to ask the Lincoln clergy for loans.[138] The division of loyalties in the city, its proximity to the coast, and especially to Hull, meant that it frequently became a battleground and the control of the city often changed hands.[139]

The Minster was obviously vulnerable: the pewter in its windows, the lead for roof and draining were assets easily realised. The building itself could provide room for a large contingent, and the houses of the Close might provide hospitality, food, valuables and victims of war, women. In May 1643 when Lincoln was held by the royalists but under siege by Manchester and Cromwell, the Close was said to be defended by 2000 men with food and ammunition. In the battle which followed the Close and the part of the town which clusters round the Minster were pillaged.[140] Later in the war the cathedral library, which had already been alight as early as 1609, was once more burned. Most of it was destroyed.[141] Some of the charred timbers can still be seen at the entrance to the Wren Library, which was subsequently built. It would appear that the books and manuscripts housed in it had already been removed, though we are less sure of where they went. Clearly the medieval library was sizeable[142] and several carts would be needed to remove the contents, which could hardly be

---

[136] Hill, *Tudor and Stuart Lincoln*, 146.

[137] Ibid, 148–9.

[138] LAO Diocesan, Additional Register 3, The Red Book, f. 226a.

[139] Hill, *Tudor and Stuart Lincoln*, 151ff.

[140] Ibid., 157–8.

[141] Ibid., 162.

[142] *Catalogue of manuscripts: Lincoln cathedral Chapter Library*, compiled R. Maxwell Woolley, Oxford 1927 *passim*; R. M. Thomson, *Catalogue*, *passim*.

done silently at night with wooden wheels scraping against the cobbles. The modern library does contain volumes owned once by sixteenth-century incumbents,[143] but a great deal that we know to have been there in 1640 was never to return. There are rumours that it all went 'down town' and much was ruined in the flooding there. A nineteenth-century manuscript records its transfer to Wallingford House in London but the reference is clearly to episcopal registers and account books which were returned when all the troubles were over.[144] It looks as though much either disappeared or was pillaged.

Little care was shown to ecclesiastical property or moveables. The bishop's palace was burned[145] and we have some indication of the destruction and melting down of metals, whether of monumental brasses or of bells or of pewter and lead. Evelyn's diary, which recounts his visit to Lincoln in 1654, records how the soldiers had gone into the cathedral church 'with axes and hammers and shut themselves in, till they had rent and torn off some large loads of metal, not sparing even the monuments of the dead'.[146] The scale of the destruction only really became apparent after the restoration of Charles II, and, with him, the Dean and Chapter. It was alleged in 1664/5 that George Shoesmithe, a glazier, and Stephen Mouton, a pewterer, had come by '16 pounds of knottes' of lead and pewter and forged them into bullets.[147] In the presentations for a visitation in 1664 it was said that George and his family were 'vehemently suspected to have secretly purloyned and conjured away much of the lead and souldere, belonging to the said churche, and many of the oald window knotts and to have sould them to diverse pewterers and other persons within the city and suburbs of Lincoln and other places to the great wrong and detriment of the church'.[148] But in spite of these suspicions Shoesmithe was still the cathedral glazier in 1670.[149]

---

[143] Wren Library, RR.1.12.

[144] Mrs Naomi Linley, a former librarian of the Wren Library, informed me that there was a reference to the library going to St Mary Wigford. Neither she nor I have so far found this reference. The Willson Collection (in the custody of the Society of Antiquaries) 786/8 p. 79 refers to 'many volumes of registers' being lodged at Wallingford House in London, where after 1660 they were bound and returned. Cathedral Acts, accounts and diocesan registers are so bound and were returned, but the cathedral manuscripts and early printed books are not mentioned. Another reference suggests this material went to Gurney House; see Williamson, *Lincoln muniments*, 7; D. M. Owen, 'Bringing home the Records; the recovery of Ely Chapter Muniments at the Restoration', *Archives* 8, no. 39, 1968, 128.

[145] Hill, *Tudor and Stuart Lincoln*, 168–9.

[146] *Diary and correspondence of John Evelyn*, ed. W. Bray, London, n.d., 207.

[147] LDC A.3.9, f. 243v.

[148] LDC Dvi. 27. 2. 2; see also *LCS* III, 645.

[149] LDC Bj. 1. 9, ff. 12v, 14v.

Between 1640 and 1660, many of the leading residentiaries had died.[150] Their voices were silenced in any case because Anglicans were not tolerated, and to add insult to injury the pulpit of the cathedral church had been removed. The Minster resounded with other preachers who linked the Word to the suppression of alehouses and horse-racing and to making provision for the poor.[151] Equally, the lands which went to providing the income of the Common Fund or the Fabric Fund were in the hands of commissioners or tenants who sought to sell them. There seems to have been a small group of recipients who came into the more valuable property. George Walker, described as a gentleman of Lincoln, came into a dozen or so properties, themselves made into units from disparate leases, between 1649 and 1653. He bought the properties outright and in most cases stood by the original leases. Other property he resold.[152]

When Charles II (1660–85) was restored, the Church of England with its institutions and its lands was restored with him – though there was no necessary presumption that the Anglican Church would have a monopoly of control over the affairs of the spirit. There was undoubtedly much goodwill towards the Church emanating from the victims of the old order: those who had lost their lands. or, more bewilderingly, their influence.[153] Evicted parish clergy were also not without their sympathisers. Sir Robert Shirley provided in his will £1,000 'to be disposed of unto such distressed parsons as have lost their estates in the service of the late King Charles!'[154] On the other hand, Charles himself, as well as many of his subjects, looked with favour on a settlement which, while it might encompass Anglicans, would not do so at the expense of other Protestants, or even, perhaps, of Catholics.[155] The restoration of the monopoly of the Church of England was not inevitable. Nor was it easy.

The Chapter Act Book which had recorded nothing between 29 October 1640 and 2 July 1660 gives the first indication of the gradual path of return. It records the appointment of dignitaries to the Minster: the Archdeacon of Lincoln was installed on 2 July 1660 and he was followed by the Subdean and in October by a Chancellor, and, most important of all, the Dean.[156]

The residentiaries were to be the Dean, the Chancellor and the Subdean. Of these, the Chancellor, John Featley, a graduate of All Souls, held the office of

---

[150] J. H. Srawley, *Michael Honywood*, Lincoln 1981, 10.

[151] Hill, *Tudor and Stuart Lincoln*, 166–9; C. Holmes, *Seventeenth-century Lincolnshire*, Lincoln 1980, 233.

[152] LDC Bij. 2.7..

[153] R. A. Beddard, 'The Restoration Church', in *The restored monarchy 1660–88*, ed. J. R. Jones, London 1979, 155–66.

[154] Bodl. Libr. MS Tanner 130, f. 24.

[155] I. M. Green, *The re-establishment of the Church of England 1660–1663*, Oxford 1978, 4–36.

[156] LDC A.3.9, ff. 207–12.

Provost and was to make enquiries into the loss of cathedral property. He was a cantankerous individual who was on bad terms with the Subdean, Robert Mapletoft, and the two of them bombarded the Dean with mutually accusatory pamphlets. It was alleged that Featley embezzled £500 from the fines of the new leases, for which as Provost he had the care, and that he profited his friends whenever he could. He also appropriated to himself a verger 'to attend on him only in honour of his person and dignity contrary to the statute'.[157] The nature of the language used and the submission of long papers of accusation and defence would have diverted the Dean and Chapter from its prime duty of restoring order. But Featley actually died in 1666 before the matter was resolved.

In contrast to the Chancellor, the Subdean Robert Mapletoft, a relative and friend of Sir Robert Shirley, and the Dean, Michael Honywood, were men of learning, principle and considerable business acumen. Honywood was able to cut his way through the details of the Common Account Book to estimate what the income and expenditure of 'the Church of Lincoln' were under Elizabeth.[158] As he set about repairing the cathedral and building a library for it at his own expense, there are signs of his working carefully on the estimates submitted.[159] Lists of the names of canons survive in his own hand and he wrote in October 1666, 'I have always above all things desired . . . to see this Church in good condition, and God's service performed with due decency and devotion.' Similarly, the Subdean was known for his godliness and his devotion to the ordered liturgical life of the 1630s.[160]

Honywood had spent the civil war abroad in the Netherlands[161] and had left behind him the living of Kegworth in Leicestershire to which his own college of Christ's in Cambridge had presented him. While abroad he indulged his hobby of collecting books and included among them the broadsides in Dutch and English about what was happening in England. His personal library included some rare manuscripts as well as books in English, Dutch, German, Italian and Spanish. He was at pains to see that the revised Book of Common Prayer was in use by 24 August 1662 (St Bartholomew's Day), not least because the penalty was deprivation.[162] But before that, it was clear that orderly liturgical worship according to the Prayer Book with singing, was being restored.

On 11 December 1660 choristers and cantors on the Burghersh Foundation were appointed, and junior and senior vicars in the following year.[163] But all

[157] LDC Dj.18 Book A, ff. 386, 404.
[158] LDC Dyii. 3.D.3.
[159] LDC Ciii 31.1.;
[160] Bodl. Libr. MS Tanner 130, ff. 17, 68–69v, 72. See also DNB, *ad hominem.*
[161] J. H. Srawley, *Michael Honywood,* 5.
[162] Ibid., 7.
[163] LDC A.3.9, ff. 216–29.

was not well either with their quality or with the provision made for them. As late as 1666, Honywood was writing to Dr William Sancroft, Dean of St Paul's and an old friend, about the choir. He said, 'Boys we want extremely in our Quire, not having above 2 or 3 worth keeping when we should have 8 ... Those quire-men we have are passable and we must keep them; but we have but 8 and should have 12.' Honywood did not disguise from his friends that the remuneration was not good but he admitted that living was cheaper than London.[164]

Lincoln was slower than St Paul's London in getting a good choir[165] and one of the reasons may have been housing. In two estimates which survive from 1663, one suggests that £100 was needed to pay the vicars choral and the choir, and the other that a further £1,000 was needed for 'vicars and singing mens houses'.[166] There were also problems with the Organist who in 1663 was so drunk that he abused the residentiaries and interrupted preaching. The organs and their loft had to be repainted and eventually replaced and an Authorised Version of the Bible had to be bought.[167] But in spite of this attempt at good order, there are indications that the lower clergy were as unruly as ever. In 1661, John Jameson, a vicar choral, was apparently not sitting in his proper place even if he continued to appear at a service, and not surprisingly he called the pompous Mr Featley rude names.[168] Shades of old controversies returned in 1664: Alexander Thompson, a Poor Clerk,

for as much as he hath seldom or never worn a surplice in the Quier since he was admitted into the said office, nor performed his duty of reading the Litany nor hath he frequented the services of the Church so often as he ought but hath absented himself and departed out of the town without the Precentor's leave, leaving the Quier unserved contrary to his duty and office

was reported at the Dean's visitation.[169] Already the bell-ringers and vergers were neglecting their duties though the bells cannot have been in place more than a year or two.[170] Rules for the ordering of preaching made in 1662[171] had to be reaffirmed as early as 1664,[172] and reordered yet again in 1670.[173]

---

[164] Bodl. Libr. MS Tanner 130, f. 17.
[165] Green, *The re-establishment of the Church of England*, 74.
[166] Bodl. Libr. MS Tanner 130, f. 17.
[167] L D C A.3.9, ff. 215, 229–229v, 237y; Srawley, *Michael Honywood*, 12.
[168] L D C A.3.9, ff. 229–229v.
[169] L D C Dvi 27.2.2.
[170] Ibid., cf. Srawley, *Michael Honywood*, 14.
[171] L C S III, 630–34.
[172] L D C A.3.9, f. 241v.
[173] L D C A.3.11, f. 8.

The lack of fervour displayed by the lower clergy was symptomatic of problems which affected the cathedral and all its personnel. At Lincoln, Anglicanism was not as popular as it appears to have been elsewhere, and guards had to be put on the Close.[174] There was also the enormous problem of putting right the Fabric of the Minister; its decay detracted from the service of God and the dignity associated with the Prayer Book services. It was estimated, in 1663, that the probable cost of the essential repairs to the church was about £2000, though Honywood himself put it at £3000.[175] The money does not appear to have been immediately forthcoming from sources earmarked for the Fabric Fund. It was, admittedly, not until 1670 that the Fabric Accounts began fully to be kept but even by that time some of the rents due were not being paid; of the arrears from the Close it was recorded that 'nothing has been received since the King's return'. In the same year legacies amounted to just £2.10s.[176] The total receipts of the fund in 1670 totalled £156[177] and it was not until 1675–6 that they amounted to £245.4s.3d.[178] In this situation the Fabric could only be repaired if individuals paid for it themselves. This is exactly what happened: in 1661, the Dean and Chapter laid aside £1,000 from the Common Fund for repairs to the church;[179] this was followed by a further £240,[180] and in 1663 by another £100.[181] Additionally, each residentiary had personally contributed, by 1663, £1,258.[182]

We may presume from the case brought against the glazier that the windows and bells were the first to be put right; but church plate was required for the decent administration of the Communion Service: it was estimated that plate and ornaments would cost £300.[183] It was not until 1673 that masons could be employed to replace the floor before the high altar, make good the steps and 'smooth out Axestrokes and hollowings' in the northern aisle leading to the cloister.[184] At a cost of £270, the wainscot behind the altar and the wooden pillars and adornments, as well as altar rails and a litany desk and repairs to the stalls, were undertaken.[185] At the same time a lot of work was put into

---

[174] LDC A.3.9, f. 217.
[175] Bodl. Libr. MS Tanner 130, ff, 68, 69v.
[176] LDC Bj.1.9, ff. 1v, 11v.
[177] Ibid., f. 16.
[178] Ibid. *ad annum.*
[179] LDC A.3.9, f. 222.
[180] Ibid., f. 231v.
[181] Ibid., f. 239.
[182] Bodl. Libr. MS Tanner 130, f. 68–69v.
[183] See above, p. 192, Bodl. Libr. MS Tanner 130, f. 68.
[184] LDC DV11 3.B.41.
[185] LDC Ciii.31.1, unnumbered letters.

repairing the bells and replacing the pulpit.[186] Such luxuries as cushions had to wait until 1688.[187]

At the same time the northern side of the cloister which had housed part of the medieval library was in ruins. Clearly there were no fabric funds immediately available for restoration of this kind. But the old order had among its adherents those whose attachment to the Anglican Church went to the limit. They had witnessed its overthrow; they had been evicted and, in some cases, expelled from England itself. As a token of their gratitude they gave in kind to the 'restoration'.

At Lincoln all the residentiaries, Honywood, Featley and Mapletoft (as we have seen) gave much; their Dean outshone them all. In addition to his contributions to the cathedral Fabric itself, he gave to the Minster the library which gracefully adorns the northern cloister. The first hint of his generosity came when an indenture was drawn up between Michael Honywood and William Evison; in it Evison agreed 'to raise up and build a Range of building designed for a library and cover it with timber and lead'. It was to take up the whole of the north cloister, and the rubbish which had accumulated there was to be removed. The library was to be of stone but inside it was to be wood-panelled. It was to have two doors of 'seasoned fir', oak was to be used for the floor and stairs and the whole was to be under the direction of Christopher Wren. It was to cost Honywood £780. A model of the library was made and Wren and Honywood worked out to the last detail the costs of painting the interior: 'a foot square gilded flat' was 2s. 8d.; 'veined work like black or white marble 16d.' The painting of shelves and wainscotting was under way by 1675 and the whole seems to have exceeded the original sum by at least £100[188] – and all this in addition to the expense of the books which were to adorn the shelves.

It is tempting to suppose that the munificence of the Dean and his colleagues was made possible by large gains accruing to the Minster through the return of purchased lands and the imposition of fines for new leases. The account books which alone would give us the true picture either do not survive or have been lost, and it is clear from such material as we have, that generosity and private wealth rather than a guilty conscience lay behind the gifts to the cathedral. The Subdean, Robert Mapletoft, was engaged in a long suit for the return of Spital in the Street; his legal fees for this property alone he put at £50, though he added, 'he cannot think (they are) so little', and he commented that he had 'given or parted with more . . . than all he ever received'. Eventually he won it

---

[186] LDC Bj.1.9, unpaginated *ad annum*.
[187] Ibid., *ad annum*.
[188] LDC Ciii.31.1, unnumbered letters. The £780 for the library does not appear to have included a £100 for wainscotting and shelving mentioned in an indenture of 13 Dec. 1675.

197

back and rebuilt its chapel at his own expense. He did not have to go to court for the return of his house, but its repair in 1663 was put at £67, and more was expected because it was 'worse than the worst'.[189] Featley, who may well have used his position as Provost to take some of the entry fines properly due to Dean and Chapter to line his own pocket[190], had some large bills to meet. He had to recover 'from John Disney the purchaser' his house at a sum of over £50, and to pay rent on another property while he did so; when he received his own house, it cost him £45 to repair it.[191] Honywood, who was not accused of embezzlement, had to go to court to reclaim his house and repair it. When all his expenses in 1663 for the Fabric, for a 'gift' to the King and for the repairs to his house were taken into account, he had parted with £2,153 'which', he wrote, 'is far more than is any way received by him as Dean of Lincoln'.[192]

In other dioceses, purchasers did not always require to be sued to release chapter property, nor did deans and chapters have to purchase back property at £700, as did Lincoln.[193] This may have been because well over £3000 of property, which had been in chapter hands, had been sold in the Interregnum,[194] but it may also suggest that there was resistance in the East Midlands either to the possession of property by, or the restoration of it to, the Anglican Church.

Other cathedral chapters were fortunate in being able to make a large number of new leases with suitable entry fines to offset other losses.[195] At Lincoln, there were new leases but fines for these, where the property was assigned to the Fabric Account, were also put to the Fabric even where they were 'formerly reserved for the residentiaries'.[196] The leasing policy of the Dean and Chapter was by law for 21 years only, and it would not, therefore, be until the 1680s that some new leases of property, either formerly purchased or where the lease had fallen in, became available and could in theory reimburse the initial generosity. Often the rent had to be wholly or partially pardoned, especially if the repairs required were great; the Subdean waived one-third of a rent due to him for this reason.[197]

The general state of the property belonging to the cathedral was not good, as the Provost's report made clear. At Aunsby, John Cotthurst had not repaired

---

[189] Bodl. Libr. MS Tanner 130, f. 69v.
[190] LDC Dj.18, f. 404.
[191] Bodl. Libr. MS Tanner 130, f. 68v.
[192] Ibid. f. 69v.
[193] Green, *The re-establishment of the Church of England*, 102–3.
[194] LDC Bij.2.7 *passim*.
[195] Green, *The re-establishment of the Church of England*, 103–7.
[196] Bodl. Libr. MS Tanner 130, f. 68.
[197] Ibid., f. 69v.

the manor house 'which is now a most despicable ruinous cottage house';[198] at Burgh in the Marsh, which had been leased for 99 years in 1562, all the fields had been enclosed and, as the Provost noted, 'unless a speedy course be taken it is probable that we may loose our land there'.[199] At Hainton, the rectory had also been enclosed and a new lease was expected to take improvements into consideration; before enclosure the rectory was said to be worth £80 p.a. but by 1660 £400 p.a.[200] In contrast to this affluence, the Provost found the chancel at Greetwell church 'full of holes', with pigeons flying about 'as in a Dovecote'. The church lacked books and Cromwell's soldiers were reported to have taken away the register: a tidy sum was needed for the repairs but the Provost had to appeal to Sir Robert Dalyson to do them on account of his lease.[201]

It is hardly surprising that against a background of crippling expense, a crumbling Minster, neglected property and some of it to be sued for, the real restoration of the Church of England was not achieved until about 1680. By that time the Minster and the library were restored and rebuilt; equally by that time there emerges a recognisable pattern of service times[202] and the re-establishment of fines for vicars and choirmen who neglected them.[203] Equally there were four residentiaries and an established pattern of weekly preaching by canons and residentiaries alike.[204] We have some suggestion that the finances of the Minster were being increased by pew rents, with seats 'over the West door' costing £6.[205] Leases were being limited in duration and entry fines charged but only slightly in excess of a single year's lease.[206] A similar picture of recovery emerges from the accounts. It was still possible for contention to occur 'for want of severall Books left in the late rebellious times and through the confusion and distraction of the same',[207] and the account books continued to follow medieval accounting practices. It was not until the eighteenth century that a modern form of accounting was introduced.[208] Yet in spite of archaic accounting, the story of recovery is traceable in finance. The Common Fund, which yielded a dividend for the year of £27.19s.5d. to each residentiary in

[198] LC 2 CC., Box 8/152941, p. 2.
[199] Ibid., p. 8.
[200] Ibid., p. 9.
[201] Ibid., p. 12.
[202] LDC A.3.11, f. 53.
[203] Ibid., ff. 20, 23v.
[204] Ibid., f. 8.
[205] Ibid., f. 68.
[206] Ibid., f. 21; C. Clay, 'The greed of Whig bishops?', *Past and Present* 87, 1980, 128–57.
[207] Ibid, ff. 70–70v.
[208] LDC Bj.4.6.

1663,[209] was to yield £84.7s.11¼d. by 1694.[210] The receipts of the Fabric Fund which stood at £170.2s.11d. between 1670 and 1671, rose to £245.4s.3d. in 1675.[211]

The presiding presence in the restoration of the Church of England to the Minster church of Lincoln was Michael Honywood. As a resident Dean, he had taken charge of the chapter and watched over the repair of the Minster and the rebuilding of its library helped by the Subdean and Chancellor. His concern for the 'good condition' of the cathedral church had borne fruit. In September 1681, at the age of 85, he died. As a scholar and bibliophile, he may sometimes have struck his contemporaries as a trifle dull, but the bequests made in his will reveal his true self: all the cathedral personnel, from the residentiaries to the sweepers, were remembered, as was his College. To the Minster he left a magnificent library and yet more to the restoration of the cathedral church.[212] His colleagues were to miss him sorely, and it is tempting to see in the complaints about the deanery which followed his death a lament for a quietly remarkable man.

Loyalty and leisure 1680–1750

The problems which confronted the English Church with the accession of a Roman Catholic, James II, did not at first seem many: there was every expectation that Anglicans would continue to enjoy a monopoly of office and access to the universities, and that neither popery nor nonconformity would interfere with the allegiance of churchmen to the Crown and, in particular, to the Stuart succession. James II, however, did not live up to Anglican expectations: his advancement of Roman Catholics, his disregard of advice on Church appointments, and finally his loss of the crown placed many Anglicans in a difficult position. Was their loyalty to the Crown simply that of allegiance to its wearer, or did legitimacy matter? For some, there could be no oath of allegiance to James' successors, William and Mary; nor was Queen Anne an acceptable alternative to the main Stuart line. Such Anglicans became non-jurors and were increasingly isolated from both the Church and the state.[213] For the rest, and these included the Dean and Chapter of Lincoln, the oath of allegiance was

---

[209] LDC Bj.3.11.
[210] LDC Bj.4.1, f. 41.
[211] LDC Bj.1.9.
[212] Srawley, *Michael Honywood*, 25.
[213] G. V. Bennett, 'Conflict in the Church', in *Britain after the Glorious Revolution 1689–1714*, ed. Geoffrey Holmes, London 1969, 155–74.

acceptable.[214] The gradual infiltration into Government of those who were not Anglicans, or who only occasionally received Communion according to the rites of the Church of England, and the recognition of the existence of nonconformist chapels and places of worship, however distasteful, was a reality which little by little they learned to live with: the loss of their spiritual monopoly meant that the ecclesiastical jurisdiction of the Dean and Chapter over some members of the Close ceased by default, as it did elsewhere.[215] It did not, however, mean that the Minster ceased to be of importance either to the individuals who held office and resided within it or to the city and diocese. There is some suggestion, as we shall see, that its fabric may have commanded the interest of the community at large, and though bishops of Lincoln ceased to have a palace there during the Interregnum, they continued to take a lively interest in the affairs of the cathedral.[216] The residentiaries also continued to devote their energies in some cases to beautifying, if not the Minster, at least their houses, and they also pursued their private and more public quarrels with an intransigence worthy of their forbears.

It was, of course, over matters of residence that tempers flared and ecclesiastical pedantry excelled: this had been of concern in the sixteenth century and it flared up again in the late seventeenth and eighteenth century. The peculiar custom of the cathedral of Lincoln, whereby only residentiaries (in an exact sense of that word) received a portion of dividend from the Common Fund, made this subject a bone of contention which never remained buried for long. Honywood's death was the signal for the first skirmishes in another long battle to begin.

There is little doubt that Archbishop Sancroft wanted his friend and correspondent James Gardiner, Subdean of Lincoln since 1671, to succeed to the deanery. Certainly Gardiner himself wrote for the Archbishop a 'job specification' which would have fitted himself. On 10 September 1681, he reminded the Archbishop that the deanery of Lincoln required:

a worthy Person who may not be hindered by other Preferments and Services from keeping the Statutable Residence of 34 weeks and 5 days to which the Oath we must administer will oblige him and which will be very requisite for the Affairs of our Church which are many and various. For besides the Business in which the Dean is concerned in common with the Chapter, which is not little, He has also Great Trust and Duty of his own, in particular the Authority of his Presence, and the good Example

---

[214] LDC A.3.12. At the end of this Chapter Book the oaths of allegiance to William and Mary and subscriptions to it are recorded.

[215] J. W. F. Hill, *Georgian Lincoln*, Cambridge 1966, 49; cf. Bennett, 'Conflict in the Church' 157–9.

[216] For their visitations see LCS III, 647–72; Bodl. Libr. MS Tanner 130, f.115; LDC Dvj.22.17(17); LDC Dvj.24(5); LDC Dvi.25(4).

of his Life will exceedingly conduce to the happy estate of our Church, and the correcting and reforming of some Corruptions that are growing amongst us.[217]

Gardiner would certainly have suited his own description, but Charles II had already promised the deanery to a former exile and close friend of Bishop Cosin, one Daniel Brevint. Brevint was an ardent supporter of the Stuarts but not to the extent of becoming a non-juror, and he was rabidly anti-papal. He saw in the liturgy of the Book of Common Prayer, even before Cosin revised it, a source of inspiration and meditation, and had written a devotional work based upon it. In contrast, in 1674, he had written *Saul and Samuel*, which was so outspoken in its criticism of the Church of Rome that it smacks of irreverence. Brevint became an ally of William and Mary and not of the exiled Stuarts; he was also an ardent supporter of the liturgical status quo and it is hardly surprising, therefore, that the deanery was his.[218] But he was 65 when he was appointed and it is very doubtful indeed whether the deanery actually commanded his attention, as distinct from his residence. Gardiner, deprived of the prize and of lower church sympathy, clearly saw him as non-resident in mind if not in body. He admitted to his friend Sancroft that the Dean was sick but he added, in 1685, that things had been in an 'ill ... state ... since the coming in of that Dean who in the space of 4 years ... has never taken one weekes paines to peruse our Statutes, or Chapter Acts, or any other Records of our Church which might informe him of his Office, and direct him of the conduct of his Government'.[219] Gardiner was to become bishop of Lincoln before the deanery again became vacant, but his caustic criticism of churchmen who did not apply themselves to their task became yet more justified with time. Brevint's successor, the former Chancellor Samuel Fuller (Dean, 1695–1699/1700), was witty enough but also often drunk, and his successor only held the deanery for little more than a year.[220] The duties of the dean were again called in question with the appointment of Richard Willis (Dean, 26 December 1701 to October 1721).

Willis was a preacher; he was neither a non-juror nor the least bit sympathetic to either high *or* Tory churchmen. He saw that the measure of toleration granted in 1689 made voluntary giving necessary, and he had been a promoter of the Society for the Propagation of the Gospel.[221] He was much appreciated by the Hanoverian court of George I and became bishop of Gloucester *while*

---

[217] Bodl. Libr. MS Tanner 130, f. 75.

[218] DNB, *ad hominem*; for other contenders for the deanery and the background to Brevint's promotion, see R. A. Beddard, 'The Commission for Ecclesiastical Promotions 1681–4', *Historical Journal* 10(1), 1967, 22, 33–4.

[219] Bodl. Libr. MS Tanner 130, f. 121.

[220] Abraham Campion, 17 Apr. 1700–21 Nov. 1701.

[221] DNB, *ad hominem*.

still dean of Lincoln. Only royal connivance prevented the chapter protesting at the non-residence of the Dean. Matters came to a head, again after a short appointment,[222] with the promotion to the deanery of Edward Gee.

Gee was born in the north and was in happy exile in London. Like Brevint, he was a defender of the new monarchy against the popery of James II, and like Willis, he was not fully resident. It was said in 1724 that the 'Dean is chiefly at Westminster, being Canon and at present Subdean there, but when here [at Lincoln] resides in his Decanal house'.[223]

All was well with Gee, until the bishop, Richard Reynolds, was able to secure the appointment of his nephew Charles as Chancellor.[224] He at once put up to the Bishop awkward questions about the Dean's absenteeism: the Chancellor, in August 1729, compared Gee's case with that of the Elizabethan dean, Francis Mallett,[225] and the Bishop, in October, had the task of adjudicating on the matter. It appeared that the Dean had not resided for two years and that the statutes were unambiguous: no one, be he a royal dignitary or an ecclesiastical one, 'had benefits . . . no other ways than that they might return Residence'. The Dean was accordingly deemed unable to receive any monies from the Common Fund, the accounts of which had not been passed in September pending the Bishop's decision.[226] The custom that distributions from the fund were made only to residents was upheld even 'to the sixte part of a Farthing'. It was alleged that the custom dated from 1306; certainly, from the later middle ages it had been enforced, and neither the demands of Queen Elizabeth nor apparently of George II availed against it.

There was, however, still room for debate on how many days constituted residence. George Reynolds as Subdean alleged that he had resided for 104 which was, in his view, 'greater residence'. He was overruled even though his relative and fellow residentiary, Charles, had a vote; and 119 days was upheld as the norm for major residence. In spite, therefore, of family and royal influence, the tradition of the Minster held: no canon could receive a portion of the common fund unless he resided. Lincoln was not a milch cow.[227]

So strict a view of residence had a number of consequences. It kept the dividend as high as possible but it also kept the number of residentiaries so low that business could be impeded. Ever one for niceties, George Reynolds asked whether three residentiaries without the Dean could style themselves 'the Dean

[222] Robert Cannon, 21 Nov. 1721–1722.
[223] *LCS* III, 657.
[224] Hill, *Georgian Lincoln*, 36 n. 4.
[225] see above, p. 175.
[226] LDC Dvj.24(5).
[227] LDC A.3.13, ff. 252, 290.

and Chapter.'[228] More seriously, could the services and sermons of the Minster be adequately performed by a mere three residentiaries?

In 1686, when three canons and Dean Brevint were in residence, divine service was said to be performed daily with singing; sermons were preached on all Sundays and 'great Holy days', and while the residentiaries preached in person, the non-resident canons who were obliged to preach on at least one Sunday either managed the task in person or found a willing deputy. Things were not so easy over Holy Communion. It was celebrated on the first Sunday in the month, and the residentiaries claimed, 'we doe heartily desire and have endeavoured to perform it oftener', but they found both their number too slight and that the potential communicants might be as few as one. This was because the inhabitants of the Close belonged to parishes adjacent to it, and the Minster was not a parish church.[229] By 1731, it was necessary to make arrangements for Morning and Evening Prayer to be read by paid deputies – this at a time when there were only three residentiaries, any of whom might be sick.[230] This arrangement had, by 1744, become the norm on Sunday 'except when any Residentiary shall chuse to read himself'.[231] Just as their predecessors had found the early rising associated with duties in choir or at the altar a trifle onerous, so by the eighteenth century Morning Prayer at 6 a.m. was better left to one who would never be considered for the office of a dignitary at all. Life in the Close was becoming more comfortable. Equally, non-resident canons paid for others to preach for them or neglected to do anything at all, rather than hazard the journey to Lincoln.[232] But as deputies became acceptable, so the whole hierarchical pyramid of the Close was put in jeopardy. At its summit was the Dean and then the residentiaries, complete with their families. In their absence the prebendal stalls by 1724 were filled with footmen and others 'of the lowest rank and Condition'. It was ordered that locks were to prevent such persons entering the stalls and, if there were to be deputies, they were to be of higher quality.[233]

The residentiaries were hardly absent on urgent business. It seems, rather, as though they regarded their chief duty as adorning the Close, rather than the Minster, with their persons and, to this end, some of them worked hard at renovating their houses. The Subdeanery was particularly well cared for by the generosity of the Gardiner family, father and son, who were thought to have made it, by the early eighteenth century, the most desirable residence in the

---

[228] Ibid., f. 250.
[229] Dvi LDC 25(4).
[230] LDC A.3.13, f. 228.
[231] Ibid., 385.
[232] LDC Dvi.22.15; LCS III, 658.
[233] LDC Dvi.24(5).

Close.[234] Yet the commitment of the residentiaries did not extend to any discernible policy of enhancing the cathedral funds.

Any increase of the Common Fund was of immediate benefit to them all as it resulted in an increase in the dividend. Unusually few properties of size paid their rent into the Common Fund; more were annexed to the Fabric Fund. A new leasing policy benefiting the latter would at the very least mean that the residentiaries did not have to subsidise repairs as they had done in Honywood's time. Critical to the maintenance of the Common Fund were the payments of septisms or the seventh part of the prebendal income from the canons who were on the foundation but who were not in residence.[235] It is clear that some prebends were too poor even to be filled after the Restoration, let alone to yield septisms: it was reported to the Bishop in 1718 that three of the prebends 'are of so small value that they have not been collated since the Restauration vizt. All Saints Saint Martins and Thorngate'.[236] Bonds were introduced to ensure payment but these were abolished by the Bishop as unseemly novelties in 1729.[237] It was important, therefore, that the Dean and Chapter followed a financially realistic leasing policy on all their properties, large or small, if the Common Fund was to increase at all.

In spite of the incentives to charge higher entry fines for their properties and increase the rents, the Dean and Chapter of Lincoln, in common with many other ecclesiastical landlords, did not increase either until the eighteenth century. By 1719, the Dean and Chapter of Exeter were beginning to take cognisance of the need to increase fines and rents, and so were Salisbury. But the vested interest of the opposition was vocal: 'What makes a den of Thieves? a Dean and Chapter and lawn sleeves.'[238]

Lazy the residentiaries of Lincoln might be; greedy they were not, nor were they financially shrewd. Even when they actually *knew* the value of their property, which was rare enough,[239] nothing was done to alter the rent or, as far as we can see, the fine. At Maltby, the Dean and Chapter had a manor with 22 acres of pasture, 36 of arable with meadows and woodland. In 1662 it was thought that the land alone was worth £25 per annum.[240] It was leased in 1690 at £4.13s.4d; in 1750 it was leased for twenty-one years at the same sum.[241] The rectory of Hainton was leased at £7 from the end of the middle ages; it was

---

[234] DNB *ad hominem.*

[235] Cole, *Chapter Acts* 12, viii.

[236] *LCS* III, 656.

[237] LDC Dvi.24(5).

[238] C. Clay, 'The greed of Whig bishops?' *Past and Present* 87, 1980, 128–57.

[239] Ibid., 139.

[240] LDC 2CC Box 8/152941, f. 164.

[241] LDC Bij.4.4, f. 208v; Bij.4.13, *ad annum.*

renewed at that sum in 1753.[242] We do not know the value of the entry fine for many leases but at least the Dean and Chapter charged £40 for Hainton in 1739.[243] Ignorance of their properties may explain in part this lack of proper management, and in 1719 the chapter took the unusual step of ordering a new book for the provost to register 'all private informations and intelligence concerning their estates'.[244] It is also possible that the chapter wished to avoid the anticlericalism which a rise in rents might provoke,[245] and that was obviously wise while the chapter were dealing with former purchasers of their property. The 'velvet glove' policy was strongly supported by Charles II,[246] but by the accession of the Hanoverians these considerations might best have given way to others; failure to increase the income of the Minster had some important consequences.

Of these the most immediate was the loss to the residentiaries: the most important was the loss to the Fabric. In 1663 each residentiary was receiving as little as £27.19s.5d.;[247] by 1694 it had risen, in spite of there being four residentiaries, to £84.7s.11¼d.;[248] in 1733 it was down to £48.2s.0½d.[249] The Fabric Accounts reveal modest surpluses from 1701 to 1719 but this was because no major works were undertaken, with nearly catastrophic results.[250] By 1725, a visitor said of the cathedral, 'It has been a most magnificent pile, but is now in a very poor condition, and has all the token of entire ruin approaching.' The cathedral surveyors, first the famous architect James Gibbs and eventually John James, reported in greater detail: Gibbs stated that 'the two towers on the west front have damaged very much the arches and split the peers below them ... and unless five of these arches are fill'd up ... with a stone wall to hinder the weight of the said towers from squeezing the peers further I believe them very much in danger'. He thought the lead-covered spires should be taken from the tower, 'for it is evident the present spires being of a considerable height makes them more lyable to be shaken with the winds'. The small spires of the cathedral were loose, the roof guttering was lying on sand, 'which is a very bad method in laying of gutters because the least weight makes an impression in the lead', and the roof 'is so bad in generall that there is no walking in the Church when it rains without

[242] LDC Bij.4,4; cf. Bij.4.13.
[243] LDC A.3.13, f. 330.
[244] LDC A.3.13, f. 113.
[245] Clay, 'The greed of the Whig bishops?', 152.
[246] Ibid., 142.
[247] LDC Bj.3.11, *ad annum*.
[248] LDC Bj.4.1.
[249] LDC Bj.4.6.
[250] LDC Bj.1.10.

being wett'. The glass and paving needed repair, the basement was foul on the south side and the vestry falling down. Gibbs concluded by saying that 'there are so many things out of repair in this Cathedral that I believe Tenn thousand pound would not make a thorough repair'. Mr James also thought it a matter of urgency that the spires be removed from the towers and concurred with most of Gibbs' recommendations.[251] To set things to rights an appeal had been launched in 1724[252] and the Bishop was asked for the stone from his ruined palace: it would save the Dean and Chapter hundreds of pounds and royal permission was duly granted.[253] Work was about to begin when on 20 September 1726 a riot began in the city which extended to the Close. Its ostensible cause was the removal of the spires. The mob broke down Pottergate and were then appeased by a senior vicar and the Subdean, who shrewdly gave them money and drink so that they returned home breaking 'some windows of several presbyterians' *en route*.[254]

The affair not only indicated how much the Fabric still required attention after the civil war in spite of Honywood's pains; it also shows how inadequate the Fabric finances were for anything other than routine expenditure of a minimal kind involving at most £300 and not £10,000.[255] Perhaps the riot also suggests a sympathy amongst the citizenry for its dominant building and a lingering goodwill towards the Church of England. But the disturbance appears to have been prompted partly by anger at the high price of grain in the county and partly by exasperation at the incompetence of the Dean and Chapter in 1722 in taking down a spire from the great steeple, instead of replacing one which had blown down.[256] In any event, the Dean and Chapter were, by 1731, in the familiar position of lending from their private purses to the Fabric Fund.[257] The huge task of restoration was commenced under a local Clerk of the Works Thomas Sympson; it was not complete by his death in 1750 and indeed it was to occupy the Dean and Chapter for the remainder of the century. The roof seems to have been improved under Sympson but there were problems with the paving of the Close, the bad state of the churchyard of St Mary Magdalen which impinged on it, and the prevalence of carts in the Minster area. The noise was such that the doors to the Minster in 1735 could not be left

[251] J. W. F. Hill, 'The western spires of Lincoln Minster and their threatened removal in 1726', *LAASR* 5, 1954, 102–67.
[252] Hill, *Georgian Lincoln*, 38.
[253] Hill, 'The western spires', 107–9.
[254] Ibid., *passim*.
[255] LDC Bj.1.11. The Fabric Accounts of 1719–30 reveal a revenue of about £325.
[256] Hill, 'The western spires', 102–3.
[257] LDC A.3.13, f. 228.

open in service time 'without indecency', with begging still constituting a problem.[258]

In the absence of effective residentiaries the task of dealing with the rioters had fallen to a Mr Cunington, a senior vicar, and a Mr Haseldine, a junior one, though the Subdean and Chancellor occasionally appeared.[259] Neither the vicars nor the choristers seem to have engaged in the drinking and other improprieties of their predecessors. For the vicars, responsibility both in the cathedral and sometimes in nearby parishes during a vacancy seemed to have wrought in them the reformation which had eluded generations of bishops. The choir also seems to have become more ambitious, and by 1724 it seems to have been taken for granted that there would be instruction in vocal *and* instrumental music. The schoolmaster continued to be paid by the city and the Dean and Chapter, as was the usher, and attendance by the choristers of school and cathedral was said to be good.[260]

Family life was also beginning to provide a stabilising influence, and to have become an accepted part of the Close. The wives, children and servants of the residentiaries were allowed to be buried in the cathedral without fee,[261] and children and choristers played in the Close provided they did not do so on Sundays or at service times.[262] No doubt the residentiaries had met socially from the very first, but in 1744, the newly elected Dean instituted a party to celebrate his protestation of major residence, an event important enough for the clerk to have reported him as saying 'I invite you my Brethren that you will vouchsafe to break of my bread with me in my Decanal house . . . for the love of God and sake of charity'.[263] Amidst such graciousness it is hard to believe that the cathedral was in danger of falling down. The marriage of generosity, taste and godliness which had characterised Honywood's tenure would return. Until it did, the residentiaries could attend to their houses and their families, and venture to divine service when the weather and the time suited them.

BOOKS FOR FURTHER READING

There is no overall history of the Minster for this period but there is much invaluable information in D. M. Williamson, *Lincoln muniments*, LMP 8, 1956. The history of the Minster in the later middle ages is well described in K. Edwards, *The English secular cathedrals in the middle ages*, Manchester 1949. 2nd edn 1967; and the subject is also

---

[258] Hill, *Georgian Lincoln*, 41–8; LDC A.3.13, f. 289; Dvi/24(5); *LCS* III, 662.
[259] Hill, *Georgian Lincoln*, 39.
[260] *LCS* III, 659–61; LDC A.3.13, f. 385.
[261] LDC A.3.13, f. 228.
[262] *LCS* III, 661.
[263] LDC A.3.13, f. 366.

treated for the period 1480–1549 in my *Secular clergy in the diocese of Lincoln*, Cambridge 1968, and *The Henrician Reformation*, Cambridge 1981. Valuable material on the cathedral which also compares it with other cathedrals will be found in Stanford E. Lehmberg, *The reformation of cathedrals*, Princeton, NJ, 1988. There is some very important and readable material in J. W. F. Hill, *Tudor and Stuart Lincoln*, Cambridge 1956, and *Georgian Lincoln*, Cambridge, 1966.

On a specialist note, it would be hard to understand the cathedral accounts without reference to Professor K. Major's 'The finances of the Dean and Chapter of Lincoln from the twelfth to the fourteenth century: a preliminary survey', *Journal of Ecclesiastical History* 5 (2), 1954, 149–67. A. F. Leach has some good material on schools in the *Victoria County History Lincolnshire II*; there is a pioneering article on the Dean and Chapter in the fifteenth and sixteenth centuries by R. B. Walker, 'Lincoln cathedral in the reign of Queen Elizabeth I', *Journal of Ecclesiastical History* 11 (2), 1960, 186 ff.

Most of the sources on which this study is based are still in manuscript form; but the early sixteenth-century Chapter Acts 1520–59 were edited by R. E. G. Cole for the Lincoln Record Society, vols. 12, 13, 15, 1915–17; much valuable material is also in H. Bradshaw and C. Wordsworth, eds., *The Statutes of Lincoln cathedral*, 3 vols., Cambridge 1892 and 1897.

7

Historical Survey,
1750–1949

✳

D A V I D M. T H O M P S O N

Introduction

Since the mid-eighteenth century the vision of the cathedral's part in the life of the Church has changed markedly. The maintenance of the Fabric has always been a major concern, and fortunately the increasing sophistication in detecting building problems has been matched by a steadily improving technology to handle them: the problem has been a corresponding increase in the cost of such work. But a cathedral is more than a building; and the issues in the changing life of the cathedral are more complex. In the eighteenth century it was sufficient to aspire to a restoration of the status quo before the civil war, although in truth the careful links established between residentiary and non-residentiary cathedral prebends and other offices in dioceses and universities, all drawn into a national network of patronage, created a world very different from anything before 1700. By the early nineteenth century, however, people were asking what a cathedral was for with a new intensity. The traditional answers were tried and found wanting; and in the ecclesiastical reforms of the 1830s cathedral revenues became an important source for redistribution of church income to support the so-called 'working clergy' in the parishes. This in turn prompted various programmes for cathedral reform, and indeed a new interest in the history of cathedral institutions which now had a practical as well as an antiquarian significance.

Yet the notion of reform can be a misleading one if it implies a return to a previous ideal. Nor is it possible to apply simple labels to whole periods and to say some were decades of corruption and others were times of revival. At all periods there have been those in the life of the cathedral who have devoted

210

themselves to it, just as there have been some spectacular examples of neglect. The story of Lincoln Minster in the modern period illustrates different views of reform. One programme of reform sought to recreate what was held to be the traditional relationship between the bishop and the council of his diocese. This was the view of men like Christopher Wordsworth (bishop of Lincoln, 1869–85) and E. W. Benson (Chancellor of Lincoln, 1872–7, subsequently bishop of Truro and archbishop of Canterbury). In his book, *The cathedral* (1878), Benson wrote that the breaking up of the cathedral system took the form of 'the drawing apart of the chapter and the bishop'.[1] But it is by no means clear that this traditional relationship ever existed in the way Wordsworth and Benson imagined. Another programme of reform sought to create a new role for the cathedral as the liturgical and preaching centre of the diocese: Edward King (bishop of Lincoln, 1885–1910) and William Butler (Dean of Lincoln, 1885–94) might be cited as examples of this. The twentieth century has tried to combine these visions, sometimes asking cathedral clergy to provide diocesan leadership in theology, or mission, or music, sometimes developing new ministries, for example in relation to industry or tourism, and always making cathedral worship not only a continuous life of prayer but also an offering of the whole life of the diocese to God. The tension throughout the modern period lies between the available financial resources and the demands made upon them.

In any history of the cathedral attention is naturally concentrated upon the Dean and Chapter. From the destruction of the bishop's palace during the civil war until the division of the diocese in 1837–9 the bishop of Lincoln's palace was at Buckden on the Great North Road near Huntingdon, which was strategically situated for transport about the largest diocese in England. From 1839 there was a new palace at Riseholme to the north of Lincoln, but it was not until Edward King's time that the bishop actually moved back into the city and restored the Old Palace. The bishop was therefore at best an occasional visitor, staying in the Old Palace only for a day or two during a visitation as Bishops Tomline and Pelham did.[2] On the other hand, although the residentiary canons conscientiously kept their three months' residence, there was no corporate presence on the part of the chapter until the end of the 1860s. The day-to-day life of the cathedral depended on the vicars choral (both priests and lay), the choir and Organist, and the various lay officials. Hence, although for the most part the chapter have left fuller records, and contained more colourful characters, it must never be forgotten that behind them were a larger and less

---

[1] E. W. Benson, *The cathedral: its necessary place in the life and work of the Church*, London 1878, 81.

[2] 'Bp. Tomline's Visitation, 1818', *LDM* 24, 1913, 169–70; 'Bp. Pelham's Visitation, 1825', *LDM* 30, 1914, 86.

obvious company, without which there would be no history to record at all. Indeed the idea of a resident chapter who really run the life of the cathedral as their primary and exclusive obligation is a late nineteenth-century or even a twentieth-century innovation. By the end of the nineteenth century the members of the chapter, who were normally appointed by the bishop (apart from the Dean, who was appointed by the Crown), usually had considerable diocesan experience, for example, Jacob Clements (Subdean, 1878–98). The development of a really resident chapter created problems for the priest-vicars, who since the fifteenth century or earlier had done duty for the prebendaries who were not resident, and caused a significant change in the dynamics of the day-to-day life of the cathedral.

Associated with this is a change in the relationship of the cathedral to the community. In Lincoln it is seen in the transformation of the cathedral from a separate, at times almost embattled, group to one much more concerned to be representative of the city and diocese as a whole. The change can be neatly illustrated by two stories nearly two centuries apart concerning the western towers of the Minster.

In 1726 James Gibbs the architect reported to the Dean and Chapter that the weight of the two western towers had damaged the arches and split the supporting piers. He advised that the wooden lead-covered spires should be taken down since they exposed the towers to greater shaking by the winds. However, when the Dean and Chapter began the work of removing the spires, there was a riot. On 20 September 1726 a mob of between 400 and 500 people from the town approached the Close, broke through the postern gate which had been left unguarded, and attacked the house of Thomas Cunington, one of the priest-vicars who was also Receiver-General of the Chapter, making him dance on Minster Green to a chorus of 'High church, low church, jump again, Cunington', or similar words. Negotiations took place, and eventually word was sent to the corporation that the spires would stand until further public satisfaction was given of the need to take them down. The reassurance was accompanied by something to drink from the Chancellor's cellars; and the spires lasted another eighty years, being taken down without popular protest in 1807.[3]

In 1921 another crisis broke concerning the towers of Lincoln cathedral. A crack was discovered in the north-west tower and in January 1922 Dean Fry wrote to *The Times* that £50,000 would be needed to remedy the faults.

[3] J. W. F. Hill, 'The western spires of Lincoln Minster', *LAASR* 5, 1954, 101–17; cf. J. W. F. Hill, *Georgian Lincoln*, Cambridge 1966, 38–41. This definitive account replaces versions such as that in H. Green, *Forgotten Lincoln*, Lincoln 1898, 99–100, which mistakes the year, and may be the source for a similar note in *LDM*, 57, 1941, 142.

Detailed reports from the Clerk of Works, the engineer and the architect soon confirmed that there was a serious risk that the west front might fall out and the two towers, both of them cracked, would fall apart. Only a small contribution towards the cost was forthcoming from the Ecclesiastical Commissioners, who had crises at other cathedrals to handle. Dean Fry, who died in 1930, raised nearly £100,000 in the last nine years of his life, much of it from North America. The repair of the tower and the transept roof was largely paid for by the descendants of those who sailed from Boston, Lincs, in the *Mayflower* and founded Boston, Mass. Lincoln was thus one of the first cathedrals to face major crises in its Fabric in the twentieth century. Now, however, the nature of the repairs and the reasons for them were publicised far and wide: and the Dean and Chapter not only appealed to the Ecclesiastical Commission but to the national and international public for support. A complete change in the relation of cathedral and people had taken place.

The modern period of the cathedral's history falls naturally into four parts. The first is the eighteenth century which has been partly discussed in the previous chapter. This was a period of calm after the turmoil of the seventeenth century. The French Revolution and the economic changes initiated by the Industrial Revolution ended this calm; but the first half of the nineteenth century saw the old order preserved in Lincoln, partly because Lincoln was only slowly affected by the growth of industry, but mainly because of the dominance of one family in the cathedral – the Pretymans. George Pretyman Tomline was bishop of Lincoln from 1787 to 1820. Within the chapter the Pretyman family's influence may be summarised by noting that for nearly three-quarters of a century, from 1793 until 1866, at least one Pretyman was a residentiary canon, and from 1814 to 1859 two were. The second period may therefore appropriately be called 'the Pretyman era'.

The period from the 1860s to the 1890s may be called 'the age of reform'. In 1800 Lincoln, although the second largest town in the county, was smaller than Boston and had a population of less than 10,000. By 1900 it was still the second largest town in the county, but now it had nearly 50,000 inhabitants and the largest town was Grimsby.[4] Industry and the railways had arrived. Church reform was the main topic of the 1830s and the reform of the cathedrals was probably the most contentious part of the package of recommendations from the Ecclesiastical Commission appointed by Sir Robert Peel in 1834.[5] John

[4] R. J. Olney, *Rural society and county government in nineteenth-century Lincolnshire*, Lincoln 1979, 2–3, 169–71.

[5] Olive J. Brose, *Church and Parliament: The reshaping of the Church of England, 1828–1860*, Stanford 1959, 125–35, 140–43; G. F. A. Best, *Temporal pillars: Queen Anne's Bounty, the Ecclesiastical Commissioners and the Church of England*, Cambridge 1964, 303–4, 331–47.

Kaye, bishop of Lincoln from 1827 to 1854, was keenly involved in the process, but its effects in Lincoln were delayed until the opportunity occurred for changes in the chapter. Bishops Jackson, Wordsworth and King by their appointments brought men to the cathedral who were able to respond to the needs of the railway age.

Finally there is the most recent period – the twentieth century, with its two faces. On one side the effects of war, and an intensely industrialised and urbanised culture, make it seem a secular century; but on the other cathedrals are probably more visited and used, both for ecclesiastical and secular occasions, than at any time since the middle ages. Improvements in building technology arrived just in time to prevent cathedrals from falling down, but at a considerable cost. So the question of the cathedral's place in church or public life has emerged in a new form.

The eighteenth century

In the early eighteenth century the three visitations of the cathedral by William Wake, bishop of Lincoln from 1705 to 1716, suggest that it was properly administered.[6] The Dean and the three residentiary canons (the Precentor, the Chancellor and the Subdean) resided for three months at a time, the turns being chosen at the annual Audit, which was the chapter meeting before the Feast of the Exaltation of the Cross on 14 September.[7] During residence the residentiary had effective control and could constitute a chapter by his presence, though certain important decisions required the consent of others. Certain patronage also fell to the canon in residence, but each canon chose a canonical farm each year, partly for its income, and partly for the rights of patronage associated with it. The choice of farms, like residence, was determined by seniority, though the rules were remarkably complex, as the occasional disputes show.

The period of canonical residence was the main obligation on a member of the chapter, but there was no sense that pluralities involved neglect. To combine a prebend with a parochial living, another cathedral prebend or an archdeaconry was common. Even so conscientious a bishop as Wake suggested to Archbishop Tenison that in view of the poverty of the bishopric the deanery, or three of the prebends, should be annexed to it.[8] It may be that he thought that annexing the deanery would provide a residence, as well as additional income, but the fact that the idea could be contemplated does not suggest that

---

[6] N. Sykes, *William Wake, Archbishop of Canterbury, 1657–1737* I, Cambridge 1957, 230–1, 204.

[7] H. Bradshaw and C. Wordsworth, *The statutes of Lincoln cathedral*, part II, Cambridge 1892, cciii. Subsequently *LCS*.

[8] Sykes, *William Wake*, I, 158.

214

Wake saw the position of dean of a cathedral as a full-time post, independent of the bishop. Indeed there might have been advantages in combining the deanery of Lincoln with the bishopric of Lincoln instead of another bishopric, as in the case of Dean Willis (1730–43), who was bishop of St David's, or Dean Yorke (1762–81), who was bishop of St David's from 1774 to 1779 and bishop of Gloucester from 1779 to 1781. Both of them resigned the deanery upon being translated to richer sees – Willis to Bath and Wells, and Yorke to Ely. Another type of plurality was to combine a prebend with a university or college office at Oxford or Cambridge. John Green, who was Dean from 1756 to 1761, was Master of Corpus Christi College, Cambridge, from 1750 to 1764, and William Richardson, who was Precentor from 1760 to 1775, was Master of Emmanuel College, Cambridge, from 1736 to 1775.[9]

It was accepted that these positions could be held in plurality with others, and one would move from house to house as need arose. This was not, in fact, very different from the habit of the gentry of spending some time in London or in Lincoln for the season, rather than spending the whole of the year in the country. The cathedral dignitaries were very much part of fashionable society, and their residence habits reflected this. In an age before even turnpike roads the difficulties of communication must never be underestimated. Pluralities brought the cathedral into closer contact with the wider world; and the links with the universities could be mutually advantageous. But there was always a fine line between bringing the world to Lincoln and being drawn away from Lincoln altogether.

When a new canon was installed he usually entertained his colleagues to a meal during his first residence. In September 1782 the Dean declared that for various good causes he had postponed his invitation to his brethren to break bread in his house until November; and a year later the Chancellor postponed the breaking of bread until the following July.[10] Prebendaries also were expected to provide entertainment, although gifts for the cathedral in lieu were gratefully received. In 1747 a contribution was made to the Fabric Fund and in 1784 it was agreed that at the installation of members of the chapter a sum should be paid for the support and increase of the library instead of the customary entertainment – 8 guineas for the Dean, 4 guineas for each residentiary, and 2 guineas for each archdeacon and prebendary. Nevertheless, the customary payments of a guinea to the junior vicars and the Organist, the patent workmen and officers of the church, and half a guinea to the boys were retained.

---

[9] DNB XXIII, 45–6 (Green); XLVIII, 251–2 (Richardson); G. G. Perry and J. H. Overton, *Biographical notes of the bishops of Lincoln from Remigius to Wordsworth*, Lincoln 1900, 340–2 (Green).
[10] Lincoln Chapter Act Book A.3.15: 16 Sept, 1782, 241; 15 Sept, 1783, 253.

Moreover, in 1808 it was insisted that the fees for the junior vicars and choir boys should be paid in cash rather than by supper at the inn.[11] Becoming a prebendary or a canon was not a cheap business. This decision was reversed in 1824, when the Dean and Chapter recorded that they had been put to very great inconvenience in complying with the 1784 order because prebendaries repeatedly came to Lincoln for installation without giving due notice of their intention. They therefore decided to 'recur to the ancient and uninterrupted usage of the Church prior to that period according to which these entertainments were always given at the Inn above the Hill on the day of Installation at the Expense of the party installed'.[12] There was no reference to what was to happen to the library!

The main work of the cathedral fell to the vicars choral. The senior vicars, in priest's orders, were originally appointed and paid by non-resident prebendaries to do duty on their behalf. By the eighteenth century there were four, holding the offices of Succentor, Sacrist, Vice-Chancellor and Provost. They were responsible for saying services when the canon in residence was not present, and under a charter of 1441 were a distinct ecclesiastical corporation. They usually held local livings in the patronage of the Dean and Chapter to supplement their relatively meagre endowment as vicars choral. The junior vicars had been in minor orders before the Reformation, but subsequently became increasingly identical with the Poor Clerks who assisted the priest at Mass. By the eighteenth century they were laymen with duties connected with the choir. Also essential were the Organist and the choir, which consisted of the boy choristers and Burghersh Chanters under the instruction of the Master of the Choristers.[13]

Then there were several offices connected with the administration or maintenance of the cathedral – the Chapter Clerk, Receiver-General, Clerk of the Works, mason, carpenter, smith and glazier: these were conveyed by patent by decision of the chapter in common and usually held for life.[14] Indeed they were treated in the same way as other property: in 1757 the chapter agreed that the pre-1700 custom of making grants of office for three lives should not be objected to but rather restored.[15] Finally, the minor offices were often more

---

[11] A.3.15: 25 Aug, 1784, 270–1; A.3.16: 19 Sept, 1808, 246. Owen Chadwick noted that the library at York was also supported by installation fees paid by prebendaries: G. E. Aylmer and R. Cant, *A history of York Minster*, Oxford 1977, 293.

[12] A.3.17: 26 Apr. 1824, 158–9.

[13] J. H. Srawley, *The original and growth of cathedral foundations*, Lincoln 1948, 14–16; A. R. Maddison, *A short account of the vicars' choral, Poor Clerks, Organists and choristers of Lincoln cathedral*, London 1878.

[14] A.3.15: Audit 1776, 167.

[15] A.3.14: 19 Sept. 1757, ff, 120a–b.

valuable as sources of profit than for the actual stipend; for example, the vergers took money from those wishing to see the cathedral. At some point in the eighteenth century officers had actually been remunerated from the Communion offerings, for in April 1793 the chapter resolved that in future no part of the Communion offerings should be distributed to any of the officers of the church but only to those poor persons on the sacrament list, and that 'untill some order shall be taken therein an adequate compensation shall be made to the Officers'.[16] Occasionally too even the profits of an office could be let out; for example, in 1830 Thomas Evans was appointed Renter of the Great Bell (Great Tom), an office which had originated when an earlier Surveyor of the Fabric had retained the profits of the bell when he fell ill rather than passing them to the Deputy Surveyor appointed and had then let them out to a third party. When Evans complained in 1842 that the perquisites from showing the bell were much less than they had been, the chapter agreed to let him off his rent provided that no one was shown up to the bell unless accompanied by Evans or his assistant.[17] Much of the story of the modern period is taken up with the gradual rationalisation and reform of this multitude of jobs.

In 1731 the language in the Chapter Act Book changed from Latin to English. The contents of the books also reveal a society in which old ways were changing, albeit slowly. The regular services in the choir, on both Sundays and weekdays, remained the primary duty of the cathedral. When in September 1735 the Bishop requested a more frequent celebration of Holy Communion, the Chancellor sent for the four senior priest-vicars for their opinion; three came and said that, realising that 'Complyance with the said order will be burthensome to the Residentiarys', they would be ready to comply with it as far as they could. The chapter resolved to leave the matter to the Dean and Subdean to point out to the Bishop as soon as they could the inconvenience which such a request involved.[18] When the question of whose duty it was to read divine service in the choir on Sundays was raised in 1746, the Dean and Chapter agreed to undertake such duty themselves, but they also agreed to appoint the two senior vicars to be their deputies 'Except when any Residentiary shall Chuse to read himself'. In relation to weekdays they noted 'that it plainly appears to them that it is and always has been from time immemorial the duty of the four Senior Vicars in their Turns to read Morning Prayer in the Chappell at the Customary Hours of Six in the Morning in the Summer and Seven in the Winter', and required them to be more diligent in performing their duty

[16] A.3.15: 5 Apr. 1793, 43.
[17] A.3.17: 11 Oct. 1830, 239; 19 Sept. 1842, 390.
[18] A.3.13: 15 Sept. 1735, 288.

personally, and not by a deputy, unless the deputy had been approved by the Dean or the senior residentiary present.[19]

The importance of the priest-vicars was clearly indicated in 1769. Because of the poor endowment of the office, they had been given preferment by the chapter to supplement their income. But they were tending not to resign their benefices when they resigned as priest-vicars, with the result that the Dean and Chapter were running out of patronage to support the office. It was therefore decided to exact resignation bonds of £500 to ensure that preferment would be available when it was needed.[20] In 1776, when new rules for the disposal of the chapter's patronage were agreed, it was noted that livings within 20 miles of Lincoln 'may be thought proper to be disposed of by the Dean & Chapter in common to those Vicars of the Church who are not otherwise provided for'; and in 1784 it was agreed that normally benefices that had been held by vicars should be given to new vicars.[21] Despite an appeal to the Bishop as Visitor to clarify the operation of these provisions in 1793, it proved necessary to make firmer rules in September 1801. It was agreed that Ashby Puerorum, Gosberton, Searby and any living within 20 miles of Lincoln should always be disposed of by the chapter in common, and reserved for senior vicars. It was also decided that when any residentiary was prevented from attending church during his residence or doing his duty at the altar, he should pay the senior vicar 20 guineas for the residence, or a portion of that in proportion to the amount of residence covered.[22]

When John Byng visited Lincoln in 1791, he thought the Communion Service 'nobly perform'd', though he was less complimentary about the voices of the lay vicars. He lamented the fact that Morning Prayers at 6 a.m. had been 'disused about 5 years ... for nobody came but those who were obliged'; though he was probably over-optimistic in his supposition that 'in old times, decent people attended the morning service, before they began, or could think of beginning, the duties of the day'. When he returned a week or two later, he also commented on the small attendance at the 9.30 a.m. service, and expected to 'live to see when none will be present at a cathedral service, but a reader, a verger, and 2 singing-boys; who will gallop it over in a few minutes'.[23] Byng's voice was one of nostalgic lament: the time was coming when others would call for more radical reform.

[19] Ibid.: 15 Sept. 1746, 381.

[20] A.3.15: 18 Sept. 1769, 85.

[21] Ibid.: Audit 1776, 165; 2 Feb. 1784, 263.

[22] A.3.16: 21 Sept. 1801, 158. The Bishop's judgment of 1793 written into the Act Book makes it clear that the 1776 decision was taken because the provision for the vicars of the church at Lincoln was insufficient: ibid.: 53.

[23] C. B. Andrews, ed., *The Torrington diaries* II, London 1935, 346, 347, 400.

Until the reorganisation of chapter revenues in 1870 there was a separate Fabric Fund for the cathedral which received the revenues of specified estates, together with any casual payments that might be made. In general the record of maintenance of the cathedral in this period was good, and this may reflect an upturn in the fortunes of the Fund. In 1731 the chapter had been lending to the Fund from their own income, and when in 1747 a new prebendary of Aylesbury was installed who, instead of an entertainment, gave 3 guineas to the Fabric Fund, they agreed that his example be commended by the Clerk to all future prebendaries, subject to the size of the prebend.[24] In 1755, following the Bishop's Visitation of the cathedral, the chapter ordered that a tenth of all fines paid to the Dean and Chapter or prebendaries should be paid into the Fabric Fund; as a result many repairs were made and a sum accumulated, part of which was invested in consols, together with the old Fabric Estate and the sum available by the lapse of the lease at Woolsthorpe and Stanwick. With the consent of the bishop, these payments were suspended in September 1788.[25] An account of the Fabric Fund between 1755 and 1779 shows that the average yield of Fabric fines and rents was about £240 p.a., and the average yield of tenths, less the payments to the Clerk of the Fabric, was about £279 p.a., giving a total of £520 p.a. In the next seven years the average yields were about £70 p.a. lower. The total spent on the Fabric between 1755 and 1786 was £9377 14s.11d, with the highest expenditure coming in the later years reaching a maximum of £1268 in 1785–6.[26]

In 1761 the chapter, possibly because of their strong Cambridge links, invited James Essex to make a survey of the cathedral and state the repairs which were necessary, and at the same time directed the east window to be glazed with stained glass according to the proposals of William Peckitt of York. The estimate of repairs submitted was the same as a list submitted in 1755, at a cost of £12,000 plus £3,000 for dressing and cleaning the walls. The initiative may have been Richardson's, since only he and the Chancellor (Charles Reynolds, who had been a member of the chapter for a long time) were present, and it is known that Essex redid the reredos at his request in 1768–9; but not many of Essex's other recommendations seem to have been acted upon.[27] The decision to fit up the room over the vestry as a Common Chamber in 1761, and to transfer the archives and muniments there, which was done the following year, seems not to have been one of his schemes.[28] An estimate of £111.19s.7d. for

---

[24] A.3.13, 18 July 1747, 392.

[25] A.3.15: 1 Apr, 1788, 326; also loose draft of Chapter Act of 16 Sept. 1788 at end of volume, not recorded in the Act Book.

[26] A.4.13: Account 1755–86.

[27] A.3.14: 9 Sept. 1761, 144b–145a; A.4.13: estimates of 1755 and 1761; *LDM* 3, 1887, 122.

[28] A.3.14: 10 Oct. 1761, fo. 146b; A.3.15: 7 Aug. 1762, 9.

lowering the earth and pavements at the west front of the cathedral to the level inside was received in 1770, an early indication of the recognition of the need to remove any cause of damp from the walls.[29]

In 1774 Essex pointed out to the Dean that the Great Tower was not designed to bear a stone spire and was incapable of supporting one. A timber and lead spire could be built like the old one, but it would be the highest in England and not suitable for an exposed position like Lincoln. The following March he offered a reduced estimate of nearly two-thirds the original cost by using the old vanes; and his revised design was accepted. The same letter also referred to the problem of the west wall, which had been repaired by Gibbs. Later in the month he explained that the west door was 16″ out of centre, which had meant that the pier on the north side was so much smaller than the south that it lacked the strength to support itself and the arch. Gibbs had built a wall to correct the tilt to the south west, but this had not been effective and Essex proposed an alternative. The Dean was clearly reluctant to act, since another letter a year later shows that the problem still had not been dealt with.[30]

The problems of securing agreement on what was an improvement are well illustrated by the classic confrontation between Precentor Gordon and Dean Cust in 1783. Even the resolutions brought before the chapter by the Dean suggest a mounting crescendo of conflict:

1st Resolved, that a letter of Dr Gordon's to Mr Jepson the receiver dated Aug.st 9th 1783 cautioning him not to pay anything on Account of certain Works going on by order of the Dean, is highly assuming, improper, and unbecoming;

2ndly That the Dean's order to Lumby to add Palisades to the posts and rails on the North side the Minister, was consistent with the usual practice of the Church in such Cases, and no more than a necessary improvement upon what was done in the year 1778.

Resolved therefore
3rdly That Doctor Gordon's taking upon himself, upon his own single authority, to countermand the orders of the Dean, with improper menaces to the Workmen, and the sawing down with his own hand great parts of these palisades, is highly irregular, presumptive, and indecent.

4thly That Dr Gordon's insinuations to the Populace that the Dean was actually stopping up an old & accustomed way to the Church, (which way, if it ever was one, was stop't up before,) were not founded in truth; and were calculated to Poison the minds of the People.

[29] A.4.13: estimate of 1770.
[30] A.4.13: Essex to Dean 14 Sept. 1774; Essex to Dean 8 Mar, 1775; Essex to Dean 29 Mar. 1775; Essex to Dean 7 Apr. 1776; Hill, *Georgian Lincoln*, 43.

5thly That the works ordered by the Dean and so much complained of by Dr Gordon, are proper, usefull and ornamental, and in most respects necessary.

Ordered, therefore, that the Expense of them (when the Bills are examined by Mr Jepson, and allowed by the Dean according to Custom in these Cases) be paid by Mr Jepson the Receiver, and placed to the account of the Fabrick.

6thly That the constant keeping open the North Door, leading from the Deanry into the Cathedral, for Boys and Girls and apprentices to play there whenever they please, is improper, and ought not to be allowed.

Ordered Therefore that the Door be opened for the admission of such as chuse to go that way to Church, when the Bells strike up, and not before, and that it be shutt again and locked the moment the Service begins, or as soon after the Dean enters the Church, as he thinks proper.[31]

The Precentor objected to the discussion of these resolutions and asked for an adjournment to the following week when the Chancellor would be present; the Subdean interrupted him while he was speaking; he moved a resolution of censure on the Dean for his conduct which was negatived by the Dean and Subdean; and then he withdrew. Matters were brought to an abrupt conclusion a month later by the death of the Dean on 16 October.

The problem of children playing and its implications for access to the cathedral (which was one aspect of this episode) was a constant one for the cathedral authorities. In 1733 the chapter had ordered that 'by reason of the many Indecencys and Disorders dayly committed in the Minster ... the Church Doors shall be from henceforth constantly Lockt Except in times of Divine Worship'. Charles Cleaver was appointed in 1755 to 'inspect the many dole boys who frequent the Minster for mischief ... and have them punished for all disorders in which he shall find them', and this became a regular office: George Hasted was appointed in 1787 'to take care of the Church during Service time, and at other times to see that the Boys do no mischief thereto by breaking Windows'. Eventually in 1788 it was resolved to shut the cathedral on Sundays except an hour before Morning and Evening Prayers.[32] Children with nothing to do are always a problem, but by the end of the century the cathedral had come to seem more of a private than a public place.

The new Dean in 1783 was Sir Richard Kaye and his appointment may explain the increased rate of building activity thereafter. In February 1784 the Dean and Chapter agreed to take estimates of the cost of paving the remainder of the church, fitting up the choir with woodwork and dressing the beams in the second transept. The Lady Bells were to be put in order and new ones hung

---

[31] A.3.15: 12 Sept. 1783, 253–5; Hill, *Georgian Lincoln*, 45–6.
[32] A.3.13, 10 May 1733, 258; A.3.14: 24 Nov. 1755, fo. 104b; A.3.15: 1 Jan. 1787, 303; 1 Apr. 1788, 326.

if necessary, and the steps into the church were to be repaired. (The repaving of the church had begun in 1780 according to Essex's proposals.) Some of Essex's other recommendations for improvements in the church were adopted. To avoid any repetition of the Gordon–Cust confrontation it was unanimously agreed that the canon in residence should not make any alterations in the Fabric, Precincts or common property without at least the consent of the other canons present.[33]

A series of improvements followed in the late 1780s. It was agreed to alter the choir and seat it in the Gothic style in September 1786. Steps were taken to ensure that the lamps around the cathedral were properly lit in 1787. In 1788 the possibility of putting iron cramps around the steeples of great Tom and Saint Hugh was investigated; and it was decided to repair the foundations and flying buttresses of the church immediately. In 1790 the walls at the entrance to the north and south aisles on the side of the choir were taken down and replaced with screens; and the ceiling of the church and the bases of the pillars were repaired where necessary. The following year it was agreed to repair the foundations with all possible speed and to pave the choir aisles with old gravestones.[34] John Byng wrote in 1791 that Lincoln was 'the finest of our cathedrals I ever saw' – 'Gothic in the highest preservation, except the loss of some saints, and of more of their heads, which a bishop of any head would restore'. He thought that the new stained glass in the east window was inferior to that in the old ones. The cloisters were in great disorder, but he was told that they were going to be repaired.[35]

William Lumby, who had been Deputy Chapter Clerk for some years and who had prepared the scheme for the Gothic seating in the choir and the plans for the repair of the manuscript library, was appointed to the newly created office of Surveyor of the Fabrick in January 1793.[36] The burial-ground on the south side of the cathedral was railed in in 1793, and the south side was paved with flagstones. But a year later the rebuilding policy seems to have been brought to an end when the chapter decided 'that no material innovations shall be made in the plan of the Church and Choir, but that only the perishing parts should be repaired, and the defective ones restored'.[37]

Internal furnishings were not neglected. Much of Essex's work had been internal. In 1788 it was agreed to purchase a pair of brass or lacquered tin

[33] A.3.15: 2 Feb. 1784, 261–2, 264–5; 15 Sept. 1784, 274; A.4.16, estimates and letters 1778–80.

[34] A.3.15: 11 Sept. 1786, 299; 1 Jan. 1787, 303; 1 Apr. 1788, 326; A.3.16: 12 Apr. 1790, 3; 14 Jan. 1791, 12; 11 Apr. 1791, 15.

[35] Andrews, *Torrington diaries* II, 346.

[36] A.3.16: 24 Jan. 1793, 39.

[37] A.3.16: 18 Sept. 1794, 73.

candlesticks to be used at the altar during candlelight prayers, and in 1793 it was decided to provide 'two or three Desks neatly covered . . . for clergymen assisting at the Altar' and to restore the elevation of the altar to its former height.[38] In 1800 the chapter accepted with thanks a picture painted by one of its prebendaries, the Revd William Peters, rector of Knipton. Peters had exhibited at the Royal Academy and his painting was of the Annunciation. It was agreed that this should be placed over the altar. The picture was moved when the reredos was altered to allow the glass in the east window to be seen: in 1950 it returned to the cathedral and was hung to the north of the choir.[39]

In the later eighteenth century a more vigorous financial policy was adopted by the chapter, though the essential defects of the system of renewing leases by fines remained for another century. But encouragement was given to the exploitation of the chapter's estates. The first enclosure bills approved by the chapter were for Fillingham and Staunton in January 1759 and there is then a steady series of enclosure bills approved, especially in the 1760s and 1770s and again in the 1790s.[40] In the 1770s gamekeepers were appointed on a number of estates, and in 1784 an order was also made about the distribution of game taken on manors belonging to the Common Estates: it was to go first to the canon in residence, who could take as much of it as he wanted at the stated price; the rest was to be divided among the other residentiaries, except that they could not send it away as presents without the consent of all. Special arrangements were made for venison from Thoresby Park ('as by ancient custom'): half went to the Provost and half to the others in the summer, and half went to the canon in residence and half to the others in winter.[41] In September 1785 new rules were adopted for granting leases, modelled on those used by the chapter of Bristol, mainly concerned to ensure that there was an accurate transcription of liabilities, fines, a schedule of tithes, etc. It was also agreed to purchase £1,000 worth of 5 per cent stock out of the balance in hand, and a few months later they appointed a firm of London bankers to handle such transactions for the Dean and Chapter. In the 1790s smaller purchases of stock were made for the Fabric and Choristers' Funds.[42] Ironically, these efforts to exploit the resources of the cathedral more effectively coincided with a period in which its revenues were used more for personal than corporate benefit.

---

[38] A.3.15: 23 Sept. 1788, 334; A.3.16: 5 Apr. 1793, 43.

[39] A.3.15: 15 Sept. 1800, 143, cf. 16 Sept. 1799, 134; *LDM* 66, 1950, 43, 267–8.

[40] A.3.14: 10 Jan. 1759, fo. 127a; 14 Jan. 1759, fo. 127b.

[41] A.3.15: 4 Feb. 1784, 265–6.

[42] A.3.15: 26 Sept. 1785, 290; 24 May 1786, 294; A.3.16: 5 Apr. 1793, 43; 18 Sept. 1794, 73.

The Pretyman era

George Pretyman was appointed bishop of Lincoln in February 1787 on the nomination of William Pitt, whose tutor he had been at Cambridge and whose secretary he had been during his early years as prime minister. Although Pretyman's father came from a Suffolk county family, the family's fortunes had been reduced by extravagance and legal costs, and he was a tradesman in Bury St Edmunds. His son's accumulation of office and the nepotism for which he became notorious are explicable partly because of the difficulties ecclesiastics receiving such preferment had in affording the style of life which was expected of them and partly because of a determination not to let the family fortunes fall again. At the time of his appointment he was barely 37, and he combined the see with the deanery of St Paul's. He was bishop for thirty-three years, until in 1820 he was translated to Winchester. In 1803 he assumed the name Tomline as a condition of inheriting an estate at Riby worth £4,000 p.a. from Marmaduke Tomline. Bishop Pretyman Tomline died in 1827 worth £200,000.[43]

Pretyman was not the first bishop of Lincoln to give patronage to his family: Richard Reynolds, who was a conscientious bishop from 1723 until 1744, appointed his son, George, as archdeacon of Lincoln in 1725, and another son, Charles, as Chancellor in 1728.[44] But Bishop Pretyman lost no time in exploiting his rights of nomination. John Pretyman, the Bishop's brother, was installed as prebendary of Aylesbury in October 1787; in November 1791 he was appointed Vicar-General and Official Principal of the Consistorial and Episcopal Court of Lincoln, and also Commissary within the archdeaconries of Lincoln and Stow; and in 1793 he became Precentor and Archdeacon of Lincoln, retaining his prebend of Aylesbury, but surrendering the legal offices assumed in 1791. In 1795 he became Master of Spital Hospital.[45] There was then a pause for a decade or so. In 1806 John Pretyman, Junior, and Henry George Pretyman, the sons of the Archdeacon, were granted the office of Registrar of the Archdeaconry of Lincoln by their father; and a burst of activity followed the appointment of George Gordon as Dean in 1810. In that year John Pretyman, Senior, acquired the prebend of Biggleswade, and his son received the prebend of Aylesbury and the Mastership of Spital Hospital which he had resigned.[46] In 1814 the Bishop's second son, who was 24 and had just taken his LL B at Cambridge, George Thomas Pretyman, was installed as Chancellor and prebendary of Stoke. A day

[43] Perry and Overton, *The bishops of Lincoln*, 346–54.
[44] Hill, *Georgian Lincoln*, 34; Perry and Overton, *The bishops of Lincoln*, 332–3.
[45] A.3.16: 22 Nov. 1791, 23; 16 Feb. 1793, 40–41; 12 Feb. 1795, 76.
[46] A.3.16: 15 Aug. 1806, 205; 20 Jul. 1810, 269; 5 Sept. 1810, 277; 15 Sept. 1810, 279–80.

or two later he and his younger brother Richard, the latter not yet ordained, were made Registrar and Actuary of the archdeaconry of Lincoln by their uncle; and Richard acquired two similar offices for the archdeaconries of Buckingham and Leicester in May. Finally in 1817 Richard, also now 24, just having taken his MA at Cambridge and been ordained priest, acquired the vicarage of Hambledon (on the presentation of his brother as canon in residence), and then the precentorship (on the death of his uncle) and the prebend of Langford Ecclesia.[47] By 1831, George Pretyman held the chancellorship and another prebend at Lincoln, a prebend at Winchester, and two rectories; and Richard Pretyman held the precentorship and another prebend at Lincoln, and three rectories.[48]

The Pretymans' accumulation of office was notorious, even in an age when pluralism was rife. What marks them out is the ruthlessness of their pursuit of personal gain, their frankness about their motives and the consequences for the cathedral of their longevity. Their ruthlessness is illustrated by the notorious cases of the Masterships of the Hospitals at Meer and Spital. Richard Pretyman was appointed Warden of Meer Hospital by his father in 1817, in circumstances which suggest that the land was ripe for exploitation. The previous Warden was given the rectory of Cardington by the Bishop, presumably to make way for his son. In 1835 the Charity Commissioners investigated the case, and Richard was taken to court on the ground that he should not have appropriated the fines for the renewal of the leases of the property to his own use. An annual rent of £32 was paid, £24 of which was distributed to six poor persons. In 1819 Richard had taken a fine of £9,000, and he received two more in 1826 and 1834, yielding a grand total of £13,147 plus £750 for the sale of timber. The Master of the Rolls declined to force Richard to repay the money to the hospital, despite the obstruction which he and the Dean and Chapter had shown to the Commissioners' investigation of the case, but a new scheme was ordered for the charity and Richard was required to pay £1,000 on his death.[49] Spital was another hospital, where the Master was John Pretyman, the bishop's nephew. For the whole of the eighteenth century the Master had been one of the residentiaries, and Edmund Venables, writing in 1889, suggested that from the mid-century the Masters 'appear . . . to have regarded the hospital not so much as a charitable trust as a benefice of which they were at liberty to make as much

[47] A.3.17: 23 Apr. 1814, 25–7; 26 Apr. 1814, 28; 12 May 1814, 29; 17 Mar. 1817, 61; 21 Jun. 1817, 64–6.

[48] *Report of the Ecclesiastical Revenues Commission, 1835*, HC, 1835, 22, 78–9.

[49] G.F.A. Best, 'The road to Hiram's Hospital', *Victorian Studies* 5, 1961–2, 143; HC 1818, 4, 175–81; 1839, 14, 468–75; 1841, 23, 254; 1852, 38, 408–9; *English reports* XLIX London 1905, 418–19; LII, 460–1; A.3.17: 23 Dec. 1839, 356.

as they could for their own profit'.[50] John Pretyman the younger was thus the first person to hold the mastership on the basis of family connection alone for more than a hundred years, and like his cousin he appropriated the fines for the renewal of leases to his own benefit. The Charity Commissioners also proceeded against him, and it was reckoned that between 1821 and 1836 his receipts amounted to £12,650 while expenditure was £926. A judgment of 1844, by which time John was dead, denied his right to appropriate revenues for his own use. The Chapter Clerk, however, was ordered to pay the costs of the suits.[51]

A letter from George Pretyman to Bishop Kaye in 1846 reveals the mixture of motives in a period of transition. The great tithes of Biggleswade had fallen in and he could therefore grant a lease for three lives 'for the benefit of my family, as my father did with Holbeach, Nettleham etc. etc. and indeed he always desired me to look at it in that light'. However, the Ecclesiastical Commission had got to hear of it and wanted to negotiate with him to get the estate for themselves. He was disinclined to do this unless Kaye pressed him, and proposed instead to grant some one, in trust, a lease to himself, with a payment of £100 to £120 p.a. to the vicar. His reasoning is fascinating:

> it was given me for the express purpose of benefitting my family, but I feel I ought to do something; I wish to endow that very poor vicarage; & wish still more to benefit my old curate: but if I do, I shd like to *have the credit of it*, & if I sell to the E. C., *they* wd get the credit, & perhaps not endow the vicarage *immediately*, which is what I am so anxious for.[52]

The wish to endow the vicarage did not extend to a permanent alienation of the property!

For Lincoln cathedral it was the length of office of the Pretyman brothers as residentiaries that was significant. George was Chancellor from 1814 to 1859 and Richard was Precentor from 1817 to 1866, a combined total of ninety-four years in office. Moreover, having acquired their preferments early in life, and not then receiving any more, the Pretymans survived at Lincoln as a reminder of a past age and an obstacle to the coming of the new. Arthur Benson wrote of the large stables and lofts, the granary and the coach-house at the Chancery 'all belonging to the time when Chancellor Pretyman . . . lived at Lincoln in such state that, an old resident told us, a footman stood behind the chair of every

---

[50] E. Venables, 'An historical notice of the Hospital of "Spital-on-the-Street", Lincolnshire', *AASR* 20, 1890, 291.

[51] Ibid., 291–92; cf. HC 1818, 4, 181–5; A.3.17: 24 Mar. 1842, 381; 16 Sept. 1844, 419.

[52] LAO Episcopal records, Kaye Correspondence, Cor B5.10.1–11: Pretyman to Kaye, 3 Jun. 1846 (unattributed manuscript quotations are taken from the muniments of the Dean and Chapter in LAO). I am grateful to my former research student Frances Knight for transcribing this letter for me; see also Best, *Victorian Studies* 5, 1961–2, 143.

guest at dinner'.[53] Throughout the whole of the period since the mid-eighteenth century the average tenure of the offices of Dean, Subdean, Chancellor and Precentor had been 15 years: apart from the Pretyman brothers who each served well over 40 years, only one person, George Gordon, Dean from 1810 to 1845, served over 30 years. The significance of this domination in a small chapter can scarcely be exaggerated. The Pretymans outlived Bishop Kaye, and so long as either lived the full implementation of the cathedral reform of 1840 was delayed.[54]

Family considerations apart, Bishop Pretyman appointed some distinguished clergy to the cathedral. He appointed William Paley as Subdean in 1795, which post he held until his death in 1805. He resigned his stall as Chancellor of Carlisle, but remained Archdeacon until 1804: he also held a non-resident prebend at St Paul's, and was rector of Bishop Wearmouth. His life therefore involved regular movement between Sunderland and Lincoln. The essential difficulty in passing judgment on this is summed up by Paley's own comment: 'Formerly the Dean of Lincoln had so much to do that he was obliged to have a subdean to help him; but now I cannot find out for the life of me that there is anything for either of us to do.'[55] This is not very different from the comment of the 'reformer', F. C. Massingberd, who reflected in his journal after deciding not to bid for the deanery in 1860 that 'with failing health, such retirement would have been welcome'.[56] Paley's reputation in Lincoln depended mainly upon his conversation: he never attended an Audit meeting of the chapter in his ten years' membership, while John Pretyman attended in six years out of twenty-three. The latter's nephews were more assiduous.

Paley's successor as Subdean was rather different. H. V. Bayley was a brilliant classical scholar, and Fellow of Trinity College, Cambridge. Venn said of him that he devoted much time and money to beautifying and renovating the cathedral. But his career was also determined by Pretyman patronage. He was appointed the bishop's Examining Chaplain after coaching his eldest son, W. E. Pretyman Tomline, for admission to Trinity; and was subsequently offered the subdeanery as a further reward in 1805. In 1811 he presented himself to the vicarage of Messingham with Bottesford, in right of his canonical farm, and eighteen months later he did the same again, this time by nominating himself to the vicarage of Great Carlton: there is no similar case in the eighteenth century. Nevertheless he made considerable improvements in Messingham and Bottesford, and ensured that there was a full-time curate for the periods he was

[53] A. C. Benson, *The life of Edward White Benson* I, London 1900, 365.
[54] A.3.17: 15 Sept, 1845, 431; A.3.18: Sept. 1866, 221.
[55] M. L. Clarke, *Paley: evidences for the man*, London 1974, 52; see also 44–7, 52–3.
[56] LAO Massingberd Correspondence 8/2, 2 Mar. 1860.

not in residence.[57] When Pretyman moved to Winchester, Bayley was given a Hampshire living, where he spent the rest of his life, resigning the subdeanery in 1828 as an exchange deal for a prebend at Westminster with Lord John Thynne, though he retained the archdeaconry of Stow and a prebendal stall at Lincoln until his death. He was sufficiently eminent to have been a candidate for the Regius Chair of Divinity at Cambridge, when John Kaye resigned in 1827 on his translation from Bristol to Lincoln.[58]

The contemporary Dean, George Gordon, also presents an ambiguous picture. He was the son of Precentor John Gordon, whose pronounced Tory opinions in the 1790s were noted by Paley. He also had a distinguished academic career at Cambridge, winning the Chancellor's Medal and being elected a Fellow of St John's in 1787. He became a prebendary and Precentor of Exeter in 1789, and Dean of Exeter in 1809. But his heart was in Lincolnshire. He became rector of Sedgbrook in 1792 and remained so until his death in 1845; and when the deanery of Lincoln became vacant in 1810 he accepted it with alacrity, turning down even the offer of the see of Peterborough in 1819. When he died in 1845 the *Gentleman's Magazine* said with marvellous understatement that 'the Dean was distinguished all his life by a zealous and careful preservation of things as they were, as well in matters connected with the minster as in politics'.[59] Gordon presented one son, the Revd George Gordon, Junior, to the vicarage of Orston, one of the Dean and Chapter's livings, in 1818, and to Hambledon (when it was vacated by Richard Pretyman) in 1819. Another son, the Revd John Gordon, was presented to Bierton with Buckland by the Dean in 1825, and to Edwinstowe in 1835.[60] Dean Gordon also presented the cathedral with gold communion plate, valued at 600 guineas, when a former set was stolen. It was said of him, as it was said of Bayley, that the charities of Lincoln would be poorer by his departure. Any simple equation between the unreformed cathedral and abuse is not therefore possible.

The same problem affected some of the priest-vicars. William Hett was a senior vicar and his pluralism (and perhaps his writings against Methodists, which made him unpopular in certain quarters) qualified him for an entry in John Wade's *Black Book*. He had five livings and paid curates for each of them: the Ecclesiastical Revenues Commission Report shows this to have given him £588 p.a. net when the curates' payments were deducted, to which must be

[57] A.3.16: 29 Apr. 1811, 290; A.3.17: 14 Dec, 1812, 11–12; W. B. Stonehouse *A Stow visitation*, ed. N.S. Harding, Lincoln 1940, 47–52.

[58] J.A. Venn, *Alumni Cantabrigienses*, part II, vol. 1, Cambridge 1940, 194; *Memoir of H. V. Bayley*, Gainsborough 1846, 9–10, 12–20, 22–32.

[59] Venn, *Alumni*, part II, vol. 3, Cambridge 1947, 89; *Gentleman's Magazine*, NS, 24(2), 1845, 317–18.

[60] A.3.17: 5 Mar. 1818, 77; 16 Feb. 1819, 87–8; 1 Jun. 1825, 171; 13 Feb. 1835, 295.

added the £2 p.a. from his prebend in the cathedral, and his share of the minor canons' revenues of £115 p.a.[61], But in 1810 he wrote to the Dean and Chapter to declare his utter astonishment that he should have lived to hear one of the senior vicars state in the vestry, in the presence of the Subdean (Bayley), 'that the whole duty of a Senior Vicar is comprehended merely in his reading his week at the Cathedral; and that, whether he attend the divine service on any other day in the month, is a matter of mere option, not of duty'. He recalled that he had been taught by Precentor Gordon and Subdean Dowbiggin some twenty-nine years before 'that it was my duty to attend the service of the Cathedral, daily & twice a day, with few & occasional exceptions, during the course of the week, the month & the year'. If, however, a senior vicar did not reside in Vicars' Court (presumably because he was living at a benefice at some distance, given to increase his income), the duties had to be shared out among the remaining residents. When he had been the junior priest-vicar, he had had to undertake a very considerable share of the duties of the cathedral for several years together on account of the poor health of his seniors. Now that he was getting older he was neither able nor willing to have any part of the duty of a junior thrown upon his shoulders. He therefore appealed to the chapter to 'restore things, in some degree, at the least, to their ancient accustomed state of *propriety* & *mutual accommodation*'. However, he concluded, if they did not agree with him, 'being a Senior Vicar of the old school' he would continue to act as heretofore – 'with diligence according to my abilities, & attention to the credit and respectability of the Church, & with a just subservience to the orders & regulations of you my much respected superiors'.[62] There is no evidence that the Dean and Chapter took action on his letter, but it aptly shows that an unsatisfactory structure did not eliminate good intentions. Hett was a pluralist but he paid curates in each of his livings.

However, reform was in the air, both in the diocese and in the country. Canon Overton wrote of Bishop Pelham that he 'left no mark upon the diocese of Lincoln; and ... during his incumbency the evils of non-residence and

---

[61] [J. Wade], *The Extraordinary Black Book* (1832), repr. New York 1970, 29, 111; *Ecclesiastical Revenues Commission 1835*, 78–9, 562–4, 572–3, 590–1. Wade's entry refers to Hett's Tory sympathies in one or two published sermons, but it is difficult to believe that his selection of examples of 'measureless rapacity' was as random as he implied.

[62] Letter from William Hett to the Dean and Chapter, 8 Sept. ?1810, L A O D C A.4.10 Bundle 79. The date could be 1816, but the fact of a chapter decision in 1808 over payments by residentiaries to priest-vicars when duty was not done (A.3.16: 19 Sept. 1808, 245) makes 1810 more likely; Hett became prebendary of Bedford Minor in 1786 (which is twenty-nine years before 1816), but it is unlikely (though not impossible) that he would have been given a prebend immediately upon appointment as a priest-vicar.

laissez-faire reached their climax'.[63] But he died in 1827, and his successor was John Kaye, bishop of Bristol and Regius Professor of Divinity at Cambridge. Kaye was a very different person, an old high churchman and a Tory, but a reformer, sympathetic to the 'Hackney phalanx' led by Joshua Watson. He and his Cambridge contemporaries, Blomfield, bishop of London, and Monk, bishop of Gloucester, became the leading trio of reforming bishops in the 1830s, concentrating particularly on the enforcement of residence. He was the first bishop of Lincoln since before 1750 to be installed and enthroned in the cathedral in person rather than by proxy.[64]

In 1831 Kaye was included in the Royal Commission appointed to investigate ecclesiastical revenues, the report of which was published in 1835. It is a necessary corrective to the general denunciation of pluralism and clerical rapacity by John Wade in his *Extraordinary Black Book* of 1832, which included details of the Pretymans in its pages.[65] The Commission's report contained figures based on the calculation of the average annual revenue for the three years ended 31 December 1831. As later critics of the report pointed out, this could be misleading, since the system of renewing leases for lives at seven-year intervals meant that only a seven-year average was really adequate: there was no such thing as an annual income. Nevertheless, it was a less misleading indicator than most of the others available to contemporaries.[66] The average net annual income of the Dean and Chapter of Lincoln was given as £6986. It was noted that the Fabric of the cathedral was sound, and that the funds for its maintenance, derived mainly from estates assigned to that purpose, were adequate. The net annual balance available to be shared among the chapter at the annual Michaelmas audit meeting was reckoned at just over £918. The four priest-vicars had a total average annual income of £115. Lincoln's net average income was roughly the same as Ely and Wells, and was exceeded by that of Canterbury, Durham, Exeter, Oxford, St Paul's, Winchester, Worcester, Westminster and Windsor. It was therefore just in the top half. The individual average net incomes of the four main offices were relatively modest; the Dean had £254, the Subdean £217, the Precentor £184 and the Chancellor £268. But when income from benefices held in plurality was added (allowing for the payment of curates), the Dean received an additional £732, the Subdean £1085, and the Chancellor £2407. By a curious coincidence the revenues of none of

[63] Perry and Overton, *The bishops of Lincoln*, 356.

[64] A.3.17: 20 Apr 1827, 194. For Kaye, see Perry and Overton, *The bishops of Lincoln*, 358–64, and also F. Knight, 'Bishop, clergy and people: some aspects of the episcopate of John Kaye, bishop of Lincoln, 1827–54', Ph.D. dissertation, Cambridge 1990.

[65] Wade, *Black Book*, 1–137, esp. 27.

[66] See P. Virgin, *The Church in an age of negligence*, Cambridge 1988, 40, 89–90.

Richard Pretyman's benefices were returned. There were fifty-one other prebendal stalls, with a combined income (excluding those permanently annexed to another office or benefice) of £1200, but it was very unevenly distributed. More than half the stalls had an annual income of less than £20, and more than a quarter had less than £10: only four had incomes of more than £75. For most of these prebendaries the only duty was to preach in the cathedral once or twice a year, a duty usually discharged in practice by the priest-vicars.[67]

By the time that the report on revenues was published, the Royal Commission had been reconstituted by Sir Robert Peel to prepare plans for the reform of the Church of England: indeed its first report on that matter had already been published. Lincoln men were keenly involved in the lobbying for church reform. Kaye as bishop was a member of the Commission. Archdeacon Bayley, formerly Subdean and described by William Palmer to Newman as 'a most leading man among the Church party', had already written to Goulburn that 'the best part of us are most willing to have a good and ample reform' and referred him to Archdeacon Goddard of Lincoln as 'the best informed and most talented of our body'.[68]

Goddard is another example of a good man promoted through a bad system. He was initially a protégé of the Grenville family and owed his ecclesiastical preferment to Bishop Pretyman, but he had been scrupulous as Archdeacon of Lincoln in seeking reform of abuses at parochial level, as his Charges indicate. In his Charge of 1833 he recognised the need to augment the incomes of many benefices, but resisted the argument for equalising the incomes of all. He responded to the attacks made on the cathedrals, particularly in Lord Henley's influential *Plan of Church reform* of 1832, with arguments which were to become commonplace over the next few years. The cathedral clergy, he argued, were originally the bishop's council and could, by appropriate reform, become so again; cathedral churches provided a model of worship, which again, if inadequately maintained at present, could be reformed; cathedrals were intended to provide places for the support of those engaged in the pursuit of learning; and lastly, he believed, it was appropriate to reward those who had exerted themselves in the service of the Church at an age when it could still bring them credit and comfort.[69] Goddard cited Pusey's *Remarks on the prospective and past benefits of cathedral institutions* with approval. Pusey's main argument had been for the development of cathedrals as centres of theological education; but in his opening pages he had argued that it was advantageous to have people

---

[67] *Ecclesiastical Revenues Commission 1835*, 44–5, 78–85.

[68] Best, *Temporal pillars*, 292–3, 298; A. Mozley, *Letters and correspondence of John Henry Newman* I, London 1891, 469–70.

[69] C. Goddard, *Charge of 1833*, London n.d., 31–48, 80–2; *Gentleman's Magazine* NS 29, May 1848, 555.

in a town who were independent of local interests, because they were only present during their period of residence; he defended an arrangement which gave parochial ministers both recognition and a period of comparative rest during their residence at the cathedral; and more generally he defended a gradation of rank among the clergy, provided it was formed upon right principles.[70]

The Ecclesiastical Commission published four reports. The first in 1835 proposed the reorganisation of dioceses, including the creation of two new ones, and the rationalisation of episcopal revenues. The second in 1836 was the one most concerned with cathedrals, since it proposed to abolish non-resident canonries, establish a norm for the number of residentiary canonries at four, and remove the separate estates for residentiary canonries in cathedrals of the Old Foundation (which included Lincoln). The third and fourth reports, which also followed swiftly in 1836, provided further detail for the main schemes and presented draft legislation. When the Commission expired with the death of William IV in 1837 a draft fifth report was ready, which responded to many of the criticisms made by the chapters, and modified the proposals further. Legislation to implement the proposals concerning dioceses had already been passed in 1836. The more complicated matters of pluralities and cathedrals were not resolved until 1838 and 1840 respectively.[71]

Kaye's membership of the Commission undoubtedly made relations between him and the chapter somewhat delicate. Both he and Goddard represented the position of moderate reform. The Bishop had discussed the relationship between the augmentation of small benefices and cathedral revenues in his Charge of 1834. He agreed with the bishop of Exeter that where prebends were endowed with the great tithes of parishes, and the prebendary had the gift of the vicarages, it would be advantageous to annex the vicarages to the prebends as they became vacant; but that was inevitably a long-term policy. In relation to the sinecure prebends he felt that the archdeaconries in the diocese had the first claim on any changed distribution of cathedral revenues; and he regarded this as a restoration, rather than a violation, of the ancient constitution of the chapter. 'Earnestly,' he said, 'most earnestly, shall I ever deprecate any change having for its object the destruction of our cathedral institutions.'[72] But though he did not favour destruction, he had to contemplate more radical change. Kaye subsequently wrote that he 'had formed no adequate conception of the destitution of the manufacturing districts and of the large towns' until he was made

[70] E. B. Pusey, *Remarks on the prospective and past benefits of cathedral institutions in the promotion of sound religious knowledge and of clerical education*, London 1833, 6–11.

[71] Best, *Temporal pillars*, 302–5.

[72] J. Kaye, *Charge of 1834*, in Works VII, ed. W. F. J. Kaye, London n.d., 146–7.

aware of the facts set out in the Commission's second report. The Commissioners therefore felt 'that the Church *must do something for itself*, before it called on the legislature to lay a tax for the supply of spiritual instruction in particular districts'. Three possibilities existed: to tax all benefices above a certain value (which he and van Mildert, bishop of Durham, had preferred); to use episcopal revenues; or to use cathedral revenues. The first was bound to incur the opposition of the clergy; episcopal revenues had already been redistributed to deal with the problems of bishops; so only the cathedral revenues were left. Two ways of using the cathedral revenues were open: either to annex stalls to populous livings, which would change the character of cathedrals and would be difficult since the need was greatest where cathedrals were fewest; or to transfer a portion of their revenues to form an augmentation fund, which was what was proposed.[73] In his Charge of 1836, Archdeacon Goddard supported the principle that the legislature, as trustee, had 'a moral right to distribute afresh whatever has public objects for its end, *whenever these objects can be shewn expressly to require it*'. Those who rigorously maintained the principle of 'an absolute indefeasible *local* claim' would find themselves upholding anomalies and inequalities which would be inconsistent both with the reputation of the Church and with its safety.[74]

The initiative in rallying cathedral bodies to protest against the proposals of the Ecclesiastical Commission was taken by the Canterbury chapter. They appointed two of their number to confer with members of other chapters on the reports as they affected cathedrals and on any proposed legislation. The fourth report, which contained the proposed legislation concerning cathedrals, was presented to Parliament on 27 June and published on 2 July 1836. The Chapters' Committee met on 8 July at St Paul's under the chairmanship of Sydney Smith, with nineteen present, representing twelve chapters. On 19 July a deputation met with the Commissioners and presented a memorial protesting against the suppression of prebends, and suggesting either annexation to needy benefices or specific appropriation or apportionment of revenues as more acceptable methods. Particular objection was taken to the idea of a common fund, and the principle of locality was deployed to justify this. It was suggested that the transfer of patronage to the bishop would not effect any significant positive change, but it would remove the advantage of having a varied disposition of ecclesiastical patronage. Above all a plea was made for consultation with those affected before any legislation was initiated and time for adequate reflection. The Commissioners replied that they were prepared to reconsider the

---

[73] J. Kaye, *Letter to the archbishop of Canterbury* (1838), in *Works* VII, 198–205 – quotations from 198 and 200.

[74] C. Goddard, *Charge of 1836*, London n.d., 3.

question of suppression or the reduction of numbers to four in each chapter, but they were not prepared to give an answer on chapter patronage. T. Manners Sutton, the Subdean (and nephew of the former archbishop of Canterbury), represented Lincoln at these meetings.[75]

The Dean and Chapter prepared a memorial for the Ecclesiastical Commissioners at the end of 1836, which was sealed on 24 January 1837. Although Pusey had published the draft petition which had been prepared at the St Paul's meeting,[76] the Lincoln memorial, like those from other cathedrals, had its own distinctive style. The Lincoln chapter protested against many of the recommendations contained in the reports with great reluctance, but with a sense that this painful alternative had been forced upon them. They regretted the lack of consultation, and hoped that a wider view might be taken of the objects of cathedrals. In their view, the influence of residentiaries necessarily depended upon their wealth, citing 'their charities, their exertions in the cause of religious education and improvement, their superintendence of local establishments' and their influence upon the character of society as evidence of their utility, and they particularly deplored the 'mischievous disposition to magnify, at their expense, the pastoral office and ministerial industry of those who are invidiously called the working clergy'. In fact, since the present constitution of cathedrals meant that nearly all their dignitaries were employed for most of the year in parochial duties, they argued

that they form a connecting link between the higher and lower grades in the ministry, raising the latter into importance, and enabled to qualify themselves the better to be in their turn 'workers together with them,' by enjoying stated intervals of comparative leisure – intervals, in which the exercise of subordinate authority attaches them to the principles by which episcopal power is upheld; while their regular attendance upon the choral services of the church secures to the public the full preservation of the most beautiful and striking solemnities of Christian worship, together with the more substantial comforts of daily prayer and thanksgiving.[77]

That passage, reflecting the arguments advanced by Pusey and Goddard, illustrates the assumptions of the age which was passing away. The way in which non-residence is made a virtue is particularly interesting: most cathedral clergy do have parochial and pastoral functions, hence their role within the cathedral relates to the worship of the church on the one hand, and leisure for reflection on the other. Christopher Wordsworth, father of a later bishop of Lincoln, argued the same case for the universities, in suggesting that they would be

---

[75] *British Magazine* 10, Aug. 1836, 225–28.

[76] *British Magazine* 10, Nov. 1836, 599–602.

[77] Printed copy in L A O V C 1.1.2; reprinted in *British Magazine* 11, May 1837, 568–74: quotations from p. 2 (570).

the poorer if professors and masters of colleges could no longer hold cathedral preferment, or indeed be incumbents, because this linked these various functions together. He rightly foresaw that the next step would be to remove the necessity for university teachers to be clergymen, which he thought would be disastrous.[78]

The chapter advanced the usual general arguments against using endowments given for one purpose in one place for another purpose in a different place, pointing out that this removed any reason for not transferring such endowments from ecclesiastical use altogether. Moreover, every one of their fifty-two stalls, save one, had produced a bishop in the last 400 years, and every cathedral in the country had had a prebendary of Lincoln as a bishop. They did not think an additional residentiary necessary. Not surprisingly they opposed the transfer of their patronage to the bishop, noting that as a result, 37 advowsons would be lost from prebendaries, 19 from the Dean, 9 from the Precentor, Chancellor and Subdean, and 31 from the body corporate. They opposed the dissolution of the minor corporations, and doubted whether the choir could manage with any fewer lay vicars. Whilst noting that the sums for the priest-vicars were too small, and would be diminished if prebends were suppressed, they felt it important for them to continue to hold benefices in the city and neighbourhood which gave them a respectable income. They regretted that there had not been 'free and open communications between bishops and their deans and chapters', which 'might have been highly advantageous', and hoped that this would now happen in the context of any change of statutes by the Visitor, i.e. the Bishop. In conclusion they reiterated their concern about promotion in the Church. Precisely because they knew that many a conscientious person entered into holy orders without any other hope or design than that of 'preaching the word', and was content to spend his life 'happy in obscurity, and rewarded by his inward sense of his usefulness', 'free from every taint of wordly ambition', they were 'the more anxious that he should not be altogether shut out from the prospect of those honours, and from that access to the higher walks of learning, which have been of old provided, in their wisdom and piety, by the nursing fathers of the church of England'.[79]

The Commission's draft fifth report offered some response to the many objections but the arguments went on for two more years, The Dean and Chapter sealed a petition to the House of Commons against the bill to effect certain recommendations of the fourth report on 4 May 1838, but the essence of the Commission's proposals was embodied in the Dean and Chapter Act of 1840.[80] This Act deprived non-residentiary prebends of any endowment (clause

[78] C. Wordsworth, *The Ecclesiastical Commission and the Universities*, London 1837, 47–59.
[79] V C 1.1.2: 3–5; *British Magazine* 11, 570–3; quotations from p. 5 (573).
[80] *British Magazine* 13, Mar. 1838, 322–34; A.3.17: 335; *British Magazine* 18, Sept. 1840, 314–38.

235

22), made provision for the appointment of up to twenty-four honorary canons in each cathedral (23), transferred the patronage of deaneries to the Crown (24), made it necessary to have been in priest's orders for at least six years before appointment to a canonry (27), removed separate estates for canonries (28), vested the separate patronage of members of the chapter in the bishop (41), restricted the patronage of chapters (44), vested the right of appointing minor canons in the chapters, with provision for making regulations for their number and emoluments (45), limited the distance at which minor canons could hold benefices to 6 miles from the cathedral (46), vested the estates of suspended canonries, deaneries and non-suspended canonries and non-residentiary prebends in the Ecclesiastical Commission (49–51), and fixed the average annual incomes for deaneries and canonries (with specified exceptions) at £1,000 and £500 respectively (66). As it affected Lincoln, the Act established a fourth canonry (17), allowed the bishop to appoint an archdeacon to the new residentiary canonry (33), allowed the new canonry to be annexed to two archdeaconries jointly in the diocese subject to certain conditions (35), and, in protecting the interests of the existing dean and canons, restricted the rights in the corporate patronage of the chapter of the new fourth canon of Lincoln for so long as any existing member of the chapter remained a member (75).

The potential for obstructing the reforms envisaged by the Act is illustrated by the problem of the fourth canonry. In November 1841, following discussion between J. J. Chalk at the Ecclesiastical Commissioners and Bishop Kaye, a draft scheme was prepared for the endowment of the fourth canonry. A transition had to be made between the present system of dividing the revenues into four parts, the Dean and canons taking one-quarter each, to the new system of dividing the revenues into six, the Dean taking two parts and the other four canons one each. Nothing could be done until one of the existing canonries became vacant, but it was agreed that as the first two canonries fell vacant two-thirds of the revenues should go to the successor and one-third to the fourth canon, and when the third canonry fell vacant two-thirds should go to the canon and one-third to the Dean.[81] When Manners Sutton died in 1844, Kaye wrote to the Commissioners saying that it would now be possible to establish a fourth canonry linked to the archdeaconry of Lincoln. However, because Archdeacon Goddard wished to retain his living at Ibstock in Leicestershire, which was now outside the diocese, it was agreed that Goddard would resign the archdeaconry and be appointed Subdean, and the Bishop would appoint a new archdeacon who would become the fourth canon. The scheme was accordingly sealed by the Commissioners on 12 November 1844.[82]

---

[81] E C File 3959: Chalk to Kaye 25 Nov. 1841; Kaye to Chalk 27 Nov. 1841.
[82] E C File 3959: Kaye to E C 28 Oct. 1844, 1 Nov. 1844; Murray to Kaye 4 Nov. 1844.

Robert Swan, the Chapter Clerk, was as obstructive as possible. First the Commissioners noted that it was impossible to get a candid account of the property of the subdeanery following Sutton's death. Then Swan tried to change the date when the scheme took effect in order to ensure that the remaining members of the chapter would get the subdeanery revenues for the year until the 1845 Audit.[83] Goddard sent a memorandum to C. K. Murray, the Secretary of the Commissioners, pointing out that the Dean had lost the use of his intellect and that therefore the Pretyman brothers constituted the chapter between them:

Have then those two sole existing members of the Chapter the power on the one hand to help themselves (*for what purpose* is not stated in Mr Swan's letter) to a whole year's profits of the Subdeanery and so in the present case to the profits also of the 4th Canon and on the other hand to dispense with the residence of the 3rd and 4th Canons?[84]

George Pretyman actually called on the Commissioners to ask what chance the chapter would have in contesting the Order in Council and the cost of appealing to the Privy Council; but the advice of the Crown Law Officers obviously convinced him that there was no chance of success so that by 31 December Kaye was writing to Murray that 'as the Chapter, that is to say the Chancellor and Precentor, have withdrawn their opposition to the Order in Council in its original form, I conclude that there will be no further obstacle to its speedy issue.'[85]

Further consultation was required to establish the procedure to be followed, and it was determined that the Archdeacon had to be appointed first, and then in a separate instrument collated to the canonry. Accordingly H. K. Bonney was installed as archdeacon of Lincoln, and presented a certificate from the Bishop for installation to the fourth canonry. Dean Gordon died in August 1845, making the next stage of the Scheme possible, and at the Audit meeting of September 1845 the Archdeacon was included in the offices for the first time. Nevertheless in 1848 the Archdeacon was denied the right to choose a canonical farm, and in 1849 it was ruled that he had no share in the income from certain chapter properties.[86] Another loser was the new Dean, for as J. G. Ward complained to the Commissioners in May 1846, his predecessor had received a quarter of the revenues, and his successor would receive double when the other

---

[83] E C File 3994 note; EC File 3959: Swan to Murray 25 Nov. 1844.

[84] E C File 3959: Goddard to Murray 7 Dec. 1844.

[85] E C File 3959: note by Pringle 20 Dec. 1844; Swan to Murray 27 Dec. 1844; Kaye to Murray 31 Dec. 1844.

[86] E C File 3959: Kaye to Murray 10 Feb. 1845; Murray to Kaye 13 Feb. 1845; minutes of Special General Meeting 8 Aug. 1845; A.3.17: 8 Feb. 1845, 421–2; 22 Feb. 1845, 423; 15 Sept. 1845, 431; 18 Sept. 1848, 476; 17 Sept. 1849, 488.

two canonries fell in: but meanwhile he had less than either and had an expensive house and hospitality to keep up.[87] He rightly guessed that he would be lucky to outlive the Pretymans. Although the complexities of this episode may seem tedious, they illustrate the fact that it was easier to pass reform legislation than to implement it.

The priest-vicars were the first group to be affected directly by the new legislation. The fourth report of the Ecclesiastical Duties and Revenues Commission in June 1836 had proposed the dissolution of the corporations of vicars choral, priest-vicars or minor canons, with adjustment of their endowments to ensure that each existing member secured a provision at least equivalent to that at present, together with much tighter restrictions on holding any chapter benefice.[88] The Lincoln priest-vicars petitioned the House of Commons against dissolution,[89] and indeed managed to avoid it for a century, but the Residence and Pluralities Act of 1838 and the Dean and Chapter Act of 1840 sank the traditional position of the priest-vicars. The limitation of pluralities to two and the prohibition on minor canons holding livings more than 6 miles from the cathedral made it impossible to reward them with the more lucrative capitular patronage; and the only alternatives were the poorer city livings in Lincoln itself. The chapter also changed the rules concerning the disposal of livings vacated by the death of a priest-vicar. A Chapter Order of 1826 had laid it down that all Dean and Chapter livings becoming vacant by the death of a senior vicar should be considered as at the disposal of the residentiary whose turn it was to present to the vacant vicarage, it being understood as before that they were to be given to one of the senior vicars. This was now altered so that if a senior vicar could no longer be presented to such a living, all the livings held by the senior vicar should be at the disposal of the residentiary whose turn it was to present to the vacant vicarage.[90] So the vicars not only lost their promotion prospects but also ran the risk of losing the livings they had.

Another effect of the Act concerned the preaching fees payable to the priest-vicars by non-resident prebendaries. One of the main duties of the prebendaries had been to preach in the cathedral on a specified Sunday each year; if they could not do their duty, the custom had been that they paid a fee to one of the priest-vicars to do duty for them. With the abolition of non-resident prebends, there was no longer a source to pay the preaching fees to the priest-vicar who substituted. Despite a plea to the Commissioners from Bishop Kaye and a

---

[87] EC File 3963: Ward to EC 30 May 1846.
[88] *Fourth Report of the Ecclesiastical Duties and Revenues Commission*, propositions 38–41, *British Magazine* 10, 1836, 207.
[89] Undated petition in VC 3,1,2, no. 7.
[90] A.3.17: 13 May 1826, 179; 19 Sept. 1842, 390.

petition from the priest-vicars, the Commission ruled that these payments were personal. The Dean and Chapter thereupon resolved to make such preaching turns in future the responsibility of the residentiary, who would pay the customary fee to the priest-vicars if he did not preach himself.[91]

A different tactic was tried in April 1851 when J. S. Gibney wrote to the Commissioners saying that he thought he ought to come under the terms of section 45 of the Dean and Chapter Act which guaranteed an income of £150 p.a. to minor canons. He stated that the Lincoln incomes remained between £40 and £50 p.a. The Estates Committee sought the opinion of the Law Officers on the relevance of the Act to minor canons in cathedrals of the Old Foundation. Their opinion was that the Act was defective in seeking to reduce the number of minor canonries, but all that could be said was that to appoint more minor canons than the statutory maximum was invalid. The Commissioners resolved at a General Meeting in November 1851 that they were not authorised to take steps to augment the incomes of minor canons in the Old Foundation. Gibney returned to the fray a year later, and asked whether the Commissioners would take over the Minor Canons' Estates and grant an annual income of £150 in return; but they replied that their powers did not extend to corporations of minor canons.[92] Even if the answer had not been in terms of the Commissioners' powers, the difficulty of producing an annual income of £600 p.a. from the priest-vicars' estates is clear. A paper listing the amount received from fines in renewal of leases by the priest-vicars between 1818 and 1839 shows that the average amount over those twenty years was £167.19s.9½d. In 1824, 1831 and 1838 there was no income from fines at all; in 1820, 1829 and 1834 it was below £12; in 1819, 1830, 1832 and 1837 it was between £20 and £100. For the remaining years it was between £100 and £200, but in the three exceptional years of 1822, 1828 and 1833 it was £384, £509 and £1141 respectively. These sums were shared among the four vicars. A table of income for 1846–52, included in the Report of the Cathedrals Commission of 1854, showed similar fluctuations: although the average income from fines was £97.15s.2d., in five of the seven years the income was below that, including 1852 when there was no income from fines at all. The high average is due to the two exceptional years of 1846 and 1851, the latter being the only year in which any income from leases for lives was received.[93] But it is also noticeable that the income is much

---

[91] EC File 3958: Kaye to Murray 30 Oct. 1841; Murray to Kaye 1 Nov. 1841; Kaye to Murray 8 Nov. 1841; Murray to Nelson 18 Feb. 1842; memorial to EC, 2 Nov. 1841, VC 3.1.2, no. 6; A.3.17: 19 Sept 1842, 390.

[92] EC File 3956: Gibney to EC 2 Apr 1851; Estates Committee to Law Officers 2 July 1851; Law Officers to Estates Committee 20 Aug. 1851; minute of 6 Nov. 1851; Gibney to EC 25 Sept. 1852; Chalk to Gibney 7 Oct. 1852.

[93] VC 1.1.1; Appendix to the *First Report of the Cathedral Commissioners, 1854*, HC 1854, 25, 909.

less in the later than the earlier period, and the significance of subventions from the Dean and Chapter had increased.

The Revolutionary and Napoleonic wars had brought Fabric activity to a stop apart from essential repairs. William Hayward, architect, was appointed Surveyor of the Fabrick in 1799 in place of William Lumby. The most significant event of these years was the removal of the spires on the western towers in 1807. Subdean Bayley was the moving spirit behind the decision: the Dean was incapacitated and the Precentor and Chancellor were absent. Although there was concern in the town, this time there was no violent opposition. Sir Joseph Banks proposed an association of inhabitants of the diocese to compel the chapter to replace them – and the spire on the central tower which had blown down in 1547 – but on taking legal advice discovered that there was no way of compelling the chapter to act.[94]

In 1828 the main bell of the cathedral, Great Tom, cracked; and efforts began to replace it. Hitherto Great Tom had hung in the north-west tower, the six Lady Bells in the central tower, and the eight bells of St Hugh in the south-west tower. William Dobson of Downham, Norfolk, was consulted and met the Dean on 3 July 1829. Subsequently he wrote to the Dean suggesting that, as he wished to place the new bell in the central tower, which he thought the finest in the whole kingdom, it ought to be made to match the tower's splendour and magnificence. He suggested a bell heavier than the 7 tons 15 cwt. of Mighty Tom at Oxford:

The commanding situation of the Building is admirably calculated for the display of such a Bell, it would be heard many miles around (if St Paul's could be heard at Windsor, may we not presume that Tom's Notes will reach the Turrets of Belvoir?) and the Clock which was evidently too powerful for the old Bell will, I am confident, be sufficiently so for a new one on the scale I have suggested.[95]

Accordingly he proposed to cast a new bell from the old one, the Lady Bells and an additional 10 cwt. of metal, making it the heaviest bell in the kingdom, and to superintend the construction of a new bell-frame. Despite making an offer 'more with a view to the acquirement of Fame than Fortune', his estimate for taking down the larger bell and peal of six, and casting them into a single bell was £280 plus £70 for additional metal. This was too much for the chapter and eventually Dobson submitted a revised estimate of £256. Work on a scaled-down version of Dobson's plan was eventually carried out by Thomas Mears of Whitechapel. The new Great Tom arrived at Lincoln on 13 April 1835, with a

[94] A.3.16: 17 May 1799, 126; 21 Sept. 1807, 225; *Memoir of Bayley*, 15–16; Hill, *Georgian Lincoln*, 271.
[95] A.4.14: Dobson to Dean 27 July 1829.

weight of 5 t. 8 cwt.; its note was A. It was hung on 30 May, and first struck by the clock on 5 June and first rung on Whit Sunday, 7 June 1835. It was clearly bigger than the old, but fell a good way short of Dobson's original ambitious scheme to rival the Kremlin.[96]

Edward Betham was appointed Surveyor of the Fabric in 1842 and in 1845 the chapter changed the account so that it was now to include provision for church services and furnishings – lights, books, cushions, etc., as well as the structure of the building. There is little record of Fabric work done, however, until 1851 when the room over the vestry ceased to be used as a Common Chamber because of its inconvenient access, and instead the vestry was made the Common Chamber and the room over the Galilee Porch used for the deposit and safe custody of archives, muniments and records.[97]

In the following year the Dean and Chapter agreed a new policy for Fabric repairs. Before any order was made for work or repairs to be done, a detailed estimate with full specification was to be obtained by the Surveyor and presented to the Dean and Chapter. No order was to be made until it had been ascertained from the Clerk of Works that the income of the Fabric Fund was sufficient to defray the expenses. Decisions about such work would normally be made at the Audit meeting in September, unless there was an emergency or the consent of every member of the chapter had been obtained. The Surveyor was also required to submit weekly statements to the Clerk of the Fabric during any work, and certify an annual statement of expenditure to the Chapter Clerk by 1 September each year.[98] The effect of this was that entries concerning the Fabric appeared more regularly in the records.

In 1853 it was agreed to repair the vestry and the chamber above it according to Mr Nicholson's estimate, with the stonework done by William Sandall at a cost of £420. £250 was also paid towards the cost of the new east window. In 1854 a two-year programme of outward repairs to the east side of the upper transept, including the semi-circular chapels and Bishop Longland's chapel and the pediments above the chapel, was agreed; plaster was to be removed from the ceiling of the five bays from the east end; and the flying buttresses of the chapter house were to be repaired. Next year it was agreed to repair the rose window at the north end of the great transept for £105, and to enquire about the cost of insuring the cathedral for £15,000. A thorough repair of half the choir roof was agreed in 1856, commencing at the west end, and £225 was set aside for external repairs to the south wall of the cathedral. A new fire-engine

---

[96] A.4.14: Dobson to Dean 10 Mar. 1830; Dean to Dobson 14 May 1830; chapter order of 1 June 1834; contract dated 6 June 1834.

[97] A.3.17: 19 Sept. 1842, 391; 15 Sept. 1845, 432; 15 Sept. 1851, 513.

[98] A.3.17: 20 Sept. 1852, 526–7.

was also purchased. In 1857 it was agreed to alter the reredos in accordance with the design of Charles Buckler of Oxford, and to provide new tiles of Derbyshire marble within the communion rails. The repairs on the south side of the cathedral were continued, provided they did not cost more than £50, but the roof repairs were discontinued for a year.[99]

These years were the last years of the old policy on cathedral estates, though the level of fines for renewal of leases was increased in the opening years of the century. In 1803 it was agreed that the fine for the renewal of a 21-year lease after seven years would be one and a half times the annual value, and that the renewal of a lease for an additional life would be two years' value if the remaining lives were under 60. These levels were increased in 1806, when it was also decided to map the property of the Dean and Chapter and the Fabric Estates. A year later restrictions were agreed on all leases in Minster Yard and the Close as they fell due so that they could only be used as private residences. It was also agreed to purchase the leases of the four Chequer houses belonging to the Fabric adjoining the Chequer Gate for 200 guineas out of the Fabric Fund, to pull them down and to let the site to the Precentor. In 1810 the fine for renewal of forty-year house leases after fourteen years was fixed at one and a half times the annual value. By 1856 the fine for the renewal of a 21-year lease was twice the annual value.[100] The period also saw an increase in the development of assets in funds rather than land. In 1808 it was agreed that, as property tax was not payable on fines paid into Funds, the Receiver-General should place the share of fines due to each residentiary into 3 per cent consols immediately unless instructed otherwise.[101] By 1824 the Dean and Chapter held £4670 worth of stock of various kinds in addition to their estates – £500 for the chapter, £3120 for the Fabric and £1050 for the choir.[102] But by the end of the 1850s it was beginning to be necessary to sell some of this stock, particularly for the choir.[103] This is but one indication of the financial squeeze which was to hit the cathedral as incomes dropped and costs rose. The twenty years' delay in adjusting to the reforms of the 1830s meant that they had to be faced in less favourable times.

[99] A.3.17: 19 Sept. 1853, 544; A.3.18: 18 Sept. 1854, 13; 17 Sept. 1855, 27; 15 Sept. 1856, 37, 39; 21 Sept. 1857, 56.
[100] A.3.16: 19 Sept. 1803, 183; 15 Sept. 1806, 211; 19 Sept. 1808, 245–6; 26 Dec. 1810, 289; A.3.18: 15 Sept. 1856, 37.
[101] A.3.16: 19 Sept. 1808, 246.
[102] A.3.17: 22 May 1824, 160.
[103] e.g. £1,000 was sold in 1856, £600 in 1859, and £800 in 1861: A.3.18: 15 Sept. 1856, 37; Audit 1859, 82; 17 Sept. 1861, 115.

The age of reform

The Act of 1840 gave the Ecclesiastical Commissioners power to take over capitular estates and regulate incomes, but in the early years the Commissioners had more than enough to do in trying to sort out episcopal estates and incomes. The Cathedrals Commission of 1852–4 failed to make any impact on the situation. Although the 1840 Act fixed average incomes for deans and canons this was easier to say than to do. After the exchanges over establishing the fourth canonry in the 1840s, the Commissioners did not trouble the Lincoln chapter about regulation of their incomes until 1860.

The problem was that the whole system of leasing ecclesiastical property was lax. Whilst in the secular world rack-renting had generally become the norm, ecclesiastical property was still usually leased either for a specified period with fines for renewal every seven years or for the lives of three named persons with fines for the replacement of deceased persons with new lives. The latter type of lease was in effect a gamble on survival. Such a system was loaded in favour of the lessee, who could make money by enclosure or tithes or exploiting other natural assets like timber or minerals. The lessor gained nothing from changes in land value or land use, apart from what could be secured through fines for renewal. Moreover, there was always a temptation for the chapter to take even an inadequate fine for renewal, since the alternative of forgoing any income until the lease fell in required both time and alternative sources of income meanwhile. The Ecclesiastical Commission offered the opportunity for the more effective exploitation of Church property by making it possible to take the long view rather than the short. But the change to the new situation could not be painless, since a period of waiting was essential to success.

It was only in the later 1850s that the Ecclesiastical Commissioners took a greater interest in trying to secure the management of the estates which the chapters had retained, and began to use powers given them by an Act of 1842.[104] A return of the chapter's income submitted in May 1860 indicates the structure of expenditure in the last years of the old regime.

The table shows the fluctuations in chapter income from year to year and the marked differences between the lean years of 1855–6 and the fat years of 1853 or 1857. It also shows the way in which the Pretymans' survival distorted the distribution of the chapter income among the Dean and canons, with the Pretymans each receiving as much as the Dean: only in 1859 with George Pretyman's death did that begin to change. Fabric receipts and expenditure more or less balanced out over the period, with expenditure slightly exceeding income; but apart from the lean years of 1855–6 it never

---

[104] Best, *Temporal pillars*, 351 n. 3, 431–5, 453–60.

Table 2. *Chapter expenditure, 1853–9*[105]

	1853	1854	1855	1856	1857	1858	1859
Dean	3087	2296	980	713	2607	2480	2177
2 pre-1840 canons	6174	4593	1960	1425	5215	4960	3415
2 post-1840 canons	3087	2296	980	713	2607	2480	2364
Total chapter	12,348	9185	3920	2851	10,429	9920	7956
Total expenditure	13,318	10,056	4744	3823	11,437	10,967	8950
Fabric receipts	1518	1189	1094	1109	1423	1346	1420
Fabric expenditure	1206	1551	988	1203	1168	1668	1411

exceeded the Dean's stipend, whereas, with the same exceptions, the incomes of the Dean and Chapter were always higher than those envisaged in the 1840 Act.

In 1860 things started to move. After the appointment of Jeremie as Subdean in 1848 there had been no change in the chapter until George Pretyman died in 1859. Charles Bird was installed as Chancellor on 16 July 1859; in January 1860 the chapter met to consider the enfranchisement of their estates, and were favourably disposed to the idea. They adjourned the meeting until 21 February to secure further information, but in the event there was no meeting then, possibly because of the illness of the Dean, who died on 28 February.[106] Meanwhile the Commissioners opened the question of the regulation of the income of the Dean and Chapter. J. J. Chalk at the Commissioners' office wrote to Robert Swan, the Chapter Clerk, on 20 March 1860 asking for a return of the income of the Dean and Chapter. Swan did not reply immediately, though he did respond to a request for the value of the deanery a few weeks later, stating that the average value for the seven years to September 1859 was £2163.7s.1d. Clearly the Commissioners' decision did not depend on receiving the return they had requested, since on 19 April the Estates Committee recommended the sealing of a scheme to regulate the incomes of the Dean and Chapter.[107] On 21 April the bishop of Lincoln wrote to Chalk asking to see the measure which was to be drawn up to redistribute the income of the Dean and Chapter. He wanted a house to be provided for the archdeacon of Lincoln, and

---

[105] E C File 3957: Swan to Chalk 14 May 1860.
[106] A.3.18: 16 July 1859, 77; 12 Jan. 1860, 88.
[107] E C File 3957: Chalk to Swan 20 Mar. 1860; Chalk to Swan 13 Apr. 1860; Swan to Chalk 16 Apr. 1860; Report of Estates Committee 19 Apr. 1860.

an endowment for the archdeaconry of Nottingham.[108] Unfortunately there is no further record of correspondence with the Bishop. After a reminder from Chalk that the return had not been received, Swan sent it on 14 May. A draft of the scheme was sent to the new Dean, Thomas Garnier, on 9 June and acknowledged on 13 June.[109]

The Dean wrote to Chalk early in July saying that the matter had been considered at the last chapter meeting and held over until September. The Commissioners noted in a minute of 12 July that the Dean was to be informed that the consent of the Dean and Chapter was not required – they had simply been given an opportunity to make observations – and the Board intended to seal the scheme on 26 July. On 20 July Bird wrote to Chalk asking whether the incomes proposed for the canons would be net – if not, he would be disposed to object – and also putting other detailed questions, e.g. whether the Fabric Fund was sufficient.[110] Chalk assured him that the incomes would be net, but by that time the chapter had already met and decided to object to the scheme.

The chapter's objections were both general and particular. They denied the Ecclesiastical Commissioners' claim to the management of the chapter's estates and said that to require a return of annual revenues was arbitrary. Furthermore, the proposal to assign a fixed annual sum was a departure from previous practice because the sums proposed fell short of the average annual income received. The amounts proposed were doubtful, since it was unclear whether they were net or subject to outgoings. The scheme made no provision for the assistance of poor benefices in the patronage of the Dean and Chapter, which they had given hitherto; the source of the income of the minor canons was uncertain; there should be a more adequate income for the choir, and 'liberal provision for the maintenance and education of the Chorister Boys'; there should be provision for the payment of the Chapter Clerk and other officers, and more ample provision for the Fabric.[111] The chapter did not seem to notice the inconsistency between complaining about lower incomes for themselves and saying that more needed to be spent on corporate purposes. Chalk replied that the scheme was consistent with those provided for Canterbury, St Paul's, Winchester, Durham, Salisbury, Lichfield, Llandaff and St David's; but it was not applicable in those cases where the estates had been transferred to the Commissioners, namely York, Carlisle, Chester, Chichester, Gloucester,

---

[108] E C File 3957: Bishop of Lincoln to Chalk 21 Apr. 1860.

[109] E C File 3957: Chalk to Swan 1 May 1860; Swan to Chalk 14 May 1860; Chalk to Dean 9 June 1860.

[110] E C File 3957: Dean to Chalk n.d. (received 7 July 1860); minute of the Board 12 July 1860; Bird to Chalk 20 July 1860.

[111] E C File 3957: Swan to E C 23 July 1860; A.3.18: 23 July 1860, 95.

Peterborough, St Asaph and Worcester. He also pointed out that the amounts of income specified were net, and that the scheme only applied to Dean and Chapter income, and not to expenditure for other purposes or officers.[112] Bird replied that for him at least Chalk's answers were satisfactory, but the Dean asked for a postponement of the sealing on the ground that there was a disposition in the chapter to transfer their estates to the Commissioners, if it could be done without affecting 'the interests of the oldest member of our Chapter, the Precentor'.[113] In September the Dean wrote that he would bring forward the subject of commutation at the audit and asked four questions: whether the Commissioners would leave in the chapter's hands the capitular estates in the town, especially around the cathedral; whether there was any possibility of better maintaining the efficiency of services in the cathedral as a portion of the choir and other expenses came out of corporate funds; whether anything could be done to augment the incomes of the minor canons; and whether any assurance could be given that the interests of Richard Pretyman would not be affected by such a step 'inasmuch as he is the principal obstacle to their taking it'.[114]

The Commissioners replied that, if the Dean and Chapter agreed to commute, the terms would be negotiable and need not affect Pretyman's pecuniary interest. There is no record of a decision on the matter at the Audit meeting on 17 September 1860, but the Subdean and the Archdeacon were absent. In December the Chapter Clerk wrote to say that the chapter had decided it was inexpedient to commute.[115] Meanwhile the Commissioners had sealed a scheme to regulate the chapter incomes on 22 November 1860. A new set of problems now arose in the Privy Council Office. It is not clear how far these problems were sparked by local opposition and how far they related to the general difficulties which the Commissioners were experiencing at this time. Bird certainly supported the scheme: he wrote in January 1861 saying that he hoped the Commissioners had not relinquished their intention of regulating the incomes, though he was concerned about securing to the executors of someone dying in the first half of the year a share of the proceeds distributed at the September Audit. He wrote again in April wanting to know what had happened, saying that he very much wanted a final settlement and dreaded 'a hostile movement on the part of those who lead the public opinion'. He

---

[112] E C File 3957: Chalk to Swan 2 Aug. 1860.
[113] E C File 23278: Dean to E C 4 Aug. 1860; see also E C File 3957: Bird to Chalk 2 Aug. 1860, Dean to Chalk 4 Aug. 1860.
[114] E C File 23278: Dean to E C 7 Sept. 1860.
[115] E C File 23278: E C to Dean 8 Sept. 1860, Chapter Clerk to E C 12 Dec. 1860; A.3.18: 17 Sept. 1860, 98.

thought that £1000 p.a. for a canon was fair, though less would be difficult.[116]

In January 1861 it became clear that there were conflicting opinions in the Privy Council Office on the proposed scheme. Chalk was told in March that the Privy Council was not satisfied that it was legally competent to make the proposed order, or any other to the same effect. The Estates Committee took legal advice, and were advised that it was not only competent for but incumbent upon the responsible authority to limit chapter incomes, so the scheme was sent back to the Privy Council Office and Lord Chichester wrote to Lord Granville to reinforce the point. However, the Privy Council Office wrote to Chalk in July enclosing a report from the Crown Law Officers saying that the Commissioners had failed to demonstrate that they had the legal power to do what they wished. As a result the scheme was stood over by the Board.[117] In November 1862 the Dean asked Chalk whether it was true that the scheme would now be approved. Chalk replied that the scheme had not been approved and was not now before the Council but, as such schemes had been approved in the past, it was always possible that with a change of government such a scheme would be approved in the future.[118] That rather desperate reply indicates the significance of the problems the Commissioners had encountered, in what Geoffrey Best called 'the fight for survival' between 1856 and 1863; for the Commissioners burnt their fingers badly over regulation of cathedral incomes in the case of Dean Duncombe of York in 1860, and their powers were only finally clarified in the Act of 1868.[119]

The problems were highlighted in further correspondence in the winter of 1862–3 with Massingberd, who had just become Chancellor. In December 1862 Massingberd queried the Commissioners' valuation of the chancellorship at £1000. A statement of the average income over the previous seven years showed it to be £953.18s.9d., but Pretyman had told him it would only be worth £500 in the coming year. Chalk claimed that calculations over the period from 1846 to 1859 showed that the Commissioners had not underestimated, while Massingberd pointed out that in the period 1860–2 the Chancellor's income had not exceed £1000 once. (The fact that the Precentor was still drawing nearly £2000 did, of course, have a depressing effect on the others.) In February the Commissioners agreed to adjust the valuation downwards slightly, and in

---

[116] E C File 3957: Bird to Chalk 26 Jan. 1861, 24 Apr. 1861.

[117] E C File 3957: Privy Council Office to Chalk 5 Mar. 1861; legal advice to the Estates Committee 29 Apr. 1861; minutes of Estates Committee 2 May 1861 and of Board 18 May 1861; Chichester to Granville 23 May 1861; Privy Council Office to Chalk 6 July 1861; Minutes of Board 19 and 25 July 1861.

[118] E C File 3957: Dean to Chalk 13 Nov. 1862; Chalk to Dean 14 Nov. 1862.

[119] Best, *Temporal pillars*, 437–41, 453–60.

March they agreed to transmit the scheme of 1860 to the Privy Council Office again. Once more it was objected to, and in November 1863 the Estates Committee decided that since the average incomes of the Dean and Chapter could not be said with certainty to exceed £2000 and £1000, the scheme should be dropped.[120]

On 25 March 1866 Richard Pretyman died, and a great obstacle to change was suddenly removed. In fact there was a complete change of personnel in the chapter in the 1860s. The records of chapter meetings start to become fuller from 1864, and whether by coincidence or not a chapter meeting held on 26 March 1866, the day after Pretyman's death, took a number of decisions which previously would have been dealt with only at the Audit meeting in September. In April 1866 the Chancellor, Subdean and Archdeacon were appointed as a Committee of Chapter to visit before the next Audit all livings in the patronage or property of the chapter under the value of £250 p.a. and to report on the best available means of gradually improving their income.[121]

The 1866 Audit meeting saw further changes. The chapter agreed to meet at least once during each period of residence, not later than the end of the second month. The Archdeacon was included within the order of presentation to benefices for the first time, and given a canonical farm; he was allowed to select a house or site within the precincts, the lease of which the chapter agreed to buy. (The purchase was completed in 1870.)[122] A new policy was adopted for the augmentation of benefices. As estates were enfranchised by the Ecclesiastical Commissioners and they drew the whole benefit of them, the chapter advised incumbents to apply to the Commissioners direct, as in the applications of Mr Jackson (Hambleton) and Dr Freeth in February 1867. In November 1867 the Archdeacon and Precentor were asked to report on the chapter finances, and at the 1868 Audit the chapter instructed the Chapter Clerk to prepare a schedule of their properties in preparation for negotiation with the Ecclesiastical Commissioners about their surrender. It was also agreed to pay the balance of the Choristers' Fund out of the chapter dividends and to appropriate 5 per cent of the dividends towards the deficiency on the Fabric Account.[123]

This reflected broader statutory changes. By an Act of Parliament which received the royal assent on 29 May 1868 all the Orders in Council made by the Ecclesiastical Commissioners in respect of cathedral and collegiate churches

---

[120] EC File 3957: Moss to EC 22 Dec. 1862; Chalk to Moss 24 Dec. 1862; Moss to EC 29 Dec. 1862; Chalk to Moss 30 Dec. 1862; Moss to Chalk 26 Jan. 1863; Chalk to Moss 29 Jan. 1863; Massingberd to EC 6 Feb. 1863; EC to Massingberd 14 Feb. 1863; Board minute 26 Mar. 1863; Privy Council Office to EC 7 July 1863; Estates Committee minute 12 Nov. 1863.

[121] A.3.18: 10 Apr. 1866, 206.

[122] A.3.18: Audit 1866, 219, 221; 18 Nov. 1870, 315.

[123] A.3.18: 1 Feb. 1867, 225–6; 11 Nov. 1867, 240; Audit 1868, 273–4.

between 1852 and 1867 were declared good in law (31 Vict. c. 19), and by a further Act later in the session (31 July 1868) the powers of the Commissioners to make schemes for the transfer and reassignment of capitular property were clarified (31 & 32 Vict. c. 114). The way was therefore clear for further negotiations to take place between the Lincoln chapter and the Commissioners. On 13 March 1869 the Archdeacon was authorised to discover from the Secretary of the Commissioners whether they were prepared to take over the estates and pay a fixed sum to the Dean and Chapter in lieu, and, having heard the Archdeacon's report, the chapter resolved to enter into negotiations. A few weeks later it was agreed that whenever a vacancy occurred in the chapter the canon vacating his canonry or his representative should be entitled to a share of the whole year's income in proportion to the interval which had elapsed between the Audit and the date of the vacancy.[124] The terms negotiated by W. A. Yool, the Commissioners' actuary, with the Dean and Chapter were sufficiently generous to require a letter of justification from him to Chalk. He explained that the sum, although large, represented the equivalent of the receipts which the chapter might expect to receive from the property to be transferred to the Commissioners. The net income of the property to be retained was £2400 p.a., so that after commutation of the rest the net income of the Dean and Chapter would be £11,600 p.a., with a prospective increase as the beneficial leases of retained premises fell in, the rack-rent value of those being £2100 more than the present reserved rents. The customary division of the Dean and Chapter's income into three distinct funds, namely the Corporate Fund, the Fabric Fund and the Choristers' Fund, with deficiencies in the latter two being made good by grants from the first, would no longer be practicable. Thus, he wrote, it had been arranged that 'as from Lady Day 1869, they shall have only one fund, taking the expenditure for the support of the Fabric and the efficient maintenance of the services upon it as a first charge, and dividing the balance'.[125] This decision was crucial for the future.

These terms were agreed by the Estates Committee on 8 July, by the General Meeting of the Commissioners on 15 July and by the Dean and Chapter on 30 July 1869. The scheme was scaled by the Commissioners on 5 August and by the Dean and Chapter on 7 August. The Crown Law Officers insisted on a Deed of Execution from the chapter as well, which was done in October, and the Order in Council was finally made on 5 February 1870 and gazetted on 8 February.[126]

[124] A.3.18: 13 Mar. 1869, 282; 20 Mar. 1869, 282; 8 May 1869, 286; EC File 23278: Chapter Clerk to EC 20 Mar. 1869.
[125] EC File 23278: Yool to Chalk, 6 July 1869.
[126] EC File 23278 ad loc. A.3.18: 30 July 1869, 288; 7 Aug. 1869, 288; 24 Jan. 1870, 296; 22 Feb. 1870, 297.

At the very last minute the Commissioners received a protest from the residents in Minster Yard, who objected to the loss of the right of enfranchisement of their leases under the new arrangements. The Estates Committee ignored the protest, but when pressed in July for a reply to the petition sent in March, they denied that the lessees had previously had a perpetual right to the renewal of their leases, which was not subject to annual review. Their maximum grievance was that they were not covered by an Act of 1860 which allowed the Commissioners to purchase the leasehold interest if they declined to sell the reversion. The Committee therefore indicated their willingness to buy the leasehold interests at prices to be determined. There is no further correspondence on the file concerning this matter.[127]

Although the agreement seemed to mark the end of a time of disagreement between the chapter and the Commissioners, it turned out to be the beginning of another and sharper period, which will be discussed below. This was due to the ambiguities of the provision for the care of the cathedral Fabric, and the outstanding problem of the priest-vicars' incomes, which henceforward became tied together in an unfortunate way. Previously there had been a clear division between the Fabric Fund and the Common Fund. Now the two were merged, with the care of the Fabric as a first charge. A capital sum of £20,000 was set aside (plus interest at 3 per cent) for expenditure on repairs, restoration and improvements to the cathedral. What no one foresaw in 1869–70 was the scale of the demand on this Fund in the next few years. The chapter continued to take liberal decisions on expenditure from the Common Fund and to spend money on the Fabric at a rate which ate away their capital.

In 1864–5 the priest-vicars discussed with the Ecclesiastical Commissioners the possibility of commuting their estates under the terms of the Cathedral Minor Canons Corporation Act. Accounts for the last fourteen years were sent in and submitted to Yool for his assessment. He advised an offer of £280 p.a. with £80 p.a. for the lay vicars, on the ground that the income of the last fourteen years had been above average (about £410 p.a.). Armed with this offer and playing on the chapter's wish to retain the property in the cathedral body, the priest-vicars persuaded the chapter to agree that any minor canon who did not hold a benefice should be paid such sum as would make up his income to £100 in any year when his canonry did not yield that.[128] The Act to amend the powers of the Ecclesiastical Commissioners which received the royal assent on

---

[127] E C File 23278: Tweed to E C 26 Jan. 1870; minute of Estates Committee, 3 Feb. 1870; petition from Close lessees, 26 Mar. 1870; Tweed to E C 14 July 1870; Estates Committee to Tweed 22 July 1870.

[128] E C File 31469: Apthorp to E C 29 July 1864; Estates Committee minute 4 Aug. 1864; Apthorp to E C 28 Feb. 1865; Yool to E C 4 Apr. 1865; Estates Committee minute 6 Apr. 1865; E C to Apthorp 13 Apr. 1865; V C 4.1.8: Gibney to Dean 3 May 1865; A.3.18: 6 May 1865, 186.

10 August 1866 (29 & 30 Vict. c. 111) provoked further correspondence, but after returns had been received from all corporations of minor canons a printed circular letter was sent in March 1869, saying that clause 18 of the 1866 Act was not sufficiently precise to enable action to be taken.[129] Presumably as a result of this, the Dean and Chapter were prevailed upon to take what turned out to be a very significant decision on 15 July 1870 when they agreed to make up the income of each minor canon to £200 p.a.[130] Since this was significantly higher than the present or forseeable value of the priest-vicars' estates, it effectively removed much of the incentive for commutation. It also became a millstone around the chapter's neck when they faced difficulties in their accounts after the commutation of their own estates.

The 1860s were also the period when the life of the cathedral was revived, and the appointments to the chapter by Bishops Jackson and Wordsworth were crucial in this process. Charles Bird was appointed Chancellor in place of George Pretyman in 1859. In one sense Bird's conception of the office, rather like that of his successor, Massingberd, was quite traditional. He had been vicar of Gainsborough (with a prebendal stall at the cathedral) since 1843, but by 1859 he was beginning to feel that it was too much for him and he wished to exchange the living for another. Instead the bishop unexpectedly made him Chancellor, the duties of which, he wrote to a friend, were 'few and easy':

I am to be instituted and installed tomorrow, D.V. (July 16th). On Sunday I am to read myself in at the cathedral. In about three months, I shall leave Gainsborough and enter into residence, and make Lincoln the place of rest for my declining years. The Chancery is a good house on the hill. The Bishop will find me plenty to do, which will be a pleasant labour, when I am able to do it.[131]

Clearly the chancellorship was regarded as a retirement job – indeed this was the main reason why it was not to be held in plurality and Bird was going to be a permanent resident in the Close. Nor was it regarded as a full-time post, which was why he expected that the Bishop would give him other things to do.

Bird was conscientious in his duties, and very much aware that he was almost the only fit person in the team. On 22 December 1859 he wrote to his brother, 'On Sunday next in the middle of my sermon, I shall suddenly become residentiary. The old Dean is too ill to preach for himself. The Archdeacon is also ill, and left Lincoln yesterday.'[132] He took care of the ordination candidates when they came to the cathedral, and he was one of the first of the cathedral

[129] EC File 35810: return from Apthorp, 10 June 1867; return from Swan, 16 July 1867; circular letter, 17 Mar. 1869; VC 4.1.56, 1866; 4.1.92 1867.
[130] A.3.18: 15 July 1870, 304.
[131] C. S. Bird, *Sketches from the life of the Revd Charles Smith Bird*, London 1864, 333.
[132] Ibid., 341.

clergy to become active in the town. Since he lived in Lincoln all year, he preached regularly in the city churches outside his period of official residence. Because of the traditional rota he preached more frequently in the cathedral than anyone else. He began a soup kitchen for the poor in the upper part of Lincoln early in 1861, and was active in promoting a Book-hawking Society for North Lincolnshire.[133] His very activity in the cathedral meant that he was more affected than many by its cold during the winter months:

I have suffered so much from the cold of our Cathedral, [he wrote in May 1862] that I have taken courage to propose to the Chapter, in the most earnest manner, the warming of our large Cathedral. They have tried Gurney stoves at York with complete success. The Dean has supported me, and after unwearied exertion I am in hopes we shall really have the stoves ready for use before next November. This is a vast comfort to me, but I feel very tired and depressed.[134]

The chapter approved the tender of the London Warming and Ventilating Company Ltd for warming the cathedral on 24 May 1862: eight stoves and pipes were to be provided for £470, with two additional ones at a cost of £115 if that proved insufficient. Sadly, they came too late for Bird, for he died on 9 November 1862. The Bishop, preaching in the cathedral on the Lancashire distress fund (to relieve the 'cotton famine'), said that Bird would have supported it. He was buried at Riseholme near Bishop Kaye.[135]

Bird was succeeded by F. C. Massingberd, rector of Ormsby. He was a reformer, a traditional high churchman, a friend of Keble and one of the earliest advocates of the revival of Convocation; though he was also an admirer of Arnold, presumably because of his view of the essential union of Church and state. Not surprisingly perhaps he served as a proctor in Convocation when it began to meet regularly again: he was so excited after the first meeting he attended in November 1852 that he could not sleep. In 1859 he published *The law of the Church and the law of the state*, setting out his view of Church–state relations, and was disappointed that it seemed to attract little attention.[136] When Ward was dying in 1860, he wondered whether to make a bid for the deanery, but did not. He wrote in his diary on 2 March 1860 with characteristic self-doubt that either Lord Sydenham, as a friend of Palmerston, or Gladstone might have been glad to help him:

But we decided to do nothing about it, and as I have always professed never to seek promotion, I must not now regret – Yet I have been feeling not quite sure whether this

---

[133] Ibid., 342–3, 344, 353, 355.
[134] Ibid., 353, 358–9.
[135] A.3.18: 24 May 1862, 124–5; Bird, *Sketches*, 372–3.
[136] LAO, Massingberd Diaries, 8/2: 19 Nov. 1852, 124–5; 20 Oct. 1859, 192.

was right – whether I might not have let my wife inform her friends – no more was needed – and with failing health, such retirement would have been welcome. Reading over Arnold's life more than ever before impressed with his nobleness of mind – And is it so wrong to covet the means of extensive usefulness?

Especially, he wondered, when probably some one else would have it 'who will not be so acceptable to the Clergy there, and not so likely to promote what one believes to be for the good of Christ's Church and His poor – Oh to do more good to *His poor* than limited means allow! What a blessing if it came in the right way!'[137]

Massingberd's ambition was not unreasonable. His friend Sir Charles Anderson, a well-known local Tory, wrote to him, 'I wish you had been Dean as I do not think you would have enlarged the Deanery. I hear the Garniers are an amiable family and we must make the best of them, but I never think a Lady Caroline is quite in her place in such proximity to a Minster.'[138] Anderson had a low view of the cathedral administration under the old regime. In an earlier letter he compared Lincoln unfavourably with York. Writing about a young relative of his who had just married, he said:

They spent their first Sunday and rec^d their first Communion in York Minster, w^h I as half Yorkshireman rejoiced in, for as our Minster is administered I cd have no pleasure in their going there. York is now well governed. The Dean has wonderfully improved everything. The Music Grand and a large Congregation every day, w^h used not to be. I give up poor old Lincoln. I never enter it. That west front quite upsets me. I can only look at it with comfort at the Side or in the Rear and feel that that facade is ruined for my Life time by the intense folly of those 4 incapables.[139]

The successful candidate was Thomas Garnier, a supporter of the Bible Society and the CMS, whom Bird liked.[140] He had been rector of Holy Trinity, Marylebone, where he had been an active town clergyman and 'though himself professedly of the Evangelical school, he celebrated divine service daily in his church, and administered the Eucharist every Sunday'.[141] He had just been appointed Dean of Ripon, but was presented by Palmerston to Lincoln. When

---

[137] Massingberd Diaries, 8/2: 2 Mar. 1860, 201–2.
[138] Massingberd Correspondence, 4/87: letter of 4 Apr., year unspecified: it is likely to have been 1860, when it would have been a few weeks before Garnier's installation.
[139] Massingberd Correspondence, 4/85: letter of 19 May, year unspecified. There is a pencil note suggesting mid-1860s, but it must be before Massingberd was Chancellor in 1862, and it is likely to have been before Bird was Chancellor in 1859, as he was previously vicar of Gainsborough where Anderson lived. The reference to the west front is to Anderson's criticism of the 'scraping' adopted by Buckler, the Cathedral Architect.
[140] Bird, *Sketches*, 346.
[141] *Gentleman's Magazine* NS 16, 1864, 256–7.

appointed he was lame from a fall in 1855, and shortly after moving to Lincoln he had another fall, which brought on paralysis. As a Liberal in politics he sympathised with many of the causes Bird supported, but died in December 1863 at the early age of fifty four. He was followed as Dean by Francis Jeune, who was installed in March 1864; but he was almost immediately made bishop of Peterborough, and in August Subdean Jeremie was installed in his place.[142] Jeremie had been Regius Professor of Divinity at Cambridge since 1850, where his lectures were described as 'those of a sound and well-read theologian, but they were lacking in vigour and originality'. Palmerston persuaded Jeremie to retain his chair at Cambridge upon appointment as Dean, which he did for six years 'to the sacrifice of his own comfort and to the injury of both his cathedral and his university', as Edmund Venables acidly wrote.[143] Anderson described him as 'one of those clever men who preach highly finished sermons, which people admire, but who do no good – a retiring shy bookworm, agreeable and kind, but as a dean utterly useless'.[144]

Initiative in reviving the life of the cathedral was not therefore to be expected from the Deanery in the 1860s; instead it came from the Chancery. Massingberd accepted the chancellorship in December 1862 on Bird's death, with the condition that he should resign Ormsby about two years later.[145] But his diary in the first twelve months is preoccupied with his worries about whether he could manage on the Chancellor's income alone, prompted (as indicated earlier) by Richard Pretyman's comments. Soon after reading himself in, he noted in his diary that the income was much more fluctuating than he had been led to suppose: 'This year supposed to be not more than £300 – How live on that without Ormsby? Incline to fear I may have done wrong. Had I declined it, might certainly have had the Archdeaconry of Stow, with £200 a year and retained my living.'[146]

He moved into the Chancery in 23 January 1863: his wife visited it first on 14 February and was 'delighted with her new house'. But it was expensive to furnish, and by Good Friday he was not so hopeful as he had been of doing a good work. 'There seem so many obstacles,' he wrote. 'Very much harrassed during my "residence" by various *little* matters and fear it may always be so.'[147] He particularly wanted to make the cathedral useful to Lincoln as a whole. In October 1863 he wrote,

[142] A.3.18: 19 Mar 1864, 156; 26 Aug. 1864, 166–7.
[143] *DNB* XXIX, 338–9 (Jeremie).
[144] Quoted in Hill, *Victorian Lincoln*, 260.
[145] Massingberd Diary, 8/2: 3 Dec. 1862, 237–8.
[146] Ibid.: 8 Jan. 1863, 240–1.
[147] Ibid.: 16 Feb. 1863, 246–7; 5 Apr. 1863, 249.

Attempted in the summer to hold service on Sunday in the Mess Room of the Stamp End Works (Messrs Clayton & Shuttleworths) which seemed likely to answer, but for the violent opposition of poor Mr Dixon, who is now since dead, and young Fardell appointed by the Precentor. It does not seem as if there were much opening here for work. Trying to arrange to have aftern Sermons in the Nave, and proposing to have catechetical classes in the Morng, Chapel. But all hangs in hand from having so many to consult.[148]

The Bishop suggested that he put his plans for catechetical lectures off in the hope that they would get an afternoon sermon in the nave. He could not decide whether it was better to wait until Advent and turn his regular sermons then into catechetical lectures, or to try to get his colleagues' consent for the lectures immediately. He was also very anxious to have some work 'below hill', and wondered about the possibility of St Benedict's.[149]

In the end he adopted a 'softly, softly' approach. By February 1864 he was writing to his son at Eton,

I have got lots of work here. I have set up a course of Lectures on the Prayer Book in the Morning Chapel of the Minster on Saturday afternoons, which are well attended. Then I have preached this morng at the Minster and in the aftern at the Foundry. So the grass does not grow under *my* feet yet.[150]

The real battle came later over the idea of a Sunday afternoon lecture in the nave during Advent. In September he thought he had got the consent of his colleagues, but at the beginning of December things turned sour. On 3 December he wrote, 'Mortified about my proposed Lecture. Precentor spoke so strongly against it to my wife, and said the Dean was so averse to it, that on my return I proposed to have it in the Morg Chapel, which quite destroys my object and makes the whole thing nugatory.' The following week, he gave his lecture, to a full chapel, but the crowds in the nave made a noise as they walked to the choir, so he wrote to the Dean.[151] The result was a triumph, for the following week he wrote,

Yesterday, being 3d Advent, delivered my 2nd Lecture, being the first *in the Nave* – probably the first Sermon delivered there since the Restoration. Bidding Pr then Sermon, the Pr for Unity and the Grace etc. I should have liked a good hearty Hymn but could not venture on more. Dean present notwithstanding his *strong objection* to the measure and dear Wife – people very attentive, seats all full and many standing – no

[148] Ibid.: 13 Oct. 1863, 252–3.
[149] Ibid.: 16 Oct. 1863, 253–6.
[150] Massingberd Correspondence, 5/12: Massingberd to his son, 22 Feb. 1864.
[151] Massingberd Diary, 8/2: 24 Sept. 1864, 261; 3 Dec. 1864, 263; 5 Dec. 1864, 264.

confusion. I think it would do well but I much doubt whether I shall get it permanently established.[152]

His doubts, however, were groundless. A year later he noted that the sermons in the nave had been taken up by the Subdean in the summer, and continued by the Archdeacon until his own residence began at Christmas; and when he was prevented by a cold from giving his first sermon, 'the Bishop kindly took it'.[153] At the Chapter Audit Meeting in 1866 the Precentor was authorised to order 200 hymn books for the nave services, and the vergers were to be given £5 each for arranging the seats for the Sunday afternoon service. The same meeting also agreed that Holy Communion should be celebrated each Sunday at 8.30 a.m., except on the first Sunday of the month.[154] His final triumph came after his death when in 1873 the chapter resolved that as it was desirable to continue the Saturday afternoon Lent lectures in the Morning Chapel which he had given and Benson was unable to reside then, they gratefully accepted Precentor Venables' offer to act as a substitute for that year.[155] Massingberd is a bridge between the old and the new. He wanted to make the cathedral more useful, but he was appointed too late in life to be really effective. But through representing the chapter in Convocation he was known to Christopher Wordsworth, who was appointed bishop of Lincoln in 1868, and fully supported Wordsworth's vision for the cathedral and diocese. When he died in 1872 the Bishop's daughter wrote that his death took away many old memories and tender associations of bygone days, though 'a quaint little touch of conservatism long remained in the little brass candlestick (relic of days before gas was introduced into Lincoln Minster) which at his desire was left in front of his stall'.[156]

The real change of direction is symbolised by Wordsworth's appointment of E. W. Benson as Massingberd's successor in 1872. It was Wordsworth's first nomination to the chapter. The two men first met in 1868, after Benson had appointed Wordsworth's son, John, as a master at Wellington College, and soon became firm friends. When Wordsworth became bishop in 1869, he made Benson his Examining Chaplain and prebendary of Heydour-cum-Walton. Benson's described Wordsworth's enthronement to his wife:

The service was very beautiful to my mind; the boys singing very carefully and very precisely, though the pointing was too complicated to allow of its being congregational enough, and the chants were not familiar. The choir was very full. There were a good

[152] Ibid.: 12 Dec. 1864, 264–5.
[153] Ibid.: 31 Dec. 1865, 273.
[154] A/3/18: Audit 1866, 221.
[155] Ibid.: 24 Feb. 1873, 365.
[156] Benson, *Life of Benson* I, 343.

many people about in the nave, and there were perhaps 100 clergy. There did not seem to have been wide enough or definite enough notice about the day, or there would have been more. And they did not get the Mayor or the laity well represented. The Dean and Chapter seem to have very little notion of how to manage to win the laity and they are deservedly unpopular though very amiable, nice people. They somehow want working into an effective institution and I do trust the Bishop will be able to lead them. He has the most fervid and the most businesslike ideas as to getting their cooperation by consulting with them, forming committees and giving them church work to do in earnest. It is only in this way that Chapters and such bodies can regain their position and do their needful work in the world and (if it is not already too late) I hope the Bishop may induce the Chapter of Lincoln to do something.[157]

Benson was brought to Lincoln to revive theological education. He concluded his first sermon as prebendary of Heydour on 1 May 1870 by asking where the schools of the prophets were at Lincoln? As they went away, the Bishop said to him:

Now, I will tell you all that is in my heart. First, you must print that sermon, and it must be called, 'Where are the schools of the Prophets?' and *then* you must look forward to this. One day, no matter how far off, you must come here as Chancellor, and you must restore the schools of the Prophets here.[158]

In offering Benson the chancellorship, Wordsworth told him that he could not offer it to anyone who would not devote himself to the study of theology, the training of theological students, and the work of Christian education, especially in Lincoln. Although Benson had some hesitation about halving his income, he shared the Bishop's view of the work of a cathedral and thought, with Lightfoot and Westcott, that Lincoln was 'exceptionally favourable for attempts to renew the Cathedral life of England'. He told Wordsworth that he would accept no other benefice or charge, whether outside or inside the city – thus he declined to stand for the Hulsean Professorship at Cambridge in 1875. After Bird he was one of the first residentiaries to have no other preferment, but he was much

---

[157] Ibid., 1, 263. This letter concluded with an oft-quoted remark about the tendency of cathedral chapters to stand on precedent: 'It may be questioned whether the Dean would think it correct to put out the Bishop's robes if they caught fire, – unless some Dean could be proved to have done it before. They would not allow a Canon's baby to be baptised in the Cathedral though there is a font there – on that ground.' In any case Benson did not think much of Dean Jeremie: in the same letter he wrote, 'I am sure I do not know what would become of the Church of England if he resigned his Professorship; it is so good of him to enjoy it and keep out some possibly dangerous thinker like Westcott for instance. All his kindliness which is great and his wit and his knowledge can't make me forgive this deadly wrong he is doing at this time. However I remember him in the Litany and hope his heart will turn.'

[158] J. H. Overton and E. Wordsworth, *Christopher Wordsworth: Bishop of Lincoln, 1807–1885*, London 1888, 285; LDM, 12, 1896, 163.

younger. His style of life was deliberately simple – he kept no horse or carriage, unlike Richard Pretyman, who would drive off after Morning Service in a post-chaise to Doncaster Races.[159]

Wordsworth held a visitation of the cathedral in 1873, the first for more than a hundred years, and in his Charge he said that a cathedral was not to be regarded merely as a magnificent Fabric, nor as a school of Church music and a model of liturgical order for a diocese, nor as a place which offered rewards for work already done, or quiet retirement for learned leisure. The salvation of the cathedral system would be the constant residence of each residentiary and the regular and efficient performance of their proper work.[160] According to the cathedral statutes, the Chancellor was responsible for theological education and Benson suggested that the title from the *Novum Registrum* – the Cancellarii Scholae – should be used. The Bishop had two rooms in the Old Palace fitted up as lecture rooms, and also promised to provide what was necessary until the fees from the students gave an adequate income. The Dean, although (in Benson's words) 'he had no preconceived affection for theological colleges', allowed the Morning Chapel of the cathedral to be fitted up for daily prayers at 7.45 a.m. (not to exceed 15 minutes). Characteristically, Benson secured the Dean and Chapter's permission for the cathedral workmen to attend these daily prayers also. Benson secured the temporary endowment of a prebendal stall for a theological tutor with a gift of £750 from his old friend, George Cubitt, MP for West Surrey and Second Church Estates Commissioner 1874–9, and appointed the Revd J. H. Crowfoot for this task. The Bishop resigned his prebendal stall of Buckden to give the new tutor a place in the cathedral and gave £100 towards the re-endowment of the stall. In 1875 an old singing-man, Mr Brook, was persuaded to resign, creating a vacancy in the vice-chancellor-ship, and Crowfoot was appointed: he was himself later Chancellor from 1898 to 1913. A second tutor, the Revd A. J. Worlledge, was appointed in 1875. In August 1877 the Bishop purchased 'Lindum Holme' as a hostel for the students, and it was opened on 1 February 1878; at the end of 1879 the old county hospital was purchased as a new hostel and opened on 1 October 1880. Benson, by now bishop of Truro, came back to preach.[161]

Benson also developed some of Massingberd's other initiatives. Two days after his installation the Dean and Chapter agreed to have full Communion Services in the middle of the day on the first and third Sunday of every month, and on the Sundays which were great festivals. The Ante-communion was also

[159] Benson, *Life of Benson* I, 344, 348–9, 352, 365, 366, 391–3.
[160] Overton and Wordsworth, *Christopher Wordsworth*, 276–7.
[161] Ibid., 285–9; Benson, *Life of Benson* I, 372–4, 376–8; A.3.18: 17 Jan. 1874, 389–90; 7 Mar. 1874, 395–6; 2 Jan. 1875, 414; 11 Jan. 1875, 415; 6 Feb. 1875, 417.

to be omitted after the Litany on the other days when Communion was early in the morning. A year later Holy Communion was to be celebrated after the Morning Service on every day for which there was a special epistle and gospel, or collect.[162] Because of the increase in the number of canons regularly resident, the senior verger was directed in December 1872 to call at the Deanery and the house of each canon residing in Lincoln every Sunday morning to discover how many seats needed to be reserved for their families at Morning Service. In July 1873 there was a reassignment of seats in the choir to take account of the families of all the canons. By December 1876 a letter in the *Lincoln Chronicle* complained that there were not enough seats for the afternoon service in the choir, because half were reserved for the prebendaries, their families and servants. Nevertheless, the scope for liturgical change was limited. Although Benson did not agree that the choir was the *raison d'être* of the cathedral, he noted after a contretemps in 1876 that 'in general & not on this occasion only the music is very evilly done'.[163]

Benson 'found his feet' as regards work among the middle classes by his Sunday afternoon sermons in the cathedral. 'It was extraordinary,' wrote Susan Wordsworth, 'what life he contrived to infuse into a somewhat languishing institution,' and she recalled a series of sermons on the Kings of Israel and Judah when the nave was crowded with intelligent listeners. Benson continued the Lent lectures, and attracted such a large audience that they adjourned to the chapter house: in 1874 he lectured on 'St Cyprian and Christian life in the third century', and in 1875 he lectured on 'Charlemagne: pictures of Christian rule and Church life at the beginning of the ninth century'.[164] In that year he also introduced the University Extension Movement, ran a Bible class for mechanics from Clayton and Shuttleworth's, and Robey's Works, and at Susan Wordsworth's suggestion began night schools in Lincoln. On the first night, Monday 18 October 1875, he found 400 men and boys waiting for admittance to the Central School in Silver Street, instead of the maximum of sixty or so they had anticipated.[165]

The climax of this was the Mission of February 1876, in which he was the leading Missioner in the church of St Peter-at-Arches. Dean Blakesley was at first suspicious, though in the event he recognized that it had been conducted with great discretion. In a revealing letter to the Subdean he said that the mischief would not arise among the artizan class, but among 'the women of the

[162] Ibid.: 30 Dec. 1872, 356–7; 15 Sept. 1873, 374; 24 Nov. 1873, 382.

[163] Ibid.: 30 Dec. 1872, 357; 14 July 1873, 371; *Lincoln Chronicle*, 1 Dec. 1876; A.4.18: 11 Jan. 1876; 16 Dec. 1876.

[164] Benson, *Life of Benson* I, 380–1.

[165] Ibid., 369–70.

NIGHT SCHOOL

FOR WORKING CLASSES.

Central National School Rooms, Silver Street.

CLASSES

FOR

ELEMENTARY INSTRUCTION

IN

READING, WRITING, ARITHMETIC,

AND OTHER SUBJECTS,

WILL BE HELD IN

THE CENTRAL NATIONAL SCHOOL ROOMS,

SILVER STREET,

Every Monday, Wednesday, & Thursday Evening through the Winter,

Commencing Monday, Oct. 18th, 1875,

FROM 7.30 TO 9 P.M.

The Classes will be conducted by Theological Students, Members
of the Universities, and other Gentlemen.

THE REV. WILLIAM MANTLE, B.A., WILL ACT AS ORGANIZING SECRETARY.

No one under the age of 14 years can be admitted. The Fee for attendance on the Course up to Christmas
will be Eighteen Pence—Half of which sum will be returned to all *punctual* attendants upon eighteen
nights, and the whole to all who shall have *punctually* attended every night.

Cards of Admission can be obtained of the SECRETARY, at his Residence, Northgate; or at the Central
National School at any time when the Night School is open.

E. W. BENSON,

Chancellor of Lincoln.

Edward R. Cousans, Printer, St. Benedict's Square, Lincoln.

8 *Handbill advertising night school classes*

UNIVERSITY EDUCATION FOR THE PEOPLE.

A PUBLIC MEETING

WILL BE HELD AT THE

CORN EXCHANGE,

ON WEDNESDAY, OCT. 28TH,

At 8 p.m.,

With the object of explaining to the Inhabitants of Lincoln the Scheme of University Lectures, in successful operation at Nottingham and other large towns.

J. RUSTON, Esq., will take the Chair.

The following Gentlemen, with others, will address the Meeting.

The Very Rev. the Dean of Lincoln;
Rev. V. H. Stanton, M.A.,
Fellow of Trinity College, Cambridge;

Rev. T. J. Lawrence,   Mr. Day,
Fellow of Downing College, Cambridge, and one of the University Lecturers;   Of Leicester (A WORKING-MAN);

The Rev. Chancellor Benson;
Rev. Hector Nelson; Rev. W. F. Clarkson;
J. G. Williams, Esq.; Mr. Edwin Teesdale.

ALL ARE INVITED.   ADMISSION FREE.

The object of this movement is to obtain for the Inhabitants of Lincoln the advantages of University instruction at a cost so small as to be within the reach of all.

FOR FULL PARTICULARS SEE OTHER BILLS.

NAMES OF COMMITTEE.

The Right Worshipful the Mayor.	Rev. H. W. Hutton.	Mr. Richard Hall.	Mr. Joseph Ruston.
The Very Rev. the Dean.	Rev. J. Mansell.	Mr. Robert Lewis.	Mr. G. H. Shipley.
The Rev. the Precentor.	Rev. W. Mantle.	Dr. George Lowe.	Mr. T. Simpson.
The Rev. the Chancellor.	Rev. J. T. Waddy.	Mr. Duncan McInniss.	Mr. Edwin Teesdale.
Rev. W. F. Clarkson.	Mr. John Barrous.	Mr. McKerchar.	Mr. Thomas Watson.
Rev. J. H. Crowfoot.	Mr. Alderman Brogden.	Mr. J. Orton.	Mr. J. T. Tweed.
Rev. John Fowler.	Mr. Henry Cooper.	Dr. Palmer.	Mr. J. G. Williams.
Rev. J. S. Gibney.	Mr. William Foster.	Mr. John Richardson.	Mr. John Winter.
Rev. G. T. Harvey.			

H. W. HUTTON, Hon. Sec.

Charles Akrill, Printer, Steam Press Office, High-st., Lincoln.

9 *Handbill for the University Extension Movement*

better classes, who will miss the excitement of the Mission week & be ready to replace it on any opportunity with an approximation to the confessional, towards which there is a constant gentle pressure on the part of a large increasing class of the clergy'.[166] He was satisfied – and surprised – by the predominance of men – but, he wrote, 'no doubt the influence of the Chancellor on men is very great; and to it I attribute the main result, & the apparent absence of the morbid hysterical religionism which has characterized revivalism so far as I have seen anything of it.'[167] The Mission was a decisive moment in the lives of both Benson and his wife, and was the culmination of his efforts to relate the cathedral to the town, since he was offered the bishopric of Truro in December that year.[168]

Benson clearly had a gift for communication with the working classes. Duncan McInnes, Secretary of the Lincoln Cooperative Society, wrote that the qualities which endeared him to them were intangible and nothing to do with his position as a clergyman. 'When *with* us he seemed to be of us, not through designing so to be, but because he couldn't help it . . . he seemed to have the faculty of looking at things with a "workman's mind".'[169] Canon Crowfoot said that during Benson's time the Chancery became a great social power in Lincoln: he and his wife set themselves to break down the social barriers of 'above hill' and 'below hill' and bring all together, a point echoed by his successor at Wellington and a later Dean of Lincoln, E. C. Wickham, who said that he threw himself into the whole life of the community and 'especially delighted in movements which brought him into contact with the leaders of labour in the city'. Crowfoot was impressed by Benson's priorities:

All classes alike were attracted to him; but whilst he took a leading part in every social movement that was set on foot, whether it was the foundation of a temperance society, or a society of mission priests, or the Cambridge lecture scheme, or night schools, or the Lincoln Mission of 1876, or the building of a County Hospital, yet he always remembered to reserve the first place for the proper work of his own office. He gave the hardest labour and consecrated the very best of his powers to the preparation of the sermons which he preached in the choir and nave, and the lectures which he gave in the Chapter House as Chancellor of the Cathedral.[170]

E. F. Benson said that his father and mother 'blew like a spring wind through the calm autumnal Close', and remarked that his mother was advanced in starting a local musical society and in her open advocacy of George Eliot's

[166] DC Ciij.3.1: Blakesley to Subdean, 2 Mar. 1876.
[167] Ibid., Blakesley to Subdean, 10 Mar. 1876.
[168] Benson, *Life of Benson* I, 378–9; A. C. Benson, *The trefoil*, London 1923, 157–8.
[169] Benson, *Life of Benson* I, 371.
[170] LDM 12, 1896, 164.

novels, which she encouraged the canons' wives to read.[171] Wickham also commented that it was the

sense that the Church in all the fulness of her historic machinery, in polity, doctrine, ritual, was a 'going concern', which attracted the future Archbishop to his work at Lincoln. He had a strong historic sense, but it was not the antiquarian, or the picturesque, or the personal, or the philosophical aspect of Church history that had supreme interest to him. He was persuaded that the old machinery had a vital relation to the needs of the day.[172]

Benson was succeeded by Edward Leeke, who married Dora Wordsworth in 1880, and remained Chancellor until 1898 when he became Subdean, retaining office until 1925.[173] Crowfoot was Chancellor from 1898 until 1913. Both men continued the work which Wordsworth and Benson had begun. The Chancellor's night schools developed into the Church House and Institute, which was opened on 3 October 1889; and Benson himself returned to open the Lincoln Cooperative Society's Free Reading Room on 2 November 1889.[174]

Benson spent only five brief years as Chancellor, though he was undoubtedly the most distinguished member of the chapter in the modern period. However, things were changing at the Deanery too. In 1872 Jeremie died and in his place Gladstone nominated J. W. Blakesley, a friend of Tennyson and one of the Apostles at Cambridge when F. D. Maurice gave the club a new direction. He was a tutor of Trinity until 1845, and then vicar of Ware, combining this with a canonry of Canterbury from 1863 on Palmerston's nomination. He represented broad churchmanship and Whig views: he was also an active member of the Committee for the Revision of the New Testament. Benson said he was 'not of an ecclesiastical turn of mind, but very valuable to ecclesiastics by his application of a critical measure of justifiableness to all they did and proposed'. Venables more sharply remarked that 'if not an ideal dean according to the modern type, for which his tone of mind and line of thought, essentially non-ecclesiastical, entirely unfitted him, he conscientiously fulfilled the duties of this office.'[175] He presided over a period of significant change in the administration of the cathedral, and was a member of the Cathedrals Commission from 1879 to 1885.

Blakesley was particularly involved in responding to the pressure from non-resident prebendaries for a greater share in the activities of the cathedral. This was linked to Wordsworth's views of cathedral reform and the investigation and interpretation of the cathedral statutes in these years. This ball began to

---

[171] E. F. Benson, *As we were*, London 1930, 69.
[172] Benson, *Life of Benson* I, 383.
[173] Overton and Wordsworth, *Christopher Wordsworth*, 279.
[174] *LDM* 5, 1889, 172, 189.
[175] Benson, *Life of Benson* II, 54; *DNB* 5, 188 (Blakesley); Hill, *Victorian Lincoln*, 261.

roll in January 1872 when the archbishops of Canterbury and York invited the Dean and one other canon of each cathedral to attend a meeting at Lambeth to discuss cathedral statutes. Chancellor Massingberd was appointed to accompany the Dean.[176] The chapter were somewhat surprised when Bishop Wordsworth indicated that he wished to be present at and take part in the installation of the new Dean in August 1872, and their reply was one of cautious compliance. More prebendaries attended Blakesley's installation than any similar event previously.[177] Wordsworth was keen to make available the cathedral statutes: the chapter agreed to a collation of the *Novum Registrum* for the private use of the Bishop and the Dean and Chapter in November 1872, on condition that it was not made public without their consent, a restriction which they removed in December.[178] The Bishop wanted to involve the non-resident prebendaries in the cathedral, just as he had involved the clergy in a diocesan synod in September 1871, much to Massingberd's delight.[179] The issue crystallised when a successor to Massingberd had to be elected as Proctor in Convocation in 1873. The chapter took counsel's advice, and all prebendaries, archdeacons and residentiary canons were summoned to the meeting to elect the chapter's representative in February. Jacob Clements, prebendary of Corringham, was elected, though Archdeacon Kaye recorded his assent 'without prejudice to any right or privilege of the said Chapter to be represented by a Residentiary Canon founded upon the ancient usages or statutes of the said Church'.[180]

Wordsworth's Visitation of the cathedral chapter later in the year asked a series of questions concerning the role of non-residentiary canons in the chapter. In reply the Dean and Chapter stated their view that recent legislation 'recognises, or has created, *a chapter consisting only of residentiary canons*', and that the only chapter meetings to which non-residentiaries were invited were those for the election of the Bishop, Dean and Proctor in Convocation; though there was grave doubt as to whether non-residentiary canons were summoned to the election of proctor in ancient times. They also noted that, although non-residentiaries were invited to assist at largely attended communions, the priest-vicars were considered to have the right of ministering in the church in place of or in conjunction with the Dean and Chapter.[181] After a long discussion of the Bishop's schedule of injunctions and directions by the chapter during the autumn, 100 copies of the Form of Installing a Canon and

[176] A.3.18: 8 Jan. 1872, 335.
[177] Ibid., 3 Aug. 1872, 341–2; 31 Aug. 1872, 343–4.
[178] Ibid., 28 Nov. 1872, 354; 30 Dec. 1872, 357.
[179] Overton and Wordsworth, *Christopher Wordsworth*, 229–32.
[180] A.3.18: 13 Jan. 1873, 359; 18 Jan. 1873, 359–60; 4 Feb. 1873, 362–4.
[181] D C C C 1.D.2.1, ad loc.

Bishop Sanderson's statute on preaching turns were printed, with the intention of giving a copy to each canon at his installation. The Bishop also reissued the statutes and presented a copy to each member of the cathedral body.[182] After his 1876 Visitation the Bishop suggested modifications in the preaching turns, but when the chapter did this without consulting the non-residentiaries, they sent a memorial to the Bishop asking for a greater part in the chapter along the lines recently adopted at Lichfield. The Bishop consulted the chapter, and the Dean's reply showed the claim of the prebendaries to a voice in the arrangement of preaching turns 'to be unhistorical & contrary to expediency & principle'.[183]

In 1879 the non-residentiaries attempted to force the Dean to summon a meeting so that their views could be laid before the Cathedrals Commission. They claimed that under the *Novum Registrum* (1440) and the *Laudum* of Bishop Alnwick (1439) all canons had a right to be involved in the government of the cathedral church, whether residentiary or not, and that the Dean and Chapter had ignored the Bishop's ruling of 1873 that 'every Canon had a right to take part in the deliberations of the Chapter on questions of general interest and importance'. An informal meeting of non-residentiaries was held at St Margaret's vicarage, Lincoln, on 8 July which resolved to ask the Dean to summon a meeting of the whole chapter to consider the matter. The Dean replied that he did not consider he had the power to summon such a meeting, but was willing to hold an informal one. This offer was declined by the non-residentiaries and the matter was referred to the Bishop's Visitation of the cathedral, but without any change.[184] The Cathedrals Commission report in 1885 included draft supplementary statutes for the cathedral which would have enabled the bishop to summon meetings of the 'Great Chapter' from time to time, and for this reason Blakesley declined to sign it. In his own evidence to the Commission he had said that he could not see what practical benefit to the church or themselves would result from involving non-resident prebendaries in the government of the cathedral: 'possibly the idea is mainly due to the enthusiasm of mediaeval revivalists, whose imagination and eloquence have enabled them to exercise great influence over the spirit of ecclesiastical dilettantism now prevailing.'[185] The Commission's proposals were never implemented; but research on the cathedral statutes in the 1880s clarified what could and could not be regarded as medieval revivalism. Henry Bradshaw, Cambridge

---

[182] A.3.18: 1 Aug. 1873, 371–2; 17 Sept. 1873, 374; 24 Nov. 1873, 381–2; 6 Dec. 1873, 385; 13 Dec. 1873, 385–6; 7 Mar. 1874, 394; Overton and Wordsworth, *Christopher Wordsworth*, 276 give the date of issue as 1874, but *LCS* I, 214 gives the date as early 1873.

[183] A.3.18: 17 Oct. 1876, 438–9.

[184] Case of the Non-Residentiary Canons or Prebendaries of Lincoln, DC CC 1.D.2.1, ff. 1–2, 11; reprinted in *Report of the Cathedrals Commission*, HC, 1884–85, 21, 418–21; A.3.21: 21 Oct. 1879, 60; 2 Dec. 1879, 63; 5 Dec. 1879, 63–4; 27 Feb. 1880, 68.

[185] *Report of the Cathedrals Commission*, HC, 1884–5, 21, 384–5, 408–9.

University Librarian, was invited to investigate the various editions of the cathedral statutes and concluded that the *Novum Registrum* of 1440 was an unratified draft which had never officially replaced the *Liber Niger* as the authorised statutes of the cathedral, notwithstanding the fact that the Dean and Chapter and the Bishop had regarded it since 1695 as authorised. Hence, although Bradshaw agreed with Bishop Wordsworth in wanting to involve a wider group of clergy in advising him, he agreed with Blakesley that this did not have any historical precedent.[186]

More radical change came in 1885 with the appointment of Edward King as Bishop and William Butler as Dean. In a striking way they offered a different approach to the revival of cathedral life from Wordsworth and Massingberd, though Benson was perhaps in the middle. Gladstone had not originally intended such a combination of high churchmen. Although he preferred King to Liddon as bishop, he approached three men before offering the deanery to Butler.[187] King's appointment was controversial for some nationally, but not as much so locally as has sometimes been implied. Precentor Venables told Gladstone that the *congé d'élire* would find a ready acquiescence when it arrived; and he was also enthusiastic about King's idea of abandoning Riseholme and restoring the Old Palace. The Dean wrote to the Bishop-elect that he was glad that his health had permitted him to preside over the election in person.[188] In fact, the last service he attended in the cathedral was Bishop Wordsworth's funeral on 25 March, and he died a month or so later, before the new bishop was enthroned. However, Archdeacon Kaye protested against the nomination and did not attend the enthronement.[189] Although Lincoln was not a particularly high church diocese, the clergy gave strong backing to King when the Church Association took him to court for alleged ritualism.[190]

Butler was a complete contrast to Blakesley. Both men were nominated by Gladstone but, in the words of his biographer, Butler came with 'the heart and lifelong experience of a parish priest':

He found a vast Cathedral with only one Celebration of Holy Communion on a Sunday, closed and unused from five p.m. on Sunday to the following morning, and one of the very first things he did was to provide an early as well as a late Celebration every

---

[186] *LCS* I, 2–9, 217–23; II, 197–223.

[187] O. Chadwick, *Edward King: Bishop of Lincoln 1885–1910*, Lincoln 1968, 12–13, 23–4.

[188] G. W. E. Russell, *Edward King*, London 1913, 86, 98, 102: there is a puzzle here since the Chapter Act Book for 20 Mar. 1886 does not record the Dean as present (A.3.21: 20 Mar. 1886, 235), which led Professor Chadwick to say that he did not turn up: *Edward King*, 17.

[189] Benson, *Life of Benson* II, 51–2, 53–4; J. Courtney, *Recollected in tranquillity*, London 1926, 87.

[190] *LDM* 5, 1889, 19. Subdean Clements undertook to gather contributions for the Bishop's defence, ibid., 5, 1889, 44.

Sunday. He never rested till he established a Sunday evening service. His parochial instinct showed itself in the care he bestowed on the workmen employed in the Cathedral. He sought them out and brought them to Confirmation and the Holy Communion.[191]

He held Bible classes and communicants' classes for the humblest of cathedral employees in his study. He made it known to the local clergy that he would be always willing, if he possibly could, to help those who were hard-pressed on Sundays. Butler also continued the involvement of cathedral clergy with educational ventures, such as the School of Art, and other activities in the city, being prepared to co-operate with all regardless of religious or political differences.[192]

Lincoln fell far short of what Butler thought a cathedral should be, especially in the provision for worship. The decoration was meagre by comparison with Worcester, from which he had come:

There was but one altar cloth, a red one, which did duty all the year round. The altar table itself was a poor thing, furnished merely with two brass candlesticks containing candles which were never lighted. A sanctuary carpet worked by ladies of the county in 1847, could not be termed a thing of beauty, although age had toned down the brilliancy of its colours.[193]

He set about improvements, securing a new marble altar (a gift from the bishop of Nottingham) and a set of altar frontals for the different seasons. A Persian carpet (made in Ushak near Smyrna specially for the cathedral) replaced the county ladies' work, which was placed in the Lady Chapel. Gifts of vases, candlesticks, and a chalice and paten from a group of lay people were received with gratitude, together with a cross from the students of the Bishop's Hostel. Archdeacon Kaye objected to the cross.[194]

The number of services was increased. The first change was the Sunday evening nave service at 6.30 p.m. Some town clergy complained at first, though it is doubtful whether it really drew people away from the town churches as they alleged.[195] For this lighting and hymn books were needed, so in November 1885 a tender of £45 was accepted to light the five bays on each side of the nave. It was decided to use Mr Thring's *Church of England Hymn Book* in

---

[191] *Life and letters of William John Butler*, London 1897, 319: most of the material for the Lincoln chapters came from the Revd A. R. Maddison, priest-vicar of Lincoln cathedral.

[192] Ibid., 320; *LDM* 10, 1894, 71–3.

[193] *Life of Butler*, 322.

[194] A.3.21: 4 Dec. 1886, 69; 19 Feb, 1887, 273–4; 19 Mar. 1887, 276; 16 Apr. 1887, 278; 27 Oct. 1888, 325–6; 9 Mar. 1889, 333; *LDM* 4, 1888, 250; 5, 1889, 3, 19.

[195] Hill, *Victorian Lincoln*, 252–3.

December and Thring, who was a prebendary, gave the cathedral 500 books. Hymn boards were ordered for the nave services in January 1886, and in July it was agreed that the first £100 from the new Visitors' Fund would be used for the expenses of fitting up the cathedral for the nave services. In June 1886 the chapter agreed to the decoration of the chancel on all great festivals.[196] Butler introduced additional celebrations of Holy Communion on Sundays and the great festivals. He also arranged for a weekly celebration of Holy Communion on Thursday mornings, which was placed in the charge of the prebendaries and priest-vicars, whose opportunity to celebrate had been reduced significantly by the more regular presence of the residentiaries, though two priest-vicars said they did not wish to celebrate then. In November 1885 the chapter agreed to a request from the Secretary of the Lincoln branch of the Church of England Working Men's Society for an early celebration of Holy Communion in the cathedral for them once a quarter.[197] More controversially, the Dean shortened the Sunday Morning Service by transferring the Litany to the afternoon; Evensong in the choir at 4 p.m was discontinued, the only Evensong being in the nave at 6.30 p.m. Some of those who had complained about the length of the Morning Service now complained of losing Evensong in the afternoon! Butler, however, took the comparison of Lincoln cathedral on a Sunday with Clapham Junction as a compliment rather than a criticism. The policy also brought results, for when he or Bishop King preached on a Sunday evening the nave was usually full, with a good representation of working men and women.[198]

A description of the Christmas services in 1886 gives some impression of the change that had already taken place:

On Christmas eve a special Evensong was held in the Choir, with an address by Canon Hutton, followed by the first part of Handel's Messiah. The Cathedral choir was augmented by voluntary helpers; the hymn, 'O come all ye faithful,' was sung after the Messiah at the end of the service, the congregation joining. A very large number of people were present. The Cathedral bells ushered in Christmas day. Early Celebration was at 7 and 8 a.m., and after Matins. The altar and reredos were beautifully decorated, a large white cross being in the centre. Scarlet Poinsettias were mixed in the decorations of the reredos, and vases of white flowers formed a row beneath the cross. The Vicars Choral were vested in cassocks for the first time and wore surplices of one uniform pattern. The Christmas hymn, 'Hark the herald angels,' was sung in procession before Matins and at second Evensong. The Dean preached. A hymn was sung in procession before the service, and the Bishop wore cope and mitre. The 'Pastoral Symphony' was played during the service. The sermon was preached by the Bishop, the

---

[196] A.3.21: 17 Oct. 1885, 213; 7 Nov. 1885, 215; 21 Dec. 1885, 225; 11 Jan. 1886, 230; 5 June 1886, 245; 13 July 1886, 250.

[197] A.3.21: 22 Sept, 1885, 204–7; 17 Oct. 1885, 211–12; 7 Nov. 1885, 214–17; 28 Nov, 1885, 221.

[198] A.3.21: 27 Apr. 1889, 338; 8 June 1889, 340: 15 July 1889, 342; *Life of Butler*, 323–8.

text being taken from Ps. 110, 3. After the service, many of the congregation passed through into the choir to look at the lighted altar and decorations. St Stephen's Day was 1st Sunday after Christmas; there were two Celebrations. Archdeacon Kaye preached on the right method of beneficence to the poor. The Precentor preached in the Nave at 3 p.m., on the two-fold revelation of the Son of Man, to the Magi in the cradle, and to S. Stephen on the Throne of Glory. The Dean preached in the Nave at second Evensong on S. Stephen's, taking for his text 'And when He had said these things He fell asleep.'[199]

An article published in the *Diocesan Magazine* a month later, however, hoped for further change. The anonymous writer welcomed the increased frequency of Holy Communion and looked forward to the time when it would be celebrated daily in the cathedral. It was suggested that several of the little chapels in the Minster should be 'rescued from their present bareness and uselessness, and fitted up with Holy Tables and kneeling chairs'. One or two might be set aside for private prayer, and others might be used as the chapels for certain diocesan societies. The author was dismayed by the fact that the choir and most of the congregation trooped out during the voluntary after the creed at the midday Sunday service: 'it cannot . . . be reasonable that the Kyrie and Creed should be exquisitely sung, while the Sursum Corda and the Gloria in Excelsis are repeated almost in a whisper by the handful of people who happen to be communicating at that time.' The Sunday Evening Service was welcomed, but the author wanted more congregational singing with 'popular hymns and popular chants, and perhaps groups of people who can sing well dotted here and there about the congregation'. Because the screen cut off the nave congregation from the altar, he suggested the installation of a nave altar, as at St Alban's Abbey or Peterborough Cathedral, which 'would give an opportunity for (choral) celebrations of Holy Communion for the poor, who do not as a rule find their way into the choir at all'. It would make the nave more impressive and increase the reverence of visitors. Finally he appealed for 'warmth of *colour* and *tone* as well as warmth of temperature' to enliven the coldness and bareness which Lincoln, in common with so many cathedrals, displayed.[200] This may have been a 'planted' article, but it indicates what reformers like Butler wanted. In 1891 Canon Crowfoot was given permission to use Bishop Fleming's chapel for the guild of St Barnabas which he had formed, though the order of service to be used had to be approved by the chapter. Two lights were authorised for use at Holy Communion in 1892, the Archdeacon dissenting.[201]

[199] *LDM* 2, 1887, 20–1.
[200] Ibid., 38–40.
[201] A.3.21: 28 Feb. 1891, 384; 2 Mar. 1891, 388; 13 July 1891, 398; 15 Sept. 1891, 403–4; 17 Oct. 1891, 405; 11 Dec. 1891, 416–17; A.3.22: 15 Oct. 1892, 26.

269

Butler died on 14 January 1894. His influence on the cathedral was readily recognised in the tributes paid to him, but it also extended more widely. As well as a readiness to help all charitable objects, he was noted for his interest in all educational matters, his encouragement of the Volunteer Movement and his interest in the Lincolnshire Exhibition and the new buildings for the School of Science and Art which that exhibition inaugurated. Some may have thought him narrow, but he was saved from real narrowness by his strong sense of justice and his capacity for friendship even with those whose views he did not share. He enjoyed good relations with the nonconformists in Lincoln, and lectured once or twice at Newland Congregational church. A nonconformist who was asked whom he liked to hear best in the cathedral replied, 'the Dean, because he *means business*'.[202]

By the 1890s the chapter generally was far more active in Lincoln. Subdean Clements was largely responsible for the improvements in the immediate surroundings of the cathedral, to be discussed below. He was one of the keen backers of the Lincoln and Peterborough Choral Festival. It was he who first proposed to commemorate the founders and benefactors of the cathedral on St Hugh's Day in 1894; and he also carried a motion for choral communions at midday on Sunday and at the great festivals in 1896, notwithstanding the Archdeacon's dissent, thereby achieving something which Butler had wanted but did not secure.[203] Jacob Clements came to the cathedral in 1878 after fifteen years as vicar of Gainsborough and four at Grantham: he was Secretary of the Diocesan Conference from 1874 to 1890, and represented the Greater Chapter in Convocation for twenty-five years, becoming one of its most senior members. He was a keen campaigner for voluntary education in Lincoln. All this meant that he was a valuable link between the diocese as a whole and the cathedral. He died in 1898.[204]

Precentor Venables devoted time and energy to the history of the cathedral and city, and helped to popularise local history in Lincoln. He had been a founder of the Cambridge Camden Society and Secretary of the Cambridge Antiquarian Society; but he also taught in the Jesus Lane Sunday School and became a curate of Julius Hare, so it could truly be said that his churchmanship was broad! Bishop Jackson made him his Examining Chaplain in 1865, and he became Precentor in 1867. He was an active supporter of the SPG, his wife being Secretary of the Ladies' Branch in Lincoln; he was a member of the

---

[202] *LDM* 10, 1894, 21–5; *Life of Butler*, 328–9, 357; J. D. Jones, *Three score years and ten*, London 1940, 198.

[203] A.3.22: 17 Nov. 1894, 120; 15 Dec. 1894, 123–4; 13 Jan. 1896, 191; 22 Feb. 1896, 196; 18 Apr. 1896, 204; 13 July 1896, 210–11; 21 Sept. 1896, 218.

[204] *LDM* 6, 1890, 165; 14, 1898, 99–101.

Committee of the School of Science and Art and of the Public Library Committee. Venables was also a scholar who wrote for various encyclopaedias and the *Dictionary of National Biography*. He died in 1895.[205]

Chancellor Leeke served longer than either of them, for after twenty-two years as Chancellor from 1877 to 1898, he followed Clements as Subdean until his death in 1925. He was very much involved in education in the town and was vicar of St Nicholas' church from 1902 to 1919. The odd one out was Archdeacon Kaye, son of Bishop Kaye. He has been described as a 'stern evangelical' by Sir Francis Hill, and he was given to preaching long and dull sermons which led Elizabeth Wordsworth on one occasion to pass the hour by thinking of all the towns ending in 'Ham'.[206] Perhaps the simpler description of him is that he was conservative, and certainly anti-ritualist. He was rector of Riseholme, and only came to live in the Close for his three months' residence. When in 1885 the remaining members of the chapter changed the dates of residence so as to begin on the first day of the month and end on the last, and also abandoned the requirement to choose three consecutive months, the Archdeacon continued to choose January, February and March. He opposed most of Butler's changes in the cathedral services, and indeed sought a review of the Dean's rights in relation to cathedral services once his successor was in office: but nothing was done.[207] Perhaps the most remarkable feature of this particular quartet, whose combined period of service to the cathedral was 141 years, is that they illustrate the profound significance of the appointments made by Bishop Jackson and Bishop Wordsworth, since all owed their offices to one or both of them.

An example of opening up of the cathedral to the diocesan clergy in this period is the story of the library. After a long silence references to the library appear once again in the Chapter Acts from the 1850s. In 1856 £25 p.a. was set aside from the Chapter Fund for the library, including the payment of Librarian's salary; and in 1857 it was agreed to print a catalogue of the cathedral library, as a result of requests made by neighbouring clergy. The Revd G. F. Apthorp, Succentor since 1844, superintended this and in 1858 he was paid £25 for compiling the index. In 1862 the two cathedral vergers were ordered to keep the library in good order, opening the windows every morning if the weather was fine, and closing them at night, sweeping the floor and dusting the books. The sum of £20 was also allocated to the Library Fund to purchase books in 1863 and next year additional shelves had to be built. At the 1866 Audit meeting, it was decided to secure the manuscripts and rare books in the library

---

[205] Ibid., 11, 1895, 51–3.
[206] J. E. Courtney, *An Oxford portrait gallery*, London 1931, 239.
[207] A.3.21: 13 July 1885, 190–1; A.3.22: 19 May 1894, 95–6; 17 Sept. 1894, 110.

by brass rods, and the Master of the Fabric was asked to effect an insurance for a moderate amount on the library: the sum of £5000 was agreed in 1868. In 1867 it was decided to open the library every Friday from 11 a.m. to 2 p.m. to enable the clergy of the diocese to use it more frequently. By now the Librarian's salary of £20 p.a. was met separately from the Common Fund, leaving £25 p.a. for library expenses.[208]

Attention was then turned to the cathedral archives. In September 1875 the Revd J. F. Wickenden's recommendations for putting the Muniment Room in order were accepted. He was made a canon in 1876 and devoted the last years of his life to this work until compelled to give up because of ill health in September 1883, when the chapter recorded their gratitude. Bishop Wordsworth's son completed the work in 1889. In November 1890 the chapter appointed a committee to consider how the library might be made more complete and more useful to the diocese, which led to the approval of new rules for its use in January 1891. Later in the year the chapter indicated their support for the establishment of a diocesan theological lending library, and this was one reason for the proposals to enlarge the library in 1892.[209] The architect's solution proved highly controversial, but it is a sign of the changing times that a major building proposal should be even in part a response to demands from the diocese as a whole.

Finally, it is necessary to turn to the problems of the Fabric in the last third of the nineteenth century. This was a period of intense activity and it precipitated the financial problems which came to a head during Butler's tenure as Dean. In 1859 J. C. Buckler was appointed Honorary Architect of the Cathedral, apparently largely at the instigation of Richard Pretyman who treated him like a member of his family because their fathers had been good friends. In 1861 Mr Ward was appointed Surveyor of the Cathedral, following the death of Mr Betham, whose widow was given a pension of £30 p.a. to acknowledge his long and faithful service.[210] Money was allocated for the repair of the west front, the completion of work at the north-east end of the cathedral, the repair of the buttresses of the chapter house, the south-west turret, the south aisle roof, the centre arch of the west front, and the buttresses and cloister ceiling.[211] In 1865 the chapter encountered further criticism from Sir Charles Anderson, when they

---

[208] A.3.18: 15 Sept. 1856, 37; 21 Sept. 1857, 56; 20 Sept. 1858, 72; 6 May 1862, 124; confirmed 15 Sept. 1862, 135; 21 Sept. 1863, 154; Audit 1864, 177; Audit 1866, 218, 220; Audit 1867, 243; Audit 1868, 273.

[209] A.3.18: 20 Sept. 1875, 423; A.3.21: 17 Sept. 1883, 150; 27 Apr. 1889, 339; LCS I: vi, viii, 5; A.3.22: 22 Nov. 1890, 374; 19 Jan. 1891, 382; 16 May 1891, 391.

[210] Hill, *Victorian Lincoln*, 267; A.3.18: 17 Sept. 1861, 115; 25 Sept. 1861, 116.

[211] A.3.18: Audit 1859, 82; 19 Sept. 1859, 84; 17 Sept. 1860, 100; 15 Sept. 1862, 135; 21 Sept. 1863, 154; Audit 1864, 177.

gave instructions for repairing the pinnacles on the west tower. He had criticised the 'scraping' of the west front at the beginning of the decade, and he and Buckler now disagreed over what should be done with the pinnacles.[212] In March 1866 Lincoln College, Oxford, was invited to contribute towards the restoration of Bishop Fleming's chapel, though Buckler was not asked for plans until August 1867. The 1866 Audit meeting decided to glaze the windows of the passage from the cathedral to the cloisters with stained glass, and to repair and clean the cloister ceiling under the library. Enquiries were made about relighting the cathedral with gas, and the cathedral was insured against fire for £30,000.[213]

The cost of Fabric repairs was beginning to cause concern and at the 1867 and 1868 Audit meetings it was agreed to pay 5 per cent of the whole income of the Dean and Chapter to the Fabric Fund until the present deficit was paid off. Nevertheless, work continued: in January 1868 the repair of the pinnacles of the south-west tower was made a priority, but the Surveyor was to do his utmost to complete the work by the summer. The roofs of the two western towers and one buttress were reported to be unsafe and ordered to be repaired; the work was to begin on the repair of the buttresses to the chapter house and the groined roof of the cloisters. However, in order to control expenditure the canon in residence was to meet with the Surveyor every Friday after Morning Service. Arrangements were also made to link the cathedral with the water main. In 1868 Buckler was asked to prepare designs for a brass rail and book boards for the stalls in the choir which needed restoration, a decision on which had been postponed in 1866. The north and south gates of the choir were restored at the expense of Archdeacon Trollope and the Dean respectively in 1869–70.[214]

The commutation of the Chapter Estates in 1870 led to major changes in policy, mainly because £20,000 was now set aside as a capital sum for the Fabric, with interest at 3 per cent p.a. available to the chapter, i.e. £600. A schedule of Fabric expenditure at Lincoln since 1840 illustrates the problems this was bound to cause. Between 1841 and 1870 the total expenditure was £31,120.11s.9d, an average annual expenditure of £1037.7s. In roughly two years out of three the expenditure was below average, but certain years pushed it up, notably 1849 and 1851. Since 1854 expenditure had only been above average in 1866 and 1867. However, in no year had the expenditure been as low as £600.[215]

---

[212] Ibid.: Audit 1865, 197; A.4.13: letter from Anderson, n.d., and letters from Buckler, 1866.

[213] A.3.18: 26 Mar. 1866, 205; Audit 1866, 218, 220; 16 Aug. 1867, 236.

[214] Ibid.: Audit 1867, 243; 1 Jan. 1868, 252–3, Audit 1868, 273, 275; 18 Nov. 1868, 278; 27 Sept. 1869, 291; 8 Apr. 1870, 300.

[215] A.4.16: schedule of Fabric expenditure, 1841–74. It should be noted that it is impossible to reconcile the figures in this schedule for 1853–9 with those quoted by Swan to the EC in 1860.

In July 1870 J. L. Pearson was appointed as cathedral architect in place of Buckler, who had resigned. The Dean and Chapter had applied to the Ecclesiastical Commissioners in May for a capital sum for roof repairs, and as a result of this their architect, Ewan Christian, inspected the cathedral. His report, dated 28 July, indicated the scale of the problems facing the chapter. He reckoned that the choir roof was in a worse state than that of the Consistory Court, which he had actually been called in to see; and several of the chapel roofs were bad, as well as that of the cloister. But he thought that the restoration of the walls was even more pressing. A lot, possibly too much, had been done in cleaning and retouching mouldings and carvings on the more prominent external walls, but very little had been done about the clerestory walls. He specifically drew attention to the masonry of the three lower stages of the two western towers, the north clerestory of the nave and presbytery, the flying buttresses over the east aisle of the south transept, the east front, the chapter house, the north-east transept, the choir clerestory, the north transept, the north clerestory of the nave, the north aisle, and the Morning Chapel. Christian concluded that the work could not be achieved except by the aid of the general public. After discussions with the Commissioners, £1300 was sent in April 1871 for the substantial repair, restoration and improvement of the cathedral Fabric. Although it is not clear, it looks as though this was a special grant and not part of the interest on the £20,000: but it opened the way for further special appeals.[216]

In July 1871 and January 1872 the chapter investigated possible reductions in expenditure, although it was agreed to proceed with restoration of the chapels in the north-west transept. A list of repairs was agreed in January 1873, including the completion of the outer portion of the Dean's Porch, the restoration of the two east pinnacles, two pinnacles of the aisles and two pinnacles of the north-west transept, the pointing of the east gable, the renewal of the lead and repair of the timber of the choir roof, the renewal of the lead of the Norman gables, and the repair of the guttering of the library roof, the roofs of the chapter house and the west part of the nave. Pearson was to certify to the Commissioners what works could be charged on the Special Fund. It was also agreed to restore the stalls in the choir. In September the chapter applied to the Commissioners for power to withdraw a sum not exceeding £2000 to meet the restoration of the Chapter house. If the application was entertained, Pearson was to report on the interior with a view to careful restoration. Leave was given to proceed with the angle pinnacle of the east end and the pinnacles of the

---

[216] A.3.18: 15 July 1870, 303–5; 8 Feb. 1871, 318; 1 Apr. 1871, 320; EC File 29480: E. Christian's report of 28 July 1870.

north transept in January 1874. Early in 1874 the chapter also agreed that the stained glass in the cathedral should follow a fixed scheme of subjects, and received a report on monuments needing restoration.[217]

It was the west front which began the problems with the Ecclesiastical Commissioners. In October 1873 Mr Smith, the Clerk of Works, was asked to prepare plans showing the extent and nature of the cracks in the two western towers; Pearson submitted a report in December 1874 and in November 1875 the chapter, having considered a civil engineer's report, resolved that the substantial repairs of the western front be commenced without delay. Instructions were given to shore up the front and tie the west wall into its present position to prevent further movement, but the chapter were not prepared to attempt to restore the structure to its original vertical position. In April 1876 Smith reported that the shoring of the south-west tower had been delayed because of severe weather. The Dean saw Pearson about ways of getting an advance from the £20,000 in the hands of the Commissioners to enable the work to proceed without borrowing money, and an application was made.[218] Christian advised the Commissioners that there was no doubt about the need for the work; but he warned that the capital sum now set aside was totally inadequate to meet the need for repairs and said that it would be improvident to spend the sum on this work when so strong a case could be made for an appeal to the County and general public. This was to be the first of a series of repeated pleas, but he was right in surmising that 'possibly the Dean & Chapter may think it best to spend all the Capital first, and go to the Public afterwards'.[219] The Estates Committee agreed to make a grant of £1400, but their letter did not suggest an appeal to the public. In January 1877 the chapter received a report on the work done. The south-west tower was plumb and upright to a height of 90′ from the ground, apart from a bulge inward and outward on the south side at a height of 65′; above 90′ the north wall leaned 8′ to the south, and the south wall 9′.5″ to the south, this bulge having displaced work done in 1868. The north-east pinnacle of the retrochoir had been restored completely, as had the pinnacle to the north east of the great transept, and the lead coverings of the choir roof had been put in good condition throughout.[220]

[217] Ibid.: 10–11 July 1871, 322; 23 Nov. 1871, 333; 8 Jan. 1872, 334; 16 Sept. 1872, 347–8; 13 Jan. 1873, 358; 15 Sept. 1873, 373; 3 Jan. 1874, 388; 17 Jan. 1874, 389; 16 May 1874, 397–8.

[218] Ibid., 11 Oct. 1873, 378; DC Ciij. 3.1: note in Benson's hand on significance of Pearson's report of Dec. 1874; A.3.18: 6 Nov. 1875, 426; 22 Apr. 1876; 27 May 1876; 3 June 1876; 30 June 1876; EC File 29480: Dean to EC 16 June 1876.

[219] EC File 29480: letter from Christian 25 July 1876.

[220] Ibid.: Estates Committee minutes 22 June 1876, 27 July 1876; A.4.18: 9 Jan. 1877; A.3.21: 16 July 1877.

In July 1878 Christian reported on the work in progress. He agreed that the works on the west front could not have safely been postponed and were therefore a legitimate charge on the capital sum. But he repeated his view, which he had represented very strongly to the chapter, that a special appeal to the public might have been made, as other cathedrals had done successfully. But he found 'an indisposition to do anything beyond what was absolutely and pressingly necessary, and for which the Capital sum will provide'. As a result the capital, 'which if carefully husbanded would probably have provided for many years of general repair', had been reduced.[221] Christian wanted the Dean and Chapter to treat the £20,000 as a capital sum to provide a regular income for ordinary repairs and make special appeals for large capital projects, but they had been steadily spending the capital sum so that they would eventually have no resources for repairs of any kind. However, since the Commissioners were prepared to regard the capital sum as a provision for extraordinary expenditure, they were not in a strong position to argue with the chapter on the principle, and instead became involved in wrangling over where to draw the line.

The chapter's programme of repairs went ahead steadily over the next few years, and between December 1878 and September 1884 they received some £8300 from the Commissioners.[222] In the same period they were making regular remissions of rent of the order of ten per cent to the tenants of chapter estates suffering bad harvests, showing the difficult time being experienced in agriculture in Lincolnshire.[223] In April 1880 the chapter accepted the offer of two new bells from Nathaniel Clayton and Mrs Charles Seely to improve the chiming of the quarters, and in November they approved a plan from Pearson to reconstruct the bell-frame in the south-west tower. A year later they accepted Pearson's plan for lowering the ground at the west front of the cathedral.[224] But in

[221] EC File 29480: report from Christian, 24 July 1878.

[222]

28 Dec.	1878	£529 4s.8d.			
28 Feb.	1879	£500	8 Feb.	1882	£1400
28 Jan.	1880	£506 16s.4d.	3 Apr.	1883	£800
7 Aug.	1880	£600	16 Aug.	1883	£400
11 Feb.	1881	£1100	20 Feb.	1884	£700
10 Aug.	1881	£1200	9 May	1884	£114 3s.5d
			2 Sept.	1884	£506
Total:					£8356 14s.5d.

A.3.21: 41, 46, 67, 82, 90, 102, 115, 138, 147, 160, 163, 166.

[223] e.g. A.3.21: 20 Jan. 1879, 43; 14 July 1879, 52; 16 Sept. 1879, 56; 12 Jan. 1880, 66 etc.

[224] A.3.21: 3 Apr. 1880, 73; 6 Nov. 1880, 86; 2 Apr. 1881, 93; 3 Dec. 1881, 110.

[224] EC File 29480: Estates Committee minute 17 Jan. 1884; letter from Christian 9 Feb. 1884; Estates Committee minute 14 Feb. 1884.

January 1884 the Estates Committee declined to make a payment towards Pearson's plan to lower the ground and widen the road along the south side and west front as part of the new plan for Minster Yard in connection with the Pottergate improvement, on which the Dean and Chapter had been co-operating with the Corporation since 1881. Christian advised that, though the lowering of the ground would be beneficial, there was more urgent work to be done on the Fabric proper. The Commissioners compromised by agreeing to pay for any underpinning which became necessary as a result of the exposure of the wall.[225]

The explosion came the following year after the report of the Cathedrals Commission was published. In their evidence to the Commission the Dean and Chapter had suggested that it would be desirable for legislation to enable chapters 'to borrow money for extensive repairs on an exceptionally large scale, when such are required for the fabric of the church or buildings attached to it', with provision for repayment by instalments over a long period. Such powers were currently enjoyed by bishops and incumbents. They said that, despite having taken £3000 of the original capital sum by the end of 1879, their architect's report suggested that they were only at the beginning of a total programme of repairs which could cost £75,000. If prosperity returned to the country it might be possible to raise a portion of this by appeal, but in the present situation it seemed hopeless even to begin unless the cost could be spread over an extended period.[226] The Royal Commission did not make such a recommendation, but did point out the extent to which cathedrals were suffering as a result of the agricultural depression. They considered that it was not possible to squeeze the incomes of cathedral clergy any more and suggested that, if the fabrics of the cathedrals were to be permanently secured, 'the question of an increase in capitular resources from property in the hands of the Ecclesiastical Commissioners must be fairly dealt with'. Accordingly they prepared a statement of claims which they considered justified and presented it to the Commissioners.[227]

Since the Commissioners' income was also affected by the depression, it was hardly surprising that they should seek to resist additional claims from the cathedrals. In the case of Lincoln their opportunity came in July 1885 when they called a halt on allocations from the capital fund and told the chapter to appeal to the diocese and to the general public. They then counter-attacked by pointing out that the return on Fabric expenditure in the Cathedrals Commission's report indicated that, of a total of £17,110 spent in the ten years

---

[225] *Report of the Cathedrals Commission on Lincoln, 1885*, HC, 1884–5, 21, 401–2.
[226] *Final Report of the Cathedrals Commission, 1885*, HC, 1884–5, 21, 459–61.
[227] EC File 29480: EC to Dean and Chapter 23 July 1885.

1874–84, £13,194 had come from the Special Repair Fund and only £3557 from the chapter's Corporate Fund – an annual average of £355. The settlement of 1870 had given the chapter an estimated net income of £11,600, only a small proportion of which was liable to fluctuation, and it was from this that the Fabric should have been maintained. The Commissioners could not understand how the chapter could regard so small an annual average as £355 as sufficient, especially as the average for the fourteen years ending with 1852 appeared to have been £1556 and for the three years ending with 1863 £1694:

The great discrepancy thus disclosed between the amounts expended on the Fabric in recent & in earlier years leads the Commissioners to doubt whether the Chapter, in dealing with this matter, may not have somewhat misapprehended the purpose for which the £20,000 was set aside under the Order in Council and have incautiously regarded that capital sum as an ordinary repair fund, rather than as a special provision for Extraordinary Expenditure![228]

There was a brief exchange of correspondence with Robert Swan, the Chapter Clerk, and then silence until January 1886 when the Dean and Subdean agreed to report on the state of expenditure on the cathedral. In March Subdean Clements visited the Commissioners, and in May the chapter ordered a rearrangement of the accounts whereby the Choir Account was to become a Domus Account including all salaries, apart from that of the Clerk of Works, and the Fabric Account was to be confined to expenditure on repairs.[229] From this it looks as though part of the problem may have been that the Fabric Account had previously carried most of the ordinary running expenses of the cathedral. A detailed response from the chapter followed. They said that the figures in the Cathedral Commission report had not been supplied by the Chapter Clerk or anyone known to them, and had presumably been supplied by the late Dean (as a member of the Commission) under some misunderstanding. The sum assumed for the maintenance of the Fabric and Services and for extensive changes, viz. £3800 plus the interest on £20,000 capital had been kept in a separate account since commutation. The Dean and Chapter had made an average annual payment of £641.12s. to the priest-vicars to raise their incomes to £200 p.a., believing that this would fall back to them and become available for the Fabric at least as soon as the £20,000 had been spent. They would welcome the commutation of the priest-vicars' estates which would remove the subsidy and make it available for the Fabric once again. Revised figures for

[228] Ibid.: Swan to EC 24 July 1885; EC to Swan 27 July 1885; Swan to EC 28 July 1885; EC to Swan 30 July 1885.
[229] A.3.21: 11 Jan. 1886, 229; 1 May 1886, 239; EC File 29480: 27 Mar. 1886.

1870–85 were enclosed, and were being sent to the Cathedral Commissioners also. These showed that the sum spent on the Fabric out of the £3800 in the last sixteen years had not been greater than in the seven years preceding commutation, but that the amount spent on the services of the church had risen from £988.6s.3d. to £1628.7s.2d., plus the sum of £641.12s. paid to the priest-vicars. Lastly they said that the depressed condition of agriculture of late years had forbidden any appeal to the diocese or to the general public for assistance in repairing the Fabric of the cathedral.[230] The figures submitted are given in Table 3.

Table 3. *Total expenditure on the Fabric, 1870–85*

Interest and capital from Commissioners	£16,637 7s.9d.
Dean and Chapter	£14,283 11s.5d.
Other sources, Corporation, gifts, etc.	£ 2236 7s.0d.
Total	£33,157 6s.2d.
Choir	£26,053 14s.2d.
Priest-vicars	£10,265 12s.0d.
Fabric: Domus	£12,573 16s.2d.
Fabric: Repairs	£33,157 6s.2d.
Total expenditure	£82,050 9s.1d.

If the sum received from the Commissioners was deducted, this left a total expenditure of £65,413.1s.4d., which was an annual average of £4088.6s.4d. from the Dean and Chapter. An additional note from Archdeacon Kaye said that the £7800 from the Corporate Account was divided in the proportion of one-third to the Dean and one-sixth to the other four canons, based on the average of the seven years before 1869; whilst the Fabric and Choir Account of £3800 was divided in the proportion of £1750 to the choir, £600 to the priest-vicars and £1450 to the Fabric. Prior to 1869 the Fabric and Choir Accounts were separate, receiving £1650 and £900 respectively. The Commissioners noted the significance of the revised figures but asked for a breakdown of the capitular income between Fabric and Services and the personal incomes of the Dean and Chapter. They pointed out that Kaye's figures implied that their personal incomes were considerably in excess of those envisaged by reforming legislation earlier in the century, and suggested that when Yool settled the terms

[230] EC File 29480: Swan to EC 3 May 1886.

of commutation in 1869 he had envisaged that the extra money on services would have come from the £7800 rather than the £3800.[231]

Christian submitted a report on the current state of the Fabric a day or so later. He noted that a very large amount of work had been done since his report in 1870, and the ground surrounding the cathedral had been lowered in conjunction with the city:

Structurally it may now be said that on the South and West Fronts, with but little exception, the walls have been substantially repaired; the serious defects which existed in the South West Tower have been effectually made good; the central Tower has been reroofed; and only the North Western Tower remains to be dealt with ... To the North and East sides generally, and to the Chapter House, the general description given in my former report will still to a great extent apply, but the work of restoration is now in hand on the North side of the Presbytery or Angels Choir.

The work had been 'excellently well done' and although very much still remained to be accomplished, he was completely satisfied with the system of restoration. Christian then went on to discuss the problem of accounts, saying that the Subdean had told him that as nearly as was practicable he had separated what properly belonged to the Fabric from the Domus Fund. But he did not think that the system was a good one, and suggested that in future the Dean and Chapter should ascertain each year the amount available from the Fabric Fund and apply it solely to structural restoration. He estimated that between £1600 and £2000 p.a. judiciously expended would 'meet all needful and pressing requirements'. How far the ordinary Fabric Fund would provide for such expenditure he could not say. Since the works needing to be done were all substantial repairs which should not be much longer postponed, he thought it would be better to use each year such portions of the special fund as were necessary to supplement the ordinary Fabric Fund. Any other work on the external structure could be met by the gradual process he had outlined, and there was not much interior work needing to be paid for at present out of the Fabric Fund. In conclusion he added that Pearson was present at his visit and they were both agreed on what needed to be done.[232]

The chapter found it hard to believe that they had been acting for seventeen years in an erroneous manner. Nevertheless, it was clear that Yool's letter of June 1869 had assumed that the net income of the Dean and Chapter would depend on the expenditure on Fabric and Services: Yool had noted that if the

[231] Ibid.: E C to Swan 14 May 1886.
[232] Ibid.: Christian to E C 13 May 1886.

income in the previous seven years on Services had been inadequate, the income for the Dean and Chapter would be less, and this comment is underlined in the Commissioners' file copy. The Estates Committee asked to inspect the cathedral accounts. The chapter for their part decided in July to calculate the means at their disposal for the expenses of choir and Fabric, and to draw up a scheme for ordinary Fabric expenses and improvements and the choir expenses. They reduced expenditure on the choir, discharged some of the cathedral workmen, and in September suspended the half-yearly grant of £12.10s. for the purchase of books for the library and decided that it was necessary to repay to the Chapter Account at once the cost of fitting up the nave, taking £200 from the Visitors' Fund and £91.14s.10d. from their Corporate Account.[233]

It will already have become clear that the questions of the Fabric expenditure and the commutation of the priest-vicars' estates were now tied together; and the lack of progress on the latter question assumed a new significance. When the Cathedrals Commission's initial enquiries were received, Provost Hutton had told Dean Blakesley in November 1879 that they were not inclined to transfer their estates to the Dean and Chapter since the present annual value was about £1200, whereas in twenty years' time, when the leases would be falling in, it might be around £1600. Even so, in November 1880 Hutton told the Dean that if the Commission wanted to abolish corporations, the minor canons would rather hand over their property to the Dean and Chapter than to the Ecclesiastical Commission; and that they would accept dissolution if they were guaranteed an income of £300 p.a. The Commission's report did recommend the dissolution of the Corporation of Priest-Vicars at Lincoln and the transfer of its property to the Dean and Chapter, but nothing was done.[234]

The priest-vicars were also unhappy about the proposal in the report on Lincoln to give recognition to the idea of a Greater Chapter, since it would give prebendaries who had relatively little contact with the cathedral more standing than they, who were regularly involved in its life; accordingly they suggested that after five or seven years' service they should be entitled to the offer of the next prebendal stall that might become vacant. The chapter did revise their policy on patronage in 1886: the principle of rotation among the canons was retained, but it was to be preceded by discussion in the chapter which would enable a presentation to be made to a priest-vicar or a prebendary. Canonical farms were given up: in fact the Dean and Chancellor had not exercised their

[233] Ibid.: Chapter Clerk to EC 9 June 1886; Estates Committee minute 8 July 1886; A.3.21: 12 July 1886, 250–1; 20 Sept. 1886, 259
[234] VC 4.1.222–3: Blakesley to Hutton 7 Nov. 1879; Hutton to Blakesley 11 Nov. 1879; 4/1/246 Hutton to Dean 24 Nov. 1880; *Final Report of the Cathedrals Commission, 1885*, HC, 1884–5, 21, 456, 458–60, 463.

options in 1885.[235] Negotiations were also resumed on the question of commutation, but once again Hutton stuck out for more than the Ecclesiastical Commissioners were prepared to consider.[236]

The priest-vicars' intransigence highlighted the issue of whether it had been right for the chapter to make payments to them at the expense of the Fabric. (Table 2 above indicates that roughly one-eighth of the total chapter expenditure between 1870 and 1885 had gone to the priest-vicars.) A. de B. Porter, the Commissioners' Financial Secretary, reported on 25 October 1886 on the Chapter Accounts, arguing that the original division of sums in the account was arbitrary, that the deficit on the Fabric had steadily worsened and so the chapter was now responsible for liabilities which it did not create. The correspondence became more acrimonious. In February 1887 the Commissioners said that the method of accounting which had allowed a deficit to accumulate on the Fabric while leaving the Dean and Chapter's income unaffected was objectionable. The Dean and Chapter's agreement with the priest-vicars seemed to be the main cause of the problem. The latter wanted to stand out for terms in excess of the present value of the property, a value enhanced by the action of the Dean and Chapter, and the Estates Committee feared that this would deprive the chapter of the power to recoup any portion of the large sums disbursed in annual subsidies. Meanwhile, the chapter had looked to the special fund to recoup the reduced income for Fabric. The Commissioners reiterated that Yool had not intended the chapter's incomes to be fixed and had clearly indicated that increased expenditure on services would have to be borne by the Dean and Chapter. They said that the priest-vicars should have been paid from the corporate revenues rather than the Fabric, and reckoned that £8000 had been lost in this way; had the Commissioners realised this, they would not have authorised payments from the Special Fund, and they intended to make no more payments until they knew the chapter's intentions.[237]

The Dean and Chapter replied by endorsing a report from Swan, in which he noted that, although there was nothing in writing (which he regretted), the understanding with Yool had been that the payments to the chapter of £2600 and £1300 were acceptable. The basic claim was that the Dean and Chapter were entitled to payments from the £20,000 so long as they were properly certified; and their current claim was for something included in Christian's 1870

[235] *Report of the Cathedrals Commission on Lincoln, 1885*, HC, 1884–5, 21, 384–5, 415; A.3.21: 20 Sept. 1886, 259–61; 10 Oct. 1886, 263–4; cf. 21 Sept. 1885, 200.

[236] VC 4.2.57 4 Oct. 1886; 4.2.59 n.d.; 4.2.60 10 Nov. 1886; 4.2.91 Porter to Hutton 7 Oct. 1886 and Hutton's reply; 4/2/90 Porter to Hutton 12 Oct. 1886 and Hutton's reply; 4.2.89 Porter to Hutton 18 Oct. 1886.

[237] EC File 29480: Porter's report of 25 Oct. 1886; Dean to EC 10 Dec. 1886, enclosing Chapter Clerk's report of 13 Nov. 1886; EC to chapter 5 Feb. 1887.

report. The Commissioners dug their heels in and declined to pay until they were satisfied that the chapter were making adequate expenditure out of their corporate revenues on the Fabric, noting that their accounting system was unfortunate because it did not prevent them taking more than their assumed statutory incomes. This immediately produced a a dispute over whether the limits laid down in the 1840 Act (as amended in 1842) were applicable in the Lincoln case. The chapter declined to accept the Commissioners' conditions and the Commissioners submitted the matter to the Law Officers of the Crown.[238]

An Opinion of 15 August 1887 stated that the Commissioners had power to make a scheme to regulate the incomes of the Dean and Chapter, but they had not done so. They could not, however, refuse consent to disbursements from the Special Fund or make conditions. The Dean and Chapter could make payments to the priest-vicars and charge them to the Fabric and the Commissioners had no duty to enquire into the details of the same. If it appeared that there was a surplus of income to the Dean and Chapter the Commissioners could make a scheme for the transfer of the surplus, but it was not important to do so if proper expenditure on the Fabric was made. The covering letter from the solicitors pointed out that the Commissioners had no remedy as to the past; and their scheme of 1860 (which was not passed) had been deficient in proposing to make up the chapter's incomes to the maximum of £2000 and £1000, rather than the minimum of £1000 and £500. But the 1870 Order in Council had been under the 1868 Act, which did allow specifically for the setting aside of a substantial sum for repairs to the Fabric.[239]

The Commissioners climbed down slowly. First they released the £600 that had caused the fuss at the end of August. In October the Estates Committee decided to report the Opinion to the Board, who transmitted it to the Dean and Chapter. Swan tried to drive home his advantage by asking the Commissioners to confirm that the 1842 Act only applied where the incomes of a Dean and Chapter were improved, which had not happened in the case of Lincoln. But the Commissioners' solicitors declined to alter their opinion.[240] The Dean and Chapter decided to test the matter by asking to pay for the restoration of the chapter house out of the Special Fund in April 1888. Pearson had been asked to prepare plans in December 1887, and the total cost was reckoned to be at least

---

[238] Ibid.: Chapter to E C 24 Mar. 1887; E C to chapter 22 Apr. 1887; Chapter Clerk to E C 23 May 1887; E C to Chapter Clerk 26 May 1887; Chapter Clerk to Dean and Chapter 1 June 1887; Estates Committee minute 23 June 1887; Chapter Clerk to E C 12 July 1887; Estates Committee minute 14 July 1887.

[239] Ibid.: Solicitor's letter of 22 Aug. 1887, enclosing Opinion of 15 Aug. 1887.

[240] Ibid.: E C to Chapter Clerk 31 Aug. 1887; Estates Committee minute 27 Oct. 1887; E C to Chapter Clerk 31 Oct. 1887; Chapter Clerk to E C 12 Dec. 1887; Solicitor's letter 31 Jan. 1888; A.3.21: 2 Sept. 1887, 284.

£7000. When the Commissioners asked for specifications, the Chapter Clerk replied that the Commission did not need them; but when the Estates Committee asked for them again Pearson sent a copy. The Committee agreed to pay subject to Christian's agreement.[241]

The chapter decided in January 1889 that when the income from the Close houses and Reserved Rents reached £220, all the surplus would be added to the sum of £3800 reserved for the Fabric; and in February they decided that the Chapter Accounts, other than those relating to the incomes of the Dean and Chapter, should be kept under three heads, Fabric, Choir and Domus. At the end of the year they asked the Commissioners how much was left in the Special Fund, and were told that it was £8676.3s.1d.[242] In February 1890 the Dean and Chapter appealed unsuccessfully to the Commissioners for money to restore the arcade on the east side of the cloisters, but they did launch a public appeal as well. The chapter then asked Pearson to provide specifications for the repair of those parts listed by him in 1874, namely the north and west face of the small north transept, parts of the choir to the right of it, and the east face of the north transept.[243] Detailed estimates were approved in May and submitted to the Commissioners, and this time it was sanctioned. Over the next three years the Special Fund was exhausted, the last payment being made in October 1893 as a contribution to the restoration of the Wren Library.[244]

The chapter's appeal was quite successful: the first list of contributions published around March 1890 began with eight contributions of 100 guineas and six of £100 (including one from the Dean and one from Canon Pretyman, son of Chancellor Pretyman). There were eleven of £50 including the Bishop, the Chancellor, the Precentor and the Subdean. By June the total raised was nearly £2500, and by the end of the year it was £3400. In 1891 a return to the House of Lords of expenditure on the Fabric since 1873 indicated that some £37,400 had been spent and less than one-sixth of that had come from public subscription. The 1890 appeal accounted for a quarter of that one-sixth. The

[241] A.3.21: 10 Dec. 1887, 296–7; 3 Apr. 1888, 310–11; *LDM* 4, 1888, 258; EC File 29480: Chapter Clerk to EC 5 Apr. 1888; EC to chapter 8 Nov. 1888; Chapter Clerk to EC 9 Nov. 1888; Estates Committee minute 15 Nov. 1888; Pearson to EC 27 Nov. 1888; Estates Committee minute 10 Dec. 1888.

[242] A.3.21: 14 Jan. 1889, 330; 10 Feb. 1889, 331–2; EC File 29480: EC to Chapter Clerk, 16 Dec. 1889.

[243] A.3.21: 8 Feb. 1890, 356; 27 Mar. 1890, 360; EC File 29480: Chapter Clerk to EC 10 Feb. 1890; Estates Committee minute 13 Feb. 1890.

[244] A.3.21: 31 May 1890, 362–3, 14 June 1890, 365; 2 Mar. 1891, 387–8; 16 May 1891, 393–4; 17 Oct. 1891, 406–8; EC File 29480: Chapter Clerk to EC 2 June 1890; Estates Committee minute 5 June 1890; Chapter to EC 26 Oct 1891; Estates Committee minute 29 Oct. 1891; Chapter to EC 8 Aug. 1893; Estates Committee minute 26 Oct. 1893.

Visitors' Fund, which had been set up in 1883 to receive payments for visiting the choir, chapter house, cloisters and tower when the vergers were forbidden to receive gratuities, contributed £1100. Eventually the appeal raised £7500.[245]

In 1892 the chapter contemplated a further ambitious scheme. At the suggestion of Alfred Shuttleworth, who lived in Eastgate House, the city proposed to widen Eastgate and clear the houses on the north side of the cathedral. The chapter supported the scheme even though it involved the demolition of Wren's Library and the building of a new one facing east. It was agreed to borrow £3000 from Smith Ellison, Bankers, repayable over fifteen years to pay for the removal and re-erection of the library according to the scheme. However, there was a fierce outcry over the proposal and despite the justifications offered, the high cost undoubtedly made the chapter ready to consider a more modest scheme. In December 1892 it was decided to repair the existing library for £900: Mr Shuttleworth contributed £400 and the rest came from the last of the Special Fund money.[246] The restoration work was completed in September 1896, when the chapter recorded their appreciation to the Subdean for his efforts in raising money and guiding the works to a successful conclusion over the last eight years. His statement of accounts was accepted with gratitude.[247]

The battles of the 1880s are a sad end to a period of considerable reform. In the previous thirty years the financial affairs of the Dean and Chapter had been put on a sounder footing: a much more systematic policy had been followed in relation to the exploitation of estates; and considerable assistance had been given for the augmentation of chapter livings and improvements in churches and parsonages. Notwithstanding the criticisms made by the Ecclesiastical Commissioners, the methods of accounting seem to have improved. But conflict came partly because the agricultural depression exposed the weak link in the Church's whole financial policy since the 1830s, namely that it depended on more efficient exploitation of income from land. When that income ceased to rise in real terms, it was necessary to decide who was to bear the cost. Actually no one decided: it was more like playing musical chairs when the music stops. The other reason for conflict was the rising cost of Fabric repairs at a time when it ceased to be acceptable on aesthetic and architectural grounds to let buildings fall down (as happened to one of the towers of Ely Cathedral in the early eighteenth century) and became technologically possible (at a price) to keep existing buildings standing. What happened at Lincoln is one illustration of a more general problem; and it was compounded by mutual suspicion

[245] A.3.21: 362; 2 June 1883, 143; *LDM* 5, 1889, 28; 6, 1890, 111–12; 7, 1891, 183; 78, 1922, 12.
[246] A.3.22: 2 Apr. 1892, 2; 17 Dec. 1892, 32; 5 Aug, 1893, 50; *LDM* 8, 1892, 74–5; Hill, *Victorian Lincoln*, 268–70; *St James' Gazette* 22 Apr. 1892.
[247] A.3.22: 21 Sept. 1896, 217–18.

between the Ecclesiastical Commissioners and the Dean and Chapter. The Commissioners accused the Dean and Chapter of putting their own interests before that of the cathedral; the Dean and Chapter blamed the Commissioners for quibbling about handing over money which really belonged to the cathedral. Now, however, the conflict was not simply over the perquisites of the Dean and canons: it was about the future of the cathedral itself.

The twentieth century

After the pace of change in the previous thirty years or so, the period following Dean Butler's death is a much quieter one. For this reason among others an account of the cathedral in the twentieth century may begin with the appointment of Dean Wickham in 1894. Edward Wickham, who was Gladstone's son-in-law, had followed Benson as Master of Wellington College, where he was a marked contrast to his predecessor, though not the inadequate successor that some suggested.[248] He was also strikingly different from Butler at Lincoln, as his biographer wrote:

To this forceful personality succeeds the modest, retiring scholar to whom anything like partisanship in religion had been all though his life anathema; the 'Christian Man of Letters', to whom thought came naturally rather than action and feeling; almost fastidious in his dread of exaggeration, as in his dislike of popularity; above all, an ardent Gladstonian in politics, the only department in which his views could even suggest the label 'Extremist'.[249]

Bishop Hicks wrote when he died in 1910 that it was as Dean of Lincoln 'that he found his true place'. He was warmly welcomed by Bishop King, who assured him that the cathedral was 'a united and happy body', and that the 'relation between the Cathedral and the city and diocese is very friendly and pleasant'.[250]

Wickham's administrative skill soon became apparent. Archdeacon Kaye's motion to reconsider the rights of the Dean in respect of cathedral services was not taken further by the chapter; but in October 1894 certain small changes in the services suggested by the Dean were approved. It was agreed to sing a hymn at the early celebration in the choir during the offertory (the Archdeacon dissenting), and to use *Hymns Ancient and Modern*.[251] In June 1901, when anti-

[248] D. Newsome, *A History of Wellington College*, London 1959, 177–230.
[249] L. Ragg, *Memoir of Edward Charles Wickham*, London 1911, 120–1.
[250] *LDM* 26, 1910, 132; Ragg, *Memoir of Wickham*, 125.
[251] A.3.22: 17 Sept. 1894, 109–10; 20 Oct. 1894, 115–16; 17 Nov. 1894, 118–19.

ritualism was again in the air, the Dean and Chapter unanimously agreed to a resolution from the Archdeacon

that in the matter of Divine Service no Bye-laws or resolutions be regarded as obligatory otherwise than as they are in accordance with the directions of the Book of Common. Prayer or the Statutes and approved customs of the Cathedral Church or with the laws of the Church and Realm.[252]

Wickham may have found his experience of handling Kaye useful in the work he did on the Committee of Convocation concerned with Prayer Book revision after 1906: for tribute was paid to 'his unwearied patience, his uniform courtesy, his unfailing fairness of mental attitude towards those with whom he did not agree, his clearness of vision and his quiet firmness of judgment'.[253]

Wickham resolved the outstanding differences with the Ecclesiastical Commissioners over the Chapter Accounts. In October 1894 the chapter appointed a Committee, consisting of the Dean, the Subdean and the Archdeacon, to review the Acts of Parliament and Orders in Council in relation to the chapter accounts, and this report was received and entered into the minutes on 6 April 1895. The report stated that the basis of any future arrangement for new members of the chapter must be the limitation of the income of the Dean and canons of Lincoln to £2000 and £1000 respectively. It was noted that the Commissioners had not made a scheme to limit the incomes formally, and that external causes soon after 1887 reduced the incomes to something not much above that. The chapter agreed to keep the accounts of the corporate income as before; and the Dean, Precentor and Archdeacon agreed to limit their incomes in accordance with the report. The Subdean and Chancellor did not so agree, but their successors agreed to limit themselves to the statutable income in 1899.[254] Wickham also sought formal clarification from the Commissioners in 1900 on the question of liability to income tax. The other members of the chapter held that their incomes should be paid free of income tax, since they were not stipendiaries but members of a corporation which paid tax collectively. Wickham disputed this, and discovered that no other cathedral took this view. As income tax had risen sharply, the adverse effect of this view on the income available for the general purposes of the cathedral was more serious. Since a majority held that they were under no statutory restriction in taking their stipends and were supported by the Chapter Clerk (who thought the chapter was as free as it was before the Dean and Chapter Act of 1840!), Wickham wanted a final decision which would prevent public criticism if the majority

[252] A.3.23: 15 June 1901, 29; 15 July 1901, 33.
[253] Ragg, *Memoir of Wickham*, 134.
[254] A.3.22: 6 Apr. 1895, 139–45; 16 Jan. 1899, 330.

287

view was mistaken and would also ensure that any increase in the corporate revenues arising from leases on neighbouring property falling in should be secured for the purposes of Fabric, choir and library. The Estates Committee, who were well aware of the difference between what Yool had told the chapter in 1869 and what he had said to them, advised that they could not act, because there was no surplus income after provision had been made for the Fabric, and that the Dean and Chapter should therefore make provision by an Act of the Chapter: but they did declare that the incomes as limited were liable to tax. The chapter accepted this in January 1901.[255]

Finally, Wickham resolved the problem of the commutation of the priest-vicars' estates. The chapter had tried again unsuccessfully during their financial difficulties in 1892, but it was judged best to wait for the leases to fall in. This happened in 1902, and so there was now no dispute about the value. Canon Hutton still stuck out for as much as he could get from both the Commissioners and the chapter, but when Porter made it clear that if the Commissioners agreed Hutton's higher figure, any pension fund would be out of the question, the priest-vicars were quick to settle. The Dean and Chapter meanwhile agreed to organise a pension fund, and final agreement was reached in July 1904.[256]

Wickham was remembered particularly for his reading and preaching. A Lincoln friend said that 'it was a privilege to hear him read the daily lessons, so quietly, but with such understanding that it was as if one had been studying a commentary on them'; and indeed he did write his *Commentary on the Epistle to the Hebrews* during this period. He was regarded as the most beautiful preacher of his day, described by one of his Wellington colleagues as 'the only preacher whom I am never tired of listening to'. He received requests for his sermons to be printed from his bishop and the humblest members of the

---

[255] EC File 23278: Kaye to EC 2 July 1900; Wickham to EC 5 July 1900; EC to Wickham 12 July 1900; Wickham to EC 20 July 1900; Precentor, Chancellor and Subdean to EC 15 Oct. 1900; Estates Committee report, 22 Nov. 1900; EC to Dean 17 Dec. 1900; Chapter to EC 15 Jan. 1901; A.3.23: 14 Jan. 1901, 6–11.

[256] A.3.22: 19 Sept. 1892, 23; VC 4. 2. 92 Hutton to EC 26 Sept. 1892; EC File 31469: Estates Committee minute 27 Oct. 1892; EC to Dean 31 Oct. 1892; Dean to EC 28 Nov. 1892; Porter to Dean 30 Nov. 1892; Dean to Porter 6 Jan. 1893; Porter to Dean 9 Jan. 1893. The final correspondence is duplicated in the EC Files and the Vicars Choral Records: EC File 31469: Hutton to EC 5 Apr. 1902 (VC 3. 2. 4. 149); EC to Hutton 9 Apr. 1902; Burton, Scorer and White to EC 13 Nov. 1902; Porter to Hutton 9 Dec. 1902 (VC 3. 2. 4. 151); Burton Scorer and White to EC 13 Dec. 1902 (VC 3. 2. 4. 152); Porter to Burton Scorer and White 16 Dec. 1902 (VC 3. 2. 4. 153); Estates Committee minute 18 Dec. 1902; Burton Scorer and White to Porter 22 Dec. 1902; Board minute 2 Apr. 1903 (Scheme approved by Privy Council 20 May 1903); A.3.23 19 Jan. 1903, 111–13; 4 Feb. 1903 114–15; 21 Mar. 1903 122–23; 13 June 1903 133–4; 4 June 1904 177–9; 16 July 1904 188–9; VC 3. 2. 4. 156 Dean to Hutton 8 June 1904; 3. 2. 4. 160 Hutton to Dean 28 June 1904; 3. 2. 4. 161 Buss to Dean 30 June 1904.

cathedral congregation. His sermons on special occasions were particularly remembered – the 700th anniversary of St Hugh, the deaths of Queen Victoria and Edward VII, the departure of the Lincolnshire Volunteers for the Boer War and their return; and Chancellor Crowfoot preaching in the cathedral on the Sunday after his death called two sermons in the closing months of his life unforgettable – that on the death of Bishop King and one in June 1910 on the 'other world' before a performance of Elgar's *Dream of Gerontius* in the cathedral.[257]

The introduction of electricity to the cathedral was another of Wickham's achievements. When the chapter approached the municipal authority for a supply of electricity for working the new organ in 1898, they had not contemplated lighting the cathedral in the near future by electric light, but a scheme for lighting the choir by electricity was approved in March 1901. Subsequently it was extended to the rest of the cathedral, and just after Wickham's death in 1910 it was put in the chapter house. The west front was lighted by electricity in 1911. Other examples of 'new technology' entering the cathedral were the purchase of a Barlock typewriter on approval in July 1909, the installation of telephones to the property of the Dean and Chapter, and discussion over the purchase of a vacuum cleaner (after correspondence with Westminster Abbey and St Paul's Cathedral) in October 1909.[258]

Wickham was also responsible for a number of special occasions during his tenure. There is no specific reference to Queen Victoria's Diamond Jubilee in the Chapter Acts (apart from a decision in July 1897 absolutely forbidding the display of Bengal or other lights of a similar character on the roofs of the Minster or the towers): the service in June 1887 had been held at the request of the Town Clerk. On Wednesday 31 January 1900 a farewell service was held for the Lincolnshire Volunteers, who were leaving for South Africa, when the Bishop preached; but when the memorial tablet for the fallen was unveiled on 5 September 1904, the Dean took the service and preached in place of the Bishop, who was not able to be present. A committee of the whole chapter was appointed to arrange the services to celebrate the 700th anniversary of the death of St Hugh and to consider the possibility of entertaining the cathedral staff. A special service was arranged for Saturday 17 November 1900 when the preacher was the bishop of Bristol, the Rt Revd Dr G. F. Browne; and it was followed by lunch at the County Rooms, and an organ recital by Dr Bennett. On Sunday 18 November the Dean preached a memorable sermon in the morning, the Subdean

---

[257] Ragg, *Memoir of Wickham*, 145–9, 157; *LDM* 26, 1910, 133–4.
[258] A.3.22: 14 July 1898, 302; 19 Sept. 1898, 310; 17 Sept. 1900, 414; A.3.23: 16 Mar. 1901, 16; 21 Jan. 1905, 217; 12 July 1909, 61; 16 Oct. 1900, 82–3; 24 Sept. 1910, 159; 28 Jan. 1911, 185; Ragg, *Memoir of Wickham*, 155.

at the special service in the afternoon, at which people were standing for want of seats, and the Bishop in the evening. Special music was provided and the cathedral choir was enlarged by the addition of several town church choirs on Sunday afternoon: a specially composed hymn by Miss E. Wordsworth was sung. Edward VII's coronation in 1902 was marked by the illumination of the Broad Tower and the firing of signal rockets at quarter-hour intervals, with two days' holiday for the cathedral workmen.[259]

Like his predecessor, Wickham was very much involved in educational affairs in the city. His particular contributions came in three areas: as Chairman of the Management Committee of the Training College for Elementary School Teachers, which was enlarged during his chairmanship; as a governnor of Lincoln Grammar School, which was reorganised and housed in a new building, largely due to his initiative; and as Vice-Chairman of the City Education Committee set up under the 1902 Education Act, where he was influential in drawing up the syllabus of religious instruction for use in council schools, and was also Chairman of the Voluntary Schools Committee. This local experience was invaluable to him in his work for Convocation in dealing with education policy in these years, particularly McKenna's abortive Education Bill of 1908. Significantly, his firm defence of the Anglican position over voluntary schools did not alienate him from local nonconformists, though his equally firm Liberalism may have assisted him here. The Lincoln Free Church Council passed a resolution after his death thanking God 'for the saintly character and life of the late Dean'. Wickham continued Butler's tradition of holding a daily service for workmen in the cathedral at 7.30 a.m., and was loved by the workmen of the cathedral. He was also actively involved in charitable work. Bishop Hicks recalled a University sermon he had preached at Oxford in the 1860s where he had pleaded not only for the deserving poor but also for the undeserving poor because 'it was precisely their moral and social faults that chiefly needed our attention': in Lincoln 'he knew the streets and alleys where homes were worst and drink rifest, and lives were at the lowest level; and he set himself . . . to make things better'.[260]

Dean Wickham's last gift to the cathedral was a settlement of the library controversy. In 1909 he offered to build a diocesan library and reading room, adjoining the north wall of the library staircase at his own expense. It was not opened until 13 May 1914, but appropriate tribute was paid both to the late

---

[259] A.3.21: 16 Apr. 1887, 278; A.3.22: 12 July 1897, 210; 17 Sept. 1900, 415; *LDM* 16, 1900, 43–4, 171, 185–6; 20, 1904, 152–4; A.3.23: 7 Jun. 1902, 72–3.

[260] Ragg, *Memoir of Wickham*, 129–44, 150–1; *LDM*, 26, 1910, 132. Canon Maddison agreed to continue the daily workmen's service in Bishop Fleming's Chapel after Wickham's death until the end of 1910; A.3.24; 24 Sept. 1910, 157; 21 Oct. 1910. 168.

Dean for his generosity and also to Canon Matthew, who had first conceived the idea of a diocesan lending library. The chapter approved new arrangements for the library, including the appointment of a Librarian and Assistant Librarian, and new rules for borrowing. In October 1914 £450 received from the British Museum for the sale of some Italian madrigals was placed to the credit of the Library Account.[261]

Edward King died on 8 March 1910, and Wickham preached a memorable sermon on the Sunday following the funeral. In the summer he paid a last visit to Switzerland, where he died on 18 August. The funerals of both men were conducted by the archbishop of Canterbury.[262] So Lincoln received a new bishop, Edward Hicks, canon of Manchester and rector of St Philip's, Salford, and a new Dean, Thomas Fry, who had been Headmaster of Berkhamsted School since 1887, within six months of each other. A new era had begun.

Edward Hicks was a radical. He became President of the Church of England Peace League in 1910; he had been a total abstainer, and an active member of both the United Kingdom Alliance and the Church of England Temperance Society for many years; and he was a supporter of women's suffrage, who agreed to become the first President of the Church League for Women's Suffrage (though he resigned when the question of the ordination of women was raised). All these issues, and others, he raised in his Primary Charge to the diocese in 1912. These sympathies made him popular with nonconformists, particularly Methodists; he was a lifelong Liberal in politics, and supported the aspirations of Labour.[263]

Fry was also an active Liberal, though it is doubtful whether his political views were 'advanced and uncompromising', as was suggested on his appointment.[264] He was well known in educational circles, and had attracted some attention in 1904 when he published an Old Testament history for schools which adopted biblical criticism. He was Chairman of the Executive of the Church Reform League and had written an essay on 'Church reform and social reform' in the collection of essays edited by Charles Gore for the League in 1898.[265] He served on the executive committee of the Christian Social Union and had been Secretary of Section A of the Pan-Anglican Congress of 1908 which dealt with social questions. Like his new bishop, he had been a total abstainer for thirty years. Canon W. E. Boulter, the Bishop's chaplain, wrote that

---

[261] A.3.24: 6 Mar. 1909, 43; 27 Apr. 1914, 337; 26 Oct. 1914, 361; *LDM* 30, 1914, 87–8.

[262] *LDM* 26, 1910, 50–61, 131–5.

[263] J. H. Fowler, ed., *The life and letters of Edward Lee Hicks*, London 1922, 191–219, 224–5, 227.

[264] *Truth*, 5 Oct. 1910, 817.

[265] C. Gore, ed., *Essays in aid of the reform of the Church*, London 1898, 291–319.

291

The two men were by no means cast in the same mould, and it was curious to observe how the one seemed here and the other there more advanced in his views. But they thoroughly understood and trusted one another, and it was a satisfaction to the Bishop to be able to count on intelligent sympathy and unfailing support from the Dean and the Cathedral body.[266]

Fry was a more forceful personality than his predecessor, and his style was very different. The Sub-organist, E. F. R. Woolley, described him as follows:

A man of small stature with a round bald head and fine broad white beard, he held himself erect and moved slowly and with dignity ... His short sermons at the sung Eucharist were admirable dissertations on the Epistles, which he delivered in a clear, precise manner. At a special service in the nave he could preach an admirable sermon, never erring on the lengthy side, and ending with a weighty sentence as he closed his manuscript. He retained all his life the somewhat autocratic manner and attitude of a Headmaster ... He was tenacious of his position as Dean of the Cathedral, and woe be to any person who did not recognize this fact ... He was not popular with the Cathedral staff; the vergers regarded him as a severe task-master and the lay clerks were rarely acknowledged by him. Twice a day the Dean would pass them outside their vestry and they would stand up and bow to him, but he passed by, looking straight ahead.[267]

The next few years saw several other changes of personnel, and also further changes in the pattern of cathedral services. A special service was arranged by the Dean and Precentor for Coronation Day 1911, and the City agreed to pay for the illumination of the central tower. The chapter also agreed to a daily celebration of Holy Communion in Lent for the first time in January 1911, and the Vestry Clerk's salary was increased because of the increased number of celebrations of Communion in the cathedral.[268] In May 1912 Precentor Bond died, and in his place Bishop Hicks appointed John Wakeford, vicar of St Margaret's, Anfield (who had also been his first prebendal appointment in December 1910). Wakeford was a high churchman and a powerful preacher, who had caused considerable controversy in ultra-Protestant Liverpool. In October 1912, within a few months of his installation, he proposed a complete change in the Sunday services: Matins and the Litany were to be said at 10.30 a.m.; the midday Communion was brought forward to 11.30 a.m., and was to be a choral Communion every week, preceded by an introit; Evensong would be sung in the choir at 3.30 p.m.; and Evensong 'of a popular or missionary character' would be sung at 6.30 p.m. with a voluntary choir. The officiating clergy in the sanctuary were also to wear copes. There would also be a weekday

[266] Fowler, *Life of Hicks*, 244; D. O. Winterbottom, *Doctor Fry*, Berkhamsted 1977, 36–7, 42.
[267] E. F. R. Woolley, *Memoirs, 1895–1920* (MS), quoted in Winterbottom, *Doctor Fry*, 43.
[268] A.3.24: 31 Jan. 1911, 189–90; 11 Apr. 1911, 211; 13 May 1911, 221; 9 June 1911, 224.

eucharist at 11.30 a.m. on Wednesdays in Bishop Fleming's chapel. Archdeacon Kaye did not vote on this occasion.[269] He attended his last chapter meeting on 15 March 1913 and died a few days later, a month or so after completing fifty years as archdeacon of Lincoln and Fourth Canon. He was replaced as archdeacon and Fourth Canon by G. W. Jeudwine, an old Oxford friend of the Bishop's, who had previously been Secretary of the Diocesan Conference and had been made archdeacon of Stow when Bond died. Wakeford was made archdeacon of Stow in his place. Lastly, when Chancellor Crowfoot retired in 1913, the Bishop appointed Canon J. O. Johnston, the Principal of Cuddesdon and biographer of Liddon, which further strengthened the Anglo-Catholic influence in the cathedral.[270]

That is an appropriate point to review the history of the Fabric up to the outbreak of the Great War. Sir Arthur Blomfield was appointed cathedral architect in April 1898, following the death of J. L. Pearson, but died just over a year later in October 1899. He was followed by C. H. Fowler, who served until his death in December 1910.[271] When in July 1898 Subdean Clements died, the chapter recorded their appreciation of his efforts to raise money by public subscription for the restoration of the chapter house, the cloisters, the north side of the choir and transepts and the improvements on the south side of the cathedral.[272] In March 1904 the chapter passed a resolution of tribute to Mr J. J. Smith, Clerk of Works for thirty years, quoting Fowler's opinion that he was

a remarkable man in many ways & his devotion to the Cathedral real & consistent & in his special office quite exceptional. The S. W. Tower of the Minster will for many centuries be an enduring monument of his skill & care. His scheme of the original Norman font showed great research and much painstaking industry.[273]

For the most part the opening decade of the new century was a quiet one for the Fabric. One new development was the reopening of the old chapter quarry and the use of Lincoln stone in the cathedral, that was much tougher than the York stone which had been used earlier. In February 1909 Fowler attended a chapter meeting to report on the condition of the vaulting in the nave: repairs were ordered to the south side and a survey of the total cost of repair throughout the nave was ordered.[274]

[269] A.3.24: 30 Oct. 1912, 284; J. Treherne, *Dangerous precincts*, London 1987, 50–70.

[270] Fowler, *Life of Hicks*, 241–2, 245–6.

[271] A.2.22: 16 Apr. 1898, 293–5; A.3.23: 23 Dec. 1910. Blomfield had designed the plans for the extensions at Wellington in the 1880s when Wickham was Master: Newsome, *History of Wellington*, 207.

[272] A.3.22: 14 July 1898, 301–2.

[273] A.3.23: 26 Mar. 1904, 164–5.

[274] *62nd Report of Lincoln Architectural Society, 1905*, xvii; A.3.24, 1 Feb. 1909, 36.

Sir Charles Nicholson followed Fowler as consulting architect in 1911, and submitted his first report in March. His first action in recommending a new heating system, because the sulphur fumes from the coke stoves were damaging the stonework, ran into difficulties when the Ecclesiastical Commissioners declined to sanction a loan on the security of the chapter's endowments. When legal advice had been taken on whether the chapter could bind their successors by taking out a loan, the Dean and Mr A. Shuttleworth handed over loans to the Chapter Clerk, and a five-year schedule of repayments at £200 p.a. was agreed in March 1913. The old coke stoves were sold to a recruiting station in the Great Central Railway's warehouse by Brayford in September 1914.[275]

In February 1912 the Dean and Chapter asked for a report from Taylor of Loughborough on the condition of the bells, because the fittings for the peal of eight in the south-west tower were in a very bad state. The report suggested using the tenor and seventh bells as service bells, replacing them by two new ones, and having the remaining six recast. Although the estimate of £739.9s.8d. for the work led to delay in making a decision, the work did go ahead. A special service was held on the west parapet of the cathedral after Evensong on Saturday 10 May 1913 to bless the bells, and the Dean met the cost out of the Special Fund (not to be confused with the old Commissioners' Special Fund).[276]

Concern over the general state of the Fabric had clearly not abated. In April 1913 the chapter agreed to discourage the holding of the Triennial Musical Festival in the cathedral, though the words 'because of the hammering involved in erecting the platform' were subsequently crossed out. In April 1914 the Dean and Chapter asked the architect whether the repair of the north-west tower could be safely left for five years, and in June they decided to set aside £200 from the Visitors' Fund each year towards its restoration, the first sum to be taken from the 1913 receipts.[277]

At first it seems to the reader of the Chapter Act Book that the outbreak of war made hardly any impact. In November 1914 the Chapter Clerk was instructed to oppose the Corporation's Bill to introduce rail-less trams (i.e. trolley-buses) in Pottergate, Minster Yard East, Northgate, etc., and in December the Chancellor was asked to report on the old question of preaching turns. Life seemed to be carrying on very much as normal. But the problem over preaching turns concerned the nomination of substitutes if a prebendary was

[275] A.3.24: 31 Jan. 1911, 187–9; 6 Mar. 1911, 198; 22 Apr. 1911, 215–16; 9 June 1911, 224–6; 9 Sept. 1911, 243; 15 Mar. 1913, 298; 27 Apr. 1914, 336; 23 Sept. 1914, 353; EC File 29480: Fry to EC 31 Jan. 1911.

[276] A.3.24: 26 Feb. 1912, 262; 20 May 1912, 272; 18 June 1912, 277; 5 May 1913, 301; 11 July 1913, 306; *69th Report of the Lincolnshire Architectural Society, 1912*, lxiii; *70th Report, 1913*, viii; *LDM* 29, 1913, 55.

[277] A.3.24: 14 Apr. 1913, 299; 5 May 1913, 300; 27 Apr. 1914, 336; 15 June 1914, 342–3.

unable to serve his turn; and in 1915 it became clear that there were pressures on the cathedral staff. In June two of the priest-vicars were given leave to become vicar and curate of St Michael's on the understanding that their cathedral duties as priest-vicars took priority. In November the Precentor reported that the priest-vicars were being canvassed in connection with Lord Derby's recruiting scheme, and the chapter agreed to place no difficulty in the way of their serving with His Majesty's Forces. The Dean and Chapter agreed to pay any difference in the salaries of other employees, except that in the case of non-combatants the chapter would need to be assured that they had been rejected for combatant service. In June 1916 the senior verger was called up for military service and it was agreed to pay an allowance to his wife. Dean Fry tried hard to persuade the authorities to send him out to the Western Front as a chaplain, but the War Office ruled that he was too old: he was nearly 70![278]

There were other minor changes. In May 1915 the Dean gave directions, on the recommendation of the Chief Constable, that the Great Clock should not strike between 8 p.m. and 7 a.m., and in September 1916 it was agreed that the cathedral bells should not be rung on Holy Cross Day (14 September) during the war. The Bishop housed half a dozen Belgians in the Old Palace at the beginning of the war, and later handed over the Palace (except the chapel and study) for use as a Red Cross hospital, moving with his family to the house of a priest-vicar absent on military service.[279]

Further changes to the pattern of cathedral services were agreed in 1916. The Sunday morning sermon was to be preached at Matins, and the Dean and Chapter agreed that a short address should be given at the Sung Eucharist by the Dean or a residentiary canon. The nave Evensong was to follow the order for the choir, but the Dean (or in his absence the canon in residence) was given the right to select and say a selection of special prayers after the third collect. Canon Jeudwine protested that the Dean and Chapter had no right to transfer the prebendaries' sermons to Matins from Holy Communion, but the Bishop as Visitor upheld the chapter's decision. It was also agreed to hold two 'services of sacred song for soldiers' in December 1916.[280]

Some significant changes in financial policy date from this period also. The form of the Chapter Accounts had been changed and a Finance Committee appointed in 1903 – at its first meeting it agreed arrangements for making certain payments by cheque; and draft estimates were submitted for the first

---

[278] Ibid.: 18 Nov. 1914, 363; 22 Dec. 1914, 366; 22 June 1915, 379–80; 15 Dec. 1915, 393–4; 19 June 1916, 416; Winterbottom, *Doctor Fry*, 47.

[279] A.3.24: 15 May 1915, 376; 18 Sept. 1916, 422; Fowler, *Life of Hicks*, 260.

[280] A.3.24: 14 Feb. 1916, 403–4; 17 Apr. 1916, 411; 25 May 1916, 414–15; 20 Nov. 1916, 430; 22 June 1917, 446.

time in 1909. Now these changes were taken further. In March 1915 the Accounts Subcommittee (the Subdean and the Archdeacon) were asked to report on expenses in connection with the choir; and it was agreed that the cathedral accounts should be audited by professional auditors in future, and that the authority of the Dean and Chapter should be required for all expenditure. In November 1916 a new form of accounts was agreed on the recommendation of the auditors. Various investments in War Loan were approved in July 1915.[281]

In April 1918 the King and Queen made a private visit to the cathedral in the course of a visit to the city of Lincoln and its foundries. They were shown round by the Dean and the Bishop, accompanied by the residentiary canons and priest-vicars; and they paused for prayer in the Soldiers' chapel. A special peal was rung, for which the ringers were paid 5 guineas extra. Later in the year on Wednesday evening, 13 November, the cathedral was packed for a special service of thanksgiving for the Armistice. The Mayor of Lincoln read the lesson and the Dean preached the sermon; and the *Diocesan Magazine* noted the remarkable contrast between 'the private and prayerful visit of the King and Queen in the spring, and the triumphant thanksgiving of the crowded congregation in the autumn'.[282]

Inevitably the war meant a lull in work on the Fabric. A. C. Benson presented the cathedral with a pulpit from the English church at Rotterdam in memory of his father in 1915, which was erected in the nave.[283] In February 1916 it was agreed to close the quarry and to remove some of the more valuable windows for safe custody during the war: the chapter also took out aircraft insurance. A report on repairs was received from Nicholson in July: the Clerk of Works died in October, and Mr R. S. Godfrey was appointed, initially from the conclusion of the war, but that was soon altered to 1 January 1917. In January 1919 he submitted a report on the mechanisation of cathedral works, and it was decided to do all work by direct labour in future rather than by hiring tradesmen. In March a lorry was purchased, which the Corporation were soon asking whether they could hire when it was not needed by the cathedral.[284]

At the end of the war it was necessary to put the chapter's finances in order.

---

[281] A.3.23: 14 Nov. 1903, 145–7; 12 Dec. 1903, 148–9; 14 Mar. 1904, 161; A.3.24: 22 Feb. 1909, 40; 22 Mar. 1915, 371–2; 19 July 1915, 381–2; 20 Nov. 1916, 428.

[282] *LDM* 24, 1918, 88–9, 214–15; A.3.25: 15 Apr. 1918, 16; Fowler, *Life of Hicks*, 258.

[283] A.3.24: 22 Feb. 1915, 370; *72nd Report of LAS, 1915*, 3; *LDM* 31, 1915, 78–9. The Chapter Acts say Amsterdam but it was clearly from Rotterdam. When a visitor criticised it as being out of keeping in a Gothic cathedral, Bishop Hicks responded that neither was he a Gothic bishop: Fowler, *Life of Hicks*, 240–1.

[284] A.3.24: 14 Feb. 1916, 404; 17 July 1916, 419; 31 Oct. 1916, 426; 20 Dec. 1916, 431; A.3.25: 20 Jan. 1919, 37; 3 Mar. 1919, 40; 20 May 1919, 46.

In the autumn of 1918 the chapter sold property worth £43,260. In 1920 they paid off the loan to the Dean for the heating installation by selling to him Northgate House, the former choir school. (At the instigation of Precentor Wakeford, the Choir School had been moved into the Burghersh Chantry, and special efforts had been made during the war to encourage more local boys to join as day boarders. However, in the end the school closed and new regulations for the choristers were approved in April 1921.)[285] Nevertheless, a significant deficit remained. In September 1920, notices to quit were served on all the tenants of houses in the Close in order to permit the renegotiation of the rents; and the balance of the Visitors' Fund was transferred to the General Account to reduce the deficit and the bank was consulted on the advisability of realising the Fund's investments to reduce the overdraft on the General Account. In October the bank drew attention to the overdraft and asked what security could be offered for the next twelve months. After consultation with the Ecclesiastical Commissioners, the Chapter Clerk was instructed in December to offer a bond of £10,000 to the bank for the repayment of the overdraft before the end of 1921. A significant portion of the following year was taken up with the negotiation of the overdraft, which included, at the insistence of the bank's Head Office, personal guarantees of £2000 each from the members of the chapter.[286] All this happened before the Fabric crisis of 1921 broke upon the chapter, but it explains why the situation was so desperate. From 1922 the members of the chapter were forgoing between 10 per cent and 20 per cent of their income in order to bolster the Special Repairs Fund. Ironically, in view of earlier discussions about liability for income tax in the 1890s, the Chapter Clerk had to engage in extensive discussions with the Chief Inspector of Taxes in order to establish that the income forgone was not liable for income tax, and this point was not conceded by the Inland Revenue until 1926. By this time, therefore, the incomes of the Dean and Chapter were between two-thirds and three-quarters of what they had been in the 1880s. The chapter eliminated the overdraft on their General Account in 1926 following the recovery of excess income tax for 1922–5, and remained in reasonable surplus thereafter. In 1927 a subcommittee, appointed to report on the future finances of the cathedral, estimated that the normal annual surplus would be £1500. In 1928 the Chapter Clerk was given a bonus because of the satisfactory balance sheet.[287]

[285] Ibid.: 24 June 1918, 22; 23 Sept. 1918, 24; 22 Oct. 1918, 27; 24 Mar. 1920, 73; 19 Apr. 1921, 104; Treherne, *Dangerous precincts*, 71–2; *LDM* 31, 1915, 172.
[286] A.3.25: 22 Sept. 1920, 84–6; 20 Oct. 1920, 89; 22 Dec. 1920, 95; 25 May 1921, 106; 21 Sept. 1921, 114; 18 Oct. 1921, 115; 22 Dec. 1921, 115; 18 Jan. 1922, 122.
[287] Ibid.: 20 Sept. 1922, 138; 30 May 1924, 157; 14 Jan. 1926, 230; 15 Mar. 1926, 237–8; 21 Apr. 1926, 243–4; 13 Sept. 1927, 293; 17 Oct. 1927, 295–6; 9 July 1928, 326.

Bishop Hicks died in August 1919, shortly after submitting his resignation, but before it actually took effect. He was succeeded by W. S. Swayne, Dean of Manchester. The new bishop was a very different man from the old, but he got on very well with Dean Fry and the other members of the chapter. (He had been warned in the first week of his episcopate to take care that neither he nor the diocese were ruled by Minster Yard.)[288] One of the earliest problems he had to deal with was the trial of Precentor Wakeford on charges of immorality in 1920–1. Wakeford was found guilty in the Consistory Court and lost his appeal to the Judicial Committee of the Privy Council, despite the flimsiness of the evidence agaisnt him. Dean Fry, who had crossed swords with him several times before, seemed convinced of his guilt: Subdean Leeke was equally convinced of his innocence.[289] The Bishop appointed Canon E. W. Blackie, vicar of Windsor, as Precentor and Archdeacon of Stow in Wakeford's place, and later made him bishop of Grantham, which underlines the extent to which the cathedral clergy were now being used in the diocese as a whole. With the cooperation of Chancellor Johnston, Bishop Swayne also established a School for Junior Clergy – those within five years of ordination – which met for three days in the Old Palace with lectures in the chapter house.[290] Johnston died in November 1923, and was succeeded by Dr J. H. Srawley, who was one of the most distinguished scholars to belong to the chapter in this century. In May 1925 Subdean Leeke died, having been a member of the chapter, first as Chancellor and then as Subdean, for forty-eight years. His association with the diocese began when he was examining chaplain to his father-in-law, Bishop Wordsworth. He was succeeded by Archdeacon Jeudwine – one of the few men to stand up to Dean Fry when he was in overbearing mood – who also served the diocese more widely in his later years as Chairman of the Dilapidations Board. Jeudwine died in October 1933.[291]

The dominating problem for the cathedral between the wars, however, was the Fabric. At the end of October 1921 the Clerk of Works reported to the Dean that there was a crack in the facade opposite the north-west tower, which indicated that there was a serious danger that the tower and the west front would collapse. Further investigations showed that the central tower was also splitting apart. On 13 January 1922 a letter from Dean Fry appeared in *The Times* saying that £50,000 would be needed to remedy the faults. On the same day a meeting was held in the chapter house with the Lord-Lieutenant, the Earl

---

[288] W. S. Swayne, *Parson's pleasure*, Edinburgh 1934, 257–61.

[289] Ibid., 272; Winterbottom, *Doctor Fry*, 46–7; Treherne, *Dangerous precincts*, 91–140, 165–6.

[290] Swayne, *Parson's pleasure*, 272, 288–9.

[291] Ibid., 291–2; Winterbottom, *Doctor Fry*, 47; A.3.25: 170; 209; 15 June 1925, 212; A.3.26: 82; 20 Oct. 1933, 83.

of Yarborough, in the chair to receive the reports of Sir Charles Nicholson and Sir Francis Fox on the state of the Fabric. The Dean explained the state of the cathedral's finances, the nature of the structural problems and the proposed solution. The cathedral had been hard hit by rising costs: its wage bill had risen from £40 per week before the war to £100 then, resulting in a considerable overdraft. In 1914 wages and materials for the Fabric cost £2400: in 1921 they were £6700. Although economies had been made and rents had been raised, there was no way in which the estimated cost of necessary repairs could be borne. The main cause of the problem was that the mortar holding together the rubble inside the walls had decayed, resulting in internal movement and the crushing of supports lower down by the weight of the towers above. The solution was grouting, using a machine that Sir Francis Fox had first devised when constructing parts of the London Underground. The repair programme proposed in 1874 had never been completed; and although the chapter had spent £20,000 on the Fabric since 1910 without an appeal, outside help was now essential. The Bishop moved and the High Sheriff seconded a resolution to raise £50,000 within the next five years and launch a national appeal for that purpose. A committee of laymen was appointed with the Lord-Lieutenant as chairman and E. Abel-Smith, Esq., as treasurer to obtain the necessary funds, and co-operate with the chapter.[292]

In July Fry wrote to the Ecclesiastical Commisioners reporting that £15,000 had been raised or promised and £10,000 paid. But, he continued,

Lincoln City is badly hit by the breaking down of foreign trade; the landowners in Lincolnshire are very heavily taxed; and of the really wealthy farmers most are nonconformists. Other cathedrals absorb the money which might have been given us, had we alone suffered. Unfortunately Sir F. Fox thinks (and I fear rightly) that the S. W. Tower will be found faulty and that the repair 30 years ago was probably only surface repair . . . Our ancestors the Normans were jerry builders.[293]

Detailed reports from the Clerk of Works (Godfrey), the engineer (Fox) and the architect (Nicholson) were submitted to confirm that there was a serious risk that the west front might fall out and the two towers, both of them cracked, would fall apart. Nicholson suggested that an annual outlay of £10,000 p.a. for five years should see the work through. He noted that only a few hundred pounds a year had been spent for the last ten years, whereas thousands had been spent at Westminster and York. 'It would be a disgrace', he concluded, 'to the present generation to allow such a fabric to become ruinous or to deteriorate

---

[292] Winterbottom, *Doctor Fry*, 49–50; *The Times*, 13 Jan. 1922, 14 Jan. 1922; *LDM* 38, 1922, 11–13; Swayne, *Parson's pleasure*, 296.
[293] EC File 29480: Fry to EC 4 July 1922.

for lack of preservative measures which would not cost a hundredth part of the capital outlay which our forefathers expended on its construction.'[294]

The Commissioners offered five annual instalments of £500 for each £10,000 spent. It was noted in the file that the Dean and Chapter now only received the statutory incomes, and that the gross receipts of the Commissioners from their estates in Lincolnshire were around £33,000. The Dean had pointed out that the members of the chapter were making personal surrenders themselves and referred to the expenditure from their own resources since 1910. His acknowledgement of the Commissioners' offer came on a postcard from New York, where he was on his first money-raising expedition.[295] Fry spent four months in America from October 1922 and raised £5000. In 1924 he made another lecture tour to the USA, raising a further £3000 in three months. It was on this visit that he stayed with Mr A. F. Bemis of Boston, who had visited Lincoln as a child with his mother. He gave £5000 for the restoration of the north and south transepts as a memorial to her, and subsequently gave £2450 to complete the work and £10,000 in 1927 to finish the central tower.[296]

In July 1924 the Appeal Committee asked all parishes to see whether they could make further special efforts in 1924, 1925 and 1926, as it was clear that more work needed to be done than originally envisaged. The response from the parishes, particularly in the country areas, was good, and the Bishop noted in 1925 that in many the giving had averaged 10*s*. per household. Nevertheless, by 1926 the total raised, exclusive of American money, was still only £41,000; and the additional repairs were reckoned at £20,000 to £25,000.[297] It was decided to appeal for an additional £20,000, and the Ecclesiastical Commissioners agreed to make a grant of £1000. They made a further grant of £1500 in 1928 in response to a further appeal for £35,000. But the overall position became increasingly desperate, not helped by the discovery of wood-beetle in the choir stalls in January 1929, and later that year the chapter agreed to take up an offer from the Commissioners of a loan of £25,000 in order to complete the work, which was later reduced to £15,000. This loan was repaid out of a grant of £20,000 made to the cathedral by the Pilgrim Trust in 1931.[298] Dean Fry, who was 80 in 1926, raised nearly £100,000 in the last nine years of his life, £33,700

---

[294] Ibid.: report from Nicholson, 1922.
[295] Ibid.: Estates Committee minute 19 Oct. 1922; Fry to EC 25 Nov. 1922.
[296] Winterbottom, *Doctor Fry*, 50–2; *LDM* 40, 1924, 148.
[297] *LDM* 40, 1924, 137; 41, 1925, 68, 103; 42, 1926, 56.
[298] EC File 29480: Jeudwine to EC 31 Mar. 1926; Estates Committee minute 15 Apr. 1926; Jeudwine to EC 14 June 1928; Estates Committee minute 21 June 1928; Chapter Clerk to EC 31 Jan. 1930; Estates Committee minute 27 Feb. 1930; Chapter Clerk to EC 25 Nov. 1930; Estates Committee minute 4 Dec. 1930; Chapter Clerk to EC 7 Apr. 1931; A.3.25: 22 Jan. 1929, 346; 20 Mar. 1929, 352; 31 Jan. 1930, 378; 31 Oct. 1930, 408–9.

of which came from America. The death of his wife in 1928 was a blow to him, but he nevertheless planned a third transatlantic voyage, this time to raise money in South America where his son was a British Consul. Although he reached Chile late in 1929, he suffered a stroke while staying with his son. He returned to Lincoln and died in February 1930.[299]

The story of the repairs of the 1920s is a fascinating one in itself, and may be found in the four reports written by the Clerk of Works, Mr R. S. Godfrey, for the Lincolnshire Architectural Society. The two west towers were completely repaired, being stitched together by concrete grouting, using a new technique that had not been available at earlier periods. The west front was secured, and the roofs and buttresses reinforced along the nave and transepts. One of the most dramatic descriptions is of the way in which the ringing of the bells in the south-west tower had caused it to shake to the point where, if it had continued, the tower would almost certainly have fallen. Before the repairs a bucket of water hung in the tower was almost emptied by vibration: after the repairs it was hardly disturbed. In another account Mr Godfrey explained how earlier repairs, more or less from the beginning, had actually made things worse. Although the early Norman arches in the western towers, displaced by the earthquake of 1185, had been supported by Early English relieving arches, the new work was not bonded into the old, so the towers continued to settle: even Essex's new arches of 1726 did not arrest the movement. The central tower never really recovered from the collapse of the spire in 1547 because the iron cramps which were inserted corroded and burst the stonework which was intended to support it. Much of the repair of the 1870s and 1880s was only refacing, and therefore did not make good the core of the walls. The detailed knowledge of earlier building techniques which was revealed was considerable. It was fitting that Godfrey should be honoured for his work by being made a CBE, and that the completion of the repairs in November 1932 should have been marked by a service of thanksgiving in the presence of the Duke and Duchess of York. Earlier on the same day a marble slab, inlaid with a bronze cross, was dedicated to the memory of Dean Fry. 'In truth,' wrote Bishop Swayne, 'the restored minster is his memorial.'[300]

Unfortunately this was not the end of the story. In 1934 the chapter decided to establish a new Special Repairs Fund in the hands of the Dean, Subdean and Precentor with three other lay trustees nominated by the Lord-Lieutenant. A

---

[299] Winterbottom, Doctor Fry, 53–4.
[300] *83rd Report of LAS*, 1926, 8–11; *85th Report of LAS*, 1928, 11–16; *86th Report of LAS*, 1929, 91–4; *88th Report of LAS*, 1931, 75–9; J. H. Srawley, *The story of Lincoln Minster*, London 1947, 74–8; Swayne, *Parson's pleasure*, 298; R. S. Godfrey, *Half-an-hour at Lincoln cathedral* [Lincoln 1931], 17–19.

301

report from Nicholson at the end of the year suggested that further urgent repairs were needed and in July 1935 work began on the east end, which was being affected by increasing vibration from traffic. In October 1935 the chapter agreed on the form of a letter to *The Times* under the signature of the Lord-Lieutenant, the Bishop and the Dean to seek contributions towards the repair of the east end and Angel Choir. By January 1936 the appeal had yielded nearly £1300, and at a meeting of the General Chapter in that month the Dean read extracts from the report of Sir Charles Peers which suggested that the cost would be £30,000. He also said that he had been converted to the idea of a Society of Friends of the Cathedral, and it was agreed to form one with the archdeacon of Lincoln as secretary. In December 1936 the chapter appealed to the Commissioners and £500 was granted. The notes in the file compare the sum with those given to other cathedrals in this period: six others were listed; the largest sums were £2000 to York in 1927 towards an appeal of £50,000, where £22,000 came from the diocese, and £1500 to Peterborough in 1927–8 towards an appeal of £30,000.[301]

At the General Chapter meeting in December 1937 the Dean reported that the funds for special repair work were nearly exhausted, but it was still necessary to complete the east window as soon as possible. The Subdean said that nearly £17,000 had been spent, of which the Dean and Chapter had contributed £2000. The Archdeacon of Lincoln stated that there were now 1040 Friends of Lincoln Cathedral, who had contributed £400. By May 1938 Nicholson was able to report that the greater part of the repair of the Angel Choir had been completed and the movement of the east wall arrested. Whilst warning that the only parts of the church that had not been dealt with were St Hugh's Choir and the eastern transepts, he held out the hope that it would be possible to return to a programme of regular and gradual repair work, instead of the extraordinary efforts of the last eighteen years. In fact it was necessary to carry out further repair work at the east end in July 1939, which put the Special Repair Fund into the red. The Fund was closed on 31 December 1939 and the overdraft was reduced as circumstances permitted: a transfer of £1000 from the Fabric Fund in January 1940 left a deficit of under £500.[302]

The Fabric crisis had highlighted the financial problems of cathedrals generally, and once again this was a spur to discussion of cathedral constitutions. The Report of a Commission of the Church Assembly on the Property and

---

[301] A 3 26: 26 Sept. 1934, 119–20; 13 Dec. 1934, 134; 31 July 1935, 158; 5 Oct. 1935, 167–8; 15 Jan. 1936, 180–2; 18 May 1936, 197; EC File 29480: Dean to EC 1 Dec. 1936; Estates Committee minute 10 Dec. 1936 and note alongside; *LDM* 52, 1936, 6–8.

[302] 2 A.3.26: 16 Dec. 1937, 266–9; 18 May 1938, 284–6; 24 July 1939, 340; 23 Oct. 1939, 352; 8 Jan. 1940, 361.

Revenues of the Church in 1924 contained considerable evidence on the financial position of cathedrals in general. Although there were difficulties in producing comparable statistics for the various cathedrals, certain common features emerged. Most cathedral chapters received an annual income from the Ecclesiastical Commissioners, as Lincoln did: those cathedrals which had opted to be re-endowed with estates calculated to provide the equivalent of the annuities had generally suffered from the fall in income from agricultural land since re-endowment. All cathedrals had suffered from the heavy increase in the cost of maintaining their regular Services and Fabric. In the latter case those difficulties had been intensified by the insufficiency of the original provision and increased building costs, and Lincoln was specifically cited as an example. The Commission believed that the emergency appeals recently made could have been avoided if a reasonably adequate annual income for this purpose had existed previously. They therefore recommended that the estates of all cathedrals should be permanently transferred to the Ecclesiastical Commission in return for stable annual incomes, and suggested the appointment of a Cathedrals Commission to examine the circumstances of each cathedral. Dean Fry, in his evidence to the Commission (in January 1922), stated that all the canons were engaged in diocesan or other work when not in residence, and that the minor canons also had other work. Since the work of a minor canon was not sufficient to occupy a man's whole time, he suggested that two minor canonries could be suppressed without loss to the cathedral. If the money required for the Fabric could be found, the ordinary income of the cathedral was sufficient to meet expenses. Nevertheless the income and expenditure statistics showed that only seven cathedrals in the country spent more on the Dean and Chapter than Lincoln, and four of those had five or six canons rather than four.[303]

A Cathedrals Commission was duly set up and it reported in 1927. Its conclusions about the appropriate constitution of cathedral chapters were similar to those of the Commission of 1879–85. They wanted to see a chapter consisting of all the canons, residentiary and non-residentiary, and suggested that there should normally be four residentiary canons, who should not have other parochial or diocesan responsibilities and should normally retire at 70. (The retirement age was eventually fixed at 75.) In order to carry out their recommendations, they proposed a permanent body of Cathedral Commissioners who would prepare new statutes in consultation with the various cathedral bodies and also administer revenues. In the Church Assembly debate on the Report in November 1927 Canon Blackie, Precentor and archdeacon of Stow, perhaps not surprisingly, disagreed with the recommendation that residentiary

---

[303] *Report of the Commission of Enquiry into the Property and Revenues of the Church*, London 1924, 32, 43, 226.

canons should not hold diocesan offices; and in the debate on the proposed Measure in July 1928 he seconded the motion for adjournment, suggesting that a formal Measure was unnecessary.[304] The Greater Chapter considered the proposed Measure in September 1928, and many of the issues that had come up in similar discussions previously emerged once more. Canon Woolley opposed the Measure as a whole and favoured reform from within. He hoped for increased participation by prebendaries in cathedral affairs, echoing the memorandum he had submitted to the Subcommission on Lincoln in 1926, which argued that the residentiaries had unwarrantably assumed control of the cathedral after 1840. Canon Boulter had supported him then and had spoken in a similar vein in the Church Assembly debate of November 1927; but Chancellor Srawley had criticised his conclusions. Canon Scott opposed the proposal to abolish the minor corporations; and the Chancellor, Subdean and seven others spoke against the Measure. Nevertheless, a motion to oppose the Measure as a whole was lost, and instead a motion to oppose a permanent Commission and to require the consent of the cathedral governing body to any scheme proposed by the Commission was carried unanimously.[305]

In the event it was agreed that the new Commission would be established for a maximum period of twelve years. Canon Blackie, by now bishop of Grantham, secured an amendment to enable the cathedral quarry to be regarded as part of the Precincts.[306] Like other cathedrals, Lincoln had to consider new arrangements for the minor canons, and a set of new statutes as such. In the Church Assembly both Bishop Blackie and the bishop of Lincoln himself had advised caution in the way corporations of minor canons were treated.[307] Nevertheless, section 13 of the Cathedrals Measure of 1931 expressly instructed the Commission to frame schemes for the compulsory transfer of the property of minor corporations to the cathedral chapter or the Ecclesiastical Commisioners. There was much correspondence again with minor canons in other cathedrals, since once more dissolution was in the air. In 1932 a scheme was prepared to transfer some property to the Commissioners and other property to the Dean and Chapter (including nos. 1–4 Vicars' Court), which was approved by the Estates

---

[304] Church Assembly Proceedings 8 (3), Autumn 1927, 347–57, 380–2; 9 (2), Summer 1928, 148–51.

[305] A.3.25: 26 Sept. 1928, 330–2; Memoranda by Canons Woolley, Boulter, and Comments by Dean Fry and Chancellor Srawley, DC CC.1.A.8; *Church Assembly Proceedings* 8 (3) 1927, 388.

[306] *Church Assembly Proceedings* 12 (1), Spring 1931, 29; final approval was given by the Assembly on 6 Feb. 1931 and it was approved by Parliament as Measure no. 7, 21 & 22 Geo. 5, 1931. The Measure was amended by a further Measure in 1934 (Measure no. 3, 24 & 25 Geo. 5, 1934).

[307] Ibid. 11 (1), Spring 1930, 56–7.

Committee of the Ecclesiastical Commission on 27 July 1933. In December 1933 the Dean and Chapter agreed to take over responsibility for maintaining the houses in Vicars' Court. The priest-vicars were allowed to live in them rent free, but subject to payment of their own rates and taxes, so long as they performed the duties of their office.[308]

With the transfer of the property the question of the dissolution of the corporation of priest-vicars became a technical one. Canon Scott's memorandum for the Cathedral Commission of 1931 had concentrated on getting the right kind of people for minor canonries. He suggested that there needed to be reasonable security of tenure, for example, for ten years in the first instance with renewals for periods of five years, and provision for preferment or pension at the close. He was concerned that there would be a tendency to experiment by appointing junior men for a few years only, which he thought would be a mistake, as experience was necessary for the singing of the services and other duties. He also felt it important that minor canons whose time was not entirely taken up with the cathedral should be free to undertake pastoral work outside; hence responsibility for the performance of cathedral duties should rest with the minor canons corporately. (There is an interesting contrast with the views of William Hett here.) Finally, he preferred to reconstitute the corporations rather than dissolve them, suggesting that those who wished to dissolve should prove that 'their continued existence is not merely an anomaly but a definite inconvenience'.[309] However, the corporation was dissolved, although they retained their distinct identity as a body. Their offices ceased to be held as freeholds, and instead they were paid stipends by the Dean and Chapter and, after considerable discussion, pensions.[310]

The more substantial question concerned new cathedral statutes. Here Canon Srawley was the key figure, for he spent considerable time on drafting in consultation with the Commission. Some of the criticisms made by the non-residentiaries had already been met before this work began. In June 1929 the Dean had reported that the Bishop was ready to appoint residentiaries to prebendal stalls, as vacancies arose: it had been held that for the residentiaries not to hold prebendal stalls was inconsistent with the original intention of the cathedral statutes. In January 1931 the General Chapter asked for a revision of the rota of preaching turns fixed by Bishop Wordsworth, so as to give more

---

[308] VC 1.3 *passim*; 26 Cathedral Commissioners to vicars choral 15 Feb. 1932; A.3.26: 3 Feb. 1933, 55–6; 28 Feb. 1933, 58; 3 Apr. 1933, 62; 10 May 1933, 65–6; EC File 31469: Estates Committee minute 27 July 1933.

[309] VC 1.3.1, undated.

[310] Statement of Priest-Vicars, 28 Feb. 1934, VC 4.6.2; A.3.26: 12 Dec. 1933, 92; 6 Jan. 1937, 220; 12 Jan. 1937, 223; 20 Apr. 1938, 283; 16 June 1938, 291; Memorandum of Dean and Chapter to Cathedrals Commission on Priest-Vicars, Feb. 1932, DC CC/1/A/9.

305

regular opportunities to all prebendaries, particularly for residentiaries other than the Chancellor. The Dean and Chapter petitioned the Bishop formally for a new statute, which was agreed in May 1931.[311]

In January 1932 the General Chapter considered a draft memorandum from Chancellor Srawley on the new statutes. They agreed to oppose the Commission's recommendation to reduce the number of prebendaries, and to support a recommendation that a suffragan bishop who was not a residentiary should rank as a dignitary and have a stall in the cathedral. After further discussion in the General Chapter in May and July 1933, the draft statutes were approved in April 1934. They were subsequently approved by Convocation and the Church Assembly, finally approved by the Dean and Chapter in March 1936, and promulgated by the King in an Order of Council dated 18 December 1936.[312] Canon Srawley wrote that the new statutes represented 'a new and better spirit than had been shown in the earlier Cathedral Commissions'. They were based on the existing customs of the Church, as modified by the lapse of time and the changes of the Reformation. Although the corporation of the priest-vicars ceased to have a separate freehold tenure and its revenues were absorbed in those of the chapter, their identity was maintained and the senior vicar retained the title of Provost. The prebendaries were made a constituent part of the Corporation of the Dean and Chapter, and were required to meet at least once a year to 'promote brotherly union among its members' and to be informed about the work and well-being of the cathedral; the Bishop, acting through the Dean, could also summon them at any time to take counsel with him on any matter. The Bishop's relation to the cathedral was made closer, and his right to celebrate Holy Communion on any Sunday or holy day after due notice was secured. The Bishop and Dean were also given permission to hold prebends and thus, in Canon Srawley's words, to 'become in the fullest sense members of the "brotherhood", in the old phrase *confratres et concanonici*'.[313] The Dean and residentiaries were forbidden to hold any benefice with the cure of souls – something aimed at, but never statutorily secured, in the nineteenth century.

Inevitably the problems of the Fabric and the new statutes dominated the early 1930s. But the life of the cathedral continued. A new source of income which appeared in this period was the BBC. In May 1934 it was decided that all fees from relays of cathedral services would go to the Dean and Chapter direct.[314] In the same year the chapter considered whether to continue the

---

[311] A/3/25: 10 June 1929, 361; 27 Mar. 1931, 428; 1 May 1931, 432–40.
[312] A/3/26: 26 Jan. 1932, 10–12; 23 May 1933, 72–4; 12 July 1933, 121–3; 4 Apr. 1934, 102; 19 Mar. 1936, 190.
[313] Srawley, *Cathedral foundations*, 18–19.
[314] A.3.26: 14 May 1934, 109.

practice of charging visitors for admission or to invite voluntary contributions. York, Winchester and Gloucester cathedrals, where no charge was
made, were consulted to see whether voluntary contributions would be liable
to income tax. (One of the ongoing problems in the early part of the century
had been whether income tax was levied on the canons individually or upon
the chapter collectively before incomes were allocated to individuals.) No
change was made then, but in September 1939 at the outbreak of war the
Minster was thrown open to provide shelter for evacuated students and children
and it was decided to discontinue charges with effect from 4 September and to
ask for voluntary contributions. They were resumed in April 1940, though
members of HM Forces and other persons in official uniform were admitted
free.[315]

The main problem affecting the precincts in the 1930s was the increase of
motor traffic and its effects on the buildings, highlighted first by the Pottergate
Arch. The Clerk of Works drew attention to the problems which were being
caused by traffic vibration in April 1934, and in 1936 the City Council diverted
traffic away from Minster Yard, though not without protest from some
residents. In 1937 agreement was reached with the Council for road widening
between Pottergate and the Wragby Road/Winnowsley Lane junction; and in
1938 the Chapter Clerk was asked to apply for the permanent diversion of
heavy traffic from Minster Yard. Discussions were still proceeding with the
City Council and the Ministry of Transport about the vibration tests necessary
to justify these steps at the outbreak of war.[316]

Whereas the First World War made almost no immediate impact on the
Chapter Act Book, the Second World War was very different. Reference has
already been made to the problems of evacuees. Another immediate problem
was air-raid protection. The Chapter Clerk had written to the Chief Constable
for advice on this as early as April 1939; and the houses in the Close were
inspected with a view to installing air-raid shelters. As soon as war broke out, it
was agreed to remove certain muniments and ornaments to other places in the
cathedral for better protection against fire. By 1941 additional fire-watchers
were being employed to support the volunteers, and a special plea was put in to
save the railings round the Dean's garden from compulsory acquisition by the
Ministry of Works.[317] The cathedral quarry was taken over by the Army in

---

[315] Ibid.: 15 Jan. 1934, 96; 8 Sept. 1939, 343; *LDM* 56, 1940, 77.

[316] A.3.26: 18 Apr. 1934, 106; 16 Dec. 1936, 219; 3 Aug. 1937, 247–8; 20 Sept. 1937, 253; 27 July
1938, 295; 8 Nov. 1938, 306; 20 Dec. 1938, 311–2; 25 Jan. 1939, 315; 20 Feb. 1939, 323; 16 May
1939, 332.

[317] Ibid.: 21 Apr. 1939, 328–9; 16 May 1939, 332; 8 Sept. 1939, 343; 1 Dec. 1941, 432.

1940. The Clerk of Works was allowed to take on work outside his cathedral duties subject to the approval of the Dean and Chapter; and the number of priest-vicars was allowed to remain at two in 1940, following the death of Canon Scott, thus reaching Dean Fry's aim over ten years earlier.[318] The Armistice Day service was not held in 1939, and instead a Remembrance Day service was held on the nearest Sunday and has continued ever since.[319] The liturgical life of the cathedral continued more or less as usual during the war, and some new initiatives were taken. In 1943 a Service of Thanksgiving for Harvest was held to which representatives of every organisation connected with farming and agriculture in the diocese were invited. Difficulties of transport made it impossible to hold one in 1944, but another was held in 1945, when representatives of the National Farmers' Union, the National Union of Agricultural Workers and the Women's Land Army presented sheaves.[320]

As early as March 1945 people were looking forward to the end of the war. A Service of Thanksgiving was prepared and copies distributed to parishes by April. A description in the *Diocesan Magazine* catches the mood when victory came:

We somehow managed to rise to the occasion when the day came, laughter grew and crowds gathered as bunting appeared in the streets and bells pealed out. Some housewives, how it is difficult to understand, managed to bake Victory Cakes, after dark groups of happy folk walked about to enjoy the illuminations, bonfires sprang up, fireworks were let off, people danced in the middle of the road holding up the traffic. There was much light hearted fun and very little drunkenness. The church services were well-attended, and it was quite like old times to see people, not dribbling but actually flowing to church.[321]

Special services were held in the cathedral both on VE Day (9 May) and on the Sunday following. Bishop Skelton wrote that the congregations 'were most impressive both in numbers and earnestness', and told how half a dozen RAF officers from Bomber Command, who must have flown over the cathedral many times during the war, motored over for the 8 a.m. Communion on VE Day and asked that they might have seats reserved for them at the Thanksgiving Service on Sunday. There was a special programme of Thanksgiving Music in the cathedral on Wednesday 19 September, which included Purcell's 'Festival Te

---

[318] Ibid.: 18 Dec. 1939, 358; 17 June 1940, 378; 3 Sept. 1940, 385; 14 Oct. 1940, 391.
[319] Ibid.: 23 Oct. 1939, 352; cf *LDM* 60, 1944, 326.
[320] *LDM* 60, 1944, 318; 61, 1945, 430.
[321] Ibid.: 61, 1945, 391.

Deum in D', Handel's 'The King shall rejoice', and three pieces by Vaughan Williams.[322]

One of the cathedral's treasures which did not require special protection was its copy of Magna Carta, because at the outbreak of war it was in the United States. In 1938 the Dean and Chapter had rather reluctantly agreed to let it be exhibited at the New York World Fair in May 1939. At first they had refused, but the Foreign Secretary had pressed them to reconsider their decision, and after taking professional advice they agreed on certain conditions – that it be transported in a fireproof safe, that it be insured by the Department of Overseas Trade for £100,000, and that it should be transported under the protection of the Foreign Office both ways. The chapter recorded that their decision had been influenced by the pressure from the Foreign Office that British interests were as much cultural as industrial, especially in relation to the development of democracy, by the fact that the two copies of Magna Carta in the British Museum were prohibited by Act of Parliament from leaving the country, and by the debt of gratitude which the Dean and Chapter owed to American citizens for their generous response to the cathedral appeal.[323] When war began the Department of Overseas Trade asked the chapter whether they would agree to its being deposited in the Library of Congress for the duration of the war at the end of the World Fair, and this was agreed on condition that the Department took full responsibility. In January 1941 they declined to allow it to be exhibited from place to place in the USA unless the Government declared that it was of urgent national importance. Eventually it was returned after the war, and the Dean spoke at the official return on 5 April 1946.[324]

In retrospect it can be seen that the war marked as sharp a dividing line in the cathedral's history as any. Immediately after the war the old order was restored, and indeed new things introduced. In December 1947 a Service of Nine Lessons and Carols was held for secondary schoolchildren in the city. 1948 saw new seats and kneelers for the choir, a new bell, and the restoration of the Dean's Eye, the thirteenth-century rose window in the north transept, to its former glory by the same mason who had restored it after the First World War, Mr Fred Strapps. In 1949 the Services chapels were redecorated, culminating in an impressive service in November when the Memorial Books containing the names of the 21,000 men who served in Bomber Groups nos. 1 and 5 were dedicated and placed in the cathedral.[325] But there were also other signs. An almost casual remark in the *Diocesan Magazine* for December 1947 expressed

[322] Ibid.: 61, 1945, 394, 423.

[323] A.3.26: 27 Oct. 1938, 317–9; 20 Dec. 1938, 309–10.

[324] Ibid.: 8 Sept. 1939, 342–3; 20 Jan. 1941, 402–3; *LDM* 62, 1946, 497.

[325] *LDM* 63, 1947, 292; 64, 1948, 69, 93, 125, 152–3, 294–5; 65, 1949, 70–1, 267, 294–5, 311–13, 323.

the hope that it might be possible to build up the congregation at the 6.30 p.m. Sunday Evening Service to the point where it would have to be moved back into the nave.[326] The world was now different from Dean Butler's time. In 1943 the Cathedral Constable, Mr C. R. Harradine, retired, and was not replaced. The description of him in the *Diocesan Magazine*, that 'he dressed like one of the old-time "Peelers" in a tall hat, frock-coat with silver buttons, and carried a silver-topped cane', reads like a reminder of a past age.[327] Fabric problems remained: Mr Godfrey showed a party of members of the Friends of Lincoln Cathedral round the building in May 1947 and demonstrated the considerable ongoing maintenance work that needed to be done; but the reports of the annual meetings of the Friends in these years show how important their establishment had been in securing a committed group of supporters to provide a steady income. By October 1947 they were 1500 strong.[328]

The 1940s mark another generational change in those most closely associated with the cathedral. Bishop Nugent Hicks had followed Bishop Swayne in 1933. He renovated and redecorated the Old Palace, and quite soon had to make appointments to the chapter. He appointed Hubert Larken as archdeacon of Lincoln in place of Bishop Hine in 1933. Soon after he appointed Arthur Greaves as Subdean, and bishop of Grantham after Bishop Blackie became the new suffragan bishop of Grimsby. The Dean felt bound to express his concern that two of the residentiaries were now suffragan bishops, the Chancellor was deeply involved with the Bishop's Hostel and the Archdeacon of Lincoln was involved with his archdeaconry, leaving no one apart from himself to devote his full time to the cathedral. In 1937 Bishop Blackie became Dean of Rochester, and so the Bishop made Bishop Greaves Precentor (which office he retained until 1959) and bishop of Grimsby, and made Archdeacon Larken Subdean, thereby meeting the Dean's earlier criticism. Larken had been Sacrist from 1927, and as one of the Masters of the Fabric was much involved in the restoration work. He inaugurated the Association of Friends of Lincoln Cathedral and remained Secretary after his retirement in 1946. The new Archdeacon of Lincoln was Kenneth Warner. Bishop Hicks was also anxious to encourage scholarship. On his initiative the Exchequer Gate was restored as a repository for the diocesan archives with the aid of generous grants from the Pilgrim Trust in recognition of the faithful work of Canon C. W. Foster. Miss Kathleen Major, Fellow and Librarian of St Hilda's College, Oxford, was appointed archivist.[329] Bishop Hicks was also the

---

[326] Ibid.: 63, 1947, 293.   [327] Ibid.: 59, 1943, 186.   [328] Ibid.: 63, 1947, 133, 237.
[329] M. Headlam, *Bishop and friend*, London [1944], 107–10, 116–7, 119–20; *LDM* 62, 1946, 483; A.3.26: 28 May 1935, 148.

moving spirit behind the service to mark the fiftieth anniversary of the consecration of Bishop King in 1935, at which the Archbishop of Canterbury preached the sermon; and he ordered that 8 March be kept as Bishop King's Day.[330] Bishop Hicks died in 1942; Bishop Skelton served from only 1942 to 1946, years dominated by the war, though it was noted that he won the esteem of the whole diocese very quickly. Bishop Owen had been Warden of Bishop's Hostel until 1936 before becoming bishop of Maidstone, but he died within a year of his confirmation in 1947.[331] In 1945 the Bishop decided to move out of the Old Palace so that it could become a diocesan retreat house, though in the event this could not be achieved immediately and it was used temporarily from 1946 to house students at the diocesan training college.[332]

Robert Mitchell succeeded Dean Fry in 1930, and served until his death in 1949. Inevitably he was a different kind of man from Fry – probably no one else could have had his boundless energy. His background was also different. He had been a member of the Anglican Evangelical Group Movement and wrote a pamphlet for them on confession and absolution in 1923. He came to Lincoln with a reputation as a preacher from St Michael's, Chester Square, in London. Canon Srawley wrote that 'he knew how to win and hold the attention of his listeners' and that on great occasions, national and others, he could preach with telling effect.[333] Ulrich Simon was not so impressed: as a student at Bishop's Hostel, Lincoln, at the time of the Munich Agreement of 1938 he heard the Dean's sermon at a solemn Thanksgiving Service:

He held the congregation spellbound by attributing the turn of events to God's wonderful providence. I ran out of my stall and feeling sick to the point of convulsion I gazed at the great west facade of the cathedral. The facade, in all its magnificence, is a sham, for it is not integral to the nave behind it. I saw in it the empty gesture of false prophecy.[334]

Mitchell, however, was not the only preacher on that Sunday to take that line, and, even if back-handedly, Simon's comment testifies to his power as a preacher. His main task as Dean was to ensure the work of restoration was completed, and this he did. His efforts helped to secure further benefactions from the Pilgrim's Trust and other sources, and as a result the cathedral has not

---

[330] Headlam, *Bishop and friend*, 117–8; *LDM* 51, 1935, 84–7; 61, 1945, 367.

[331] *LDM* 62, 1946, 493, 511.

[332] Ibid.: 65, 1945, 406; 62, 1946, 517.

[333] Ibid.: 61, 1949, 222.

[334] U. Simon, *Sitting in judgement, 1913–1963*, London 1978, 63. I owe this reference to my former research student, Andrew Chandler.

had to face such a critical situation again. Like several of his predecessors, he took an active part in city life, particularly in education, but also latterly in what would now be called tourism: he was nominated to the City Development and Publicity Committee in 1939.[335]

The 'anchor man' of the chapter in these years was probably the Chancellor, Canon J. H. Srawley. He served from 1923 to 1947, and died in January 1954. His work in Bishop's Hostel and in the preparation of the new statutes has already been mentioned. He was a liturgical scholar of distinction, and in some ways exactly the kind of man whose talents have thrived best in the opportunities offered by the cathedrals of the Church of England in the modern period.

The new Dean appointed in 1949 was the Rt Revd D. C. Dunlop, bishop of Jarrow, who had previously been Provost of St Mary's Cathedral, Edinburgh. Following the provisions of the new statutes of 1936 he was given the prebend of Aylesbury, which had been attached to the deanery until 1245 and was also vacant. In his installation sermon, he addressed the question, 'What is a cathedral for?' His answer was that the first duty of the cathedral foundation was to maintain the worship of God, day by day, week by week, not only in its own name 'but in the name of, and on behalf of, the whole Christian Family of the Diocese'. Moreover, it was vital that this was corporate worship, for the Church was the body of Christ:

For centuries (he concluded) Lincoln Minster has by its very appearance witnessed to man's citizenship of heaven. For centuries its worship has gone up to God taking with it the work and hopes and fears and vows of both illustrious and common folk. May it long continue before God a place pleasing to him, a place of which he may say 'Here will I dwell, for I have a delight therein.'[336]

This vision has been the inspiration of the cathedral in the later twentieth century.

Conclusion

The quarter of a millennium considered in this chapter may truly be said to be the most marked period of change in the history of Lincoln Minster. Part of this represents changes in the history of the Church of England and its place in the nation; and part represents changes in the history of Lincoln, particularly in the economic basis of the city.

At one level the story of Lincoln in this period fits a stereotypical picture. The eighteenth-century quiet of the cathedral led gently into the situation

[335] *LDM* 65, 1949, 221; A/3/26, 23 Oct 1939, 352–3.
[336] *LDM* 66, 1950, 19, 70–3.

where, because of the Pretymans, it became a particularly obvious example of traditional corruption, justifying the kind of reform undertaken in the 1830s. By the early nineteenth century the alliance between cathedral and Toryism seemed solid. Dean Gordon regularly proposed the Conservative MP Colonel Sibthorp for election. Robert Swan, the Chapter Clerk, was the embodiment of the local Tory cause for much of the century and the key to much local Tory influence. A Liberal canvass of Lincoln in 1855 found no support forthcoming from any Anglican clergyman.[337] Even as late as June 1870 there is an intriguing piece of evidence in the priest-vicars' records on the back of a letter from their solicitors about the leases they owned. It was a standard letter about the Mid-Lincolnshire Registration which read as follows:

It is not our intention to send Mr Cooling round to the Overseers this year to assist in making out their Lists of Voters, as it is hoped by this time each Overseer is well acquainted with his duty in that respect.

We shall however be glad if you will inform us *before the 20th of July next* whether there are any persons in your Parish favourable to the Conservative Cause, who are entitled to be on the Register, for whom we shall be glad to make Claims, and to see that their names are placed on the lists now about to be made out.[338]

Yet this alliance clearly survived the reforms of the 1830s; and those reforms did not sweep away the Pretymans – they merely made a repetition more difficult. The Muncipal Corporations Act in Lincoln resulted in a reformers' victory, though this proved temporary; and the Cathedral Close, included in the city after 1835, remained a Tory stronghold. Lincoln, however, was not a town dominated by clerical influence: its parliamentary representation in the mid-nineteenth century was often split, with the pollbooks not showing clear social correlations among the freemen.[339] Moreover, reformers and anti-reformers in the cathedral were not easily distinguishable by background and circumstances. In the later part of the century the cathedral clergy included several Liberal sympathisers.

The interesting politics of cathedral reform are internal to the Church not external to it. Even the simplified view of ecclesiastical parties is not much help. There were some old high churchmen: very much later there were some obvious tractarians; but there were many in between and only a few evangelicals. Little of the change at Lincoln before 1885 can be attributed to the Oxford Movement; Massingberd was a high churchman of the old school and Benson represented a

---

[337] Hill, *Georgian Lincoln*, 271; *Victorian Lincoln*, 258; R. J. Olney, *Rural society and county government*, 165.

[338] Letter from Burton and Soar, 22 June 1870: VC.4.1.97.

[339] Hill, *Victorian Lincoln*, 18–46; J. R. Vincent, *Pollbooks*, Cambridge 1967, 130–2.

Cambridge attitude, which was different – and there tended to be more Cambridge than Oxford men at Lincoln anyway.

More important than the parties are the problems of status – between bishop and chapter, within the chapter, between chapter and minor canons. These were important because what was being forged in the nineteenth century was a new conception of what a cathedral might be. Trollope, in his series of essays on the clergy of the Church of England, wrote that if there was anyone who had not been a dean who could distinctly define the duties of a dean, 'he must be one who has studied ecclesiastical subjects very deeply', and he went on to remark that 'the lines of deans have fallen in pleasant places'.[340] He was vigorously denounced by Dean Alford in the *Contemporary Review*: but Alford did not provide an alternative justification for the function of cathedrals. Indeed, an essay in the same journal a month or two later not only defended the status quo but wanted more money diverted to cathedrals to develop music and learning.[341]

The story of the priest-vicars shows very clearly the way in which a group of men who had been largely responsible for carrying on the daily worship of the cathedral in earlier times were more or less literally displaced by the residentiary canons, when they actually began to reside for longer periods than their official period of residence and to carry out duties that they had probably never carried out regularly in the history of the cathedral before. This accentuated all kinds of personal resentments between the two bodies. It also illustrates the difficulty of carrying out Church reform by consent.

Cathedrals have, on the whole, been neglected in the history of nineteenth-century Church reforms. Neither the bitter criticism of John Wade's *Extraordinary Black Book* nor the gently humorous defence offered by Trollope's Barsetshire novels goes very far in making it possible to understand the changes. Lincoln is a long way from Barchester, but the story of Precentor Pretyman and Meer Hospital could have formed the basis for Hiram's Hospital in *The Warden*, though there is no evidence that it did.[342] Trollope made one vital point when he made the theme of that novel the contrast between a structure which deserved criticism and clergy who were honest and honourable. In his *Autobiography* he wrote that he had been struck by two opposite evils: one was the possession by the Church of certain funds and endowments intended for charitable purposes, which had been allowed to become 'incomes for idle

---

[340] A. Trollope, *Clergymen of the Church of England*, ed. R. ap Roberts, Leicester 1974, 31, 34.

[341] 'Mr Anthony Trollope and the English clergy', *Contemporary Review* 2, 1866, 240–62; 'Cathedral life and cathedral reform', ibid. 488–513.

[342] G. F. A. Best, *Victorian Studies* 5, 1961–2, 135–50. Professor Best's study of the Ecclesiastical Commissioners, *Temporal pillars* (Cambridge 1964), gives a view of cathedral reform from the centre, but inevitably leaves the details largely untouched.

Church dignitaries'; the other was the undeserved severity of the newspapers on the recipients of those incomes, 'who could hardly be considered to be the chief sinners in the matter'. 'It is seldom,' wrote Trollope, that such a man 'will be the first to find out that his services are overpaid ... Satire, though it may exaggerate the vice it lashes, is not justified in creating it in order that it may be lashed.'[343]

Central to the problem of cathedral reform was money. The suppression of non-resident prebends and elimination of pluralities took a lot of money away from the cathedral clergy, and was a prime source for increasing the incomes of what were usually called 'the working clergy' of the Church of England; but it did not affect the finances of the cathedral building. The Fabric Estates at Lincoln had always been kept separate. Improved administration helped cathedral revenues, but its impact was delayed and then countered by agricultural depression. Much of the story concerned the politics of dealing with newly established central administrative machinery – an aspect which tends to be overlooked. In the end the Fabric posed the crucial question: how could the money be found to keep a medieval building like Lincoln standing? The pressure to maintain the Fabric forced the cathedral chapter into an awareness of its dependence upon the generosity of a wider public. By the 1920s probably more people had given money to the cathedral in the previous half-century than at any period in its history. In this sense, if no other, its support was democratised.

The deficiencies of cathedral legislation and the cumbersome nature of the Ecclesiastical Commissioners also resulted in an unfortunate triangular tussle between the chapter, the priest-vicars and the Commission at Lincoln. The chapter had accepted compulsory commutation of their estates after 1870 under the 1840 Act, but there was no similar power to deal with the minor corporations. The recommendations of the 1885 Cathedral Commission report on this subject were never carried into effect. Consequently the chapter, having generously agreed to supplement the priest-vicars' incomes in 1870, found themselves landed with a burden at a time of agricultural depression and increasing pressure on their income for other purposes, particularly the Fabric. The priest-vicars fended off pressures for commutation until they could secure relatively favourable terms in 1903. The effect of this was to poison relations between the chapter and the Ecclesiastical Commission, who thought that the members of the chapter were drawing higher incomes than they should. This suspicion of the chapter was disastrous in the 1920s, when in fact inflation had started to erode the real value of chapter incomes significantly. The ability of each of the three parties involved to play the other two off against each other makes

[343] A. Trollope, *Autobiography*, ed. B. A. Booth, Berkeley 1947, 78–80.

fascinating material for an ecclesiastical novel, but it did not contribute to the advancement of the cathedral's mission. Only in 1990 did the state at last agree to make some financial provision for the support of cathedral fabric, nearly fifteen years after it did the same for other church buildings.

From the 1870s until the 1930s the cathedral established a new kind of preaching ministry on Sunday evenings, which was probably at its peak during the episcopate of Edward King. The quality of worship was obviously transformed in the same period. The latter changes may now be seen to have been more important than the former. But the understanding of the role of the Church of England itself has also been changing. There is a much stronger sense of the independence of the Church from the state than in former times, exemplified by the development of the Church Assembly and more recently the General Synod. Bishops like Wordsworth and King would have welcomed the principle, even if they might have been surprised by some of the consequences. It is an interesting coincidence that when a new bishop had to be elected in 1932 at the time the new statutes were being considered, two canons protested on principle at the right of the Crown to dictate a nominee to the chapter: they were Canon Boulter and Canon Srawley, each totally dedicated to the life of the cathedral and diocese.[344]

That change has also affected the cathedral's relations with other churches. It has been noted already that from the late nineteenth century the cathedral became less stand-offish towards nonconformists. In 1949 the Methodist Local Preachers' Mutual Aid Association presented to the cathedral a specially bound and inscribed Bible for the nave as part of their centenary celebrations.[345] It is impossible to imagine that happening a century earlier. More recently bishops of Lincoln have nominated Free Church ministers exercising a ministry as industrial missioners in the diocese to honorary canonries in the cathedral. Thus Dean Dunlop's vision of the cathedral offering worship 'on behalf of the whole Christian people in this county'[346] has a wider reference than some of his predecessors might have envisaged. The implications of that vision as it stretches to involve all people in a society where active Christian commitment is declining are the main task of the cathedral today and tomorrow.

In the end, however, it is impossible to escape from the significance of the building. D. H. Lawrence offers one picture of that in his novel, *The Rainbow*, in his description of Will Brangwen's impression:

Away from time, always outside of time! Between east and west, between dawn and sunset, the church lay like a seed in silence, dark befor

---

[344] A.3.26: 22 Dec. 1932, 49.
[345] *LDM* 65, 1949, 267.
[346] Ibid.: 66, 1950, 71.

death. Containing birth and death, potential with all the noise and transition of life, the cathedral remained hushed, a great, involved seed, whereof the flower would be radiant life inconceivable, but whose beginning and end were the circle of silence. Spanned round with the rainbow, the jewelled gloom folded music upon silence, light upon darkness, fecundity upon death, as a seed folds leaf upon leaf and silence upon the root and the flower, hushing up the secret of all between its parts, the death out of which it fell, the life into which it has dropped, the immortality it involves, and the death it will embrace again.

Here in the church, 'before' and 'after' were folded together, all was contained in oneness ... And there was no time nor life nor death, but only this, the timeless consummation, where the thrust from earth met the thrust from earth and the arch was locked on the keystone of ecstasy. This was all, this was everything.[347]

Another picture was offered in a war-time soliloquy by the philosopher and broadcaster, C. E. M. Joad. He wrote of the affectionate curiosity of the Gothic sculptors who carved devils and demons to express the mischief that is in all things, and snails, ducks, foxes and geese to show the kinship of humanity with all creation. He pondered on the remoteness of the spirit which carved 500 stone roses, each of them different from any other, from modern moods:

I have not the descriptive powers to do justice to the wonder of this place, to the meticulous care and varied richness of the masses of the detail, and to the spaciousness of design which yet holds the vast structure together and enables the eye to apprehend the intricacies of the parts, without ceasing to be aware of the unity of the whole. I can only testify to the overwhelming impression of majesty and beauty that it conveys. Perhaps something must be allowed for my own mood in which discontent with a civilisation which, I know, could produce no building of an even comparable impressiveness, and horror of the background of our times which enhanced both the serenity and the remoteness of the Cathedral, combined to invest the whole experience with a feeling of nostalgia for a past in which such creations were possible.[348]

Such descriptions express the way in which the cathedral embodies human aspirations after the eternal; but the emphasis nevertheless remains on the human feelings. Bishop Swayne in his address at the Thanksgiving Service in November 1932 struck a rather different note. He recognised that a great cathedral was a national monument, and was also a supreme work of art:

But it is the appeal of a work of art which embodies a life, which itself is a living thing. A great Christian Cathedral is no mere museum piece. It is not a dead thing to be treasured and protected without alteration, diminution or addition. It lives. It dominates its own material. It royally asserts itself as it will. It is the home of an idea, a faith, a spirit. To that faith and spirit the future belongs, and they can never suffer themselves

[347] D. H. Lawrence, *The Rainbow*, London 1915, 189–90.
[348] *LDM* 59, 1943, 175.

to be dominated by the hand of the past, beautifully though that hand may have wrought in its own day.[349]

A history, therefore, is always inadequate to do justice to the life of a cathedral such as Lincoln, for it runs the risk of becoming entangled in personal and corporate rivalries, and the problems of finance, and missing the point of what the building is for. Bishop Swayne expressed that point in these words: 'This Church of St Mary the Virgin, on Lincoln's sovereign hill, stands for the faith of the Incarnation. That is its supreme importance.'[350]

[349] Ibid.: 48, 1932, 182.
[350] Ibid.

Select bibliography

✳

This includes the major works devoted to the history of the cathedral and a brief account of the manuscript sources on which the history is based.

MANUSCRIPT SOURCES

The muniments of the Dean and Chapter were briefly described in *First Report of the Commissioners of Public Records*, 1800, p. 337, and at greater length by J. A. Bennett in *Historical Manuscripts Commission Twelfth Report*, Appendix 9, 1891. Canon C. W. Foster and Miss Major in the course of their work on the *Registrum Antiquissimum* (see below, Lincoln Record Society) checked and tidied the contents of the Muniment Room. The establishment of the Lincolnshire Archives Office in 1948 made more detailed checking and description possible and a classified list was prepared for the use of readers in the office. At the same time detailed descriptions were included in the published reports of the Archives Office:

4 952–3 Muniments of the Dean and Chapter, a classified list, 37–69, based on a check of the inventory made by Canon Wordsworth;

5 953–4 Episcopal records in the muniments, 58–61;

7 955–6 Chapter Clerk's Office, the Ark of the canon in residence, 58–9;

9 1957–8 Vicars Choral Records, 52–54.

A summary of this work, and of the history of the muniments is given in D. M. Williamson (Owen), LMP *Lincoln muniments* 8, 1956. Dr Nicholas Bennett (now Cathedral Librarian) is currently engaged on amplifying and extending the list of muniments with a view to publication.

Important material relating to the cathedral is included in the episcopal registers and visitation books: K. Major, *A handlist of the records of the bishops of Lincoln and the archdeacons of Lincoln and Stow*, Oxford 1953.

A number of these materials, as well as some of the chapter's own archives, have been published by the Lincoln Record Society (founded 1910) and Canterbury and York Society:

319

LRS vols. 3, 6, 9, 1912–14, ed. W. P. W. Phillimore and F. N. Davis, *Rotuli Hugonis de Welles episcopi Lincolniensis.*

LRS vol. 11, 1914, ed. F. N. Davis, *Rotuli Roberti Grosseteste episcopi Lincolniensis – necnon Rotulus Henrici de Lexington episcopi Lincolniensis.*

LRS vol. 20, 1925, ed. F. N. Davis, C. W. Foster and A. H. Thompson, *Rotuli Ricardi Gravesend episcopi Lincolniensis.*

LRS vols. 39, 43, 48, 59, 60, 64, 69, 76, 1948–86, ed. R. M. T. Hill, *The Rolls and Register of Bishop Oliver Sutton.*

LRS vols. 57, 58, 74, 1963–82, ed. M. Archer, *Bishop Repingdon's Register.*

Canterbury and York Society, vol. 73, 1984, ed. N. H. Bennett, *The Register of Richard Fleming* vol. 1

LRS vol. 2, 1912, ed. C. W. Foster, *Lincoln episcopal records in the time of Thomas Cooper 1571–1584.*

LRS vols. 12, 13, 15, 1915–17, ed. R. E. G. Cole, *The Chapter Acts of the cathedral church of Lincoln, 1520–1559.*

LRS, vols. 27, 28, 29, 32, 34, 41, 42, 46, 51, 62, 67, 78, 1931–73 ed. C. W. Foster and K. Major, *Registrum Antiquissimum of the cathedral church of Lincoln.*

LRS Parish Register Section II, 1913, ed. C. W. Foster, *The parish registers of St Margaret in the Close, Lincoln.*

PRINTED SOURCES

Anon, *An historical account of the antiquities in the cathedral church of St Mary, Lincoln, abridged from William of Malmesbury, Matthew Paris, etc.*, Lincoln 1771.

Anon, *Anthems for two, three, four, five, six, seven and eight voices as they are now performed in the cathedrals in York, in Durham and in Lincoln, collected and sold by T. Ellway*, T. Gent, York 1736.

Anon, *A collection of anthems used in the cathedral church of Lincoln.* Lincoln 1827.

Anon, *Lincoln cathedral, an exact copy of all the ancient monumental inscriptions*, W. and B. Brooke, London, 1851.

Apthorp, G. F. *A catalogue of the books and manuscripts in the library of Lincoln cathedral*, Lincoln, 1859.

Archer, Margaret *Register of Bishop Repingdon of Lincoln*, 3 vols., LRS 57, 58, 74.
  'Philip Repingdon, bishop of Lincoln, and his cathedral chapter', *University of Birmingham Historical Journal* 4, 81–103.

Arnold, T., ed., *Henrici Archidiaconi Huntendunensis Historia Anglorum: de contemptu mundi*, 1879, 297–320.

Archaeological Journal, vol. 103 for 1946, London, 1947: part iv, Lincoln cathedral, pp. 101–56:
  Clapham, A. W. 'The cathedral buildings, library, Close, Exchequer Gate and Diocesan Record Office'.

Saxl, F. 'The eleventh-century design for the west front' [includes a conjectural reconstruction of the first cathedral based by W. Frank 1 on drawings made by R. S. Godfrey for the reinforcement of the structure in 1922].

Lafond, Jean, 'The stained-glass decoration of Lincoln cathedral in the thirteenth century'.

Bailey, John 'The struggle and the light, the built legacy of St Hugh', Grosseteste lecture, Lincoln 1985

'St Hugh's church at Lincoln', *Architectural History* 1991.

Bassett, Steven, 'Lincoln and the Anglo-Saxon see of Lindsey', *Anglo-Saxon England* X, 1990, 1–32.

Bell J. and W. H. Kynaston, *Incunabula in the Lincoln cathedral library*, Lincoln 1925.

Benson, A. C. *Life and times of Edward White Benson, London, 1900*, The Trefoil, London, 1923.

Benson, E. F. *As we were*, London 1930.

Benson, E. W. *The cathedral, its necessary place in the life and work of the church*, London, 1878.

Bilson, J. 'Plan of the first cathedral church of Lincoln', *Archaeologia* 62, 1911, 553–64.

'The beginnings of Gothic architecture', *Journal of Royal Institute of British Architects*, 3rd series, 6, 1899, 316–17.

Bird, C. S. *Sketches from the life of the Reverend Charles Smith Bird*, London 1864.

Binnall, P. B. G. 1864, 'Notes on the medieval altars and chapels in Lincoln cathedral', *Antiquaries' Journal* 42, 1962, 68–80

Blethen, H. T. 'Bishop Williams, the altar controversy and the royal supremacy', *The Welsh History Review*, 9, 142–54.

Bloxam, M. H. 'On the tombs in Lincoln cathedral', *AASR* 18, 1885–6, 103.

Bond, L. H. 'Lincoln cathedral', Royal Archaeological Institute programme of summer meeting, 1974, 76–80.

Bowker, M. *The secular clergy in the diocese of Lincoln 1495–1520*, Cambridge 1968.

The Henrician Reformation: the diocese of Lincoln under John Longland, 1521–1547, Cambridge 1981.

Bradshaw, H. and C. Wordsworth *The Lincoln Cathedral Statutes* [*LCS*]: Part 1 *The Black Book*, Cambridge 1892; Part 2 (2 vols.), Cambridge 1897.

British Archaeological Association transactions for the year 1982, Medieval Architecture at Lincoln cathedral, ed. T. A. Heslop and V. Sekules, London 1986

Jones, M. J. 'Archaeology in Lincoln'.

Gem, R. 'Lincoln Minster: Ecclesia Pulchra Ecclesia Fortis'.

Kidson, P. 'St Hugh's Choir'.

Laxton, R. R. 'The trusses of St Hugh's Choir roof'.

Foot N., C. D. Litton and W. G. Simpson 'The high roofs of the east end of Lincoln'.

Park, D. 'The medieval painted decoration of Lincoln cathedral'.

Russell, G. 'The thirteenth-century west window of Lincoln cathedral'.

Dean, M. 'The Angel Choir and its local influence'.

Glenn, V. 'The sculpture of the Angel Choir at Lincoln'.

Stocker, D. 'The shrine of Little St Hugh'.

Sekules, V. 'The tomb of Christ and the development of the sacrament: Easter sepulchres reconsidered'.

Major, K. 'Houses in Minster Yard: documentary sources'.

Cocke, T. 'The architectural history of Lincoln cathedral from the dissolution to the twentieth century'.

Brooke, C. N. L. 'Continental influences on English cathedral chapters in the eleventh and twelfth centuries'. *XIe Congrès des sciences historiques, Stockholm, 1960, résumé des communications*, 120–1.

Brooks, F. W. and F. Oakley, 'The campaign of Lincoln', *AASR* 36, 1921–2, 295–312.

Bruce-Mitford, R. 'The chapter house vestibule graves at Lincoln, and the body of St Hugh of Avalon', reprinted from F. G. Emmison and W. B. Stephens, *Tribute to an antiquary* (Marc Fitch), London 1976.

Buckler, J. C. *A description and defence of the restoration of the exterior of Lincoln cathedral*, Oxford 1866.

Bumpus, T. F. *The cathedrals of England and Wales I*, London 1905.

Callus, D. A., ed., *Robert Grosseteste scholar and bishop*, Oxford 1955, includes Appendix 1: K. Major, 'The *familia* of Robert Grosseteste', 216–41; Appendix 2: E. W. Kemp, 'The attempted canonization of Robert Grosseteste', 241–6; Appendix 3: J. W. F. Hill, 'The tomb of Robert Grosseteste with an account of its opening in 1782', 246–50.

Carley, J. P. 'John Leland and the contents of pre-dissolution libraries: Lincoln', *TCBS* 9, 1989, 330–57.

Cheney, C. R. 'List of feast days to be observed by workmen in the cathedral of Lincoln', *BIHR* 34, 1964, 147.

Cole, R. E. G. 'Proceedings relative to the canonization of Robert Grosseteste bishop of Lincoln', *AASR* 33, 1915–16, 1–28.

'Proceedings relative to the canonization of John de Dalderby', *AASR* 33, 1915–16, 243–76.

'Some papal provisions in the cathedral church of Lincoln, AD 1300–1320', *AASR* 34, 1917–18, 219–28.

Colyer, C. and B. Gilmour, 'St Paul in the Bail, Lincoln', *Current Archaeology* 63, 1968, 102–5.

Crossley, P. 'Lincoln and the Baltic: the fortunes of a theory', in E. Fernie and P. Crossley, eds., *Medieval architecture and its intellectual context*, London 1990, 169–80.

Dahmus, J. F. ed., *The metropolitan visitation of William Courteney archbishop of Canterbury 1381–1396*, Urbana, Illinois University Press, 1950.

Deanesley, M. *The Lollard Bible*, Cambridge 1920.

Delamare, R. *Le De officiis ecclesiasticis de Jean d'Avranches*, U. Chevallier, Bibliothèque Liturgique vol. 22, Paris 1923.

Dimock, J. F. 'Recorded history of Lincoln cathedral', *AASR* 10, 1869–70, 190–201.

Giraldi Cambrensis Opera VII, *RS* 1877, especially the obit roll, 153–64 and Schalby's narrative, 193–216.

Doggett, N. 'The Anglo-Saxon see and cathedral of Dorchester on Thames, the evidence reconsidered', *Oxoniensia* 51, 1986, 49–61.

Douglas, D. 'The Norman episcopate before the conquest', *Cambridge Historical Journal* 13, 1957, 101–15.

Douie, D. L. and Farmer, H. eds., *Magna Vita Sancti Hugonis*, Nelson Medieval Texts, 2 vols., London 1961.

Edwards, K. *The English secular cathedrals in the middle ages*, Manchester 1949; 2nd edition 1967.

Farmer, D. H. 'The canonization of St Hugh of Lincoln', *LASR* 6, 1955–6, 86–117.

  St Hugh of Lincoln, London 1985.

  'The cult and canonization of St Hugh', in H. Mayr-Harting, ed., *St Hugh of Lincoln*, Oxford 1987, 75–87.

Fiennes, Oliver 'Bad dreams and bright visions', a lecture given by the retiring Dean to the Greater Chapter of Lincoln, St Hugh's Day, 1988. Not published.

Foster, C. W. 'Lincolnshire wills proved in the Prerogative court of Canterbury 1384–1468 and 1471–1490', *AASR* 41, 1932–33, 61–114, 179–218.

  Index of the wills and administrations of the Dean and Chapter and the prebendal peculiars of Lincoln, British Record Society Index Library 57, 1930.

Foster, C. W. and A. Hamilton Thompson, 'Chantry certificates for Lincoln and Lincolnshire', *AASR* 34, 1922.

Foster, P., *et al.*, 'The prebendal manor house at Nassington', *Northamptonshire Archaeological Journal* 146 (for the year 1989), 1991, 555–8.

Fowler, J. H. *The life and letters of Edward Lee Hicks*, London 1922.

Freeman, A. 'The organs of Lincoln Cathedral', *The Organ* 2, 1928.

Garton, C. *Lincoln School, a summary honours board*, Lincoln 1988.

Gibbons, A. *Early Lincoln wills*, privately printed, Lincoln 1888.

Godfrey, R. S. *Half-an-hour at Lincoln cathedral*, Lincoln 1931.

Greenway, D. E. J. Le Neve, *Fasti Ecclesie Anglicane 1066–1300 III Lincoln*, London 1977.

Hamilton, N. E. S. A. *Willelmi Malmsburiensis monachi de gestis pontificum Anglorum*, *RS* 1870.

Headlam, M. *Bishop and friend*, London 1944.

Heslop, T. A. 'The iconography of the Angel Choir at Lincoln cathedral', in E. Fernie and P. Crossley, *Medieval architecture*, London 1990, 151–8.

Hill, J. W. F. 'Lincoln castle, constables and guard', *AASR* 40, 1932–33.

  'The western spires of Lincoln Minster and their threatened removal in 1726', *LASR* 4, 1954, 101–7.

  Medieval Lincoln, Cambridge 1948; reprint with corrections in introduction, Stamford 1990.

  Tudor and Stuart Lincoln, Cambridge 1956.

  Georgian Lincoln, Cambridge 1966.

  Victorian Lincoln, Cambridge 1974.

Hunt, R. W. 'English learning in the late twelfth century', *TRHS*, 4th series, 19, 1936, 19–42.

Jacob, E. F. and H. C. Johnson, *The register of Henry Chichele II*, Oxford and Canterbury and York Society 1938.

Johnson, C. *Hugh the Chanter, history of the church of York, 1066–1127*, Nelson Medieval Texts 1961.

Johnston, J. O. 'Sermons in Lincoln cathedral', *AASR* 33, 1915–16, 277–303.

Jones-Baker, D. 'Medieval and Tudor musicians in Hertfordshire, the graffiti evidence', in D. Jones-Baker, *Hertfordshire in history*, Herts. Local History Council, Hertford, 1991 [incorporates part of a Grosseteste memorial lecture on the medieval musical graffiti in the cathedral].

Kemp, E. W. *Canonization and authority in the western church*, Oxford 1948. See also Callus, *Grosseteste*

King, H. P. F. *J. Le Neve Fasti Ecclesie Anglicane, 1300–1541, I Lincoln*, London 1962.

Kirwan, L. *The music of Lincoln cathedral*, London 1977.

Kuttner, S. and E. Rathbone, 'Anglo-Norman canonists of the twelfth century, an introductory survey', *Traditio* 7, 1949–51, 279–359.

Kynaston, W. H. *Catalogue of foreign books in the chapter library of Lincoln cathedral*, London 1937, facsimile reprint 1972.

Lehmberg, S. E. *The reformation of cathedrals*. Princeton, N. J., 1988.

Le Neve, John *Fasti ecclesie anglicane* – corrected and continued to the present time by T. Duffus Hardy, 3 vols., Oxford 1954. See also D. E. Greenway, H. P. F. King.

Le Patourel, J. *The Norman empire*. Oxford 1976.

Lincoln Civic Trust, *Survey of ancient houses in Lincoln*, in progress:
  Jones, Stanley, Kathleen Major and Joan Varley
    I Priorygate to Pottergate, Lincoln 1984 (with Christopher Johnson).
    II Houses to the south and west of the Minster, Lincoln 1987.
    III Houses in Eastgate, Priorygate and James Street, Lincoln 1990.

Lincoln Diocesan Magazine 1885 – in progress. The series contains a number of anonymous contributions on cathedral services, notably in vol, 2, 1887, and vol, 5, 1889. In addition there are the following outstanding papers:
    Clements, J. H. 'Defence of Bishop King', 5, 1889.
    Anon., 'Dean Butler', 10, 1894.
    Crowfoot, J. H. 'Archbishop Benson', 12, 1896.
    Anon., 'Bishop Tomline's Visitation of 1801', 24, 1913.
    Anon., 'Bishop Pelham's Visitation of 1825', 30, 1914.
    Anon., 'William Peters' reredos, 1800', 16, 1950.
    [I am grateful to Mrs Varley for abstracting references to the cathedral from the *Diocesan Magazine*.]

Lincoln Minster Pamplets, Friends of Lincoln cathedral
  1st series, ed. K. Major:
    1 Srawley, J. H. *The origin and growth of cathedral foundations*, 1948.
    2 Srawley, J. H. *The book of John de Schalby*, 1949.
    3 Cave, C. P. *Roof bosses in Lincoln Minister*, 1950.
    4 Hill, R. M. T. *Oliver Sutton, Dean of Lincoln, later bishop of Lincoln*, 1950.
    5 Srawley, J. H. *Michael Honywood, Dean of Lincoln*, 1951.

6 Gardner, Arthur *Lincoln Angels*, 1952.

7 Srawley, J. H. Robert *Grosseteste, bishop of Lincoln*, 1953.

8 Williamson (Owen), D. M. *Lincoln muniments*, 1956.

Unnumbered:

Anderson, M. D. *The choir stalls of Lincoln Minster*, 1951.

2nd series, ed. J. Varley:

1 Froude, J. A. *St Hugh of Lincoln*, introduction by F. M. Powicke, 1959.

2 Zarnecki, G. *Romanesque sculpture at Lincoln cathedral*, 2nd edn, revised 1970.

3 Binnall, P. B. G. *Nineteenth-century stained glass in Lincoln Minster*, 1966.

4 Chadwick, W. O. *Edward King, bishop of Lincoln*, 1968.

5 Griffiths, D. N. *Lincoln cathedral library*, 1971.

6 Harvey, J. H. *Catherine Swynford's Chantry*, 1972.

7 Major, K. *Minster Yard*, 1974.

Honeywood Press, publications of Lincoln cathedral library:

Parker, J. W. *'If nothing hinders' an account of the office of a canon of Lincoln cathedral*, 1983.

Brighton, C. R. *Lincoln cathedral cloister bosses*, 1985.

Foreville, R. *Saint Gilbert of Sempringham*, translated by K. F. Dockrill, 1986.

Garton, C., translator, *The metrical life of St. Hugh*, 1986.

Arundale, R. L., *Richard Neile, bishop of Lincoln*, 1987.

Zarnecki, George *Romanesque Lincoln, the sculpture of the cathedral*, 1988.

Alldrid, N. and D. Tripp *The Latin and French inscriptions of Lincoln Minster*, 1990.

Linnell, N. 'Michael Honywood and Lincoln cathedral library', in D. Marcombe and C. S. Knighton, *Close encounters: English cathedrals and society since 1540*, University of Nottingham 1991, 72–87.

Luard, H. R. *R. Grosseteste Epistole*, R S 1861.

Mackinnon, H. 'William de Montibus, a medieval teacher', in T. A. Sandquist and M. R. Powicke, *Essays in medieval history presented to Bertie Wilkinson*, Toronto 1969, 32–45.

Macready, H. and F. H. Thompson, eds. *Art and patronage in the English Romanesque*, Society of Antiquaries of London, 1986, includes T. A. Heslop, 'Seals as evidence for metal working in England', 50–60 (the chapter seal), N. Stratford, 'Niello in England in the twelfth century', 28–49 (the chapter seal).

Maddison, A. R. *A short account of the vicars choral, Poor Clerks, Organists and choristers of Lincoln cathedral from the twelfth century to the accession of Edward VI*, London 1878.

The Vice-Chancellorship of Lincoln cathedral, Lincoln 1879.

'Lincoln cathedral choir 1558–1642', *AASR* 18, 1885–6.

'A Visitation of Lincoln cathedral', *Archaeological Journal* 46, 1889.

'Lincoln cathedral choir 1750–1875', *AASR* 21, 1891–2, 208–26.

'A ramble through the parish of St Mary Magdalene', *AASR* 21, 10–43.

'A ramble through the parish of St Margaret within the Close', *AASR* 22, 1893–4, 1–31.

'A catalogue of manuscripts belonging to Lincoln cathedral in the fifteenth century', *AASR* 23, 1895–6, 248–53.

'Papers discovered underneath the organ case of Lincoln cathedral', *AASR* 24, 1897–98, 122–30.

(with others) *Life and letters of William John Butler*, London 1897.

Major, K. 'The office of Chapter Clerk', in M. V. Ruffer and A. J. Taylor, *Medieval studies presented to Rose Graham*, Oxford 1950, 163–88.

'The finances of the Dean and Chapter of Lincoln from the twelfth to the fourteenth century', *JEH*, 1954, 149–67.

see also Manuscript sources: Lincoln Minster Pamphlets, Lincoln Civic Trust: Callus, Grosseteste.

Massingberd, W. O. 'Lincoln cathedral charters', *AASR* 26, 1901–2, 18–96, 321–68; *AASR* 27, 1903–4, 1–91.

Mayr-Harting, H., ed., *Saint Hugh of Lincoln*, Oxford 1987:

Farmer, D. H., 'The cult and canonization of St Hugh', 75–87.

Stocker, D. A., 'The mystery of the shrines of St Hugh', 89–124.

Memoirs illustrative of the history and antiquities of the county and city of Lincoln communicated at the annual meeting of the Archaeological Institute of Great Britain and Ireland held at Lincoln, July 1848, London 1850 includes:

Winston, C. 'An account of the painted glass in Lincoln cathedral', 90–124.

Penrose, F. C. 'An inquiry into the system of proportions which prevail in the nave of Lincoln cathedral', 125–38.

Boole, G. 'Philosophical remains of Bishop Grosseteste', 139–44.

Cockerell, C. C. R. 'Ancient sculpture in Lincoln cathedral', 215–40.

Bonney, H. K. 'A short dissertation upon the monuments at the upper end of the north-eastern part of the presbytery', 241–7.

Tennyson d'Eyncourt, C. 'Memoir on the leaden plate, the memorial of William d'Eyncourt preserved in the cathedral library', 248–52.

Willson, E. J. 'Notices of the ancient deanery, Lincoln', 291–3.

Pretyman, C. and A. Way, 'Testamentary documents preserved in the chapter muniment room in Lincoln Minster, comprising the wills and inventories of effects of Richard de Ravenser, archdeacon of Lincoln, 1386', 310–27.

See also *Archaeological Journal* 103 for 1946.

Moor, C. 'Roman cardinals at Lincoln', *AASR* 29, 1907–8, 337–60.

Morgan, N. J. *The medieval painted glass of Lincoln cathedral*, British Academy, Corpus Vitrearum Medii Aevi, 1983.

Nicholson, W. A. 'On the character of the arch formed by the elastic stone beam between the western towers of Lincoln cathedral', *Lincolnshire Topographical Society* 1841–2.

Nordstrom, F. 'Peterborough, Lincoln, and the science of Robert Grosseteste', *Art Bulletin* 37, 1955, 241–72.

Overton, J. H. and E. Wordsworth, *Christopher Wordsworth bishop of Lincoln, 1807–1885*, London, 1888

Owen (Williamson), D. M. 'The Norman cathedral at Lincoln', *Anglo-Norman Studies* 6, Woodbridge, Suffolk, 1984, 188–99.

See also Manuscript sources, Lincoln Minster Pamphlets.

Parsons, D., ed., *Eleanor of Castile 1290–1990: essays to commemorate the 700th anniversary of her death: 28 November 1290*. Stamford, Paul Watkins, in association with the University of Leicester Department of Adult Education, 1991. Includes papers on the memorials by Nicola Coldstream and Phillip Lindley.

Perry, G. G. 'Some episcopal visitations of Lincoln cathedral', *Archaeological Journal* 38, 1881, 1–20.

Perry, G. G. and J. H. Overton, *Biographical notes of the bishops of Lincoln from Remigius to Wordsworth*, Lincoln 1900.

Poole, G. A. 'Architectural history of Lincoln Minster', *AASR* 4, 1857, 8–48.
'The tomb of Remigius', *AASR* 14, 1877–78, 21–25.

Ragg, L. *Memoir of Edward Charles Wickham*, London 1911.

Report of the Cathedrals Commission on Lincoln 1885. HC XXI, 1884–5.

Richter, M. (general ed.), *Giraldus Cambrensis Speculum Duorum*. Board of Celtic Studies, University of Wales, history and law series, no. 27, Cardiff 1974.

Russell, G. W. E. *Edward King*, London 1913.

Scott, F. S. 'Earl Waltheof of Northumberland', *Archaeologia Aeliana*, 4th series, 30, 1952, 148–213.

Scott, G. G. (communicated by E. Venables), 'Some notes of an examination of the choir of Lincoln cathedral, with a view to determining the chronology of St Hugh's work', *AASR* 12, 1873–4.

Sharpe, E. 'On Lincoln cathedral', *AASR* 9, 1867–8, 179–90.

Shull, V. 'Clerical drama in Lincoln cathedral, 1318–1561', *Publications of Modern Language Society of America*, 3, 1937.

Simpson, W. G. 'Work on the survey and dating of the roofs of Lincoln cathedral during 1988', *Archaeological Journal* 146, for 1989, 1991, 582–3.

Southern, R. W. *Robert Grosseteste: the growth of an English mind in medieval Europe*. Oxford 1986.

Spear, D. S. 'The Norman empire and the secular clergy, 1066–1204', *Journal of British Studies* 21, 1981–2, 1–10.

Srawley, J. H. *The story of Lincoln Minster*. London 1933.

Stocker, D. 'The tomb and shrine of Bishop Grosseteste in Lincoln cathedral', in W. M. Ormrod, ed., *England in the thirteenth century*. Woodbridge 1986, 143–8.

Stocker, D. and P. Everson, 'Rubbish recycled: a study of the re-use of stone in Lincolnshire', in D. Parsons, ed., *Quarrying and building in England AD 43–1525*. Royal Archaeological Institute, 1990.

Swayne, W. S. *Parson's pleasure*, Edinburgh, 1934.

Sympson, E. M. 'The choir screen or pulpitum in Lincoln cathedral', *AASR* 24, 1897–8, 457–66.

Thomson, Rodney M. *Catalogue of the manuscripts of Lincoln cathedral chapter library*, D. S. Brewer, Cambridge, for the Dean and Chapter, 1989.

Treherne, J. *Dangerous precincts*, London 1987.

Trollope, E. 'The Norman sculpture of Lincoln cathedral', *AASR* 8, 1865–6, 279–93.
'Little St Hugh of Lincoln', *AASR* 15, 1879–80, 126–30.

Venables, E. 'Notes of an examination of the choir of Lincoln cathedral', *Archaeological Journal* 32, 1875.

'Architectural history of Lincoln cathedral', *Archaeological Journal*, 40, 1883, 159–92.

'The Vicars' Court', *AASR* 17, 1883–4, 235–50.

'Antony Beeke's register of the prebendaries of Lincoln', *Archaeological Journal* 42, 1885, 461–75.

'Recent discoveries of the foundations of the apse of St Hugh's cathedral', *AASR* 18, 1885–6, 87–95.

'A survey of the houses in the Minster Close', *AASR* 19, 1887–8, 43–75.

'Opening of the tomb of Bishop Oliver Sutton', *AASR* 19, 354–7; *Archaeological Journal* 46.

'Bosses of the eastern walk of the cloisters of Lincoln', *AASR* 20, 1889–90, 179.

'An historical notice of the hospital of Spital on the Street', *AASR* 20, 1889–90.

'Some account of the old houses in Lincoln Close pulled down in March 1892', *AASR* 21, 1891–2, 43–8.

'The shrine and head of St Hugh of Lincoln', *AASR* 21, 1891–2, 131–51; repeated in *Archaeological Journal* 50, 1893, 37–61.

'The memorial slabs formerly in the cloisters of Lincoln Minster', *AASR* 21, 1891–2, 190–4.

Walcott, M. E. C. *Memorials of Lincoln and the cathedral*, Lincoln 1866.

Walker, R. B. 'Lincoln cathedral in the reign of Queen Elizabeth I', *JEH* 11, 1960, 186–201.

Ward, Anne, *The Lincolnshire Rising 1536*, East Midland District Workers' Educational Association, Nottingham 1986.

West, J. E. *Cathedral organists*, 2nd edn, London 1921.

Westlake, H. F. *Parish gilds of medieval England*, London 1919.

Wickenden, J. F. 'The choir stalls of Lincoln cathedral', *AASR* 15, 1879–80, 179–97; repeated in *Archaeological Journal* 38, 1881, 42–61.

'Contents of the muniment room at Lincoln cathedral', *Archaeological Journal* 38, 1881, 309–28.

Wild, Charles, *Guide to Lincoln cathedral*, Lincoln 1819; republished by Britton.

Willis, Browne, *A survey of the cathedrals of Lincoln, Ely, Oxford and Peterborough*, London 1730.

Winston, C. 'On the glazing of the north rose window of Lincoln cathedral', *Archaeological Journal* 14, 1857, 111–20.

Winterbottom, D. O., *Doctor Fry*, Berkhamsted, 1977.

Woodward, R. *Boy on a hill. Memorials of a childhood and youth in Lincoln between the wars*, Gainsborough 1984.

Woolley, R. M. *Catalogue of the manuscripts of Lincoln cathedral library*, London 1927.

Wordsworth, C., bishop of Lincoln, *Statuta Ecclesie Cathedralis Lincolniensis* (a reprint of the *Novum Registrum* and *Laudum*), London 1873.

Wordsworth, C., canon of Lincoln, 'Inventories of plate, vestments, etc., belonging to the cathedral church of the Blessed Mary of Lincoln', *Archaeologia* 53, 1892.

Notes on medieval services in England, with an index of Lincoln ceremonies, London 1899.

Index

❀

Note: Places not identified by county are in the pre-1972 county of Lincolnshire.

329